THE JUVENILE OFFENDER

The Holbrook Press Criminal Justice Series

THE JUVENILE OFFENDER
Control, Correction, and Treatment

Clemens Bartollas
Sangamon State University

Stuart J. Miller
Washington and Jefferson College

Holbrook Press

Allyn and Bacon, Inc.

Boston   London   Sydney   Toronto

CREDITS (Additional to those listed in text)

Cartoons pages 19, 101, 110, 198, 245, 249, 259, 267, 337
by Gloria Grolla

Photos page 33 by John White/EPA-Documerica; page 46
Melissa Hayes; page 196 Steve Hansen/Stock, Boston

Printed in the United States of America

Library of Congress Cataloging in Publication Data

Bartollas, Clemens.
  The juvenile offender.

    Bibliography: p.
  Includes index.
    1. Juvenile corrections—United States. 2. Juvenile
delinquency—United States. 3. Juvenile justice,
Administration of—United States. I. Miller,
Stuart J., 1938–   joint author. II. Title.
HV9104.B349   364.36′0973   77-26976
ISBN 0-205-06069-2

DEDICATION

To Jean and JoAnn,
our wives

Contents

PART II INSTITUTIONALIZATION

Foreword

Throughout the world youth crime and its "correction" are viewed as social problems of great concern. However, the priority accorded youth problems reflects less a concern with understanding the difficulties youths encounter in their socialization for legitimate adult roles than on how to control young people so that their behavior will not offend or interfere with adult society. As populations become older it can be anticipated that efforts to coercively control youths will increase, since the interests and activities of young people contrast substantially with those of older persons. Because few efforts have been made to overcome the negatives associated with age-homogeneous grouping, linking social mechanisms across age groups are almost wholly lacking. Many students of youth socialization have remarked in recent years that some of the more urbane societies appear to "not like children or youth" because the social policies and programs for them reflect far greater concern with coercive social control than with enhancing youth socialization for adult roles.

The period of the 60s offered youth new opportunities for participation in the societal mainstream, but those opportunities were abruptly terminated in the early 70s in an arbitrary manner. One consequence of that change has been a rapid escalation of the number of youths of all social classes who are apathetic, alienated, and hostile. While many middle-class youths are increasingly engaged in narrow, career-related behavior, there has emerged a tiny minority of young adults who wholly reject the system and engage in serious terrorist activity. The economic recession and subsequent unemployment of large numbers of youth was also an important contributing factor to the behavior observed in the 70s.

In recent years, people have become increasingly apprehensive about crime and public safety, even though such increased fears are often not based on actual risk. As a result of these fears, many jurisdictions have proposed and quickly implemented mandatory long term incarceration for offenders—despite the overwhelming evidence that these programs are relatively ineffective in social restoration and despite the known fact that many offenders engage in more serious criminal behavior subsequent to institutionalization. Even the escalating costs of custody have not dissuaded many from increased use of these more "heroic" methods of intervention.

In this social context of conflict, contradiction, and confusion, Bartollas and Miller offer a thorough and comprehensive presentation of contemporary juvenile corrections in the United States. Much of the contemporary literature on juvenile corrections is fragmented and not readily available to professionals in the field. The authors drew together much of that literature and organized this book so as to facilitate understanding of juvenile corrections today. The reader follows youth into and through the juvenile system from initial contact with police to the juvenile court, diversion programs, disposition and post-disposition processing into a variety of community-based and institutional programs. The focus of the authors is more on the processes of how juveniles are corrected than on the organization and operation of the system per se.

There are many valid criticisms that can be made about the operation of juvenile corrections today because of its costliness and its relative ineffectiveness in achieving positive goals for youth. In their analysis Bartollas and Miller show that far greater effort is directed toward routine processing and custody than toward treatment and restoration. Society appears to expect organizations in juvenile corrections to solve most of the problems of youth assigned to them, but they must do so with limited resources, inadequate technologies, and often in social environments that are antithetical to the appropriate delivery of services known to be effective. At the same time, society refuses to provide legitimate roles for youth subsequent to their experience in juvenile corrections, so that any progress that is made is quickly undone when youth return to crime-ridden and opportunity-less environments. Little wonder that the response of youth is further hostility and continuing criminal behavior.

It seems quite clear that all youth-serving organizations—including juvenile corrections—must do far more to facilitate greater implementation of the conditions necessary for adolescent socialization for legitimate roles in a post-industrial democratic society. Adherence to the law cannot be based solely on the fear of punishment; yet, in many ways, public schools, juvenile courts, and juvenile correctional agencies operate on this assumption. We speak of the juvenile justice system in a glib manner as if such really existed, but from the perspective of thousands or perhaps millions of youths in many countries, the system is viewed as one only for control and punishment, not "justice!" Nonetheless, the ideal of justice must be fundamental to juvenile corrections in a democratic society, for without it people will not conform to the values and norms that are essential to the viable continuance of that society.

In many ways society, through its actions in the juvenile corrections system, appears willing to show youths that social institutions and persons with power will be reinforced in their power at the expense of serving youths or meeting their needs. The public school may not provide an adequate education for students, but if youths express their concern by nonattendance or disruption, they are charged as truants or vandals. No one enjoins the school to provide an effective educational environment. Thus far court decisions have tended to enforce the organizational prerogatives far more than youth rights to an education, service, or opportunity. Even in the case of the family, it is the parents whose authority is usually unequivocally supported when there is a charge of incorrigibility. The juvenile is the target for incarceration or treatment, not the parents or the family as a group. One wonders how incorrigibility could ever be successfully resolved by incarceration of a child, and yet that continues to be the practice in many jurisdictions.

Guided by an ideal of justice, one is led to inquire into the nature of law governing the processing of youth into and through the so-called juvenile justice system. Nearly half of all cases processed in the United States in the mid-1970s were for behavior that was not considered law-violating for adults. Moreover, these statutes grant broad discretion to various personnel in the system with few or no requirements for accountability. Little explicit attention is given in most juvenile codes to the rights of youth, to mechanisms for effective and prompt processing, trial, and service delivery, or to periodic review of the actions and non-actions of personnel. We need to examine far more rigorously the formulation, administration, and consequences of contemporary juvenile law and determine whose interests are *really* served by laws referred to as the Juvenile Code.

Bartollas and Miller provide a critical analysis of contemporary juvenile corrections. Such is necessary if we are to modify the existing system toward one which could be more effective. They conclude with a series of policy alternatives and prerequisites for a system oriented to justice for youth. Their suggestions deserve our serious attention today!

Rosemary C. Sarri
Professor of Social Work
University of Michigan
Ann Arbor, Michigan

Preface

Who exactly is a juvenile offender? The authors use the terms "juvenile offender" and "juvenile delinquent" to refer to any person under the age of 18 who violates an ordinance or statute and is caught. However, many who are processed through the juvenile justice system fall outside this definition. The abused, the dependent and neglected, the mentally ill, and the mentally retarded are subjected to the workings of the system as if they were offenders.

Our purpose is to explore and define the important and emerging component of juvenile corrections in the United States. As a field of study, juvenile corrections has been neglected and a definitive study has not been made. Debate exists about the scope of juvenile corrections. Some believe that juvenile corrections involves only a study of juvenile institutionalization; others feel that the processing of any or all who come through the juvenile justice system should come under the purview of juvenile corrections. Because the writers regard the basic focus of juvenile corrections as the control, correction, and treatment of both juvenile offenders and the aforementioned groups, we have accepted the latter definition.

The writers judge that the history of juvenile corrections, the processing of youth, the philosophy of juvenile justice, the detention of juveniles, and the diversion of youth from the juvenile justice system into a nonsystem all come under the purview of juvenile corrections. We have been concerned, moreover, to depict the fascinating and sometimes tragic world of the juvenile offender, to describe the jobs and problems of those practitioners in the justice system who work with youths, and to address the important issues inherent in juvenile corrections.

We believe that the basic mission of juvenile corrections is to correct or rehabilitate youthful offenders so that they will neither return to the juvenile justice system nor continue into the life of an adult criminal. One of the primary foci of this book is therefore to examine the present effectiveness of juvenile corrections in accomplishing this mission.

The book will follow juvenile offenders through the justice system, beginning with the police pickup of misbehaving juveniles, including those youths caught in a criminal act. The options available to the police range in severity from warning and release, through intake into the juvenile court, to detention in an appropriate facility. Youths delivered to the court may be released after intake procedures, turned over to social agencies, or held for official hearings. Juveniles who are held for official action appear before a judge in the fact-finding or adjudicatory stage of the court's proceedings; once offenders are declared delinquent, judges have a number of options. The most widely exercised is probation, under which juveniles are permitted to remain at home, to attend school, and to participate in community activities. However, juvenile offenders who commit serious offenses or who have committed previous offenses may be sent to a juvenile correctional institution. There, they frequently undergo some kind of treatment directed toward rehabilitation, and, when deemed ready by the staff or some other board, they are released. The final step usually consists of aftercare for those youngsters released to the community.

Our intent, then, is to bring into focus the several components of juvenile corrections. The authors admittedly have certain biases, but they believe those biases do no more than reflect the controversy over the issues and positions currently articulated in juvenile justice.

Acknowledgments

Many have contributed to the writing of this book. The authors are profoundly grateful to Mildred Rose who skillfully edited the manuscript. She performed countless miracles in shaping the work from rough to final copy. Lynn Thorkildson, John Vargas, and David Johnson are some of the practitioners who contributed to our understanding of the juvenile justice system. John Hall, Gail Truitt, Frank Kopecky, Robert Crane, Gary Storm, Robert Pilgrim, S. Burkett Milner, Sidney Burrell, Donna Hamparian, Sandy Martin, Mike Brown, and Mike Townsend are the colleagues whose helpful critiques have been widely utilized. The insights of John Hall have been especially helpful in the writing of this book. Martha Schultz, Gerald Melton, and Carolyn Dallas faithfully served as research assistants during various phases of the project. Sue Farris, Sue Kunkel, Jane Lang, Donna Dragon, Martha Spangler, and Barbara Clutter typed many drafts and performed other administrative tasks that enabled the authors to keep the manuscript moving without interruption. We are grateful also to Richard Carle, our editor at Holbrook, for his assistance and patience. Finally, we would like to thank Sangamon State University for its support of one of the authors who was granted released time to complete this project, and to Sangamon State University and Washington and Jefferson College for their assistance in the various typing and xeroxing phases of this book.

part I

THE SYSTEM
AND EARLY DECISION MAKING

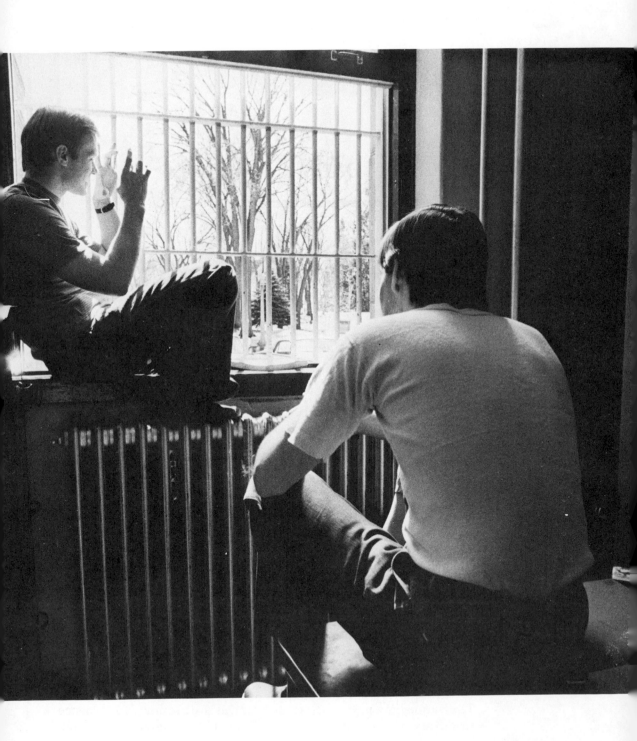

1

Introduction to Juvenile Corrections

Juvenile corrections in the United States, the basic theme of this book, deals with the procedures used to correct the behavior of juveniles who violate the law. To accomplish its mission of rehabilitating youthful offenders, juvenile corrections must be concerned with the impact of external and internal forces on the juvenile justice system, for these forces provide the context, or setting, in which juvenile corrections is carried out in this country. The assumed rise of youth crime, the national movement to improve standards in juvenile justice, the conflicting philosophies and strategies for treating offenders, and the fragmentation of the juvenile justice system are the most important components of these forces. They affect nearly every youth who is picked up by the police, processed by the court, committed to training schools, and placed on aftercare. This chapter will provide an overview of each of these forces.

RISE OF CRIME IN THE UNITED STATES

The alarming rise in crime is considered by many to be the number one domestic problem. The president and local public officials all inform us of the seriousness and pervasiveness of the crime problem. Daily, the media bombard the citizen with news of violence and predatory activity. The *Uniform Crime Reports* documents this rise in crime with evidence that index offenses (murder, forcible rape, robbery, aggravated assault,

3

burglary, larceny, and motor vehicle theft) have more than doubled in the past fifteen years and have increased 37 percent in the past five years. The *Uniform Crime Reports* for 1976 also records index offenses increased one percent and violent offenses decreased 4 percent over those of 1975.[1]

The public is becoming increasingly intolerant of the crime problem in the United States. Judges are reacting by giving longer sentences and by placing fewer offenders on probation. Parole boards are now less frequently persuaded that technically eligible inmates should be freed. The result is that every state in the union, except California, showed a rise in the number of people behind bars in 1975; the 250,000 men and women in prison at the start of 1976 was the largest number on record in this country; and this figure mushroomed to 275,000 by the start of 1977.[2] The state of Illinois, for example, is confining 150 more persons than it is releasing each month.

RISE OF YOUTH CRIME

The evidence is mixed on the rise of youth crime. Statistical studies and the media testify to a dramatic rise in youth crime, but self-report and victimization studies challenge this.

Youth crime, according to the *Uniform Crime Reports,* has skyrocketed the past two decades. Arrests among juveniles under the age of eighteen rose more than 144 percent from 1960 to 1975, with murder increasing 211 percent, forcible rape 102 percent, robbery 375 percent, aggravated assault 240 percent, larceny 166 percent, and motor vehicle theft 24 percent. Other categories in which youth crime increased during this period, as listed by the *Uniform Crime Reports,* are:

Forgery and counterfeiting	154 percent
Fraud and embezzlement	262 percent
Stolen property—buying, receiving, and possessing	637 percent
Weapons—carrying and possessing	114 percent
Prostitution and commercialized vice	373 percent
Offenses against family and children	373 percent
Driving under the influence	508 percent
Violation of liquor laws	192 percent
Violation of narcotic drug laws	4,417 percent[3]

The offenses committed by youths in 1976 included nearly all those committed by adults, as 24.9 percent of all those arrested were juveniles under the age of eighteen. Indeed, youth crime accounted for more than 46 percent of all arrests for property crimes (burglary, larceny-theft, and motor vehicle theft). Eighteen-year-olds had the highest rate of violent crime of any age group; seventeen-year-olds ranked second; sixteen-year-olds, third; and thirteen- to fourteen-year-olds, fourth.[4] See Figure 1-1 for the percentage of total crime committed by juvenile offenders in 1976.

The increased violence and vandalism in our elementary and secondary schools is another shocking indicator of the rise of youth crime. Senator Birch Bayh, Chairman of the Subcommittee to Investigate Juvenile Delinquency, reported the following increases in violence and vandalism in schools between 1970 and 1973.

Homicides increased by 18.5 percent.

Rapes and attempted rapes increased by 40.1 percent.

Robberies increased by 36.7 percent.

Assaults on students increased by 85.3 percent.

Assaults on teachers increased by 11.8 percent.

Burglaries of school buildings increased by 11.8 percent.[5]

FIGURE 1-1   Percentage of Total Arrests of Juveniles under Eighteen

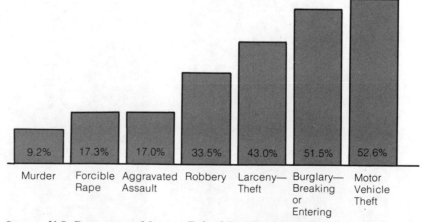

Murder	Forcible Rape	Aggravated Assault	Robbery	Larceny— Theft	Burglary— Breaking or Entering	Motor Vehicle Theft
9.2%	17.3%	17.0%	33.5%	43.0%	51.5%	52.6%

Source: U.S. Department of Justice, Federal Bureau of Investigation, *Uniform Crime Reports, 1976* (Washington, D.C.: U.S. Government Printing Office, 1977), p. 183. Reported by 10,119 agencies with a 1976 estimated population of 175,499,000.

Senator Bayh noted in his report to the U.S. Senate that 70,000 assaults on teachers take place annually in this country and that school vandalism costs in excess of one-half billion dollars per year. To illustrate the magnitude of the problem, he reported that during the three years of the survey, 362 teachers were asaulted in Dayton, Ohio, and 252 were attacked in Kansas City, Missouri.

Another testimony to the rise of youth crime is found in the news media. The *New York Times,* for example, informed its readers on November 30, 1975 that sixty-four fifteen-year-olds were arrested for murder in New York City in 1973 and 1974. These accounts of violent crime offer further chilling evidence:

> Miami, Florida, August: Three boys—two aged thirteen and one twelve—have been charged with first-degree murder in the death of a homeless derelict who was sprinkled with lighter fluid and set afire.
>
> Hornell, New York, October: Two fifteen-year-old boys were picked up by authorities on charges that they struck and killed Daniel Swift, a twenty-five-year-old policeman, last night with a car they were trying to steal.
>
> Chicago, Illinois, October: Two sisters, thirteen and fifteen years old, were named in delinquency proceedings today for the slaying of their father, the police said. The two confessed the shootings after they quarreled with him over a beating he had given them.[6]

Radio and television also do their best to alert the public to the pervasiveness and danger of youth crime and sometimes sensationalize stories of violent youth crime.

The findings of self-report and victimization studies, however, debate this dramatic rise of youth crime. Martin Gold and David Reimer, for example, found in a national survey of self-reported youth crime in 1972 that the seriousness and frequency of delinquent behavior of thirteen- to sixteen-year-old boys was lower than the delinquent behavior of that age group had been in 1967. This study further concluded that youth crime began to level off in the 1960s and is less of a problem than it was a few years back.[7]

The Institute for Juvenile Research in Illinois in 1976 completed a three-year study of self-report youth crime throughout the state. Alan Berger, in his discussion of this research, noted that the extent of youth crime among boys closely parallels the findings of similar studies conducted across the country over a decade ago, which would indicate that youth crime among boys has not greatly increased. This study, on the other hand, did show a marked increase over the past decade of youth crime among girls.[8]

A national victimization study published in 1976 found that "violent crimes—robbery, rape, and assault—showed no significant change in victimization rate from 1973–1974" and that the overall number of victimizations among all ages rose by 7.5 percent primarily because of household larceny and personal larceny without contact.[9] In comparison with the *Uniform Crime Reports* for the same period, which reported an 11.3 percent increase in violent crimes and an 18.3 percent rise in property crimes among all ages, the national victimization study gives a much more conservative estimate of the extent of crime in our society. Thus, it would appear that this study raises serious doubt about the increase of violent youth crime and, at least, some doubt about a great increase in youth crime.

Some reseachers also contend that the great increase in the 1970s of ten- to eighteen-year-olds, who are in the crime-prone years, will result in more juvenile crime even if the juvenile crime rate remains static. Consequently, the general population has been misled into believing that a greater proportion of juveniles is involved in crime because the amount of youth crime has gone up.

Part of the problem in assessing the extent of youth crime lies in the amount of hidden delinquency, which includes crimes committed by juveniles who are not caught and unreported juvenile crimes. We simply do not know whether or not there is more hidden delinquency than there was one, five, ten, or thirty years ago. Neither do we know whether or not the percentage of juveniles involved in hidden crime has increased.

To determine whether or not youth crime has increased, we additionally need to be certain about the reliability of the statistics on juvenile delinquency. As any researcher knows, these statistics often reflect only the responses of families, police, and community members to children who simply do not want to conform. They further reflect changes in community policies and police effectiveness. Formerly hidden socially unacceptable behavior has become known because of increased police activity. Also, police and community may pay more attention to known juvenile offenders who have records. These youths may be brought to the attention of the juvenile court more frequently than other lawbreaking youths whom the community does not consider "bad."[10]

However, although the evidence concerning the rise of youth crime is conflicting and there is no way to estimate the amount of hidden delinquency or the reliability of statistics, it appears that there has been, in fact, a gradual rise of youth crime over the past twenty years or so. Moreover, the evidence seems to indicate that youth crime did indeed begin to level off in the mid-1970s and that it should decrease in the 1980s because of the declining birthrate.

But let there be no question about it, youth crime—as well as adult crime—is a serious problem today. One of society's responses to teenage crime is to blame it on a unit or institution of society. Parents blame the schools. Religion is accused of failing to create a sense of morality. Law enforcement officers are chastised for failing to keep youth out of trouble. And, of course, everyone blames parents for coddling and permissiveness. Now society is charging officials in the justice system to correct and control the behavior of juvenile offenders.

THE NATIONAL MOVEMENT TO IMPROVE STANDARDS IN JUVENILE JUSTICE

In response to this challenge from society, a number of professional organizations, national and state commissions, and other groups have prepared standards, models, and guidelines to improve the fairness and effectiveness of the juvenile justice system. The President's Commission on Law Enforcement and the Administration of Justice, the National Advisory Commission on Criminal Justice Standards and Goals, and many state standards and goals projects have examined juvenile justice in the context of the total criminal justice system. In addition, the National Council on Crime and Delinquency, the National Conference of Commissioners on Uniform State Laws, the International Association of Chiefs of Police, and the American Correctional Association have examined juvenile justice from various perspectives or have concentrated on specific aspects of the juvenile justice system.

This emphasis was accelerated in the mid-1970s as three important groups began to develop standards for juvenile justice and delinquency prevention. The first, the Institute of Judicial Administration and the American Bar Association Joint Commission on Juvenile Justice Standards (IJA/ABA Joint Commission), completed a five-year project in 1977 that carefully reviewed the premises on which the juvenile justice system is based and the procedures used in youth corrections. The twenty-three volumes of IJA/ABA standards are being submitted to the American Bar Association and, if approved there, will be submitted to state and local bar associations. The second group, the Juvenile Justice Task Force, is part of the second phase of the 1973 National Advisory Commission on Criminal Justice Standards and Goals. This task force is charged with formulating a set of objectives and advisory standards that will serve as a model for state and local agencies in their attempts to improve the juvenile justice system. The Standards Committee, the third group, was established by Section 208(e) of the Juvenile Justice and Delinquency Prevention Act of 1974; its purpose was to recommend to the president and Congress a set of standards for the administration of juvenile justice.[11]

The combined efforts of these commissions and organizations to update the philosophy and standards of juvenile justice have been impressive. However, the conflicting standards proposed by these groups have done much to reduce their overall impact. For example, the National Council on Crime and Delinquency and others recommend the removal of status offenders from the auspices of the juvenile court, while the National Council of Juvenile Court Judges opposes their removal. The Juvenile Justice Standards Project recommends determinate sentencing and a specific length of confinement for juveniles who have committed serious crimes; yet, the National Council of Juvenile Court Judges, the U.S. Supreme Court decisions, and all the national commissions support indeterminate sentencing for juveniles. The National Advisory Commission on Criminal Justice Standards and Goals places a heavy emphasis on community-based corrections with the recommendation that only hard-core juveniles be incarcerated, but the Juvenile Justice Task Force has taken a much more moderate position on the institutionalization of troublesome juveniles and does not appear to be nearly as enamored of community-based corrections.

CONTEMPORARY STRATEGIES OF TREATMENT

Juvenile corrections is handicapped by this lack of agreement on how to treat juvenile offenders. A major part of the reason why no single policy or set of policies presently guides the handling of offenders is that nearly everyone has an opinion on what can be done to correct the behavior of law-violating juveniles. Indeed, pet theories and folk remedies are in vogue throughout our society.

Also contributing to the lack of policy agreement is the fact that euphemisms abound in juvenile justice philosophy. The following terms used in adult courts were changed verbally to apply to juvenile courts but no change of intent was involved:

A *trial* became an *adjudicatory hearing.*
Parole became *aftercare.*
Sentence to imprisonment became *commitment.*
Holding in jail became *detention.*
Sentencing hearing became *dispositional hearing.*
Indictment became *petition.*
Jail became *shelter.*
Arrest became *take into custody.*

Finally, rhetoric is divorced from reality in juvenile justice philosophy. For example, a recently appointed commissioner of youth corrections commented shortly after assuming office that the easiest thing for him would be to "preach reformation and practice punishment."[12] This split between promise and performance also can be seen in the policy of administrators of community-based programs promising more than they can deliver.

Philosophical Underpinnings of Juvenile Corrections

Four philosophical approaches to treating children in trouble have developed in this century: *parens patriae,* due process, reintegration, and punishment.

Parens Patriae.   The *parens patriae* philosophy, which emerged with the founding of the juvenile court, was summed up by the Committee of the Chicago Bar Association that sponsored the act.

> The fundamental idea of the juvenile court law is that the state must step in and exercise guardianship over a child found under such adverse social or individual conditions as to encourage the development of crime. . . . The juvenile court law proposes a plan whereby he may be treated, not as a criminal, or legally charged with crime, but as a ward of the state, to receive practically the care, custody, and discipline that are accorded the neglected and dependent child, and which, as the act states, "shall approximate as nearly as may be that which should be given by its parents."[13]

The state, represented by the child-saving juvenile court, was to deal with children separately from the rigorous formalities of criminal law. An informal and flexible procedure was to be substituted in which the fatherly and benevolent juvenile judge would gently and in a friendly manner probe the roots of the child's difficulties; once a child's problems were determined, the decision would be made as how to best meet his needs. The objective of the whole process was to help children in trouble to adjust to themselves and to their environment.

According to Dunham, the purposes of the juvenile court were "to understand the child, to diagnose his difficulty, to treat his condition, and to fit him back into the community."[14] The court, acting in lieu of a child's parents, was most concerned about treating a child for his problem. This concept of individualized justice was based on viewing delinquency as a symptom of some underlying conflict. Thus, determinism was assumed, and punishment for wrongdoing was foreign to juvenile court philosophy.

The juvenile court, then, was to serve as a social clinic, designed to meet children's needs and to serve their best interests. The task of the court was to discover the pathology of the child and to call upon the scientific expert to provide the cure. Child-saving reformers, a term used by Anthony Platt, were confident that the combination of the *parens patriae* philosophy and the treatment provided by the scientific expert could lead to the salvation of wayward children.[15]

Due Process.   Since the very beginning of the juvenile court, the *parens patriae* philosophy has been challenged by proponents of the due process or constitutional argument. Although the due process philosophy was not to have significant impact until the Supreme Court decisions of the 1960s and early 1970s, its basic emphasis was to give children better protection through the application of a greater number of due process provisions and procedural safeguards.

The due process approach holds that the state must justify interfering with a child's life; that current diagnostic and treatment techniques are not sufficiently developed to warrant effective intervention on the part of the juvenile court; and that children in need of help are different from children accused of crime and therefore need to be dealt with differently.[16]

Due process philosophy, in contrast to *parens patriae* philosophy, presumes neither guilt nor need; it presumes the innocence of the child as its primary concern is the establishment of accuracy and fairness in the juvenile court process. In short, due process philosophy is fearful that decisions of the juvenile court will be based on imperfect or inaccurate handling.

Reintegration.   The Corrections Task Force of the President's Commission on Law Enforcement and Administration of Justice recommended in 1967 the use of community-based corrections for all but the hard-core offenders. The task and challenge of corrections, according to this task force, is to keep youthful offenders in the community and to help reintegrate them into community living.

> The task for corrections, therefore, includes building or rebuilding solid ties between the offender and the community, integrating or reintegrating the offender into community life—restoring family ties, obtaining employment and education, securing in the large sense a place for the offender in the routine functioning of society. . . . This requires not only efforts directed toward changing the individual offender, which have been almost the exclusive focus of rehabilitation, but also mobilization and change of the community and its institutions.[17]

Reintegration philosophy is characterized by a strong concern with both the offender and the community. Offenders are permitted to make choices so that they may test the alternatives offered in the community. Their motivation to change is supposed to arise from their perception that new and viable behaviors are available to them. Confinement is used as little as possible, since community supervision is considered far superior. The ideal staff member does not exist in this approach; all staff are equally important for the change-producing skills they bring to the teamwork effort.[18]

Reintegration philosophy is used much less in juvenile corrections than in adult corrections; nevertheless, it provides the underpinnings of some of the present models of treating juvenile offenders.

Punishment. The fourth philosophical approach to dealing with youthful offenders emphasizes punishment as the remedy for misconduct. This approach actually goes back to the eighteenth and nineteenth centuries, but it has gained popularity in the 1970s because of the rise of youth crime. Although this approach has had different connotations at various times, supporters today maintain that punishment is beneficial because it is educative and moral. Offenders are taught not to commit further crimes, while noncriminal citizenry receive a demonstration of what happens to a person who breaks the law.

The supporters of the punishment approach claim that the juvenile court has abandoned punishment in favor of individual rehabilitation. They assume free will as they argue for severity and certainty of punishment and advocate a greater use of prisons and incarceration. Other basic assumptions behind this approach are that young people who engage in delinquent behavior are abnormal, few in number, and possess character defects; that antisocial behavior reflects a character defect that can be corrected through punishment; and that punishment can be helpful in teaching responsibility, diligence, and honesty; therefore, the juvenile justice system ought to become more effective so that youthful offenders can be apprehended and punished with greater speed, efficiency, and certainty.

Correctional Models   What can be done to correct the behavior of juvenile offenders? Four basic models have emerged to answer this question: the medical model, the adjustment model, the crime control model, and the least-restrictive model. Each model combines philosophical assumptions, scientific knowledge, and folklore to develop a strategy for correcting youthful offenders. The conflicts among the advocates of these positions are of serious concern to students of juvenile corrections.

The Medical Model.   The followers of the medical model contend that crime is caused by a factor that can be identified, isolated, treated, and cured. They believe that wayward youths who have committed any type of crime should be treated as though they had a disease. Punishment should be avoided because it only reinforces the image these youths have of themselves as unloveable and does nothing to solve their problem. By diagnosing the causes of their behavior and by providing the cure, proponents believe that they can deter youth in trouble from committing additional crimes. This model also assumes that juvenile lawbreakers do not have the ability to exercise freedom of choice or to use reason and that the criminal is fundamentally different from the noncriminal.

The psychoanalytic school of the medical model, for example, claims that juveniles become involved in crime because of emotional problems and that these youths need trained therapists to help them solve their problems. Only through intensive psychotherapy can lawbreakers discover the insight and the strength to free themselves from the causes of their unlawful behavior. In addition, the medical model postulates that a lack of love in early childhood may cause violent behavior. This emotional deprivation leads some juvenile or adult offenders to strike out compulsively at others later in life. They are driven to commit these acts and cannot help themselves, even though they know the acts are wrong.

The medical model also contends that the legal definition of delinquency should be broad and that victimless crimes and status offenses as well as crimes against victims, should remain on the books. Police power should be shared with those competent in diagnosis and knowledgeable about human growth and development. This model does not believe in the frequent use of detention facilities; these facilities should be reserved for children who need special care and custody. The medical model is, therefore, much more concerned with the psychological and social conditions of offenders than with their crimes and states that juvenile court decisions should be based solely upon the needs of the child.

The Adjustment Model.   Emerging from the medical model, with several assumptions in common with it, the adjustment model holds that offenders are different from nonoffenders, need to be treated, and can be given the "cure" by a scientific expert (a person trained in a particular counseling technique). Both the medical and adjustment models use the insights of clients, although the adjustment model places more emphasis on the present than on the past. In addition, it postulates that the character and background of juvenile offenders do not explain their criminal behavior but only create personal problems that lead them into trouble. Although the personal problems of the offenders may create pressure on them to violate the law, the adjustment model affirms that they still are able to be responsible and to make law-abiding decisions. Thus, unlike the medical model, the adjustment model assumes that troublesome youths are reasonable and capable of responsible decision making.

According to this model, juvenile offenders need treatment. The therapies used are those that enable individuals to change by helping them to adjust and grow. The emphasis is placed upon the youth being responsible at the present time; that is, while adolescents cannot change the facts of their emotional and social deprivations of the past, they can demonstrate responsible behavior in the present and avoid using their past problems as an excuse for delinquent behavior. Reality therapy, transactional analysis, guided group interaction, positive peer culture, milieu therapy, and others are all used to help clients cope more effectively with their personal problems, their peers, and their environment. Offenders are shown that their maladjustive behaviors get them into difficulty, and they are provided with alternatives that will allow them to get along with others. These therapies are not based on punishment any more than are those in the medical model, since punishment is seen only to increase the individual's alienation and behavior problems.

The adjustment model also believes in a broad legal definition of delinquency and concurs with the medical model that police power should be shared with scientific experts. Moreover, instead of emphasizing the needs of the child, as the medical model does, the adjustment model is primarily concerned with helping youths reintegrate themselves into society by becoming more responsible in their decision making. Finally, the adjustment model discourages the wide use of juvenile detention.

The Crime Control Model.   The crime control model has been far more popular in the adult criminal justice system than in the juvenile justice system, but the apparent increase in youth crime is leading many to argue that it should be applied to youths as well. Proponents of this model believe that the various methods of rehabilitating juvenile offenders have failed and that treating juvenile lawbreakers in the United States amounts to "coddling" them. The supporters of this position believe very strongly that discipline and punishment are the most effective means of deterring crime. Judge Robert Garner of the Orange County, California Superior Court stated this position forcibly when he said:

> It is in the law that we find our children in an environment where the child is not taught responsibility for behavior but rather is protected against the natural consequences of his actions. Under present juvenile court laws, a youth is permitted to get away with something he knows is wrong,

without punishment. . . . With its guardianship philosophy and its total abandonment of the punitive approach, the juvenile court has produced a large segment of our youth population completely without any respect for law and order. . . .

. A new kind of juvenile court would serve notice on the young criminal offender that he will receive certainty of punishment for a violation of law. The judge will be the stern conscience of society. Until our young people realize this, the juvenile crime rate is going to soar. Punishment is based on fear, and fear has apparently become, in this modern day, a nasty word.[19]

The crime control model is grounded in the conviction that the number one priority of justice should be the protection of the life and property of the innocent from the predatory. The violence of youth crime is making people afraid to walk the streets; too many women are being raped, too many old people are being victimized, and too much property is being destroyed. A small percentage of the youth population, perhaps 5 to 10 percent, is committing the major proportion of serious youth crime and is casting a pall of terror over their communities.

The crime control model sharply challenges the efficacy of keeping troublesome youths in the community. It holds that citizens deserve protection from youthful criminals; that coddling juvenile offenders only reinforces their negative behavior; and that these offenders must be punished to "purge" their unwanted behavior. Consequently, advocates are quick to isolate juvenile offenders, especially those who have committed serious crimes, in detention homes, jails, and training schools. The use of mandatory-sentencing laws that specify an extended length of punishment for serious youth crimes is a recent "hardline," or crime control, position.

Philosophically, the crime control model assumes that only the behavior of offenders makes them different from other youths. Their lawbreaking activities make it clear that they have chosen to be different from their peers. Certainly implicit in this assumption is the conviction that most youths obey the law. A second assumption is that lawbreakers are able to choose, can reason, and are not controlled by any past or present forces; that is, they are not driven to crime by forces beyond their control (inadequate family life, emotional deprivation, or social environment). A third assumption is that punishment will effectively control behavior. But, following the "proper" punishment, the offender ought to be returned to normal community living.

The advocates of the crime control model also believe in a broad legal definition of delinquency. A great deal of confidence is placed in the police as highly respected participants in the process of administering juvenile justice. That the punishment should fit the crime rather than the treatment fit the offender is another of this model's premises. Since the repression of crime is the ultimate goal, efficiency in detecting and processing juvenile offenders is given the highest priority; law-breaking youths, within this concept, should be processed quickly and dealt with harshly in an attempt to discourage further antisocial behavior.[20]

The Least-Restrictive Model.   The least-restrictive model first became popular in the 1960s. When professionals and students became aware of the extent of youth crime, the negative impact of delinquency labels, and the criminogenic and violent nature of juvenile institutions, many began to reappraise what should be done with juvenile lawbreakers. Studies on hidden delinquency and middle-class lawbreaking also taught a valuable lesson—nearly all juveniles break the law, but only a few are caught.

Matza, Schur, and others developed a theoretical framework for the least-restrictive model.[21] The philosophy behind this model is that fate and chance are the only reasons why many juveniles are caught. The lucky break the law and get away with it, but those who are caught are labeled and processed through the juvenile justice system. A great many of these offenders, according to this viewpoint, begin to live up to their labels, which then become self-fulfilling prophecies. Offenders become committed to delinquent behavior, particularly when they are placed in juvenile institutions or detention facilities with youths who have committed much more serious crimes.

For these reasons, supporters of this model urge a least-restrictive philosophy—don't do any more than necessary with youthful offenders. If possible, leave them alone.[22] If their offense is too serious to permit this course of action, use every available resource before placing them in detention or in institutions. Keeping status offenders (juveniles who have only run away, violated a curfew, been ungovernable at home, or been truant from school) out of the juvenile justice system is one of the more predominant concerns of proponents. Providing juveniles with all the procedural safeguards given to adults is also a vital concern. Adherents, of course, urge the use of community resources in working with juvenile offenders, an approach believed by many to be the best for youth correction.

The basic assumptions of the least-restrictive model are quite different from those of the first three. First, this model assumes that the vast majority of juvenile offenders are not greatly different in behavior or background from lawbreakers who are not caught and processed. Second, this model presupposes that the stigma imposed by society and processing through the juvenile justice system are important factors in continuing unlawful behavior. Third, the model upholds the position that offenders exercise freedom, possess reason, and are capable of choice. Some youths, of course, have stronger criminogenic pushes than others (lower-class ghetto youth growing up in a hard-drug area versus the upper-middle-class youth surrounded by law-abiding friends), but still, lawbreaking is a deliberate choice made by the individual. Fourth, supporters claim that firm and kind guidance in the community can limit future violations of most offenders. Finally, this model recognizes that although some youths need detention because of violent or destructive behavior, the vast majority do not.

The least-restrictive model strongly recommends that victimless crimes and status offenses be removed from the law books. Although proponents of this model are suspicious of police power because they feel that the police are too quick to process troublesome youths, treatment experts receive the most severe criticisms. The least-restrictive model challenges the ability of the rehabilitation ideal to provide a "cure" for juvenile misbehavior. This model, in fact, contends that treatment never ends; it just goes on and on. Additionally, adherents of this model question how youths can be rehabilitated when they have not been integrated into the community in the first place.

These are the basic models within which juvenile corrections carries out its mission. The first two, the medical model and the adjustment model, are committed to the treatment concept. They are much more concerned with ensuring that juvenile offenders receive the necessary therapy than with institutionalizing them. The crime control model, on the other hand, is a punishment model that contends that juveniles must pay for their crimes. Obviously, proponents of this model encourage the institutionalization of juvenile offenders. They are also critical of the briefness of the stays in juvenile institutions imposed on some violent offenders. The least-restrictive model encourages diversionary programs and community-based corrections. Advocates of this approach to correcting juveniles want to do everything possible to keep all but the hard core out of training schools. They also have been vocal about the failure of the rehabilitation ideal, especially in an institutional setting. See Table 1-1 for a further comparison of the four models.

Not surprisingly, rarely is anyone single-mindedly devoted to one of these approaches; rather, juvenile justice practitioners tend to pick and choose from each in designing their own approach to troublesome juveniles. Nevertheless, practitioners—whether they be judges, probation officers, juvenile officers (police officers), or institutional staff members—ordinarily favor one model more than the others. Their different approaches to treatment and their lack of respect for those who follow a different course create inefficiency and confusion in correcting juvenile offenders.

Least
Restrictive

Crime
Control

Adjustment   Medical

TABLE 1-1   Correctional Models

The Model	Cause of Problem Behavior	Does It Punish?	Does It Treat?
Least Restrictive	No real problem exists. Delinquency is normal behavior. Eliminate some laws.	no	no
Crime Control	Permissiveness by parents and society	yes	no
Adjustment	Personal problems and general irresponsibility	no	yes
Medical	Background problems, such as emotional deprivation	no	yes

FRAGMENTATION IN THE JUVENILE JUSTICE SYSTEM

The lack of cooperation and communication among some practitioners also exists on a much larger scale among the juvenile justice subsystems. The total juvenile justice system is made up of the police (a juvenile division in larger law enforcement agencies), the juvenile court, juvenile probation, community-based corrections, juvenile institutions, and aftercare (parole). Ideally, these agencies are interrelated so that the flow of justice moves in the following sequence: law violation, police, judicial process, disposition, and rehabilitation. See Figure 1-2 for this intended flow of justice.

In reality, however, cooperation and communication are lacking among the subsystems, so that the entire system has become disjointed and fragmented. In fact, the fragmentation is so great that both the juvenile and the adult justice systems are frequently referred to as nonsystems. Pettit and Holmberg comment on this fragmentation:

> Despite the improvements, however, a vacuum continuously appeared between the various parts of the system, each of which was functioning independently. For example, judges just do not know what the problems of the prison are, nor does the police officer understand the role of the probation and parole office. Survey data collected on a statewide group of criminal law and justice system personnel showed that of the seventeen separate components of the system, the only people who had realistic information about each part as well as the whole were those who had experience in each—the criminals. And as could be expected, the lack of information and understanding among the various parts of the system bred distrust.[23]

Actually, juvenile corrections is more fragmented than adult corrections. Police, courts, and corrections tend to deal with juvenile offenders in quite different ways. An offender may be referred to social work agencies in one jurisdiction; responded to in another as an adult criminal; and in still another, be dealt with by the juvenile court. In some jurisdictions offenses are ignored in favor of dealing with the youths' emotional problems; other jurisdictions use all available community resources before committing youths to juvenile institutions; others are quick to commit offenders to juvenile institutions for even minor offenses; and others place juveniles in adult facilities.[24]

Fragmentation is caused by several factors. The first is the lack of a common goal among the segments of the juvenile justice system. Therefore, each subsystem selects its own goals, which, unfortunately, may change with each new police chief, juvenile judge, chief probation

FIGURE 1-2   Process and Impact of Juvenile Justice System

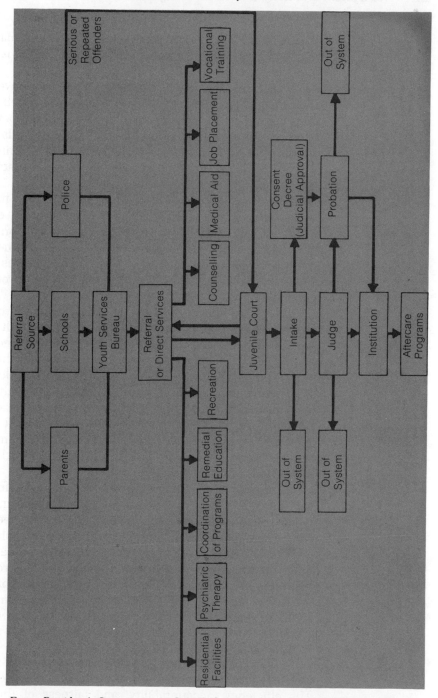

From: President's Commission on Law Enforcement and the Administration of Justice, *The Challenge of Crime in a Free Society* (Washington, D.C.: U.S. Government Printing Office, 1967), p. 89.

officer, or institutional superintendent. Indeed, the goals of justice itself may be changed in a community if a violent crime is committed by a juvenile.

A second cause of fragmentation is that local governments control their own affairs and set their own standards, which are often reflections of local biases rather than of professional competence. Local bias becomes quite apparent when the goals and standards of such commissions as the National Advisory Commission for Criminal Justice Standards and Goals are compared with the actual practices in juvenile corrections.

The consequences of such fragmentation are manifest in duplicated services and soaring costs to taxpayers. An example of such duplication is the establishment of identical recreation programs for the same adolescents. Duplication costs also result when a family with multiple problems is seen by several different agencies at the same time. The usual outcome is that the agencies work at cross-purposes with each other.

Negative impact on juvenile offenders is another possible consequence of fragmentation. Some youths who are guilty of minor crimes are placed in training schools with youths who have committed serious crimes. Such offenders may not be able to protect themselves against more antisocial delinquents, and, even if they are able to protect themselves, their institutional stay probably will result in their learning even more about crime. Too, more sophisticated offenders are able to play off agencies against one another as they avoid attempts to change their behavior. This disjointed system thus results in some boys and girls being sentenced to inappropriate institutions or in their being able to avoid needed treatment.

Fragmentation also creates tension among professionals working with juvenile offenders. Conflict particularly arises among the juvenile judge and the police when the police may want to see the "one-person crime wave" put away and the judge disagrees and places the youth on probation. Probation officers, in addition, become unhappy when judges neither read their reports nor follow their recommendations. Institutional social workers and aftercare specialists often disagree over the decision of when a youth should be released and to whom. The aftercare specialist may challenge the placement recommendation of the social worker because he feels that the youth has not had sufficient confinement.

Obviously, juvenile corrections can function effectively only to the degree that each segment of the system takes into account its subparts. The efficiency, accountability, and fairness of the system depend greatly upon the coordination and communication among the subsystems. As long as so many jurisdictions continue to go their own ways, the juvenile justice system will remain disjointed and fragmented. Consequently, one of the real challenges facing juvenile justice practitioners is to create a systematic, coordinated, and smoothly running system.

SUMMARY

The public is presently reacting to the rise in youth crime. Daily, the media informs the public how unsafe the streets are, how many elderly people are being victimized, how many women are being raped, and how much property is being stolen and destroyed by young people who are seemingly beyond the control of our social institutions. Juvenile corrections is being given the mandate to rehabilitate these youthful offenders. This challenge has created a furor of activity to bring about a more just and humane juvenile justice system. However, the conflicting philosophies and methods of juvenile corrections and the fragmentation of the juvenile justice system make it very difficult to succeed in the mission of rehabilitating juveniles in trouble. How effective juvenile corrections is in meeting this challenge is one of the basic considerations of this book.

QUESTIONS

1. What are the advantages and disadvantages of the medical, adjustment, crime control, and least-restrictive models?

2. If you were working with juvenile offenders, what strategy or model would you employ? Why?

3. Do you feel that it is possible to rehabilitate youthful offenders? Explain.

4. What can be done to overcome the fragmentation of the juvenile justice system? Be specific.

5. In your opinion, how much has youth crime risen? Why has it risen? How do you believe it could be stopped?

ENDNOTES

1. U.S. Department of Justice, Federal Bureau of Investigation, *Uniform Crime Reports, 1976* (Washington, D.C.: U.S. Government Printing Office, 1977), p. 10.
2. *Corrections Magazine* 3 (March 1977): 4.
3. U.S. Department of Justice, *Uniform Crime Reports,* p. 182. These statistics were taken from 2,726 agencies representing a 1975 estimated population of 96,429,000.
4. Ibid., p. 183. The statistics were taken from 10,119 agencies representing a 1976 estimated population of 175,499,000.
5. Birch Bayh, *Congressional Record,* 121, 17 April 1975.
6. Willard A. Heaps, *Juvenile Justice* (New York: Seabury Press, 1974), pp. 4–5.
7. Martin Gold and David J. Reimer, *Changing Patterns of Delinquent Behavior among Americans 13 to 16 Years Old, 1967–1972* (Ann Arbor, Mich.: Institute for Social Research, University of Michigan, 1974).
8. Alan Berger made these comments at a seminar on Delinquency Prevention at Sangamon State University, February 1977.
9. "National Victimization Survey Finds No Increase in Violent Street Crimes from 1973 to 1974," *Criminal Justice Newsletter,* 7, no. 12.
10. Martin R. Haskell and Lewis Yablonsky, *Juvenile Delinquency* (Chicago: Rand-McNally College Publishing Company, 1970), p. 265.
11. Wilfred W. Nuernberger and Richard Van Duizlend, "Development of Standards for Juvenile Justice: An Overview," *Juvenile Justice* 28 (February 1977): 3–6.
12. Benedict S. Alper, *Prisons Inside-Out* (Cambridge, Mass.: Ballinger Publishing Company, 1974), p. 145.
13. Roscoe Pound, "The Juvenile Court and the Law," *National Probation and Parole Association Yearbook* 1 (1944): 4.
14. Warren H. Dunham, "The Juvenile Court: Contradictory Orientations in Processing Offenders," *Law and Contemporary Problems* 23 (Summer 1958).
15. Anthony M. Platt, *The Child Savers* (Chicago: University of Chicago Press, 1969).
16. Frederic L. Faust and Paul J. Brantingham, eds., *Juvenile Justice Philosophy* (St. Paul, Minn.: West Publishing Company, 1974), pp. 574–575.
17. President's Commission on Law Enforcement and Administration of Justice, *Task Force Report: Corrections* (Washington, D.C.: U.S. Government Printing Office, 1967).
18. Vincent O'Leary and David Duffee, "Correctional Policy: A Classification of Goals Designed for Change," *Crime and Delinquency* 16 and 17 (October 1971): 377–385.
19. Heaps, *Juvenile Justice,* p. 161.
20. Daniel Katkin, Drew Hyman, and John Kramer, *Juvenile Delinquency and the Juvenile Justice System* (North Scituate, Mass.: Duxbury Press, 1976), pp. 97–98.
21. David Matza, *Delinquency and Drift* (New York: John Wiley & Sons, 1964); Edwin M. Schur, *Radical Non-Intervention: Rethinking the Delinquency Problem* (Englewood Cliffs, N.J.: Prentice-Hall, 1973).
22. Schur, *Radical Non-Intervention.*

23. M. L. Pettit and B. K. Holmberg, "Let's Put It All Together: An Integrated Approach to Criminal Law and Justice," *Journal of Police Science and Administration* 1 (March 1973): 113.
24. Alan R. Coffey, *Juvenile Corrections: Treatment and Rehabilitation* (Englewood Cliffs, N.J.: Prentice-Hall, 1975), p. 3.

REFERENCES

Faust, Frederic L., and Brantingham, Paul J., eds. *Juvenile Justice Philosophy.* St. Paul, Minn.: West Publishing Company, 1974.
  Contains excellent materials on the history and philosophy of the juvenile court.

Gold, Martin, and Reimer, David J., "Changing Patterns of Delinquent Behavior among Americans 13 to 16 Years Old, 1967–1972." Ann Arbor, Mich.: Institute for Social Research, University of Michigan, 1974.
  An extremely interesting self-report study that describes the changing patterns of adolescent behavior.

Katkin, Daniel; Hyman, Drew; and Kramer, John. *Juvenile Delinquency and the Juvenile Justice System.* North Scituate, Mass.: Duxbury Press, 1976.
  Develops three models of the juvenile justice system that are similar to the correctional models found in this chapter.

Nuernberger, Wilfred W., and Van Duizlend, Richard. "Development of Standards for Juvenile Justice: An Overview." *Juvenile Justice* 28 (February 1977): 3–6.
  This article summarizes the efforts to develop standards in juvenile corrections.

Pettit, M. L., and Holmberg, B. K. "Let's Put It All Together: An Integrated Approach to Criminal Law and Justice." *Journal of Police Science and Administration* 1 (March 1975).
  Clearly describes the fragmentation of the criminal justice system.

Schur, Edwin M. *Radical Non-Intervention: Rethinking the Delinquency Problem.* Englewood Cliffs, N.J.: Prentice-Hall, 1973.
  This book has become a definitive study for those interested in the least-restrictive model.

U.S. Department of Justice, Federal Bureau of Investigation. *Uniform Crime Reports, 1976.* Washington, D.C.: U.S. Government Printing Office, 1977.
  Contains many statistics on crime in the United States.

2

Profile of
the Juvenile Offender

Juvenile lawbreaking, in official terms, is a violation of the legal or social norms of society that evokes official response from one or more elements of the juvenile justice system. Delinquency, then, does not officially occur until officials respond. This means that official delinquency and actual juvenile lawbreaking are two vastly different situations.

UNDETECTED JUVENILE LAWBREAKING

The various studies on officially undetected delinquency have found that adolescents should not be divided into offenders and nonoffenders, since the majority of youths occasionally commit minor offenses.[1] The evidence, in fact, suggests that the youth who never violates the law is a rarity. Some are minor offenders, some break the law regularly, a few commit violent or predatory crimes, and a few support themselves through crime and are committed to it as a way of life.[2]

Figure 2-1 shows the types and proportion of juvenile offenders in the population. The circle demonstrates that conforming juveniles who do not become involved in crimes are actually a minority; the majority break the law in minor ways but are not discovered. The more serious offenders are the ones most likely to be processed by law enforcement officers.

The literature on undetected delinquency has a high degree of consensus on the following findings:

FIGURE 2-1   Juvenile Lawbreaking in American Society.

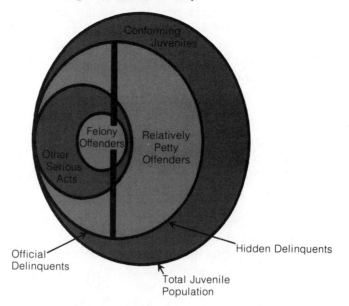

Source: Don C. Gibbons, *Delinquent Behavior,* 2nd ed., © 1976, p. 34. Reprinted by permission of Prentice-Hall, Inc., Englewood Cliffs, New Jersey.

1. There is considerable undetected delinquency, and apprehension is low, probably less than 10 percent.
2. When self-reported information on illegal acts is obtained from both middle- and lower-class juveniles, it becomes clear that both are involved in considerable illegal behavior.
3. The fact that the juvenile court must deal with dependency and neglect cases as well as with juvenile lawbreaking tends to give a false impression of the relationship between lower-class membership and delinquency.
4. Although most undetected lawbreaking would be handled informally or dismissed if brought to the attention of the juvenile court, not all hidden delinquency in this country involves minor offenses; a significant number of serious crimes are committed each year by juveniles who elude apprehension by the police.[3]

OFFICIAL JUVENILE OFFENDERS

In 1976, of the total arrests 7,912,348, 24.9 percent (1,973,254) were of those under eighteen.[4] Juveniles, as previously noted, accounted for more than 46 percent of all arrests for property crimes (burglary, larceny, theft, and motor vehicle theft). The percentage of juveniles arrested increases each year from ten through sixteen and then generally declines each year from seventeen through twenty. Sixteen- and eighteen- year-olds are arrested more frequently than individuals of any other age. Eighteen-year-olds traditionally have the highest rate of violent crime of any age group, seventeen-year-olds rank second, and sixteen-year-olds either third or fourth.

Sex and Youth Crime
More than five times as many males as females under eighteen were arrested: 1,387,424 males and 380,622 females. Although delinquency has been predominantly a boys' problem, the reported rise in female delinquency will be evaluated later in this chapter.

Race and Youth Crime
The racial distribution of arrests of juveniles under eighteen was as follows: 1,407,153 were white, 406,231 were black, 15,748 were American Indian, 612 were Chinese, 1,047 were Japanese, and 17,834 belonged to other racial groups. The significance of these statistics lies in the fact that although three times as many whites as blacks were arrested (76.1 percent of the total arrests were whites, compared to 22 percent black), institutionalization in juvenile facilities was equal between whites and blacks.

Geography and Youth Crime
Also of interest is the fact that 1,626,321 were city arrests, 718,250 suburban arrests, and 114,769 rural arrests. It is significant that over one out of three juvenile arrests were suburban. This matter of middle-class delinquency will be considered later in this chapter.

TYPES OF OFFENDERS

Classification schemes certainly fail to do justice to the everchanging nature of the adolescent. Troublesome youths cannot easily be placed in neat categories. Therefore, classification merely acquaints the student with the various types of processed youths.

The literature is replete with methods for classifying juvenile offenders. Classification by offense, behavior, psychological dynamics, and perception of the world have been the categories used most often when referring to delinquent behavior. For example, Schafer developed the following typology of criminal behavior: occasional criminals, professional criminals, abnormal criminals, and habitual criminals.[5] Hirsh divided delinquent activity into the following offenses: incorrigibility, truancy, larceny—ranging from petty larceny to armed

FIGURE 2-2

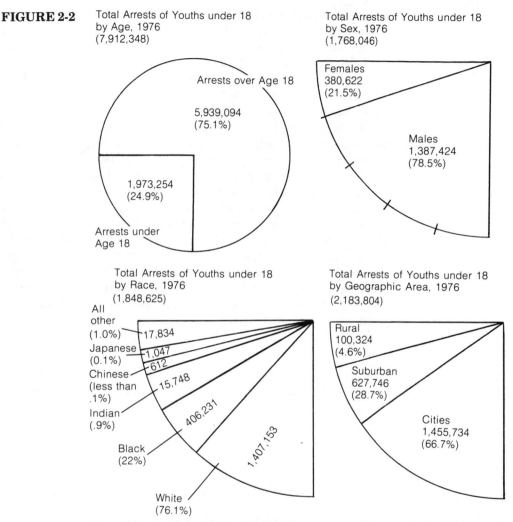

Total Arrests of Youths under 18
by Age, 1976
(7,912,348)

Arrests over Age 18

5,939,094
(75.1%)

1,973,254
(24.9%)

Arrests under
Age 18

Total Arrests of Youths under 18
by Sex, 1976
(1,768,046)

Females
380,622
(21.5%)

Males
1,387,424
(78.5%)

Total Arrests of Youths under 18
by Race, 1976
(1,848,625)

All other (1.0%) — 17,834
Japanese (0.1%) — 1,047
Chinese (less than .1%) — 612
Indian (.9%) — 15,748
Black (22%) — 406,231
White (76.1%) — 1,407,153

Total Arrests of Youths under 18
by Geographic Area, 1976
(2,183,804)

Rural
100,324
(4.6%)

Suburban
627,746
(28.7%)

Cities
1,455,734
(66.7%)

Adapted from tables in Section 4 U.S. Department of Justice, Federal Bureau of Investigation, *Uniform Crime Reports,* 1976 (Washington, D.C.: U.S. Government Printing Office, 1977), pp. 170–214. Statistics presented in Figure 2-2 vary by category because the data base for each category is different. Percentages do not always add up to 100 because of rounding error.

robbery—destruction of property, violence—using such weapons as knives and guns—and sex offenses.[6] Quay developed the following system to evaluate the institutional behavior of juvenile offenders: inadequate-immature—consisting of youths who behave in childish and irresponsible ways; neurotic-conflict; and unsocialized or subcultural delinquency—has been involved in gang delinquency and adheres to values of delinquent peer group.[7] The I-Level (Interpersonal Maturity Classification system) has become one of the most widely used ways to classify both institutionalized and noninstitutionalized youthful offenders. This classification scheme attempts to discover the world view of offenders, focusing on their perception of self, others, and the world; it ranges from I₁ (infantile in interpersonal maturity) to I₇ (Christ-like).[8] Both the Quay and I-Level Classification systems will be further explained and evaluated in future chapters.

Even though these and many other classification schemes exist, the writers of this book wish to suggest classification based upon the perception of offenders. This scheme has not been methodologically tested, but it is based upon the authors' many years of working with juvenile offenders. The chief types of offenders, according to this classification, are the noncriminal youth, the situational offender, and the chronic offender. Noncriminal youths are further classified as status offenders, dependent and neglected youths, naive offenders, and emotionally disturbed offenders. Chronic offenders include those youths who are products of delinquent subcultures and those who are inducted into a delinquent career by being processed through the system. (See Table 2-1.) Future chapters will consider how these youths are handled by the juvenile justice system.

The Noncriminal Youth

The youths classified as noncriminal do not consider themselves to be delinquents. They are typically members of multiple-problem

TABLE 2-1   Types of Juvenile Offenders

Noncriminal Youths

    Status Offenders
    Dependent and Neglected Children
    Naive Offenders
    Emotionally Disturbed Children

Situational Offenders

Chronic Offenders

    Delinquent Subculture Products
    Noncriminal or Situational Offenders
        Committed to a Delinquent Career

families or they have no families at all. Most of these youths are emotionally deprived; some have been abused or battered by parents.

The Status Offender. *Status offender* is a legal description applied to a juvenile who commits acts that are law violations only for juveniles. Approximately half of all juvenile arrests each year are for such acts as truancy, waywardness, and running away from home. Juveniles who commit minor acts that are illegal only because they are underage are known as PINS (persons in need of supervision), MINS (minors in need of supervision), CINS (children in need of supervision), and predelinquent, incorrigible, ungovernable, beyond control, unruly, and wayward children. The following is a fairly complete description of status offenders:

> Uncontrollable or beyond control of parents, guardians or custodian; habitually disobedient or refuses to obey reasonable and proper (lawful) orders of parents, guardians, or custodians; incorrigible or ungovernable; wayward; runaway; habitually truant; persistently violates rules and regulations of school; idle, dissolute or immoral life or conduct; injuring or endangering welfare, morals, and/or health of self or others; associates with criminal or immoral persons; frequents taverns, or uses alcohol; engages in any calling, occupation, or exhibition punishable by law; wanders the streets in the nighttime; violation of law only applicable to children; violation of juvenile court order.[9]

Status offenders tend to place the blame for their problems on their parents. They feel that their need for a warm, accepting, and meaningful relationship with parental figures is not satisfied. Even though their material needs may have been provided for very well, they feel rejected and neglected. They come to resent their parents who seem to have problems in expressing warmth and love to their children. Parents, in turn, come to shun their defiant and demanding children. The consequences often are verbal altercations between parents and child or even physical violence, with the child striking or pushing the parent.

These parents soon realize that they are losing control of their children, who will no longer accept restrictions on their behavior. As a result, the parents may call the police to intervene when they view their children's behavior as excessive, abusive, or unmanageable. Sometimes, parents ask police to act because their youngster is "going around with the wrong crowd" or is dating someone who is "bad" or embarrassing to the family.

Feeling unloved and full of internal turmoil, status offenders tend to resent and reject the limits outsiders place on their behavior. They especially strike out at the school because they feel that the "rule enforcers" there are making too many demands on them. The end result is poor schoolwork, truancy, conflict with teachers, and fights with peers. Some status offenders, interestingly enough, admit that they know they are intelligent and have the capacity to do excellent academic work.

Their anger, resulting from early rejection and continued conflicts with "significant others," frequently results in overt violation of the law. Although they turn to unlawful activities because they either want attention from their parents or want to embarrass them, they do not look upon themselves as delinquents and often do not consider the consequences of their behavior. Indeed, when processed through the juvenile justice system, they are usually quick to tell practitioners that they are not like "those other kids." Thus, their emotional conflicts with parents and "significant others" predispose them to behavior that draws them into the justice system, but they do not consider themselves delinquent or bad.

Illustrations of striking out against parents include drunkenness, unauthorized use of motor vehicles and credit cards, and forgery of family checks. Status offenders, especially girls, have a propensity for running away from home. In recent years, this type of offender also has seemed to be drifting toward drug use. Alcohol and marijuana appear to be the most popular drugs for middle-class status offenders, while alcohol, marijuana, and substances that can be sniffed (paint, gasoline, aerosols, and glue) are leading in popularity with lower-class status offenders.[10] Other ways to gain attention or express resentment involve theft and sexual deviation. Middle-class youngsters often shoplift items they have in abundance at home; girls sometimes can hold the possibility of their sexual promiscuity as a weapon over the heads of parents.

Dependent and Neglected Children. Neglect cases usually involve children abandoned by parents or whose parents fail to care properly for them. Dependency cases generally concern parents' complete lack of physical, emotional, and financial ability to provide for their children. These adolescents, whose homes are inadequate or nonexistent, often have not committed any crimes, but are referred to the juvenile court because there is no other place to send them. They often also have been victims of child abuse.

These youths usually are aware of the unsatisfactory nature of their homes, and, if placed in a foster home, they may resent or even come to hate their parents. Yet they may remain hopeful that someday their parents will open their arms and homes to them. For example, frequently such a child will run away from a foster placement and return to one of the parents. These youths may become involved in truancy, shoplifting, or other crimes, but they do not consider them-

selves as delinquents. They usually blame their problems on the lack of parental support or on poor foster parents.

Dependent and neglected children who end up in the juvenile justice system normally have had problems in a number of foster and group homes. The child welfare department, not knowing what to do with them, may turn to the juvenile court and use it as a dumping ground for these "dead-endies." A child welfare worker, in the following statement, explains why in one case the department had to turn to the juvenile court. The child involved had sex problems and a history of shifting from one home to another.

> Now we're going downhill. . . . With these tougher kids—hard-to-place kids—you have to place them in a home that may not be the best home, but she [the foster mother] will tolerate him so he has to be placed there. With a boy like Gino, especially if there are young girls in the family, the foster mother comes to feel he's going to do something to the girls and she can't tolerate it. Hence it becomes almost impossible to find a place that will take the boy.[11]

It is difficult to estimate how many dependent and neglected children are involved in the juvenile justice system. Part of the problem relates to the many different methods of handling these children. For example, forty-one states do not separate dependent and neglected children from delinquents in detention facilities, and seventeen states allow these "throwaway children" to be housed with delinquents in juvenile institutions.[12] Some states, such as Illinois, separate the child welfare department from the juvenile court. In other states, juvenile court codes no longer permit the institutionalization of these children. Still, thousands of dependent and neglected children are confined in county jails each year; others are placed in detention centers and have their best interests entrusted to the juvenile court.

Naive Offenders. Mentally retarded children are included in the category of naive offenders. Some mentally retarded children originally were sent to a state school for the retarded, but were then referred to the juvenile justice system because they adjusted poorly. Others were referred directly to the justice system because no other resource was available. These youths often had not committed a crime; they were victimized by the fact that no other placement was available. Of course, some mentally retarded children do break the law.

Some mentally retarded youths are truly naive offenders, for they do not know when they are doing something wrong. Others suspect that they may be doing something wrong, but only on a low level of consciousness. That is, the morals and values of society are not understood by these youths. Consequently, they do not perceive themselves as delinquents and sometimes are quite baffled when placed with juvenile offenders in the juvenile justice system.

The number of mentally retarded children processed through the justice system each year is unknown because of the lack of statistics. But, even if such statistics were available, a significant problem would arise in identifying these children. Their scores on intelligence tests may vary by several points each time the tests are administered, which makes it difficult to know whether the youths are under or over an arbitrary cutoff point (for example, an I.Q. of 70). Not all naive offenders, of course, are mentally retarded. Many are of normal intelligence but simply are unaware of the various laws.

Emotionally Disturbed Children.   The final type of noncriminal juvenile is the emotionally disturbed youth. Definition of this psychiatric term may vary somewhat, but youths whose emotional problems severely interfere with their everyday functioning and whose behaviors bring them into the justice system are generally included in this broad category. Even if statistics on the number of disturbed youths were available, the vagueness of the term would challenge the validity of any such information.

The two most important characteristics of emotionally disturbed offenders are their psychological states and their acting-out behavior, manifested either in persistent behavior problems or in their involvement in heinous crimes. These youths are labeled emotionally disturbed, prepsychotic, psychotic, or schizophrenic by psychiatrists and clinical psychologists. Psychological evaluations record that they have poor self-concepts, anxiety symptoms, neurotic guilt, little self-awareness, restricted ego capacities, and a high degree of rejection; are unable to control impulses; resist authority; have pathological relationships with family members; have a tendency to act out inadequacies; and have many internal conflicts.[13]

These youths also have either continual behavior problems or are involved in shocking crimes. Persistent-behavior-problem youths are initially referred to mental health services because they are unable to function in everyday life. They seem to react more negatively than the typical unruly child to the rejection and neglect received at home. They appear to have difficulties in relating to and forming friendships with peers. Often, they make inappropriate interpersonal overtures to both the same and the opposite sex. In short, the community looks upon them as a nuisance and sometimes as a danger. They usually are referred for out-patient care in a community mental health facility and may spend some time as patients in psychiatric hospitals. During treatment they probably receive tranquilizers and are exposed to various types of psychiatric intervention, psychological testing, and casework methods.

A few of these emotionally disturbed youths do commit violent and shocking crimes that seem totally out of character. They have not previously been troublemakers; indeed, they may have done well in school, been active in the church and scouts, and been considered fine young people by the community. Nevertheless, these juveniles apparently have been full of repressed rage and they unleash it one day toward a parent, a sibling, a neighbor, a teacher, or a schoolmate.

Lisa Richette tells of a youth whose anger toward his parents mounted over the years. They expected perfection from him and yet they would run through the house naked, leave pornographic books around the house, and even have sexual intercourse in front of him. To contain his rage, he retreated into religion, which made him feel even more guilty about their behavior. He finally took matters into his own hands and killed his parents.[14]

Another youth was considered an ideal young man. His teachers thought very highly of him, he had never been in any trouble with the law, and he seemed to have a happy home life. Yet he took a shotgun, shot his parents repeatedly, and then quartered them. The community was shocked. How could this quiet, well-mannered youth from a good middle-class home do such a thing? In working with him, it became abundantly clear to the counselor why he had exploded. Although he had always been polite and compliant, he had been full of rage against his parents. One night he simply lost control of himself. Typical of youngsters who kill their parents, he then repressed the event and dissociated himself from the crime.

These youths often do not know what to make of their own behavior. It is, of course, much easier for an adolescent to explain away behavior problems than it is to dismiss a violent crime. Consequently, disturbed youths who have commited violent crimes frequently deal with them by repressing and denying them. Even when there is proof that the youth killed a parent or friend, the disturbed youth may deal with it by blotting it from his memory and detaching himself from this event. But, these youths seem to be filled with confusion and self-doubt over what they have done. One youth verbalized this when he said, "I don't know why I did that. I hope that I'm not crazy like my father."

Emotionally disturbed youths are distinguished from other noncriminal youths by an internal drive that seems to cause them to lose control of themselves. They are, then, capable of committing horrible and bizarre crimes because they lack internal controls. However, neither the disturbed youth nor other types of noncriminal youths perceive themselves to be delinquent and are not committed to crime as a way of life. Personal problems rather than a desire for gain or the wish to please peers, are generally the reason for their presence in the justice system.

The Situational Offender

Neither do situational offenders look upon themselves as committed to crime. They do drift in and out of crime because of boredom, group pressure, or financial need. Yet, other than for occasional excursions into the deviant world, these youths remain law-abiding. But let there be no question about it: they can become involved in serious antisocial behavior, such as armed robbery, burglary, auto theft, rape, and even homicide.

David Matza has developed the drift hypothesis to explain the behavior of these youths. The "bind of law," according to Matza, has to be neutralized before the juvenile offender is put into drift. Following the act of giving himself the "moral holiday implicit in drift," the offender must learn from others that the crime is something that is fairly easy to do. Once juveniles are successfully involved in law-violating behavior, they probably have the ability to repeat the crime. As Matza notes, only "clowns and fools . . . like to engage in activities that they do badly." If juveniles are too apprehensive or are fearful that they will be arrested, they may not have the will to repeat the crime. Thus, Matza believes that the situational offender is in limbo between convention and crime; influenced by the group, he evades decision and commitment.[15]

Situational offenders may be middle-class adolescents who are simply bored and seeking new thrills. They, therefore, become involved in drinking, the use of marijuana and other drugs, sexual activity, and destruction of property. Lower-class situational offenders may be on the periphery of gangs or may come from extremely deprived areas. The former tend to commit crimes to gain acceptance of peers, while the latter most often steal to eat, to have clothes, and to have a little money in their pockets. Situational offenses range from armed robbery, burglary, and battery to petty theft, joyriding, and malicious mischief.

Situational offenders all seem to be dependent on the peer group. Whether they are affluent middle-class youths destroying property just for kicks, adolescents involved in a drug culture, or lower-class juveniles robbing a liquor store, the group very much influences their behavior. This emotional hold enables them to neutralize the "bind of law," to develop the necessary fatalistic feeling to commit a new infraction, and to activate the will to repeat a crime.[16]

Situational offenders continue to drift in and out of lawbreaking until one of several things happens. They may outgrow the desire to commit crime. They grow up and begin to assume the responsibilities of adults—college, work, marriage, and family. Or, they may be apprehended by the police and processed by the juvenile courts; this may either deter them from future antisocial behavior or it may be the start of their being labeled delinquent or bad kids. Evidence exists that youths who are processed by the system and labeled delinquent are apt to continue their negative behavior. Youths who choose to live up to their labels have passed the threshold from situational to chronic offender.

Becoming a chronic offender means conversion to delinquent values. Matza also has explored this matter of conversion. He believes that juvenile offenders have freedom of choice (they have free will and are not controlled by internal or external forces) and that their decision making is a crucial variable in their career. In *Becoming Deviant*, Matza states that he believes that three stages are involved in becoming committed to delinquent values. The first is *affinity*—being around criminal activity and chronic offenders. This exposure to criminal attitudes, norms, and friends makes the juvenile more favorably inclined toward antisocial behavior. But only in the second stage, *conversion*, do youths clearly decide upon crime as a way of life. An act of will is involved when youthful offenders commit themselves to antisocial behavior. They must decide to pursue a delinquent career, to perceive themselves as criminals, and to make crime a way of life. In the third stage, *signification*, offenders actually begin to stand up for and model themselves after career delinquents.[17]

The Chronic Offender   The chronic offender is known by many labels: serious delinquent, violent offender, dangerous offender, hard-core delinquent, and career delinquent. Nevertheless, whatever the label, the predominant characteristic of these youths is their commitment to crime and their involvement in one crime after another, often very serious crimes against persons and property. Their initial participation in crime constitutes the budding of a life-style centered around violence and "making it big" in the criminal world. Chronic offenders expect to engage in criminal careers for at least several years, if not for the rest of their lives.

Chronic offenders become committed to criminal careers through one of two routes. In the first, noncriminal and situational offenders move from casual involvement with other offenders on the streets, to being processed with them through the system, to perceiving crime as a way of life, and finally to being willing to stand up for this involvement. Usually these youths have been picked up by the police many times, have been in courts and the detention halls several times, and have had one or more institutional stays. The decisions they make at each stage move them closer to a delinquent career.

The second route is quite different. Some youths become absorbed in crime before they have contact with the justice system. These offenders often grow up in a ghetto area and, surrounded by vice and crime, become involved with peers in unlawful acts at an early age. Frequently, they come from impoverished families. They tend to feel that life is a struggle and that only the strong survive; therefore, they are always on guard against being hurt or exploited by others and develop a hostile and suspicious view of the world around them. They seem to accept a commitment to crime without any apparent episodes of decision making.

How numerous are chronic offenders? In *Delinquency in a Birth Cohort,* Wolfgang, Figlio, and Sellin have provided the most authoritative answer to this question. These researchers studied all of the boys born in Philadelphia in 1945 who continued to live there from their tenth to their eighteenth birthday. Of the nearly ten thousand making up the cohort, 35 percent had incurred one or more police contacts. Tracing the boys through school and police records, these researchers became aware that this delinquent group could be subdivided into single offenders, multiple offenders, and chronic offenders. Although approximately half of those who committed a single offense later became involved in a second, only 6.3 percent committed more than five violations, Wolfgang and his associates found that 627 chronic offenders were responsible for over half of all offenses and two of every three serious offenses committed in Philadelphia.[18]

James Collins, Jr., has used a 10 percent sample (or 971 individuals) of the Wolfgang et al. study and followed this smaller cohort to age thirty. He found that the follow-up sample contained 14.8 percent, or 144, chronic offenders who committed 74 percent of all offenses and an even higher percentage of serious ones.[19] Data also revealed that youths who early became chronic offenders committed 82 percent more offenses than those who became chronic offenders only later (14.1 for the first group and 8.7 for the second).

The President's Commission on Law Enforcement and Administration of Justice placed the blame for youth violence on lower-class, ghetto, male repeaters. The Commission concluded:

1. Violent crime is primarily a phenomenon of large cities. This is a factor of central importance.
2. Violent crime in the city is overwhelmingly committed by males.
3. Violent crime in the city is concentrated especially among youths between the ages of fifteen and twenty-four.
4. Violent crime is committed primarily by individuals at the lower end of the occupational and income scale.
5. Violent crime in the cities stems disproportionately from the ghetto slums.
6. By far the highest proportion of all serious violence is committed by repeaters.[20]

Similiarly, Wolfgang et al. found that nonwhites were much more likely than whites to be chronic offenders and that lower-class boys were more likely than middle-class boys to be chronic offenders. Data also revealed that the group of chronic offenders made more residential moves, had lower I.Q. scores, included a greater percentage of mentally retarded youths, and had less education then either single or multiple offenders.[21]

Thus, these studies present a picture of a few youths committing half or more of all juvenile offenses and an even higher percentage of the violent juvenile offenses in the community. Lower-class boys are responsible for much of the violent youth crime in this country.

CHANGING NATURE OF JUVENILE CRIME

Youth crime in the late 1970s differs from that of the early 1960s. Increasingly visible middle-class crime, rising female crime, the return of the juvenile gang, and the widespread use of drugs are all new characteristics of youth crime in this country.

The Middle-Class Offender   Average citizens, if faced with the question of the degree of anti-social behavior among middle-class youths, probably would take one of two extreme positions. They would either say that middle-class youths are relatively free of unlawful behavior and that the delinquent problem rests solely in lower-class neighborhoods, or they would contend that middle-class juvenile offenders are involved in extensive antisocial behavior, including sexual promiscuity, heavy drinking, drug use, and serious vandalism.

Prior to the 1960s, the answer was thought to be clear. The deprivations and circumstances of lower-class living were believed to drive youths to unlawful behavior, and studies concentrated almost entirely on lower-class youth. But during the past decade and a half, researchers have been examining the middle class very carefully to see whether or not they, too, are heavily engaged in crime. The truth appears to lie somewhere between the belief that the middle class is not particularly involved in crime and the belief that they are extensively involved. Few researchers question that suburban youth crime has increased; in fact, the nearly three-to-one ratio of city to suburban arrests of juveniles under the age of eighteen would undoubtedly be reduced even further if police patrolled middle-class neighborhoods as much as they do lower-class ones and used the same criteria in arresting middle-class as for lower-class youths. However, most studies do find middle-class offenses to be petty in nature.[22]

Who are these middle-class lawbreakers? The first type is the boy or girl with family problems. These youths tend to be loners and their offenses usually are running away, truancy, and/or ungovernable behavior at home. When they become involved with shoplifting, unacceptable sexual behavior, or drugs, they are normally only seeking a reaction from their parents—attention, embarassment, or anger. These incorrigible youths were described earlier in this chapter.

Those in the second category are also in conflict with their parents, but these youths are much more amenable to peer group influence. Instead of focusing on parental rejection and neglect, they seem to channel some of their anger toward parents into a critique of parental values and way of life. One of these adolescents said, after he was arrested on a drug and disorderly charge:

> If I have to be like my old man, working all the time and only concerned about making money, not giving a damn about anyone other than himself—and if they make him a big shot in the church and in the neighborhood—if that's what the straight world is, man, then I don't want any of it.[23]

The offenses of these juveniles generally are confined to drug use and unacceptable sexual behavior. Any additional offenses are usually drug related. The disorderly charge against the above youth, for example, probably arose from his reaction to the drug bust. Even though they may be into everything but hard drugs, the majority of these youths seem to escape the correctional funnel of the juvenile justice system.

The third type of middle-class lawbreaker is very different from the first two types. Satiated with affluence, these youths basically are bored with their lives and are seeking new thrills. While they generally have no serious problems with parents, they are very much concerned with bringing more excitement to their lives. Therefore, they become involved in senseless destruction of property, shoplifting, joyriding in "borrowed" cars, traffic offenses, alcohol use, and other drug offenses. This group, interestingly enough, seems more likely to use alcohol than other types of drugs.

These lawbreakers are even less frequently processed through the juvenile justice system than those in the second group. One reason, of course, is that their parents usually are important people who will do whatever is necessary to extricate their children. They pay the damages, apologize to the right people, and pull the necessary strings.

The fourth group of middle-class offenders is involved in many of the same activities as the third group, but it is made up of juveniles who have only recently moved up to middle-class status. Their fathers, who formerly held lower-class jobs, have been promoted to middle-class positions, such as lower-management, plant foremen, and skilled workers. The children, however, still have many lower-class characteristics, such as toughness, callousness, physical prowess, and desire for danger.[24] These adolescents tend to cluster in gangs and, if the gang has an antisocial leader, the group sometimes becomes involved in serious delinquent behavior—for example, auto theft or assault. This group, needless to say, cannot always stay ahead of the law. When apprehended, they do not have parents with either the clout or the necessary resources to rescue them. Therefore, they often are confined.

Of the four groups of middle-class lawbreakers, then, the first and fourth are usually the ones processed by the juvenile justice system. As coming chapters will document, both types have considerable difficulty surviving in juvenile facilities.

The Female Juvenile Offender

Juvenile crime among girls under eighteen, according to the *Uniform Crime Reports,* more than tripled between 1960 and 1975. Arrests increased from 70,925 in 1960 to 251,008 in 1975, a rise of 251.9 percent. In general, violent crime (murder, robbery, and aggravated assault) among girls increased more than 503.5 percent, and property crime (burglary, larceny-theft, and motor vehicle theft) rose 420.4 percent. The most rapidly increasing crimes committed by females are shown in Table 2-2.

In *Sisters in Crime,* Freda Adler argues that crime among girls is going up because they are abandoning the traditional triad of incorrigibility, running away, and promiscuity and are becoming involved in

TABLE 2-2

Crime	1960	1975	Percent Change
Larceny-Theft	13,661	76,128	457.3
Aggravated Assault	676	3,637	438.0
Robbery	355	2,651	648.8
Stolen Property (buying, receiving, possessing)	189	1,747	824.3
Driving under the Influence	63	596	846.0
Narcotics Violations	195	10,682	5,377.9

Source: U.S. Department of Justice, Federal Bureau of Investigation, *Uniform Crime Reports, 1975* (Washington, D.C.: U.S. Government Printing Office, 1976), p. 183. Data reported by 2,726 agencies representing an estimated 1975 population of 96,428,998.

more aggressive and antisocial behavior.[25] She provides several quotations to substantiate her case:

> "I know it's happening, but I'll be damned if it still doesn't shock me when I see it," explained one exasperated sergeant who was slumped in the chair of a district precinct house in Washington, D.C.* He was talking about the new problems which girls have created for police. "Last week, for instance, we get a call of a disturbance at the high school. A fight . . . after school. So we get down there and pull up and here is a hell of a crowd yelling and screaming at the kids in the center, who are fighting. I push my way through the crowd—they're going crazy like it is really a mean fight and when I get to the middle . . . I liked to fell over. Here are two husky broads, and they are fighting . . . now I don't mean any hair-pulling face-scratching kind of thing; I mean two broads squared off and duking it out. Throwing jabs and hooking in at each other and handling themselves like a couple of goddamned pro sparring partners. I mean, I got to ask myself, What the hell is going on? What in the name of God is happening to these girls any more"

In New York, Gladys Polikoff has spent the last quarter of a century working with adolescent girls who have been apprehended by, and are being processed through, the Youth Aid Division of the police department:

> It's difficult to put a finger on exactly what is happening, but something quite drastic has taken place out there.* Through the fifties, we'd get an occasional girl . . . for shoplifting . . . mostly it was because the girl had taken something for kicks or on a dare . . . strictly a spur-of-the-moment sort of thing. Now, of course, girl shoplifters are quite common; and they are taking specific things for resale or for their own use in a very methodical way. Girls we're seeing now are involved in a whole new range of activities . . . like extortion. A group of girls ganging up on another girl and shaking her down for money. I mean, that was simply unheard of just a few years ago. Now, you don't get the name-calling, hair-pulling that used to go on between girls . . . you get vicious physical assault.

The increasingly violent female adolescent, according to Adler, is particularly visible in correctional institutions:

> At Muncy State Prison for Women in northwestern Pennsylvania, for instance, there has been a radical change in the inmate population.*
> Sue Goodwin, a prison official who has formerly worked as a probation officer in two major urban areas, feels the change in the general attitude of her charges has become glaringly apparent.
> "In the first place," she explained, "there is no question that the

---

*From *Sisters in Crime* by Freda Adler. Copyright © 1975. Used with permission of McGraw-Hill Book Company.

adolescents are the hardest inmates to handle. They are the most exuberant, and the ones who rebel the most. And now we have begun to get a whole new breed of adolescent inmates . . . very violent ones. They are no longer the .frightened, docile prisoners that women have traditionally been. Instead, they come in here and, within the first two weeks, they have to let everyone know that they are the 'baddest ass' in the place."

Finally, Adler cites gang activity as an indicator of greater violence among adolescent girls. In Philadelphia, female cliques, ranging from a few to several dozen, engage in typical male gang activity:

> Deborah is a fifteen-year-old who has been a member of such a group for a number of years.* She comes from the 21st-and-Montgomery section of the city—a rugged area, with dilapidated housing, a high crime rate, and widespread unemployment. A student at William Penn High School, she began her involvement with gangs as a hanger-on with the Valley Gang, an all-male gang from the same area. Although currently connected with a church organization seeking to break down the gangs and gang involvement, she feels no shame about her activities in the past. Her words are spoken with a hint of pride as she tells about her effectiveness on the streets and in violence-oriented gang operations.
>
> She, along with the other girls of her group, did much street fighting, usually rivaling the other male gangs of the area. "A lotta times we'd go down to Norris Street, in enemy territory, and fight their girls. But we never shot anybody," she said, pointing out that, instead, the girls liked to confine their efforts to the use of fists and, only occasionally, pipes, clubs, and bricks as weapons. She admitted to having used a knife on special occasions. "The way it was, if any of the other girls got messed up bad, it was because they asked for it. I mean, now we might beat them up or threaten to stab them, but we weren't like the boys . . . they're mean; they used guns and all. We never used guns."

Adler notes that almost a third (twenty-three) of the eighty-five male gangs in Philadelphia have female branches. However, the Black Persuaders and the Sedgewick Sisters are two exclusively female groups with no male affiliation. Adler predicts that these may be a harbinger of numerous girl gangs in the future.

Although few would challenge the contention of the *Uniform Crime Reports* and *Sisters in Crime* that crime among females of all ages has increased, several studies contest the idea that violence among women and girls has increased. Rita Simon states that "the proportion of female arrests for violent crimes has changed hardly at all over the past two decades."[26] Some evidence, in fact, is available that female arrests for murder-manslaughter and aggravated assault have decreased.[27]

The two most popular explanations for increased female involve-

---

*From *Sisters in Crime* by Freda Adler. Copyright © 1975. Used with permission of McGraw-Hill Book Company.

ment are role reversal and role validation. Adler claims that the feeling of emancipation is so strong and deep with contemporary women that role reversal is taking place. As a result, women want a greater piece of the pie and, according to Adler, are becoming more willing to do anything men do in order to realize this goal.[28]

However, little evidence exists that role reversal is having any impact on adolescent girls. Both Weiss and Simon concur that role validation theory is a better explanation of female adolescent involvement in crime. Role validation theory proposes that female antisocial behavior is an illegitimate expression of femininity rather than of masculinity. Weiss, using self-report data gathered from juvenile girls in the San Francisco Bay area, found that girls who occupy the most traditional feminine roles are more involved in lawbreaking than those who pursue the less feminine or more masculine roles.[29]

The Return of the Gang

From the late 1940s through the 1950s, teenage gangs in nearly every urban area struck terror in the hearts of citizens. When gangs began to reduce their activities and even to disappear from some urban areas in the 1960s, some observers thought that the problem of teenage gangs was coming to an end. Gang activity in New York City, especially, decreased significantly in the 1960s. The major sociological reason related to the demise of gangs appears to be the use of hard-core drugs, while minor reasons include the civil rights movement, riots, growth of militant organizations, Vietnam, and an exodus from the ghettos.[30]

A current leader of a large Bronx gang reflects on the lack of gangs in the 1960s: "You can't keep a brother interested in clicking [gang activities] if he's high or nodding."[31] Another youth, who was a heroin addict for several years in New York City during the 1960s, also blames drugs for the lack of gang activity.

> My brother was a big gang member. But we did not go for that kind of thing. Man, we were on drugs. That was cool. We were too busy trying to score to buy our drugs to fool around with gang activity. It was everybody for himself.

As one city after another reported serious problems with gangs in the early 1970s, it became apparent that the gangs had returned. But, while almost matching the violence of gangs of the 1950s, the gangs of the 1970s seem as equally intent on making money from crime. Present-day gangs tend to extort local merchants, engage in robberies, shake down students for money, intimidate local residents, and sell stolen goods. The security manager of a large grocery store in Brooklyn remarked:

These gangs know exactly what they're doing. They send guys in here to watch the cash registers. They note who's getting a lot of change. Out in the parking lot, other kids try to rip them off.

They'll send two guys in here. One guy deliberately acts very suspicious, to draw our attention; meanwhile, his confederate is boosting (stealing) stuff. We lose about $800 a week in meat they steal from us.

You know what happens with it? They have a regular "meat route" nearby, a list of people they sell the meat to. They'll even take orders before going out to grab the stuff.[32]

To investigate gangs in the mid-1970s, Walter B. Miller conducted a national survey of gangs in major urban cities in this country. Through interviews, questionnaires, and visits to the site, Miller came to the conclusion that youth gangs are now a problem of the utmost seriousness. He found that hundreds and thousands of gang members are terrorizing whole communities, are keeping many urban schools in a state of occupation as they exploit and intimidate both teachers and students, and are committing as much as one-third of all violent juvenile crimes.[33]

Miller found from his initial research that professionals in the justice system reported problems with youth gangs in ten of the fifteen largest metropolitan areas. Respondents in six cities—New York, Philadelphia, Los Angeles, Chicago, Detroit, and San Francisco—considered gang problems to be extremely serious. Dr. Miller estimates from available data that the number of gangs in these six cities range from 760 to 2,700 and include from 28,500 to 81,500 gang members.

Miller also reported the experience with gangs of these six cities from 1965 to 1975. New York appeared to experience a lull in gang violence between 1965 and 1971, followed by a dramatic rise in the number of gangs and gang crimes up to 1973. The number of reported gangs, gang members, and gang-member arrests leveled off and remained at this high level, but the number of gang-related killings declined markedly after 1973. Chicago experienced the rise and fall of a number of supergangs between 1965 and 1973, with gang killings peaking in 1969. Smaller and more traditional gangs and rising gang-member arrest rates characterized gang activity in Chicago between 1973 and 1975. In Los Angeles, Hispanic gangs created problems between 1965 and 1971, primarily in established Hispanic communities. Black gangs began to increase around 1972, and they contributed the bulk of the record numbers of gang killings there in the mid-1970s. In Philadelphia, problems with gangs, that were mostly black, were intense throughout the 1960s; police reported an average of about forty gang-related killings each year. The numbers of gang-related killings decreased in the 1970s, but the number of gangs and gang members in Philadelphia continued to remain at a high level. Detroit reported a decline in the gang situation during the first part of the 1960s; a small number of larger gangs experienced growth between 1968 and 1973; and a proliferation of small gangs occurred between 1973 and 1975. San Francisco also saw a decline in black gangs early in the 1960s, with the corresponding establishment of a small number of highly criminal Chinese gangs. The numbers of the relatively small Asian gangs, especially Filipino, increased between 1971 and 1974. Killings increased among the Chinese gangs, but then a decline in the violence of Chinese gangs occurred between 1973 and 1975. A resurgence of black gangs seemed to be evident during this time.

Gang members have a number of assault techniques (see Table 2-3). Significantly, in the mid-1970s the rate of murder by firearms or

TABLE 2-3 Major Forms of Assaultive Encounters: Gang Member Participants, 1973–1975

| Form | EXISTENCE REPORTED | | | | | | No. Cities Reporting Form |
	New York City	Chi-cago	Los Ange-les	Phila-del-phia	De-troit	San Fran-cisco	
Planned Rumble: pre-arranged encounter be-tween sizable rival groups	R	R	R	O	R	-	5
Rumble: encounter between rival groups, generally sizable	O	R	R	R	R	R	6
Warfare: continuing pattern of retaliatory engagements by members of rival groups; various forms	O	R	O	R	O	R	6
Foray: smaller bands engage rival bands	R	R	R	R	O	O	6
Hit: smaller bands attack one or two gang rivals	O	R	R	R	R	O	6
Fair Fight/Execution: single gang member engages single rival	-	R	R	R	R	O	5
Punitive Assault: gang members assault or kill present or potential members of own gang	O	O	O	R	-	-	4
Number of Forms Reported per City	6	7	7	7	6	5	

R = Reported by respondent
O = Reported by other source

Source: From Walter B. Miller, *Violence by Youth Gangs and Youth Groups as a Crime Problem in Major American Cities* (Washington, D.C.: U.S. Government Printing Office, 1975), p. 90.

other weapons was higher than ever before. For example, the five cities that have the most serious gang problems averaged at least 175 gang-related killings a year between 1972 and 1974. Furthermore, research shows that fighting among gang members is the dominant form of gang violence; in fact, forays by small bands, armed and often motorized, seem to have replaced the classic "rumble." However, the increasing victimization of adults and children appears to be a definite trend in the late 1970s.

Gang members, whether they are involved in assaults on others or in the destruction of community property, seem to be motivated by desire for material gain and for control over public facilities. The control of public facilities often stems from the defense of honor and the local turf.

Social characteristics of gang members in the 1970s resemble those reported for past periods. Members are primarily male, range in age from about ten to twenty-one, come from low-income communities, and are largely black and Hispanic, although gangs of a variety of Asian origins seem to be on the increase (see Table 2-4). There is also some evidence that even younger youths are becoming involved in gangs.

Gangs are active at the elementary, junior, and high school levels. In fact, gangs sometimes take control of a school itself or part of its facilities. This control has permitted gangs to set disciplinary policy and to collect fees from other students for the privilege of attending school, traversing the corridors, and avoiding gang beatings. They have also forbidden teachers and other school staff to report these activities to authorities. Many city schools have had to adopt extreme security measures to protect themselves from gang violence.

As a result of gang activity and violence, the three largest cities recorded approximately 13,000 gang-member arrests in a single year,

TABLE 2-4   Major Ethnic Categories of Gang Members in Six Cities

	Number	Percent
Black	29,000	47.6
Hispanic	22,000	36.1
Non-Hispanic White	5,400	8.8
Asian	4,600	7.5
	61,000	100.0

Source: Walter B. Miller, *Violence by Youth Gangs and Youth Groups as a Crime Problem in Major American Cities* (Washington, D.C.: U.S. Government Printing Office, 1975), p. 66.

nearly half of which were for violent crimes. To cope with the problem of gangs, some cities have established gang intelligence units (GIU), but in Chicago and Philadelphia the units were abandoned because they were ineffective. Nor have they been particularly effective elsewhere. The fact of the matter is that law enforcement agencies do not know how to police and control juvenile gangs.

In 1975, Miller predicted that in the late 1970s and early 1980s gang problems will worsen in Los Angeles, Detroit, and San Francisco, improve in Philadelphia, and remain stable in New York and Chicago. He does not see any immediate relief from gang violence and predatory activity in this country.

He concludes his excellent study with these words:

> The basic question—"How serious are problems posed by youth gangs and youth groups today, and what priority should be granted gang problems among a multitude of current crime problems?"—must be approached with considerable caution, owing to a persisting tendency to exaggerate the seriousness of gang activity, and to represent the "gang of today" as more violent than at any time in the past. Exercising such caution, the materials presented in this report appear amply to support the conclusion that youth-gang violence is more lethal today than ever before, that the security of a wider sector of the citizenry is threatened by gangs to a greater degree than ever before, and that violence and other illegal activities by members of youth gangs and groups in the United States of the mid-1970s represents a crime problem of the first magnitude which shows little prospect of early abatement.[34]

The Increased Use of Drugs   Drug use in this country is pervasive among young people. (See Table 2-5.) According to the National Advisory Commission on Criminal Justice Standards and Goals, there are several types of drug users:

1. *Experimental User* is curious about drugs and occasionally uses them to test their effects.
2. *Social or Recreational User* occasionally takes drugs to socialize with friends.
3. *Seeker* spends a lot of time and money in obtaining drugs, and they play an important role in the user's life. However, despite heavy and regular use, the addict may still remain functional and be able to meet social and academic responsibilities.
4. *Self-medicating User* uses tranquilizers or stimulants as a habitual response to loneliness, boredom, frustration, and stress.
5. *Dysfunctional Drug User* is dominated by drugs, and the process of securing and using them interferes with the life of this user.[35]

TABLE 2-5   Total Arrest Trends by Sex, 1960–1975

Offense Charged	Males under 18			Females under 18		
	1960	1975	Percent Change	1960	1975	Percent Change
Narcotic drug laws	1,263	55,182	+4,269.1	195	10,682	+5,377.9
Liquor laws	14,687	39,095	+ 166.2	2,289	10,433	+ 355.8
Drunkenness	11,719	19,091	+ 62.9	1,362	2,987	+ 119.3

Source: U.S. Department of Justice, Federal Bureau of Investigation, *Uniform Crime Reports, 1975* (Washington, D.C.: U.S. Government Printing Office, 1975), p. 183.

Adolescents generally prefer substances that are not too costly. Beer and marijuana meet this criterion better than hard drugs. Availability and potency are also important in drug use, for these substances are likely to be used as means to other ends, especially for achieving excitement. For example, marijuana, alcohol, and other drugs used at football games, rock concerts, parties, outings, dances, and similar activities provide additional excitement to that already inherent in such activities or in some cases produce excitement when it seems to be lacking.[36]

In addition to excitement, experience-enhancing substances also serve the purpose of exploration. They enable the youth to experience new social orbits, mating relations, and unfamiliar places. Narcotic substances are used least of all to escape or retreat from the external world into an inner and private self.

The succession of drug-alcohol fads is often quite rapid. In the second half of the 1970s, wine has become popular with many juveniles; hard liquor too has become popular again in some teenage circles. Beer continues to be highly popular among male adolescents from working class homes. Nevertheless, marijuana continues to be the drug of choice for the majority of youth; no other drug has approached its popularity for the mass of juveniles.

Gold and Reimer feel that the reason for the increased use of drugs is greater tolerance of drugs by parents. Male drug users seem to be granted more autonomy by their parents than non-drug users, while girls' greater drug use largely depends upon their dating boys who use drugs. The fact that both boys and girls perceive of the use of marijuana as normal is also important in the increased use of drugs.[37]

SUMMARY

This chapter covered a wide terrain. It moved from a discussion of recognized and hidden juvenile lawbreaking to an examination of the different types of juvenile offenders and concluded with a profile of changing juvenile crime. Offenders were divided into the noncriminal, the situational, and the chronic. The changing profile of juvenile crime included the increase of middle-class and female offenders, the return of urban gangs, and the increase in drug use. Undoubtedly, the types and profiles of juvenile offenders will continue to change. Countertrends will sometimes make the prevailing trends hard to interpret. Nevertheless, offenders of the types described in this chapter appear to be the youths with which society must deal if it is to maintain law and order. The degree of success in the 1970s will largely determine the degree of safeness of our streets in the 1980s and 1990s.

QUESTIONS

1. What types of youths are included in the authors' classification scheme contained in this chapter? Are there any advantages in classifying youthful offenders in this manner? What are the disadvantages?

2. What can be done to keep noncriminal youths out of the system?

3. What should society do about chronic offenders? Is there any way they can be rehabilitated?

4. What can an urban school dominated by predatory gangs do to make the environment safer for both pupils and teachers?

5. Do you believe that role reversal has anything to do with the rise of crime among juvenile girls?

6. What are the problems with identifying commitment as the basic difference between situational and chronic offenders?

ENDNOTES

1. LaMar T. Empey, *Studies in Delinquency: Alternatives to Incarceration* (Washington, D.C.: U.S. Department of Health, Education and Welfare, Office of Juvenile Delinquency and Youth Development, 1967), pp. 27–32; Maynard L. Erickson and LaMar T. Empey, "Court Records, Undetected Delinquency and Decision-Making," *Journal of Criminal Law, Criminology and Police Science* 54 (December 1963): 456–469.
2. William T. Pink and Mervin F. White, "Delinquency Prevention: The State of the Art," in *The Juvenile Justice System,* edited by Malcolm W. Klein (Beverley Hills, Calif.: Sage Publications, 1976), p. 9.
3. LaMar T. Empey, "Contemporary Programs for Adjudicated Juvenile Offenders: Problems of Theory, Practice, and Research," in *Juvenile Justice Management,* edited by Adams et al. (Springfield, Ill,: Charles C Thomas Company, 1973), pp. 425–493.
4. U.S. Department of Justice, Federal Bureau of Investigation, *Uniform Crime Reports, 1976* (Washington, D.C.: U.S. Government Printing Office, 1977), p. 181. Data reported by 10,119 agencies with a 1976 estimated population of 175,499,000. The following statistics on sex, race, and geographic location of crime are taken from the *Uniform Crime Reports, 1976,* pp. 180–214.
5. Stephen Schafer, *Theories in Criminology: Past and Present Philosophies of the Crime Problem* (New York: Random House, 1969), pp. 175–177.
6. Nathaniel Hirsh, *Dynamic Causes of Juvenile Crime* (Cambridge, Mass.: Sci-Art Publisher, 1937).
7. Roy Gerard, "Institutional Innovations in Juvenile Corrections," *Federal Probation* (December 1970), pp. 38–40.
8. M. Q. Warren, "The Community Treatment Project: History and Prospect," in *Law Enforcement, Science and Technology,* edited by S. A. Yefsky (Washington, D.C.: Thompson Book Company, 1967), pp. 191–200.
9. *Phase I Assessment of Youth Service Bureaus, Summary Report of Youth Service Bureau Research Group for LEAA* (Boston: Boston University, 1975), p. 13.
10. George H. Byars, "Some Facts about Sniffing Phenomenon," *Juvenile Justice* 26 (May 1975): 27–34.
11. President's Commission on Law Enforcement and Administration of Justice, *Task Force Report: Juvenile Delinquency and Youth Crime* (Washington, D.C.: U.S. Government Printing Office, 1967), p. 27.
12. Rosemary C. Sarri and Robert D. Vinter, "Justice for Whom? Varieties of Juvenile Correctional Approaches," in Klein, *Juvenile Justice System,* p. 190.
13. Clemens Bartollas et al. *Juvenile Victimization: The Institutional Paradox* (New York: Halsted Press, A Sage Publication, 1976), p. 152.
14. Lisa Aversa Richette, *The Throwaway Children* (New York: J. B. Lippincott Company, 1969).
15. The following discussion on delinquency and drift is adapted from David Matza, *Delinquency and Drift* (New York: John Wiley & Sons, 1964), pp. 184–190.
16. *Ibid.*
17. David Matza, *Becoming Deviant* (Englewood Cliffs, N.J.: Prentice-Hall, 1969), pp. 90–117.

18. Marvin E. Wolfgang, Robert M. Figlio, and Thorstein Sellin, *Delinquency in a Birth Cohort* (Chicago: University of Chicago Press, 1972).

19. James Collins, "Chronic Offender Careers," (Unpublished paper presented to the American Society of Criminology, Tucson, Arizona, 4–7 November 1976), p. 5.

20. President's Commission on Law Enforcement and Administration of Justice, *Task Force Report: Corrections* (Washington, D.C.: U.S. Government Printing Office, 1967).

21. Wolfgang, Figlio, and Sellin, *Delinquency,* p. 30.

22. Edmund Vaz, *Middle-Class Delinquency* (New York: Harper & Row, 1967).

23. Paul H. Hahn, *The Juvenile Offender and the Law* (Cincinnati, Ohio: W. H. Anderson Company, 1969), p. 114.

24. Leon F. Fannin and Marshall B. Clinard, "Differences in the Conception of Self as a Male among Lower and Middle Class Delinquents," in Vaz, *Middle-Class Delinquency,* p. 110.

25. Freda Adler, *Sisters in Crime* (New York: McGraw-Hill Book Company, 1975), p. 106.

26. Rita Simon, *Women and Crime* (Lexington, Mass.: D. C. Heath and Company, 1975), p. 46.

27. Joseph Weis, "Middle-Class Female Delinquency" (Unpublished paper presented at the Annual Meeting of the American Society of Criminology, Toronto, November 1975), p. 4.

28. Adler, *Sisters in Crime.*

29. Weis, "Female Delinquency."

30. Craig Collins, "Youth Gangs of the 70s," *Police Chief* 42 (September 1975): 50.

31. Ibid., p. 5.

32. Ibid., p. 201.

33. Walter B. Miller, *Violence by Youth Gangs and Youth Groups as a Crime Problem in Major American Cities* (Washington, D.C.: U.S. Government Printing Office, August 1975). The following materials are chiefly taken from Chapter 15 of Miller's excellent gang study.

34. Ibid., p. 205.

35. National Advisory Commission on Criminal Justice Standards and Goals, *Community Crime Prevention* (Washington, D.C.: U.S. Government Printing Office, 1973).

36. Walter B. Miller, "Adolescent Subculture and Drug Use," *Proceedings of International Seminar, Sociocultural Factors in Nonmedical Drug Use,* Institute of Criminal Justice and Criminology, University of Maryland, College Park, Md. (3–5 November 1975), pp. 67–68.

37. Martin Gold and David J. Reimer, *Changing Patterns of Delinquent Behavior among Americans Thirteen to Sixteen Years Old, 1967–1972* (Ann Arbor, Mich.: Institute for Social Research, University of Michigan, 1974), pp. 60–68.

REFERENCES

Adler, Freda. *Sisters in Crime.* New York: McGraw-Hill Book Company, 1975. *The role reversal thesis of this book has been heavily criticized, but it is still interesting and informative reading.*

Miller, Walter B. *Violence by Youth Gangs and Youth Groups as a Crime Problem in Major American Cities.* Washington, D.C.: U.S. Government Printing Office, 1975.

> *An excellent national gang study that presents the most authoritative source on gangs in this country.*

Vaz, Edmund. *Middle-Class Juvenile Delinquency.* New York: Harper & Row, 1967.

> *A very good selection of articles on middle-class crime.*

Wolfgang, Marvin E.; Figlio, Robert M., and Sellin, Thorstein. *Delinquency in a Birth Cohort.* Chicago: University of Chicago, 1972.

> *One of the important sources for students interested in youth crime in this country.*

3

The Police
and the Juvenile

When asked about the effectiveness of the juvenile justice system in treating delinquents, a Los Angeles police officer responded:

I don't want to sound like a hard-ass, but we have some really bad young hoodlums on the streets in L.A. These aren't the nickel-and-dime kid shoplifters; they are hard core. Some of them have dozens of arrests, but they're still out there ripping off people. Some of them have killed people, but they are still out there. The juvenile justice system doesn't take care of the dangerous kids—they are on probation, on parole, on bail, on the street. They are in gangs, with a hard-core leader and a few other psychopaths. They pull pretty good kids into their web—peer pressure or whatever it's called. These good kids start imitating the hard core, and pretty soon there is a bigger gang. And then the gangs start in on each other—you've seen the paper—someone is always getting cut up or killed in a gang war. And then there is a need for revenge and another killing and so on. The system probably wouldn't do much. These punks are into juvenile hall and out twenty minutes later; seriously, some of these hoodlums are back on the street before I finish the paperwork. If you are going to correct kids, they have to get their hands whacked the first time they put them in the cookie jar, not six months later. Juvenile justice is slow. Jesus, the rights these kids have got. They have more rights than I have: lawyers, witnesses, the whole bag. I'm not talking about the mickey mouse cases; I mean the hoodlums.*

*This excerpt is from Chapter 5, "The Police View of the Justice System," by Robert M. Carter is reprinted from *The Juvenile Justice System* (Vol. V, *Sage Criminal Justice System Annuals*) M. W. Klein, Editor © 1976, p. 124 by permission of the publisher, Sage Publications, Inc.

The intent of this chapter is to describe police-juvenile relations, including the history, the attitudes of juveniles toward the police, the attitudes of the police toward juvenile offenders, police discretion, formal and informal disposition of juvenile offenders, processing juvenile offenders, the rights of juveniles, the juvenile officer, the juvenile unit, police programs for juvenile offenders, and issues in police-juvenile relations.

HISTORY OF POLICE-JUVENILE RELATIONS

Over the past two centuries, police-juvenile relations have changed markedly. In the 1800s troublesome youths were confronted by officers walking the beat. The youth was sometimes treated as an erring child and received a slap on the wrist. Or, the offender might be taken to the parish priest for admonition and spiritual guidance. At other times, the adolescent experienced the same treatment as an adult offender. Needless to say, this inconsistent, and sometimes harsh, treatment resulted in a mistrust of the police.

As far back as 1914, the New York City Police Department recognized the problem and provided adolescents with a chance to get to know local police. In the 1930s, August Vollmer, in Berkeley, California, introduced the concept of a youth bureau in a police department and emphasized the importance of crime prevention by the police. Youth bureaus were soon established in many large urban police departments as the need arose for greater police specialization in the area of juvenile law enforcement. These specialized units were known by various names: crime prevention bureaus, juvenile bureaus, youth aid bureaus, juvenile control bureaus, and juvenile divisions. The Police Athletic League (PAL) was also formed in New York City in the 1930s and swiftly spread to other cities.

The development of an urbanized society, the rise in youth crime, changing court decisions, and new legislation resulted in increased specialization as police-juvenile relations moved into the post–World War II era. A significant philosophical change was that of regarding police as helpful rather than punitive. Juvenile law enforcement officers began to expend considerable effort in developing the duties, standards, procedures, and training necessary for working with juveniles. A group of police juvenile officers organized the Central States Juvenile Officers Association in 1955, and the International Juvenile Officers Association was founded in 1957.

Beginning in the 1960s, older adolescents and young adults were enlisted as auxiliary police in some police departments. They were called white hats, youth patrols, teens on patrol, and police-buddy patrols. The police also began to invest human resources in police-community relations in an effort to improve juveniles' attitudes toward law enforcement officials. These programs were directed at both pre-delinquent and delinquent young people. Some police departments even developed counseling and diversionary resources of their own to meet community needs. Furthermore, the police began to divert trou-blemaking youths to social agencies and to youth service bureaus during the late 1960s.

Recent court decisions have affected police-juvenile relations by ruling that police must provide juveniles with the due process and procedural safeguards guaranteed by the Fourteenth Amendment, with the result that procedures for taking adolescents into custody, keeping juvenile records, fingerprinting juveniles, and photographing them have come under close scrutiny.

JUVENILE ATTITUDES TOWARD THE POLICE

Several studies have investigated youth attitudes toward the police. Both Portune and Bouma concentrated on measuring the attitudes of junior high youths. In 1971 Robert Portune concluded from his study of almost 1,000 junior high students in Cincinnati that:

Attitudes vary by age. Portune found that hostility toward the law and police increased from grades seven through nine.

Attitudes vary by race. The whites surveyed had much more favorable attitudes than blacks.

Attitudes vary by sex. The girls had more favorable attitudes than the boys.

Attitudes vary by academic performance in school. The better students had more favorable attitudes than the poor students.

Attitudes vary by socioeconomic class. The higher the occupational status of the father, the more favorable was the child's attitude toward the police.[1]

In a more detailed study, Bouma and his associates administered 10,000 questionnaires to Michigan schoolchildren in ten cities. These students, most of whom were in grades seven through nine, were asked about their attitudes, their parents' attitudes, and their friends' attitudes toward the police. This study, which agreed with all of the major findings of Portune's research, additionally established that:

1. Even though hostility toward the police significantly increased as students moved through their junior high years, the majority of

students would still cooperate with the police if they saw someone other than a friend commit a crime.

2. Most youths perceived friends to be more antagonistic toward the police than they were, and they perceived attitudes of parents toward the police to be quite similar to their own.

3. A majority of students felt that the police were "pretty nice guys." In fact, over half of all students felt that the police are criticized too often.

4. One-third of the white and two-thirds of the black youths believed the police accused students of things they did not do.

5. Although two out of every three students felt that the city would be better off with more policemen, only 8 percent felt that they would like to be police officers.[2]

Understandably, Portune and Bouma found that juveniles with police contacts were more negative toward the police than those without. Chapman, in a study of 133 delinquent and 133 nondelinquent boys in Dayton, also reported that juvenile offenders were more negative toward the police.[3] The Center for Criminal Justice of the Harvard Law School, in studying the recidivism rates in Massachusetts following the closing of training schools in that state, found that status offenders tend to be more positive toward the police than juveniles charged with other offenses. Additionally, the Center for Criminal Justice found that youths who come from white-collar families and who attend school regularly are also more likely to be positive toward the police.[4] Finally, Giordano, in matching 119 boys who had contact with the juvenile justice system with 119 who had not, discovered little difference in how both groups felt about the police. But, she went on to say, juvenile attitudes toward police seem to be affected more by high levels of delinquent activity and by peers than by the degree of contact a youth has with the system.[5]

Two different studies reported that gang members are extremely hostile toward the police. In a representative statement, one gang leader blasted the police with these words:

> They don't want us in the recreation centers, they don't want us on the streets, they don't want us hanging around the soda fountains. Where the hell do they want us? Home watching TV? We're too old for TV and too young for the bars. We get tired of just hanging around and we have to let off steam—even if it means fighting, stealing cars, breaking windows. They think we're all bad, some kind of punks.[6]

A member of another gang made this complaint about the police:

> Every time something happens in this neighborhood, them mother fucking cops come looking for me! I may not be doing nothing, but if somebody

gets beat or something gets stole they'll always be coming right to my place to find out what's going on![7]

Emerging from these studies is a fairly clear picture: Young people in general are fairly positive toward the police. Specifically, younger youths tend to be more positive than older ones, whites usually are more positive than blacks, and girls tend to be more positive than boys. A good attitude also seems to be related to social class, for middle-class youths normally are more positive in their attitudes than lower-class youths. Juveniles who have not had contact with the police tend to be more positive than those who have had police contacts. Typically, most hostile toward the police are those youths committed to a delinquent career and involved in youth gangs. In addition to these findings, law enforcement officers who anticipate hostile feelings from adolescents often respond to them in such a way that hostility is generated. Their anticipations, then, can result in a self-fulfilling prophecy.

Law enforcement agencies, fortunately, are making a major effort to build better relations with both delinquent and nondelinquent juveniles. Several of these programs for youthful offenders will be described later in this chapter. Hopefully, the attitudes of youth will improve even more as the police continue a positive emphasis on police-juvenile relations.

POLICE ATTITUDES TOWARD JUVENILES

Police attitudes toward juveniles are affected both by the pressures juveniles place upon them and by the occupational determinants of police work. The greatest pressure in policing juveniles is the strain that youthful lawbreaking and misbehavior places upon law enforcement agencies. It has been estimated, for example, that 50 to 75 percent of police agency work directly or indirectly affects adolescents.[8] In handling juveniles who come to the attention of the police, law enforcement officers must learn to discriminate between dangerous, hard-core offenders and harmless, misbehaving juveniles. Mistakes at this point can cost a police officer his life. It is not easy to take any juveniles into custody; the incorrigibility of the status offender, the special problems of arresting the juvenile girl, and the contaminating influence of peers all create difficult situations. The growing conflict between those who want to "lock the kids up" and those who state unequivocally that juveniles must be kept out of the correctional system also creates pressures on the police officer. Finally, the police are aware that many communities lack the resources for dealing with the juvenile offender. Consequently, even though police officers may have strong reservations about placing a runaway youth in the county jail, they may have no other alternative.

The police are held accountable for maintaining law and order. Skolnick notes that the police follow the crime control model more often than the due process model. Police are socialized in such a way that they begin to see themselves as craftsmen in their ability to recognize and to apprehend criminals. As they daily come in contact with victims, they soon become aware of the danger inherent in their jobs. They are taught that they must be alert to typical assailants who point to trouble or danger. They also must defend the authority of their position and therefore must quickly quash any verbal or physical abuse from either teenagers or adults. Finally, they must always be suspicious.[9]

In view of the pressures created by youth crime and the occupational determinants of police work, it would seem that the police officer would have considerable animosity toward law-violating juveniles. However, Walter Miller, in his national survey of youth gangs, did not find this to be true. Lengthy interviews with practitioners in the justice system revealed that five different approaches, or operating philosophies, could be used in dealing with youth crime: (1) strong service orientation (actual hostility to law enforcement elements); (2) combined approach (service orientation predominant); (3) combined approach (approximately equal elements of service orientation and law enforcement); (4) combined approach (law enforcement orientation predominant); (5) strong law enforcement approach (hostility to service elements).[10]

Table 3-1 shows that a higher proportion (41 percent) preferred the fourth approach over any other, with equal proportions (20.5 percent) choosing the third and fifth approaches. Significantly, a similar proportion (18 percent) favored the second, and, not surprisingly, none of the police favored the pure service approach.

Although the majority of the police (62 percent) favored predominantly law enforcement or hard-line orientations, a sizeable minority (38 percent) preferred the even mix or primarily service-oriented approaches. In addition, only one out of every five police officers in the study favored a purely hard-line law enforcement approach to youth crime. Therefore, these police—most of whom were working with violent, and often intractable, gang members—favored a much higher degree of acceptance of the service philosophy and the agencies in dealing with youth crime than might be expected, according to the law-and-order image of police.

To generalize too much from Miller's small sample of urban police officers is risky. Nevertheless, the proportions in each group do seem representative of the many police officers we have taught. It is not unreasonable, therefore, to conclude that the animosity supposedly

TABLE 3-1   Police versus Nonpolice: Five Approaches

APPROACH	POLICE		NON-POLICE	
	Number	*Percent*	*Number*	*Percent*
1 Pure Service	0	0.0	8	16.7
2 Service Predominant	7	16.9	19	39.6
3 Equal Elements of Both	8	20.5	9	18.7
4 Law-Enforcement Predominant	16	41.0	9	18.7
5 Hard-Line Law-Enforcement	8	20.5	3	6.2
Totals	39	98.9	48	99.9

Source: Walter B. Miller, *Violence by Youth Gangs and Youth Groups as a Crime Problem in Major American Cities* (Washington, D.C.: U.S. Government Printing Office, 1975).

characterizing police-juvenile relations may be exaggerated. Perhaps the various police programs designed to improve police-juvenile relations and the specialized juvenile officers trained to relate to troublesome youths are beginning to have a positive impact on both juveniles and police officers in the way they view each other.

POLICE DISCRETION

Police discretion refers to "the choice between two or more possible means of handling a situation confronting the police officer."[11] Discretion is important, for the law enforcement officer takes the responsibility of being an on-the-spot prosecutor, judge, and correctional system in dealing with the misbehaving adolescent. The police actually act as a court of first instance in controlling the initial sorting-out of juveniles. In a real sense, the police officer is a legal and social traffic director who can use his wide discretion to either detour youths from or involve them in the juvenile justice system.

Wattenberg and Bufe found, from their study of the files of the Detroit Police Department, that the first contact with a police officer was highly influential on a youth's future deposition to delinquency.[12] Lohman concurs:

The process of rehabilitation begins from the first moment the offender comes into contact with the policeman. The youngster who gets himself into trouble generally wants to get himself out of it, too. If the first contact he has with the law is both friendly and understanding, he will probably be more amenable to the treatment he is going to get. . . . If the officer is really in charge of the situation and of himself, the child's attitudes will cool gradually, and the job at hand will be easier as a result. This, then, is probably the most important part in rehabilitation an officer can play: to remember that he is the first step in a continuous process which has as its goal the making of a delinquent into a good citizen.[13]

Because the police are crucial in determining which cases will be processed into the system, police discretion has come under attack. Judge Breitel warned:

Discretion—even legally permissible discretion—involves great hazard. It makes easy the arbitrary, the discriminatory, and the oppressive. It produces inequality of treatment. It offers a fertile bed for corruption. It is conducive to the development of a police state—or, at least, a police-minded state.[14]

To exercise at least some control over police discretion, many jurisdictions have developed guidelines for its proper use in juvenile encounters. The National Advisory Commission on Criminal Justice Standards and Goals, for example, recommended that each juvenile court jurisdiction should work out policies and procedures with local police agenices for governing the discretionary authority of police officers.[15]

However, most of the time the police contact with a juvenile is impersonal and consists simply of police commands such as "Get off the corner," "Break it up," or "Go home." Most studies estimate that only 10 to 20 percent of police-juvenile encounters become official contacts.[16] Bordua's 1964 study of the Detroit police, for example, found only 5,282 official contacts out of 106,000 encounters.[17]

The police officer's disposition of the misbehaving youngster is mainly determined by six factors. The first and the most important appears to be the nature of the offense. If a juvenile commits a serious offense, referral to the juvenile court is likely.[18]

Second, the interaction between the law enforcement officer and the juvenile is also an important variable. Piliavin and Briar discovered that the youth's deference to the policeman is very influential in determining disposition.[19] If a youth is polite and respectful, the probability of informal disposition is greatly enhanced. But if the juvenile is hostile, Piliavin and Briar found, police judge him as bad and in need of the attention of the juvenile court. Werthman and Piliavin shed additional light on police-juvenile relations when they reported that black gang members regard the police as enemies who discriminate against blacks and invade their "turf"; thus, they display hostility and scorn for the police. The consequence of these hostile attitudes is a high rate of court referrals.[20]

Third, individual factors, such as prior arrest records, age, previous offenses, peer relationships, family situations, and conduct of parents, generally have a bearing on how the law enforcement officer handles the juvenile.[21]

Fourth, race often is a major variable in influencing the handling of offenders, although there is considerable disagreement among the various studies concerning its importance. It is difficult to appraise race as a variable for two reasons: blacks appear to be involved in more serious crimes than whites, and, therefore, receive more court referrals; also, communities tend to differ in racial discrimination.[22] The strongest testimony for the support of race as a determining variable is found in the studies of Thornberry and of Wolfgang and associates that concerned Philadelphia. Thornberry found that blacks are processed more than whites, even when the seriousness of their offenses is controlled. [23] Wolfgang's study concluded "that the most significant factor related to a boy's not being remediated by the police, but being processed to the full extent of the juvenile justice system, is his being nonwhite."[24]

Fifth, external pressures in the community usually have some influence on police discretion. Attitudes of the press and the public, the status of the complainant or victim, and the conditions of the existing referral agencies (available resources, length of the waiting list, and local juvenile-court handling of such referrals) usually influence police processing of juvenile lawbreakers.[25]

Sixth, the internal policy of local police departments is also important. Wilson, in his study of the way two police departments handled juvenile lawbreaking, found that the more professional police department had higher numbers of juveniles referred to the juvenile court.[26] Hence, this study suggests that the greater the professionalism of a department, the less the discretion in handling juvenile offenders. Too, the strategy developed by a law enforcement agency influences what the officer does in the field. Some larger departments quickly turn the juvenile offender over to the juvenile control unit, social service bureau, or social service unit of the police department. And the law enforcement officer, of course, is sensitive to the wishes of supervisors and, ultimately, to those of the chief.

INFORMAL AND FORMAL DISPOSITIONS
OF JUVENILE OFFENDERS

When investigating a complaint or arriving at a scene of criminal activity, a juvenile or patrol officer has at least five options. First, the juvenile can be questioned and released to the community. This informal encounter can be brief or can involve an interview at the police station. The law enforcement officer often will opt to give the juvenile an informal reprimand.

Second, the misbehaving youngster can be taken to the station, have the contact recorded, be given an official reprimand, and then be released to the community; this is sometimes called a *station adjustment*. If the police officer deems it necessary and policy permits, the juvenile can be placed under police supervision; that is, the youth remains under the supervision of the police department until released from this police-imposed probation.

The third option is to release the youth and make a referral to a youth service bureau, a mental health agency, or some type of social agency, such as Child Welfare, Big Brothers, Big Sisters, or the Y.M.C.A. With this option, the police officer chooses to divert the youth from the juvenile justice system.

A fourth option is to issue a citation and refer the youth to the juvenile court. A conference of chiefs of police agreed that this type of referral should be made when the offense is serious, when the youth has a history of repeated delinquent behavior, when diversionary programming has failed, or when the officer believes that the youth or his family are in need of aid.[27]

The fifth and final option is to issue a citation, refer the youth to the juvenile court, and take him to the detention hall. In communities that do not have a detention facility, youths must be taken to the county jail or the police lock-up. Obviously, taking children out of their homes and placing them in a detention home should be a last resort.

PROCESSING JUVENILE OFFENDERS

Of the various types of noncriminal youths, the retarded and emotionally disturbed are occasionally difficult or even dangerous to handle. The police also must spend considerable time in the homes of the dependent and neglected. But status offenders take the most time and present the most problems. They run away, create problems in school, are in conflict with parents, are reported for sexually unacceptable behavior, and sometimes become involved with drugs. These youths must be handled very carefully, for they usually are resistant to or even defiant toward authority. The law officer must be exceedingly careful so that a minor offense, such as a curfew violation, for example, does not become a charge of resisting an officer, disorderly conduct, or worse.

Police officers particularly do not like to take juvenile girls into custody for several reasons. Male police officers tend to feel awkward with misbehaving juvenile females. Too, police officers are often injured in attempting to arrest women, and juvenile females are considered more unpredictable than adult women. A sergeant taking a college course verbalized this: "The only times I have been hurt as a police officer is trying to arrest a woman. You've got to really watch yourself with women because they can hurt you." He went on to say that juvenile girls represent an even more dangerous arrest situation.

The police officer can be an important figure in saving the situational offender from deeper involvement in delinquent behavior. The officer who is called to break up a crowd, to check out a party, or to control rowdy behavior sometimes finds that more serious antisocial behavior is occurring. The officer must then decide on the most beneficial dispositional alternatives for the youths involved. However, high-risk factors exist for the police officer who must intervene in group lawbreaking, as group behavior is often quite unpredictable. In working with youthful offenders, the police also need to be especially aware of the impact of narcotics. A police officer's knowledge of alcohol, hallucinogens, depressants, inhalants, and hard drugs and the impact they have on the human organism can be useful in recognizing reactions and saving the lives of juveniles on drugs.

Gang intelligence units (GIU) have the most difficult task in policing juvenile offenders. Both the city government and the police administrators usually put pressure on the unit to crack down on gangs, yet, unit participants know that violent gang members have few qualms about killing police officers; they also are aware that combatting these youth gangs is equivalent to taking on organized crime. The consequence of these pressures is that gang intelligence units sometimes have resorted to harassment and gestapo-like tactics, including stirring up intergang conflict by spreading rumors and by dropping members of one gang deep in the "turf" of another gang, by issuing citations to gang members for minor traffic violations, and stopping gang members on the street for interrogation.[28]

Sherman cites a report of a University of Chicago church group that catalogued the more gruesome tactics of the GIU in Chicago. In one startling incident reported by this church group, several rifles had been reported stolen from the ROTC unit of a Chicago high school. The

GIU assumed the Blackstone Rangers had taken them, and a GIU officer picked up Mickey Cogwell, a top Ranger leader. The GIU officer took Cogwell, a known nonswimmer, out on the rocks that extended into the lake at 43rd Street and asked where the guns were. When the

FIGURE 3-1   Police-Juvenile Dispositional Alternatives

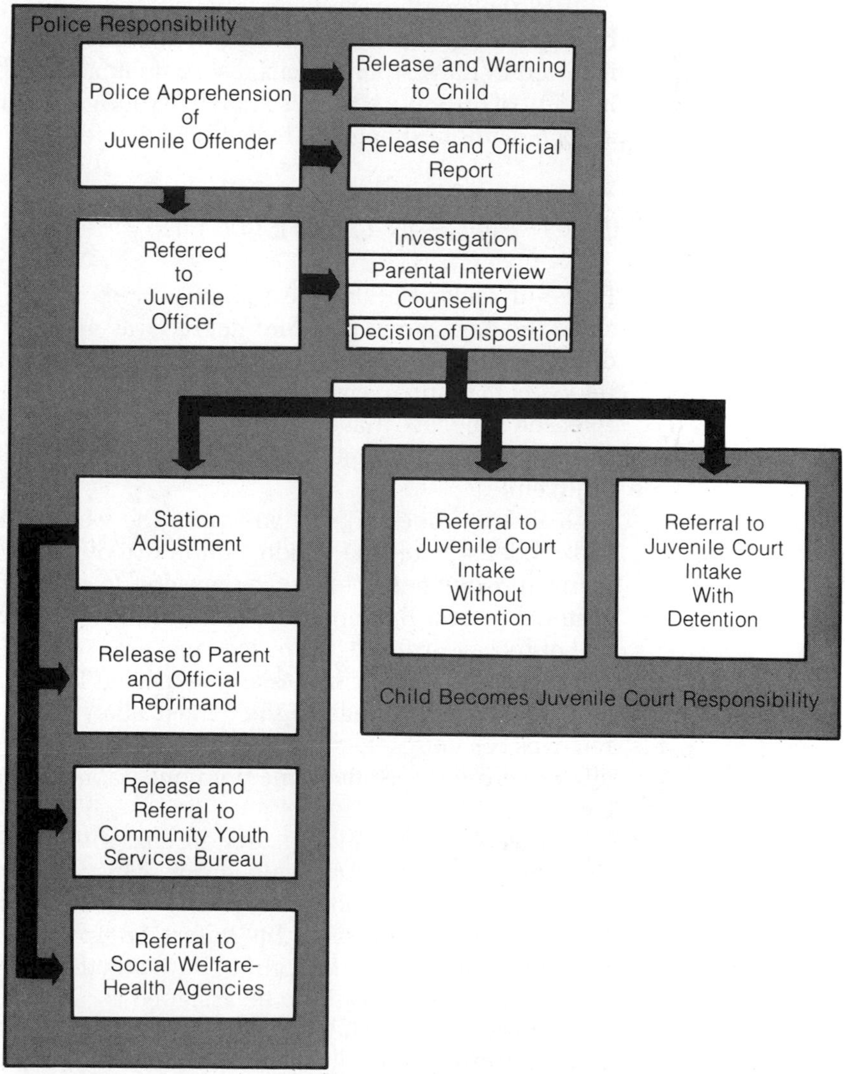

From: Richard Kobetz and Betty B. Bosarge, *Juvenile Justice Administration* (Gaithersburg, Md.: International Association of Chiefs of Police Press, 1973), p. 142.

GIU officer received no answer, he said, "Down on your knees, Cogwell." The youth refused to move. He was then beaten to his knees. The officer asked again, "Where are the guns?" No answer. He then pointed a gun at Cogwell's head, but the youth still refused to answer. The GIU officer fired the gun, barely missing the youth. He said, "We'll kill you if you don't tell us." The guns were later found in the white community. Cogwell has taken a lie detector test verifying his description of this incident.[29]

We believe that the average police officer is usually above reproach in responding to the lawbreaking youth, but some officers do become involved in harassment, racial discrimination, and brutality. When an incident of brutality becomes known to youngsters in a neighborhood or school, it unquestionably creates negative feelings toward the police.

RIGHTS OF THE JUVENILE IN CUSTODY

Police-juvenile relations have changed radically in most departments since the days when the third degree was given at the station. Some departments, not surprisingly, do lag behind others and are much more reluctant to grant due process rights to juveniles under arrest. But there is reason to believe that the majority of the law enforcement agencies in this country are attempting to comply with court decisions on the rights of juveniles.

Twenty-nine jurisdictions avoid the word "arrest." Ten of these jurisdictions state that "taking into custody" is not an "arrest."[30] In many jurisdictions the word is avoided to protect the youth from a criminal record. But since a youth taken into custody is, for all intents and purposes, arrested, the police must grant him all privileges ordinarily granted to an adult who is arrested. That is, the police must inform the juvenile of his legal rights; must allow him to contact parents, relatives, or counsel; must ensure that he appears before a judicial officer within a specified time; and must abide by fair treatment standards.

Juveniles taken into custody are also entitled to the rights stated in the 1966 *Miranda* v. *Arizona* decision. This U.S. Supreme Court decision does not allow a confession to be used in court unless the individual has been advised of his rights before interrogation, especially of the right to remain silent, the right to have an attorney present when he is questioned, and the right to be assigned an attorney by the state if he cannot afford one.[31] The right against self-incrimination and the right to counsel were specifically made applicable to juveniles in *In re Gault*.[32]

However, in the *Gault* decision, the U.S. Supreme Court failed to clarify whether or not a juvenile could waive the protection of the

FIGURE 3-2   Taking a Juvenile into Custody

Source: John Stevens

Miranda rules and failed to state what is necessary for a youth to intelligently and knowingly waive his *Miranda* rights. If he is under the influence of drugs or alcohol or is in a state of shock his ability to waive his rights may be impaired.

The first duty of the juvenile officer, or the arresting officer, if the department does not have a juvenile division, is to contact the child's parents to let them know that the youth is in police custody. The officer can do this by telephone or in person, but the parents should be informed as soon as possible.

Even though the Supreme Court has not ruled on the matter, it is reasonable to assume that the due process protections against unlawful search and seizure can be extended to juveniles, and several state and municipal courts have decided to so extend these constitutional safeguards. Yet, problems are created when attempts are made to determine whether or not a youth has the maturity and judgment necessary to waive his rights by consenting to a search. This decision ultimately rests with the discretion of the police officer.

Interviewing

Interview methods have also come under close scrutiny. Field interrogation and stopping and questioning youngsters should follow the same rules that are applied to adults in stop-and-frisk. Interrogators at the police station not only should guarantee juveniles all their rights but also should avoid physical abuse, profanity, and derogatory remarks. Since it has been estimated that 50 percent of juveniles interrogated by the police confess what they have done, advising youthful suspects of their rights is extremely important. This must be done regardless of age, immediately on arrest, prior to taking any written statement, at the start of each new period of questioning, and by each officer questioning the suspect.

Fingerprinting and Photographing

Fingerprinting, photographing, and placing juveniles in line-ups are highly controversial procedures. While some states forbid both fingerprinting and photographing of juveniles except by order of the court, the police department usually determines policy. It is not unusual for some jurisdictions to fingerprint all juveniles taken into custody and suspected of serious wrongdoing. The Juvenile Justice and Delinquency Prevention Act of 1974 recommended that fingerprints should not be done without the written consent of the juvenile judge. Juvenile fingerprints should not be recorded in the criminal section of the fingerprint registry and they should be destroyed after their purpose has been served.[33]

FIGURE 3-3   Fingerprinting of a Juvenile

The practice of photographing adolescents is less widespread than fingerprinting, and placing a juvenile in a line-up is done only occasionally. The Juvenile Justice and Delinquency Prevention Act recommended that a photograph should not be taken without the written consent of the juvenile judge and that the name or picture of any juvenile should not be made public by the media.

Before these three procedures—fingerprinting, photographing, and appearing in line-ups—juveniles should be advised of their right to counsel and to have these show-ups conducted in the presence of counsel. Although opponents argue that these techniques should be abolished because of their association with criminal proceedings, the procedures nevertheless continue to be used because of the need for positive identification.

Record
Keeping   Juvenile record keeping is another sensitive issue. Some jurisdictions maintain, in addition to a police record of each contact, a central juvenile index that is widely used by local agencies that pool their information. The objection to such police records is that even though juvenile records may be kept separately from adult records, they will not be expunged and will be available to label the individual in later years. Gough relates the incident of a highly respected and capable police juvenile sergeant whose files indicated that he had been picked up for child molesting: when he was fourteen years old, he had kissed his thirteen year-old girl friend in public and consequently was charged "with conduct arousing or tending to arouse the passions of a child under the age of fourteen years." Instead of being erased, this "offense" was retained on the police sergeant's records, and came back to haunt him as an adult.[34]

Guidelines   The National Advisory Commission on Criminal Justice Standards and Goals recommends the following guidelines for protection of the rights of the juvenile in custody:

> When police have taken custody of a minor, and prior to disposition . . ., the following guidelines should be observed.
>
> 1. Under the provisions of *Gault* and *Miranda,* police should first warn juveniles of their right to counsel and the right to remain silent while under custodial questioning.
>
> 2. The second act after apprehending a minor should be the notification of his parents.
>
> 3. Extrajudicial statements to police or court officers not made in the presence of parents or counsel should be inadmissible in court.
>
> 4. Juveniles should not be fingerprinted or photographed or otherwise routed through the usual adult booking process.
>
> 5. Juvenile records should be maintained physically separate from adult case records.[35]

IMPROVING RELATIONS WITH JUVENILES

The nature of juvenile justice police work is dependent on the philosophy of top administration, the size of the city, the problems in the community, and the orientation of the particular police department. Particularly in large cities, juvenile divisions staffed by officers trained in juvenile work handle youthful lawbreaking. But there are both advantages and disadvantages to assigning officers to special duty with juveniles.

The major advantage is that juvenile specialists, because of additional training, more specialized knowledge, and greater familiarity with youth crime, can do a better job. Too, they can develop useful contacts in the community, have better communication with the juvenile court, and be available for assistance in training other officers in the special procedures and problems in handling juveniles.

The disadvantages of specialization include the danger that nonspecialized personnel may ignore matters they themselves should handle. They may say, for example, "Forget it; that's a job for 'diaper dicks'." Another disadvantage is the tendency to divorce the juvenile division from the rest of the police department; juvenile officers who feel alienated may begin to operate on their own. Finally, the executive policymaker can become overdependent on the selective and biased point of view of the juvenile specialist.[36]

The New Breed of Juvenile Officer

Juvenile officers usually are in a better position to create positive relationships with youngsters than are nonspecialized officers because of their training and experience. However, their ability to maintain these relationships depends upon personal resources: native intelligence, ability to create a rapport with youth, patience, and an understanding of the basic dynamics of human behavior. Furthermore, juvenile officers need to be highly committed to helping adolescents rather than punishing them, particularly by referring youths and their parents to the proper agency as soon as possible.

The juvenile officer should volunteer for the position and be interested in this type of work; he should be young, in good physical condition, and morally and emotionally well-adjusted. A major difficulty encountered in recruiting top-quality juvenile officers is that in many police departments the position is not considered desirable; indeed, many juvenile officers feel stigmatized by being involved in what is often seen as relatively undemanding and unimportant police work.

Two critical factors must be kept in mind in training juvenile officers. First, the officers must receive training before assuming their field duties, for they cannot be expected to perform efficiently without adequate job preparation. Second, choice of subject matter is extremely important during the training process. Courses should cover the philosophy of juvenile police work, the scope of a juvenile unit, juvenile law, relationships between the juvenile unit and other police units, interviewing, dispositional alternatives, community resources prevention of juvenile lawbreaking through community organization, and understanding of the predisposing factors in juvenile lawbreaking.[37]

Wattenberg and Bufe describe the effective juvenile officer:

As might be expected he has a genuine interest in young people, which shows itself in extra effort on their behalf. He is a good police officer, tending to give each task the time it requires to do a thorough job; he works well with his fellow-officers. In his dealing with juveniles he is calm, manly, firm and patient. He talks well to them, wording his remarks to their level. He keeps his promises to young people and exerts "salesmanship" in support of a law-abiding course of action. He presents a good appearance and keeps his records well. Outside activities, suprisingly, did not loom as important. In fact, so strong an allegiance to an outside organization as to unduly influence dispositions appeared on the negative side. Leadership ability did not appear to be critically essential. However, competence in speaking and writing were highly important. So was willingness to work hard with parents. As to disposition, the key attribute was a tendency to judge cases on their merits as contrasted with a policy of either quickly filing charges with the juvenile court or being reluctant to do so.[38]

In 1970, the International Association of Chiefs of Police mailed a questionnaire to 1,991 administrators of law enforcement agencies in all fifty states; 1,471, or 73.9 percent, were returned. This sample of some 40,000 law enforcement agencies in the country indicated that 5,557 officers were assigned to juvenile work out of a total of 203,877 police officers. In addition, 781, or 55.8 percent of the departments responding, had juvenile units. Qualifications for the juvenile unit usually included a high school diploma (63.8 percent) and some prior police experience (81.1 percent). However, few departments required both a written and an oral examination (22.1 percent) for appointment to the position of juvenile officer; even fewer required either a written examination (4.4 percent) or an oral examination (12.8 percent) for appointment to juvenile work. Also, fewer than half of the responding departments required the officer to have formal classroom training in juvenile work (45.5 percent).[39]

The Juvenile Unit   Juvenile units are designated variously: crime prevention bureau, juvenile bureau, youth aid bureau, juvenile control division, juvenile division, or juvenile unit. Regardless of the name, however, the functions of juvenile units are roughly comparable throughout the country.

Detection of Youth Crime, Potential Lawbreakers, and Conditions Conducive to Lawbreaking.[40]   These elements are of prime importance in the development of a delinquency-prevention program. If juvenile officers are to know "who is doing what" and "who is about to do what," they must have access to all available sources of information.

The school, in particular, is a valuable source. Therefore, a good relationship must be developed with child-guidance counselors. Social agencies are also a valuable source of information about conditions that contribute to juvenile lawbreaking, as are the juvenile court and probation department. Parents, relatives, and friends of juvenile offenders are helpful in determining why these youths have misbehaved. Patrol activities of juvenile officers will also yield needed information, particularly when the officer visits local hangouts and talks with local merchants and citizens of the community.

Investigation of Juvenile Lawbreaking.   Such investigations should be as prompt, thorough, and complete as possible. It is important to discover all the offenses a youth has committed and any associates involved. A group of informants can be very helpful, not only in preventing delinquency, but also in investigating juvenile crime. All available tools, such as departmental and school records and the services of probation and aftercare departments and social agencies, should be used in making an investigation. Interviews should be held with the youth himself, his companions in crime, his parents, the victim, and anyone else who may have relevant information. Cases usually assigned to the juvenile unit for investigation involve bicycle thefts, family-related situations (such as desertion, neglect, or abuse), adults responsible for or accused of contributing to the delinquency of minors, offenses committed on school property, possession or sale of obscene pictures, drug offenses among adolescents, sex offenses (except forcible rape), and disorderly behavior by juveniles.

Disposition or Referral of Cases.   This is probably one of the most important functions of the police department, and the services of the juvenile division or unit are especially crucial in effecting treatment for misbehaving youth. In the more serious cases, referrals are made to the probation department and the juvenile court. Social agencies, both public and private, can be used for the minor cases. Big Brothers and Big Sisters, for example, are instrumental in helping many adolescents turn away from criminal careers. The youth service bureau is also an extremely valuable referral source for status offenders. Nor should religious agencies be overlooked, for some churches and clergy provide excellent services in working with youths. Recreation agencies, such as the Y.M.C.A., Y.W.C.A., and Boys Clubs, are excellent referrals for certain juveniles. And, should a department have one, the social service unit can have very positive results in dealing with youthful offenders and their families.

The various dispositions exercised by juvenile divisions are:

Application for Petition—the youth must be brought before the juvenile court.

Transfer of Cases—the case is transferred to another agency that has jurisdiction.

Referral to Other Agencies: Action Suspended—no further action is taken if it is determined that juveniles and their parents can effect a satisfactory solution.

Insufficient Evidence—if evidence conflicts or there is reasonable doubt as to the guilt of a juvenile, no further action is taken.

Exoneration—juveniles are cleared of all involvement if the investigation clearly indicates that they are not responsible for the crime.

Voluntary Police Supervision—a valuable aid if a department has such a service. It is used if it can be determined that guidance from the police department may help to keep a youth out of the juvenile court.

Adult, Not Juvenile, Status—if the investigation proves that the person is over the juvenile court age limit, then he will be handled as an adult, and the case will be transferred to another police division.

Unfit—a recommendation is made to the juvenile court that the juvenile be remanded for trial as an adult because of the seriousness of the offense or because of an extensive criminal career.

Detention—is always protective, never punitive, and the juvenile is held no longer than is necessary for effective placement or to bring him to the attention of the juvenile court.[41]

Protection of the Juvenile.   Protection has a number of aspects, particularly patrol of streets and places especially dangerous for juveniles, and cooperation between juvenile units and civic betterment groups to secure the revocation of the licenses of undesirable businesses. Youth victimization by other juveniles, another area in which protection is greatly needed, is a serious problem in some areas and can be mitigated by increased patrolling. Additionally, the apprehension and prosecution of adults involved in offenses against minors can make the streets safer. Finally, protection is needed against unwarranted publicity at a time when the hard-line approach is uppermost. It is the job of the juvenile unit not only to protect the juveniles of their community against unfair and untrue stories, but also to generate favorable media publicity, particularly by bringing to the attention of the media the good work of a juvenile or a group of juveniles.

Community Organization.   The juvenile divisions of police departments can provide invaluable youth services that will assure juveniles of safer and more wholesome lives. Juvenile divisions can also give encouragement and counsel to community leaders as they try to organize the community, and they can provide moral support to community leaders in their fight against such individuals as absentee landlords who try to circumvent community-betterment efforts.

INNOVATIVE POLICE-JUVENILE PROGRAMS

Because of their concern with improving relations with juveniles and decreasing youth crime, law enforcement agencies have committed much time and money during the past two decades to the development of three basic types of police-juvenile programs—programs that will bring about better attitudes toward the law and the police among pre-delinquent youth; diversionary programs; and police-juvenile offender programs. The prevention and diversion programs will be discussed in Chapter 7; this chapter will briefly summarize a few of the police-juvenile offender programs.

School-Community Guidance Centers

The School-Community Guidance Center program in Dallas, Texas was established to deal more effectively with truancy. The basic plan called for police officers to take into custody those students who were absent from school without parental knowledge or consent and deliver them to a junior high school that housed the pilot program. Personnel of the program (a police officer, a probation officer, and a visiting teacher) then attempted to ascertain why the student was a truant and to motivate him to go to school. This program was so successful that several others are now in operation.

Drug Abuse Rehabilitation Training (DART)

The police and probation departments of Burbank, California are cooperating in a drug abuse rehabilitation training program for the juvenile drug offender. Although this three-hour weekly series is under the auspices of the Burbank, California, Drug Abuse Council, police officers take part in the presentations. The police department sends drug offenders and their parents (who are required to attend with their children) to these seminars before deciding upon disposition of their cases.

Police Supervision of Offenders

Some police departments place youthful offenders under police supervision. This is a debatable function of the police, but some departments use this type of supervision in the hope that it will prevent these juveniles from becoming more deeply involved in the juvenile justice system. Those law enforcement agencies that use police supervision require offenders to make periodic progress reports at the police station.

Police Athletic League   In operation since the second decade of this century, the Police Athletic League programs include delinquency prevention, diversion from the juvenile justice system, and working with youthful offenders. An extensive recreational program, leadership training, full and part-time employment opportunities, and moral training for boys and girls between seven and twenty-one years old are its chief components.

ISSUES IN POLICE-JUVENILE RELATIONS

The administrative decision on how deeply to become involved in juvenile work and the informal nature of decision making in police-juvenile relations are two important issues.

Degree of Involvement in Juvenile Work   A controversy exists among police administrators over how extensively their departments should become involved in juvenile work. Some chiefs, for example, absolutely refuse to permit the department to have anything to do with juvenile work. Some agree to a juvenile division and assign officers to it, but they have no real interest in juvenile work and do their best to isolate themselves from it. These chiefs tend to let juvenile divisions go their own way as long as they do not bring public embarassment to the department. But other chiefs encourage the juvenile division to sponsor such activities as the Police Athletic League, and a few become actively involved in police-juvenile work, supporting prevention, diversion, and offenders' programs; encouraging the initiation of police-juvenile dialogues; and designing policy that elevates the juvenile officer and the juvenile division to the level of other units of the department.

Conversations with police administrators lead to the conclusion that the trend in the late 1970s is for police departments to move away from deep involvement in juvenile work. Juvenile divisions in many jurisdictions are only handling "missings," dependent and neglect cases, and child abuse. In these police departments, detective bureaus are assuming responsibility for juvenile and adult investigations.

The quality of police-juvenile relations in a community seems to rest on this issue. Generally, a good case can be made for the argument that the more specialized a department is in its juvenile work and the more juvenile programs it sponsors, the less brutality, corruption, discrimination, and abuse of due process rights of juveniles will be found. Furthermore, it would appear that the present attitudes of police and youths toward each other can be traced to the greater involvement of law enforcement agencies in service-oriented juvenile work.

Informal Nature of Decision Making

It is often thought that decision making about youths is limited to the formal justice system. Nothing is further from the truth. As noted in this chapter, the majority of juvenile offenders are informally warned and released, put under surveillance, scolded, or threatened by the police, all without a written record. A large number of youths are also informally adjudicated outside the court without a petition. And the unofficial offenses of a smaller number of youths are overlooked and not recorded by the probation officer because he wants to give them another chance. Informal decision making also is involved when a police officer takes a youth home instead of to the police station because he knows the youngster's father, or the juvenile judge dismisses the petition because the girl's family belongs to the same country club he does. Similarly, the probation officer does not return the youth to the juvenile court for violation of probation because he knows that the judge will just continue his probation, or the institutional staff worker recommends a youth for release because he helped the staff member paint his house.

The list of instances that demonstrate how the informal system intrudes on the formal correction of juvenile behavior is endless. Decision making ought to be confined to the formal system, for the informal system leads to unfairness, inefficiency, and corruption; police officers permit factors other than the offense to influence their decision; institutional staff members play favorites with some youths and exploit others; and judges tend to give middle-class youths the breaks they deny lower-class juveniles. However, the pressures of the system, the personalities of practitioners, and the society in which we live all lead to the continuation of the informal system. Therefore, we need to be certain that the informal system of juvenile corrections does not deny social justice to youthful offenders nor create greater victimization of the innocent in the community.

SUMMARY

Beginning with the history of police-juvenile relations, this chapter covered a number of topics related to juvenile law enforcement. Police attitudes toward juveniles and juvenile attitudes toward the police were examined. The animosity each has for the other seems to be exaggerated from the available evidence. Because law enforcement officers take on the responsibilities of prosecutor, judge, and correctional system in their contacts with juveniles, attention was given to the most important variables influencing the disposition of the misbehaving youth, and the five basic disposition alternatives were discussed. The rights of the juvenile taken into custody were considered, especially those pertaining to confessions, fingerprinting, photographing, and record keeping. The final section of the chapter was devoted to the methods law enforcement agencies use to improve relations with juveniles. Clearly, law enforcement for juveniles has come a long way the past two centuries.

QUESTIONS

1. How have the police contributed to hostile reactions from adolescents?

2. Do the police have too much discretion in dealing with juvenile lawbreakers? What are the advantages and disadvantages of limiting discretion? How could discretion be limited?

3. What rights does a juvenile have when taken into custody?

4. Would you consider a career as a juvenile officer? What do you think would be the frustrations and rewards of the job?

5. What other programs could police use to control juvenile lawbreaking?

ENDNOTES

1. Robert Portune, *Changing Adolescent Attitude toward Police* (Cincinnati: W. H. Anderson Company, 1971).
2. Donald H. Bouma, *Kids and Cops* (Grand Rapids, Mich.: William E. Eerdman Publishing Company, 1969), pp. 69–79.
3. Ibid.
4. Robert B. Coates et al., "Exploratory Analysis of Recidivism and Cohort Data on the Massachusetts Youth Correctional System" (Cambridge, Mass.: Center for Criminal Justice, Harvard Law School, 1975), p. 52.
5. Peggy C. Giordano, "The Sense of Injustice: An Analysis of Juveniles' Reactions to the Justice System," *Criminology* 14 (May 1976): 105–106.
6. Roul Tunley, *Kids, Crime and Chaos: A World Report on Juvenile Delinquency* (New York: Harper Press, 1962), p. 40.
7. Carl Werthman and Irving Piliavin, "Gang Members and the Police," in *The Police*, edited by David J. Bordua (New York: John Wiley & Sons, 1967), p. 70.
8. John P. Kenney and Dan G. Pursuit, *Police Work with Juveniles*, (Springfield, Ill.: Charles C Thomas, 1965), p. 5.
9. Jerome Skolnick, *Justice without Trial* (New York: John Wiley & Sons, 1966).
10. Walter B. Miller, *Operating Philosophies of Criminal Justice and Youth Service Professionals in Twelve Major Cities* (Cambridge, Mass.: Center for Criminal Justice, Harvard Law School), p. 4.

11. Richard W. Kobetz and Betty B. Bosarge, *Juvenile Justice Administration* (Gaithersburg, Md.: International Association of Chiefs of Police, 1973).
12. William W. Wattenberg and Noel Bufe, "The Effectiveness of Police Bureau Officers," in *Prevention of Delinquency: Problems and Programs,* edited by John R. Stratton and Robert M. Terry (New York: Macmillan Company, 1968).
13. J. D. Lohman, *The Handling of Juveniles from Offense to Disposition,* original draft mimeograph (Washington, D.C.: U.S. Government Printing Office, 1963).
14. Charles Breitel, "Controls in Criminal Law Enforcement," *University of Chicago Law Review* 27 (Spring1960): 427.
15. National Advisory Commission on Criminal Justice Standards and Goals, *Corrections* (Washington, D.C.: U.S. Government Printing Office, 1973), pp. 389–436.
16. James Q. Wilson, "Dilemmas of Police Administration," *Public Administration Review* 28 (September–October 1968).
17. David J. Bordua, "Recent Trends: Deviant Behavior and Social Control," *The Annals* 359 (January 1967): 149–163.
18. Robert M. Terry, "Discrimination in the Handling of Juvenile Offenders by Social Control Agencies," *Journal of Research in Crime and Delinquency* 4 (July 1967): 218–230; Nathan Goldman, *The Differential Selection of Juvenile Offenders for Court Appearance* (New York: National Council on Crime and Delinquency, 1963), pp. 35–47.
19. Irving Piliavin and Scott Briar, "Police Encounters with Juveniles," *American Journal of Sociology* 70 (September 1976): 206–214.
20. Werthman and Piliavin, "Gang Members and the Police," pp. 56–98.
21. James T. Carey et al., *The Handling of Juveniles from Offense to Disposition* (Washington, D.C.: U.S. Government Printing Office, 1976), p. 419; A. W. McEachern and Riva Bauzer, "Factors Related in Disposition in Juvenile-Police Contacts," in *Juvenile Gangs in Context,* edited by Malcolm W. Klein (Englewood Cliffs, N.J.: Prentice-Hall), pp. 148–160; Thorstein Sellin and Marvin E. Wolfgang, *The Measurement of Delinquency* (New York: John Wiley & Sons, 1964), pp. 95–105; Theodore N. Ferdinand and Elmer G. Luchterhand, "Inner City Youths, the Police, the Juvenile Court and Justice," *Social Problems* 17 (Spring): 510–527.
22. Terry, "Discrimination," pp. 218–220.
23. Terence P. Thornberry, "Race, Socioeconomic Status and Sentencing in the Juvenile Justice System," *Journal of Criminal Law and Criminology* 64 (March 1973): 90–98.
24. Marvin E. Wolfgang, Robert M. Figlio, and Thorstein Sellin, *Delinquency in a Birth Cohort* (Chicago: University of Chicago Press, 1972), p. 252.
25. Carey, et al., *Handling of Juveniles,* p. 419; Goldman, *Differential Selection,* pp. 93–124.
26. Wilson, "Dilemmas of Police Administration," p. 19.
27. U.S. Department of Health, Education and Welfare, *Police Services for Juveniles,* Children's Bureau Publication, no. 344 (Washington, D.C.: U.S. Government Printing Office, 1954), p. 20.
28. Lawrence W. Sherman, "Youth Workers, Police and the Gangs: Chicago 1956–1970" (Master's thesis, University of Chicago, 1970), p. 28.
29. Ibid.
30. Jurisdictions that avoid the word "arrest" are: Alaska, District of Columbia, Florida, Georgia, Guam, Idaho, Indiana, Kansas, Kentucky, Maryland, Michigan, Minnesota, Missouri, Montana, Nevada, New Hampshire, New Jersey, New Mexico, Ohio, Oklahoma, Oregon, Puerto Rico, Rhode Island,

Texas, Utah, Virgin Islands, Washington, Wisconsin, and Wyoming. Jurisdictions that state taking into custody is an arrest: Georgia, Guam, Kentucky, Minnesota, Missouri, New Mexico, Oregon, Virgin Islands, Wisconsin, and Wyoming.

31. 384 U.S. 436 (1966).
32. 387 U.S. (1967)
33. Edward Eldefonso, *Law Enforcement and the Youthful Offender,* 2d ed. (New York: John Wiley & Sons, 1973).
34. Aidan R. Gough, "The Expungement of Adjudication Records of Juvenile and Adult Offenders: A Problem of Status," *Washington University Law Quarterly* 2 (April 1966): 173.
35. National Advisory Commission, *Corrections,* p. 764.
36. Kobetz and Bosarge, *Juvenile Justice Administration,* p. 154.
37. U.S. Department of Health, Education and Welfare, *Police Services for Juveniles,* pp. 42–43.
38. Wattenberg and Bufe, "Effectiveness of Police Bureau Officers," p. 171.
39. Kobetz and Bosarge, *Juvenile Justice Administration,* pp. 43–61.
40. This list of the functions of a juvenile unit is found in Kenney and Pursuit, *Police Work with Juveniles,* pp. 75–84.
41. Ibid., pp. 81–82.

REFERENCES

Bouma, Donald H. *Kids and Cops.* Grand Rapids, Mich.: William E. Eerdmans Publishing Company, 1969.
An interesting account of police-juvenile relations in a Michigan city.

Eldefonso, Edward. *Law Enforcement and the Youthful Offender.* 2d ed. New York: John Wiley & Sons, 1973.
Describes well the procedures used by law enforcement agencies in dealing with juvenile offenders.

Kenney, John P., and Pursuit, Dan G. *Police Work with Juveniles,* Springfield, Ill.: Charles C Thomas Company, 1965.
A classic in police-juvenile relations.

Kobetz, Richard W. *The Police Role and Juvenile Delinquency.* Gaithersberg, Md.: International Association of Chiefs of Police, 1971.
Includes a good discussion of the juvenile unit and the juvenile officer.

Portune, Robert. *Changing Adolescent Attitudes toward Police.* Cincinnati:W. H. Anderson Company, 1971.
Examines the attitudes of juveniles toward the police in Cincinnati, Ohio.

Pursuit, Dan G.; Gerletti, John D.; Brown, Robert M., Jr.; and Ward, Steven M. *Police Programs for Preventing Crime and Delinquency.* Springfield, Ill.: Charles C Thomas Company, 1972.
Discusses many interesting police prevention and community relations programs.

4

The Juvenile Court

The juvenile court has received both fanatical support and strident criticism since its inception at the turn of the century. Supporters claim that the informal setting of the juvenile court, coupled with the fatherly demeanor of the juvenile judge, enables misbehaving children to be treated for their problems rather than punished. Similarly, youths are saved by the kindly parent, the state, from placement with adult criminals in correctional facilities. The purpose of the court, as expressed in the *Commonwealth* v. *Fisher* decision in 1905, "is not for the punishment of offenders but for the salvation of children . . . whose salvation may become the duty of the state."[1]

Critics of the juvenile court sharply challenge the claim that these idealistic goals are realized to any extent. They say, in essence, that the juvenile court has not succeeded in rehabilitating juvenile offenders, in reducing or even stemming the rise of youth crime, or in bringing justice and compassion to youthful offenders.[2] Some investigators accuse the juvenile court of doing great harm to troubled children.[3]

To allow a fair evaluation of the juvenile court, this chapter will present its historical development, the procedures involved in its administration, a description of its personnel, and several important issues presently facing it.

CREATION OF THE JUVENILE COURT: TWO INTERPRETATIONS

In 1899, the juvenile court was born in Cook County (Chicago) when the Illinois legislature passed the Juvenile Court Act. Anthony Platt, in *The Child Savers,* discusses what is a widely supported interpretation of the origin of the juvenile court. He claims that the Chicago court was created only because it satisfied several diverse interest groups. He also sees the court as an expression of middle-class values and of the philosophy of conservative political groups. Platt, in challenging the idea that the juvenile court was revolutionary, says:

> The child-saving movement was not so much a break with the past as an affirmation of faith in traditional institutions. Parental authority, education at home, and the virtues of rural life were emphasized because they were in decline at this time. The child-saving movement was, in part, a crusade which, through emphasizing the dependence of the social order on the proper socialization of children, implicitly elevated the nuclear family and, more especially, the role of women as stalwarts of the family. The child-savers were prohibitionists, in a general sense, who believed that social progress depended on efficient law enforcement, strict supervision of children's leisure and recreation, and the regulation of illicit pleasures. What seemingly began as a movement to humanize the lives of adolescents soon developed into a program of moral absolutism through which youths were to be saved from movies, pornography, cigarettes, alcohol, and anything else which might possibly rob them of their innocence.[4]

Platt reminds his readers that it was no accident that the behaviors the child savers selected to be penalized—sexual license, roaming the streets, drinking, begging, fighting, frequenting dance halls and movies, and staying out late at night—were found primarily in lower-class children. From the very beginnings, according to this interpretation, juvenile justice generated class favoritism that resulted in poor children being processed through the system, while middle-class children were more likely to be excused.

In their excellent essay, Faust and Brantingham present a broader interpretation of the origin of the juvenile court.[5] They state that the invention of the court can be understood when the following factors are taken into consideration: the pressures for social change existing in the late nineteenth century in the United States, the prevalent philosophical views on crime and correction, the implications of these conditions and positions taken for handling children in trouble, and a legal catalyst.

Pressures for Social Change   Certain social and economic conditions in the last thirty years of the nineteenth century acted as a major impetus to the founding of the juvenile court. Many citizens were incensed greatly during this period by the treatment of children; the county jail system, in particular, was one of their grievances. County jails in Illinois housed hundreds of children during the 1880s and 1890s. The jails were regarded as moral plague spots and considered highly injurious to troubled youth.

Urban disenchantment also was an important issue. The population of Chicago literally exploded, tripling between 1880 and 1900. This staggering growth brought many problems of urban life—filth and corruption, masses of poor, rise of crime, and corruption in city government. These social ailments created considerable urban disenchantment and were a precipitating factor in the birth of the juvenile court.

Another important social change was the revolution in the status of middle-class women and the rise of female influence in politics. Child saving, in fact, became an important area in which women could express themselves and could develop their strengths; it became an avocation for some middle-class women who wanted something to do outside the home.

Philosophical Views

The second elements, according to Faust and Brantingham, were the theoretical and philosophical developments in correctional theory. The classical school of criminology, constructed around assumptions of free will, responsibility, lack of discretion, due process trial procedures, and punishment, largely was abandoned by penologists. The positive school of criminology was substituted in its place. Supporters of positivism believed in determinism, looked to the scientific expert, and attempted to discover why offenders committed crimes. In positivism, the way was open for the use of the treatment model, or the therapeutic state, in the juvenile court. Once the juvenile court discovered a child's problem, the scientific expert could provide the cure; children were treated rather than punished. Reformers were confident that the combination of the treatment model and the juvenile court would lead to the salvation of wayward children.

Middle-class religious humanitarianism also was an important motivating factor. Christians were challenged by such writers as Charles Dickens and Mary Carpenter to rescue children from the degrading slums. Slum conditions were believed to foster ignorance, misery, squalor, vice and criminality. Many of the well-known child savers were ministers; most child-saving institutions were private charities supported, at least in part, by religious denominations.

Implications of Philosophy

The third element in the creation of the juvenile court involved the philosophical positions of the child savers. These reformers believed that excluding children from criminal proceedings sheltered them not only from adult offenders but also from the stigma of criminality. Preventive intervention should take place so that youths did not become committed to criminal careers. The end result of this strategy was to construct an effective treatment program for the needs of the wayward child.

The Legal Catalyst   The fourth element was a legal catalyst. This catalyst provided a rationale for the informal procedures of juvenile justice and the expanding state power over children. The *parens patriae* doctrine, under which the state accepted parental responsibility for children, was used to justify the casual fact-finding and dispositional activities undertaken by the juvenile court. The kindly parent, the state, could thus justify relying heavily on psychological and medical examinations rather than on trial by evidence. The *parens patriae* terminology also was used as a shield behind which the juvenile court could stand—largely immune to attacks from appellate courts. Consequently, once the *parens patriae* rhetoric was applied to juvenile proceedings, the institution of the juvenile court followed. (See Figure 4-1.)

DEVELOPMENT OF THE JUVENILE COURT

Juvenile courts spread rapidly across the country. Thirty-one states instituted them by 1905, and by 1928, only two states did not have a juvenile court statute. The original act and amendments that followed the act brought the neglected, the dependent, and the delinquent together under one roof. The last category was made up of both status offenders and actual violators of the criminal law. Misbehaving children, rather than being considered criminal, were offered assistance and guidance. Hearings were informal and nonpublic, records generally were confidential, children were detained separately from adults, and a probation staff was appointed.

Disregarding due process safeguards because of the civil jurisdiction of the court, reformers proposed that the noncriminal aspects of the proceedings be echoed in the physical surroundings of the court:

> The courtroom should be not a courtroom at all; just a room, with a table and two chairs, where the judge and the child, the probation officer and the parents, as occasion arises, come into close contact, and where in a more or less informal way the whole story may be talked over.[6]

Reformers advocated that the judge sit at a desk rather than on a bench and that he occasionally "put his arm around his shoulder and

FIGURE 4-1   Model of Invention

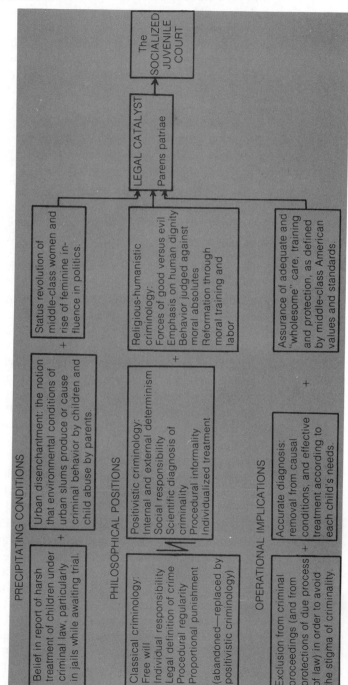

From: Frederic L. Faust and Paul J. Brantingham, *Juvenile Justice Philosophy* (St. Paul, Minn.: West Publishing Company, 1974), pp. 562–563. Reprinted with permission.

draw the lad to him."[7] However, these kindly parents and sympathetic judges ought not to lose any of their judicial dignity. The goals of the court were to investigate, diagnose, and prescribe treatment. Lawyers were believed unnecessary because the basic objective was not to become involved in an adversary trial, but to determine the best treatment plan for children in trouble. Since delinquency was thought of almost as a disease or sickness, this plan was to be devised by physicians and psychiatrists.

Some of the basic assumptions of the juvenile court were that the troubles of children were produced by an evil environment, especially poor parental care; that the juvenile court should function as a social clinic designed to serve the best interests of the child; that children brought before the court should be given the same care, supervision, and discipline provided by a good parent; that children should not be stigmatized as criminals; and that the rights to shelter, protection, and proper guardianship are the only rights of children. These assumptions were operationalized into the following principles: the informal procedures of the court were to fulfill the needs evidenced by the child's behavior and condition; the individual needs of each child warranted treatment uniquely planned for him; and the use of a residential setting offered protective supervision and constructive activity.[8]

The Critical Response

Of the various critics of this approach to juveniles in trouble, the constitutionalists have had the greatest impact. The constitutionalists basically contended that the juvenile court was unconstitutional because the principles of a fair trial and of individual rights were denied. Although their argument was met and beaten back in state after state, it began to have a greater impact in the early 1960s. Supported by those who were disenchanted by the *parens patriae* court, the constitutionalists were able to influence the legislatures of California, New York, and Illinois to alter their juvenile court statutes substantially and to try to give children better protection and procedural rights.

The fundamental assumptions of the constitutionalist model are that children in need of help are different from children who break the law and must be dealt with through separate judicial proceedings; that current diagnostic and treatment techniques are not sufficiently developed to ensure that the delinquent can be treated and cured of his misbehavior; and that the state must justify interfering with a child's life when his freedom is at stake, for children should not be stigmatized. Children also have procedural rights as well as the rights of shelter, protection, and guardianship. Constitutionalists recommended that these assumptions be incorporated into the juvenile court by the establishment of separate procedures for dealing with dependent and neglected children and with those accused of crime; by the use of various informal adjustments to avoid official court action as much as possible; and by the provision of rigorous procedural safeguards and rights for children in trouble at the adjudicatory stage of the juvenile court proceedings.[9]

Changes in Legal Norms: Import of *In re Gault* **and Other Cases**

A series of decisions by the U.S. Supreme Court in the 1960s and early 1970s accelerated rapidly the influence of the constitutionalists in the juvenile court. The first major case was *Kent* v. *United States.* In this 1966 case, the juvenile court had transferred Kent's case to the adult court without an evidentiary hearing. Also, Kent had not been present when the court decided to waive jurisdiction, and his attorney had not been permitted to examine the social investigation of the youth that the court used in deciding to waive jurisdiction.[10] Justice Fortas, in the decision, stated:

> There is evidence, in fact, that there may be grounds for concern that the child receives the worst of both worlds; that he gets neither the protection accorded to adults nor the solicitous care and regenerative treatment postulated for children.[11]

The Court decided that withholding Kent's record essentially meant a denial of counsel. The court also held that a juvenile has a constitutional right to be represented by counsel; that a youth charged with a felony has a right to a hearing; and that this hearing must "measure up to the essentials of due process and fair treatment." Finally, a youth's attorneys must have access to his social or probation records.

In May of 1967, the U.S. Supreme Court reversed the conviction of a minor in the case of *In re Gault.* This has been one of the most influential and far-reaching decisions to affect the juvenile court. The Court in this case overruled the supreme court of Arizona for its dismissal of a writ of habeas corpus. This writ had sought the release of Gerald Gault, who had been adjudicated to the State Industrial School by the Juvenile Court of Gila County, Arizona.

Gault, a fifteen-year-old Arizona boy, and a friend, Ronald Lewis, were taken into custody on June 8, 1964, on a verbal complaint made by a neighbor. The neighbor had accused the boys of making lewd and indecent remarks to her over the phone. Gault's parents were not notified that he was taken into custody; he was not advised of his right to counsel; he was not advised that he could remain silent; and no notice of charges was made either to Gerald or his parents. Additionally, the complainant was not present at either of the hearings. In spite of considerable confusion about whether or not Gerald had made the alleged phone call, what he had said over the phone, and what he had said to the judge during the course of the two hearings, Judge McGhee committed him to the State Industrial School "for the period of his minority (that is, until twenty-one) unless sooner discharged by due process of law."

The U.S. Supreme Court, in overruling the Arizona Supreme Court, considered which of the following should be rights of juveniles:

1. Notice of the charges.
2. Right to counsel.
3. Right to confrontation and cross-examination.
4. Privilege against self-incrimination.
5. Right to a transcript of the proceedings.
6. Right to appellate review.[12]

Mr. Justice Fortas, in delivering the Court's opinion, recalled other cases that had provided juveniles with due process of law. In both *Haley* v. *Ohio* (1948) and *Gallegos* v. *Colorado* (1962), the U.S. Supreme Court prohibited the use of confessions coerced from juveniles, and in *Kent* v. *United States,* as previously mentioned, the Court gave the juvenile the right to be represented by counsel. Justice Fortas concluded this review of legal precedent with the sweeping statement that juveniles have those fundamental rights incorporated in the due process clause of the Fourteenth Amendment of the Constitution.

The *In Re Gault* decision answered in the affirmative the question of whether or not a juvenile has the right to due process safeguards in proceedings where a finding of delinquency can lead to institutional confinement. The decision also stated that a juvenile has the right of notice of the charges, right to counsel, right to confrontation and cross-examination, and privilege against self-incrimination. But the Supreme Court did not decide that juveniles have the right to a transcript of the proceedings or the right to appellate review.

In rejecting these latter two rights, the Court clearly did not want to make the informal juvenile hearing into an adversary trial. The cautiousness of this decision was expressed in a footnote that said the decision did not apply to pre-adjudication or post-adjudication treatment of juveniles. Several other important issues were also left unanswered:

1. May a judge consider hearsay in juvenile court?
2. Does the exclusionary evidence principle derived from the Fourth Amendment apply?

3. What is the constitutionally required burden of proof necessary to support a finding of delinquency?
4. Is a jury trial required?
5. Does the requirement of a "speedy and public trial" obtain in juvenile court?[13]

Since *In re Gault,* the U.S. Supreme Court has made other important decisions concerning the juvenile court. For example, *In the Matter of Samuel Winship* (1970), the court decided that juveniles are entitled to proof "beyond a reasonable doubt." The "preponderance of evidence" is not a sufficient basis for a decision when youths are charged with acts that would be criminal if committed by adults.[14]

The *Winship* case involved a New York boy who was sent to a state training school at the age of twelve for taking $112 from a woman's purse. The commitment was based on a New York statute that permitted juvenile court decisions on the basis of a "preponderance of evidence"—a standard much less strict than "beyond a reasonable doubt."

The *Winship* case not only expanded *In re Gault,* but also reflected other concerns of the U.S. Supreme Court. The Court desired both to protect juveniles at adjudicatory hearings and to maintain the confidentiality, informality, flexibility, and speed of the juvenile process in the pre-judicial and post-adjudicative states. The Court obviously did not want to bring too much rigidity and impersonality to the juvenile hearing.

The U.S. Supreme Court, in both *McKeiver* v. *Pennsylvania* (1971) and *In re Barbara Burrus* (1971), denied the right of juveniles to have jury trials.[15] The significance of this decision is that the Court indicated an unwillingness to apply further procedural safeguards to juvenile proceedings. This especially appears to be true concerning the pre-adjudicatory and post-adjudicatory treatment of juveniles.

Bail is still denied to juveniles in all but nine states; Alabama, Arkansas, Colorado, Georgia, Massachusetts, Michigan, North Carolina, South Dakota, and West Virginia allow bail. Even though few juveniles are released on bail, most juvenile court statutes do limit the time that accused juveniles may be held in custody before their hearings. The California Juvenile Code, for example, states:

> Upon delivery to the probation officer of a minor who has been taken into temporary custody under the provisions of this article, the probation officer shall *immediately investigate* the circumstances of the minor and the facts surrounding his being taken into custody and shall *immediately release* such minor to the custody of his parent, guardian, or responsible relative (except under certain specified conditions). . . . If the probation officer determines that the minor shall be retained in custody, he shall

immediately file a petition . . . with the Clerk of the Juvenile Court, who shall set the matter for hearing on the Detention Hearing Calendar.[16]

The *In re Gault* and *Winship* decisions have unquestionably effected profound changes in the legal status of the juvenile justice system. However, the *McKeiver* decision and the more conservative stance of the U.S. Supreme Court since 1971 raise some question about whether or not this ultimate appellate court will be willing to change these legal norms much more. These court decisions of course have received varying endorsements from juvenile courts across the country. Some juvenile courts gave procedural rights to juveniles even before the U.S. Supreme Court decisions, but others have lagged far behind in implementing these decisions.

NATURE OF JUVENILE COURT SERVICES

The jurisdiction of the juvenile court, despite variation among and even within states, generally includes delinquency, neglect, and dependency cases. Children's courts may also deal with cases concerning adoption, termination of parental rights, appointment of guardians for minors, custody, contributing to delinquency or neglect, and nonsupport. The three basic stages of the juvenile court process are intake, adjudication, and dispositional hearings. The juvenile court also holds detention hearings.

Statistics The number of children appearing before the juvenile court significantly increased from the late 1950s until the early 1970s, when it began to level off, primarily because many jurisdictions directed status offenders away from their courts. (See Table 4-1.)

Although these statistics indicate a dramatic increase in crimes disposed of by juvenile courts, less than 4 percent of the youthful population appeared in juvenile court in 1972. Even adding the number of adolescents who appear in juvenile court sometime during their teenage years, appearances before juvenile court still involve only a small minority of American adolescents—perhaps one boy in every six and one girl in every nine. In addition, half of the court referrals are considered so minor that they are handled informally.[17]

Another important statistic is the maximum age over which the juvenile court has jurisdiction. As Table 4-2 indicates, thirty-two states and the District of Columbia have set seventeen as the maximum age over which the juvenile court has jurisdiction.

TABLE 4-1   Juvenile Court Cases and Child Population, 1957–1972

Year	Delinquency Cases	Population Ages 10–17	Percent
1957	440,000	22,173,000	2.0
1958	470,000	23,433,000	2.0
1959	483,000	24,607,000	2.0
1960	510,000	25,368,000	2.0
1961	503,000	26,056,000	1.9
1962	555,000	26,056,000	2.1
1963	601,000	28,989,000	2.1
1964	686,000	29,244,000	2.3
1965	697,000	29,536,000	2.7
1966	745,000	30,124,000	2.5
1967	811,000	30,837,000	2.6
1968	900,000	31,566,000	2.8
1969	988,500	32,157,000	3.1
1970	1,052,000	32,614,000	3.2
1971	1,125,000	32,969,000	3.4
1972	1,112,500	33,120,000	3.4

From: U.S. Department of Health, Education and Welfare, *Juvenile Court Statistics, 1972* (Washington, D.C.: U.S. Government Printing Office, 1973.)

Since 1967, when the President's Commission on Law Enforcement and the Administration of Justice recommended that juvenile codes be updated, thirty-three states have undertaken substantive revisions; additional legislation is also being sought in many of these states.[18] The most progressive changes are the proposals in Utah and Massachusetts for the removal of status offenders from the juvenile justice system. Seven states, New York, California, Illinois, Colorado, Kansas, Vermont, and Oklahoma, have banned the commitment to institutions of first-offense status offenders.

Another important statistic concerns the choice of the juvenile court to handle delinquency cases by a judicial (filing a petition) or nonjudicial (dismissing or diverting to nonjudicial agencies) method. Table 4-3 indicates that in 1971, 52 percent of the delinquency cases were handled by nonjudicial methods. Yet, a wide variance is evident in the rural juvenile court (42 percent) and the semiurban court (67 percent) use of nonjudicial methods. Children in trouble clearly have a better chance of having their cases dismissed or diverted to nonjudicial agencies in urban or semiurban locales than in rural areas. Obviously,

TABLE 4-2 Maximum Age at Which the Juvenile Court Has Original Jurisdiction in Delinquency Cases, by States

State	Age Limit	State	Age Limit
Alabama	15	Montana	17
Alaska	17	Nebraska	17
Arizona	17	Nevada	17
Arkansas	17	New Hampshire	16
California	17	New Jersey	17
Colorado	17	New Mexico	17
Connecticut	15	New York	15
Delaware	17	North Carolina	15
District of Columbia	17	North Dakota	17
Florida	16	Ohio	17
Georgia	16	Oklahoma	15
Hawaii	17	Oregon	17
Idaho	17	Pennsylvania	17
Illinois	16	Rhode Island	17
Indiana	17	South Carolina	16
Iowa	17	South Dakota	17
Kansas	17	Tennessee	17
Kentucky	17	Texas	16
Louisiana	16	Utah	17
Maine	16	Vermont	15
Maryland	16	Virginia	17
Massachusetts	16	Washington	17
Michigan	16	West Virginia	17
Minnesota	17	Wisconsin	17
Mississippi	17	Wyoming	17
Missouri	16		

From: National Criminal Justice Information and Statistics Service, *Children in Custody: A Report on the Juvenile Detention and Correctional Facility Census of 1971* (Washington, D.C.: Law Enforcement Assistance Administration, 1974), p. 1.

urban and semiurban courts have more resources for diverting youths than do rural courts. That rural judges are more conservative or punishment-oriented than urban or semiurban judges may also be a factor.

The Detention Hearing Acts that govern the juvenile court normally require that the police either take children to the court or to a detention facility or release them to parents. The criteria for detention are based on the need to protect the child and to insure public safety. An initial decision to detain can cover only a short period of time, usually forty-eight to seventy-two hours; before this period is over, either a detention hearing must be held before

TABLE 4-3   Delinquency Cases Disposed of by Urban, Semiurban, and Rural Juvenile Courts, United States, 1971.

Type of Court	Total	Judicial		Nonjudicial	
	Number	Number	Percent	Number	Percent
Total	1,125,000	475,000	42	650,000	58
Urban	717,000	320,000	45	397,000	55
Semiurban	313,000	110,000	33	221,000	67
Rural	77,000	45,000	58	32,000	42

From: U.S. Department of Health, Education and Welfare, *Juvenile Court Statistics, 1971* (Washington, D.C.: U.S. Government Printing Office, 1972), p. 8.

a judge or the intake unit of the court must decide whether or not to file a petition. Although juvenile court acts differ concerning the nature of the judicial detention hearing, it generally is agreed that the finding of the juvenile judge must be supported by evidence. As already noted, juvenile court acts are supposed to insure children of the right to counsel, the privilege against self-incrimination, and a notice of the charges.

Juveniles awaiting hearings and disposition decisions are held in three types of facilities. The first is the detention hall or detention home, which physically restricts the youth for a short period. The second, shelter care, is physically nonrestrictive and is available for those who have no homes; that is, shelter care ordinarily is reserved for those juveniles who require emergency care because of the collapse of family living. It is sometimes also used for those who require juvenile court intervention. The third type of facility is the jail or police lockup. But regardless of the place of detention, this resource must be used only as a *last* resort. The *Report of the Advisory Committee on Standards for the Administration of Juvenile Justice* offers the following criteria for determining when to detain juveniles in secure facilities:

1. They are fugitives from another jurisdiction.
2. They request protection in writing in circumstances that present an immediate threat of serious physical injury.
3. They are charged with murder in the first or second degree.
4. They are charged with a serious property crime or a crime of

violence other than first or second degree murder which if committed by an adult would be a felony, and:

a. They are already detained or on conditioned release in connection with another delinquency proceeding.

b. They have a demonstrable recent record of willful failures to appear at family court proceedings.

c. They have a demonstrable recent record of violent conduct resulting in physical injury to others. . . .

d. They have a demonstrable recent record of adjudications for serious property offenses. . . .

e. There is no less restrictive alternative that will reduce the risk of flight, or of serious harm to property or to the physical safety of the juvenile or others.[19]

Intake   Intake is essentially a preliminary screening process "to determine whether the court should take action and if so what action or whether the matter should be referred elsewhere."[20] Thirty-five states include mandatory intake procedures in their juvenile court statutes. Typically, larger courts handle the intake function through a specialized intake unit; probation officers or sometimes even judges screen incoming cases in smaller courts.

Intake procedures follow complaints against children. Courts tend to differ from jurisdiction to jurisdiction on who is permitted to sign the complaint. Generally, most complaints are brought by the police, although they may be initiated and signed by the victim or by an incorrigible youngster's parents. In Illinois, parents, victims, probation staff, social service agencies, neighbors, or anyone else may go directly to the court to file a complaint. Complaints may also be brought against school offenders by school officials and truant officers.

After the complaint is received by the juvenile court, the intake unit must first decide whether or not the court has statutorial jurisdiction. If the statutorial guidelines are unclear, the intake officer should seek the advice of the prosecuting attorney. Once legal jurisdiction is decided, the second step is to conduct a preliminary interview and investigation to determine whether the case should be adjudicated nonjudicially or petitioned to the court, an evaluation procedure that varies from jurisdiction to jurisdiction, principally because so many juvenile courts have failed to provide written guidelines.

The Intake Unit. The intake unit has various options for the disposal of cases: (1) outright dismissal of the complaint; (2) informal adjustment (chiefly, diversion to a nonjudicial agency); (3) informal probation; (4) consent decree; and (5) filing of a petition.

Outright dismissal of the complaint occurs if legal jurisdiction does not exist. Informal adjustment is a more complicated process, which may involve restitution, warnings, or diversion to youth service bureaus or social agencies. Generally, the diversionary, or noncourt, agency supervises diverted youths and then reports to the intake unit on their progress; status offenders and children with minor offenses usually are placed under this option.

Informal probation involves the casual supervision of a youth by a probation officer, who reserves judgment on the need for filing a petition until he or the intake officer sees how the youth fares during the informal probation period. Both the President's Task Force on Juvenile Delinquency and Youth Crime and the U.S. Children's Bureau advocated abolishing informal probation because the legal rights of juveniles are violated, but the National Advisory Committee on Criminal Justice Standards and Goals supported its use. In the midst of this controversy, nearly 20 percent of juvenile cases still are placed on informal probation.[21] Supporters maintain that informal probation saves judicial time and avoids the "evils" of adjudication.

A consent decree, defined "as a formal agreement between the child and the court in which the child is placed under the court's supervision without a formal finding of delinquency,"[22] provides an intermediate step between informal handling and probation or institutionalization. It not only eases the case load of the court, but also provides protection against the stigma of delinquency. The National Advisory Commission on Criminal Justice Standards and Goals recommended that this decree should be enforced for a period of no longer than six months; that its use should not result in the removal of the child from his family; and that it should be based upon sufficient evidence.[23]

If none of these options is satisfactory, the intake unit can always choose to file a petition. Table 4-3 notes that 43 percent of the delinquency cases in 1971 were disposed of by filing a petition. Figure 4-2 shows the disposition of the Intake Department of the Juvenile Court of Sangamon County, Illinois. The Advisory Counsel of Judges of the National Council of Crime and Delinquency recommended the following guidelines for filing a petition for adjudication:

1. Cases in which it is necessary to make a factual determination on the question of delinquency or neglect;
2. Cases likely to involve commitment or change of custody;
3. Cases in which either a parent or child indicates a desire to appear before a judge;
4. Cases that have a serious impact on the community;
5. Cases in which the child or parent refuses normal cooperation;

FIGURE 4-2 Juvenile Court Intake Decisions and Dispositions

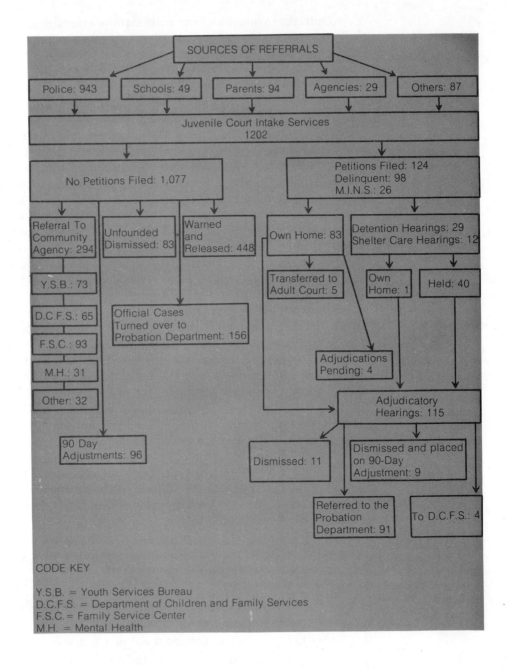

From: "Annual Report, 1 January–31 December 1976," Seventh Judicial Circuit, Intake Department, Sangamon County, Illinois, p. 9.

6. Cases in which the court must determine whether or not a child in custody or detention should so remain; and

7. Cases in which two or more children are involved in the same delinquent act and it has already been determined that at least one of them is to be handled judicially.[24]

Pre-judicial handling in the intake unit is vulnerable to misuse, as coercion in the name of treatment is a possible outcome of informal methods. Also unacceptable is the use of detention solely for deterrence. Furthermore, including a youth's demeanor and attitude among the criteria for pre-judicial disposition is questionable because there is a grey area of uncertainty about what the juvenile is actually feeling. Juveniles sometimes will act remorseful or "hard" when they feel the opposite.

The Adjudicatory Stage

Once a petition is filed, the youth appears before the judge in the adjudication, or fact-finding, stage of the court's proceedings. This stage, as previously stated, has undergone great change since *In re Gault.* Although some courts have resisted the various procedural and due process protections, most courts handle this stage of the juvenile proceedings differently than before the *Gault* decision. The present trend, at least in large urban juvenile courts, is to hold bifurcated, or split, hearings at the adjudicatory stage. In fact, bifurcated hearings were made mandatory in California in 1961.

Since youths are entitled to proof "beyond a reasonable doubt" when charged with an act that would constitute a crime if committed by an adult, the judge is expected to follow the rules of evidence and to dismiss hearsay from the proceedings. This means that the evidence must be relevant and must contribute to the belief or disbelief of the act in question. Hearsay is dismissed because it may be unreliable or may be unfair, inasmuch as it cannot be cross-examined. Fox, in this regard, has noted "that the cornerstone of procedural reform in the juvenile court is the right to be represented by a lawyer."[25]

In addition to the defense attorney the child is entitled to have (unless this right is waived), the prosecutor or state's attorney also may become involved. Duties of the prosecutor include being present at probable cause hearings, law violation fact-finding hearings, and waiver hearings; assisting intake officers in jurisdictional determinations; attending probation revocation hearings; and engaging in plea bargaining with defense attorneys if court rules permit.

Juveniles are assured the right to a speedy, private trial, with only the parents, probation officer, police officer, defense attorney, prosecutor, victim or person who signed the complaint, and the judge present. The press is neither invited nor permitted to publish the findings of this hearing.

In spite of this theory of what the adjudicatory stage is, the typical hearing sometimes falls far short of granting juveniles due process and procedural safeguards. Frequently, the hearing is overly brief. The rapidity with which cases are heard in large courts constitutes what Lemert refers to as "the three-minute children's hour."[26] In California, the Governor's Commission on Juvenile Justice found that the average time spent on a juvenile hearing is approximately ten to fifteen minutes.[27]

Representation by counsel can also be a legal charade. By the way they phrase the question of legal representation or even by the tone of voice, judges can persuade parents to waive the right of counsel. Defense attorneys, too, can perform their role without really affecting the "justice" going on in the courtroom. Private attorneys, who often feel awkward or out of place in a juvenile court, are not always certain whether to rely more heavily on legal defenses and defend the children to the limit or to help the judge in showing the juveniles the wrongness of their ways. Hence, they may have some reservations about trying to have juveniles released on technical grounds.

Public defenders are even less likely to provide their clients with an adequate defense. As in adult justice cases, public defenders are limited in the time they can spend with clients. Morover, many are more concerned with maintaining good relations with the judge and the prosecutor than with defending children. Thus, they are easily coopted and quickly move their cases in and out of the courtroom. Further, they are amenable to plea bargaining, now an unhappy fact of life in many juvenile courts. When the prosecutor wishes to make a deal, children are urged to admit the allegations against them or to plead guilty to a lesser charge, in order to receive a less severe sentence.

Some judges are prime destroyers of constitutional safeguards and may even consider themselves above the law. Committed to the philosophy of *parens patriae* and individualized justice, they not only resent outsiders who seem to be telling them how to run their courts, but they also refuse to grant any or few of the procedural safeguards to children in their courtroom. These judges, indeed, run their courts as if *Gault* never happened.

**The
Disposition
Stage**

The disposition stage of the court's proceedings normally is quite different from the fact-finding stage, especially when it is held at a different time. The judge, in determining what to do with a delinquent juvenile, is not limited as much by constitutional safeguards; rules of evidence are relaxed; and probation officers can report their findings in

Look son, I'm a Public Defender not Perry Mason—Let's not waste our time with pleas of innocence!

a hearsay form. The judge usually reads a social study of the youth, prepared by a probation officer, that includes such factors as school attendance and grades, family structure and support, degree of maturity and sense of responsibility, relationships with peers, participation in community activities, and attitudes toward authority figures. Juveniles are permitted to have legal counsel in this final stage of the proceedings, and counsel should have the right to challenge the facts of the social study.

Judicial decision making at the dispositional stage has been the subject of many studies. Although it has produced a sizeable body of literature, the findings are inconsistent in evaluating the impact on judicial decisions of race, sex, social class, home situations, and school attendance. One reason for this volume of conflicting testimony is that juvenile court systems vary from jurisdiction to jurisdiction in regard to the ability, background, and perspective of staff members; organizational structure; statutory and procedural constraints; and community expectations.

Thomas and Fitch, in what is probably the most extensive study on judicial decision making, reviewed cases processed between 1966 and 1973 in a metropolitan area of Virginia. Their study yielded a sample of 1,522 juveniles who had come before the court one or more times during this period. Thomas and Fitch found that even when the type of offense was controlled, males were treated more harshly than females, blacks more harshly than whites, school drop-outs more harshly than those who had stayed in school, and those from broken homes more harshly than those from intact homes. Youths from lower socioeconomic backgrounds tended to be treated more harshly when they were charged with either feloniés or status offenses, but all social classes were dealt with in a more equitable fashion when the offense was a misdemeanor. Still, youths from the upper social classes were much more likely to be put on probation for misdemeanors than were those from lower social classes. Status offense complaints received from parents or guardians resulted in harsher treatment than those received from other sources. Finally, the three judges who heard most of the cases in this sample varied considerably in the sanctions they gave for the various offenses under consideration.[28]

Judicial Alternatives. The alternatives available in juvenile courts vary significantly in number. But juvenile judges, though limited by available resources, have a vast amount of discretion in decision making; in fact, the only major restraint is that the choice must be made from the alternatives authorized by the applicable juvenile court act.

1. *Dismissal* is certainly the most desirable disposition; the fact-finding stage may have shown the youth to be guilty, but the judge can decide, for a variety of reasons, to dismiss the case.
2. *Fine or restitution* also is usually very desirable. The youths may be required to work off their debt for a few hours each week, but their lives are not seriously interrupted.
3. *Psychiatric therapy* as an outpatient, whether in the court clinic, the community mental health clinic, or with a private therapist, is intended to be a treatment-oriented decision and is typically reserved for middle-class youths to keep them from being disposed

to unfitting placements. Actually, psychiatric counseling is not usually a very effective placement decision. If parents can afford it, it probably already has been tried unsuccessfully.

4. *Probation* seems to be a fairly popular decision with misbehaving juveniles as well as a good treatment alternative for the court. The judge can give the child a suspended sentence, place him on probation, and assure the youth that his sentence will be served if problems arise while he is on probation. The probation officer can be directed by the judge to involve the youth in special programs, such as alternative schools, speech therapy, or learning disability programs. Some probation officers are often able to become valuable role models and to provide the type of positive support some of these youths need.

5. *Private foster homes* are more restrictive inasmuch as youths are removed from their natural homes. These placements are used more frequently for status offenders and dependent neglected children. The intent is to remove children from homes where they have been abused and traumatized and place them in homes where love, kindness, and concern predominate. But foster care does not always live up to its billing.

6. *Community-based correctional programs,* to which juveniles are assigned during the day and from which they return home in the evening, offer another judicial alternative. Failure to participate in these day programs once assigned ordinarily means a return to the court. Unfortunately, these facilities are limited in number and primarily are clustered in a few states.

7. *Group homes and halfway houses* are found in many communities. They are not as desirable as community-based day facilities because youths are taken from their natural homes to live in these facilities. Group homes are located in the community and are usually for short-term placement. Participation in such community activities as schools, clubs, and recreational activities may be included. Juveniles, interestingly enough, seem to be more negative about this type of placement than any other judicial alternative in the community.

8. *Short-term residential facilities* in other communities, whether under state, county, religious, or other auspices, are among the more punitively oriented judicial alternatives. Boys' homes, children's homes, residential schools for the retarded, and ranches, camps, and work programs are included in this category. Some of these placements unquestionably are more treatment-oriented than others; still, youths are taken away from their own communities, are placed in detention for a definite period of time or until they satisfy the "keepers" that they are ready to return home, and must experience at least to some degree the pains of imprisonment.

9. *Mental hospitals* certainly are even more on the restrictive side of the continuum. Even if placement is made to a modern facility, surrounded by attractive landscape and lawn, patients are processed, humiliated, and often destroyed in the great name of the therapeutic state. Indeed, many inmates—youngsters as well as the aged—walk hunched over, learn to pay a thousand-and-one deferences to staff, and gradually accept their "no person" status.

10. *Placement in a training school* is even more punitive, although judges may send youths to several different types of detention. The end-of-the-line facility, if the state has one, is much different from a first-of-the-line or minimum security training school. Some juveniles, as forthcoming chapters indicate, find placement in these schools boring, humiliating, and overwhelming. Many choose to run at the first opportunity. Others, thwarted in runaway attempts and seeing no other alternative, choose to take their own lives.

11. The juvenile judge can elect to remand the youth to *adult court;* that is, the juvenile court can release jurisdiction over the youth and transfer the case to adult court. Criminal proceedings may then follow. This is the most punitive choice. It may result if the judge receives considerable pressure from both the prosecutor's office and the community. Refusing to transfer the publicized case can place a judge's political future in jeopardy.

ADMINISTRATION OF JUVENILE COURT SERVICES

The structure of the juvenile court varies from jurisdiction to jurisdiction. Special and separate juvenile courts sometimes devote their total effort to the legal problems of children in a specific geographical area; the Denver Juvenile Court, the Boston Juvenile Court, and the Juvenile Court for Orleans Parish in Louisiana are examples. A separate court is organized statewide in several states, and only juvenile judges sit on cases in the various districts of those states. Connecticut and Utah use this structure. In other states, juvenile offenders are handled exclusively by family court judges. These family courts hear both juvenile jurisdiction cases and some domestic relations cases. New York, Delaware, and Rhode Island use statewide family courts, although New York does not administer family courts on a statewide basis.[29]

More typically, juvenile courts are part of a circuit, district, county, superior, common pleas, probation, or municipal court. This broad-based trial court may be either the highest court of general trial jurisdiction, as in Florida and California, or the lower trial court where lesser criminal and limited-claim civil matters are heard. This structure is found in Maine, New Hampshire, and Arkansas.

There are yet other variations of the court structure. In Michigan and much of Kansas, juvenile matters are considered by a juvenile or family court, while the juvenile judge in other counties is a member of a trial court bench that hears a variety of criminal, civil, probate, and juvenile cases. Alabama, Louisiana, and Colorado employ this hybrid structure.[30]

Nationally, juvenile courts presently are being affected by a movement toward a single trial court, inclusive of all courts where initial trials take place. In a massive court reorganization in Cook County, Illinois, 208 courts became the circuit court for Cook County. The juvenile court, which had already long been part of the circuit court in Cook County, was not changed by the reorganization. The juvenile court of the District of Columbia, however, was absorbed into the new single trial court for the District.

The Juvenile Court and Politics

The juvenile court is pervaded by politics. In fact, throughout its history, the policy of the juvenile court has reflected the demands of various agencies and interest groups.

On the local level, the court, as evidenced by the many welfare functions assigned to it, is expected to function more as a social agency than as a judicial agency. But, because it has both a punitive and a rehabilitative goal, the court is in the position of not being able to perform either role to anyone's satisfaction. The juvenile court thus becomes a convenient scapegoat as citizens' groups skirmish between soft-line ("kids will be kids") and hard-line ("let's lock up every young hoodlum") extremes.

The juvenile court must also cope with a complex network of intergovernmental relations at the local, regional, state, and federal levels. The juvenile court usually receives its resources from the municipal or county governments, augmented by some state assistance. The juvenile court is responsible to the municipal government for those services the local governing body assigns it, but only the state legislature has the authority to determine the jurisdiction of the juvenile court. The court, then, receives its mandates from one level of government, the legislature, but other levels of government, the municipal or county councils, decide how far the court should go in carrying out the legislature's mandates. Not suprisingly, then, the juvenile court often finds itself unable to cope with the conflicting demands.[31]

The court's ability to manage this confusing web of intergovernmental relations is reduced even further because of its inferior location in the hierarchy of courts. Attorneys and social workers both tend to rank the juvenile court low in their esteem compared to other types of courts. Relatively few attorneys aspire to be juvenile court judges, and those who do often view it only as a step toward higher office.

Adding to the pressures on the juvenile court is the fact that its proceedings are subject to review and supervision by the higher courts. This, of course, reminds the juvenile court that it is, above all, a judicial agency that is expected to preserve the rule of law as well as to serve the welfare needs of the local community. Therefore, in addition to appeasing diverse citizens' groups in the community, the juvenile court must also satisfy the legal community that proper respect is being given to the institution of law.[32]

Juvenile court judges, confronted by all the inconsistent demands made upon them, find it difficult to know how to handle best this difficult situation. Judges are also political animals who prefer to remain in office. They like "good press" and to see their names in print—as long as the reference is positive. Some judges, in fact, even court the press; they want to have good relations with the police, probation department, school officials, welfare department, newspaper editors, and the average man on the street. Judges, in short, want to be reelected.[33]

In the face of these public and political pressures, some judges are quick to pursue the politically expedient path. Others stand firm on what they feel is right, regardless of the consequences. Rubin illustrates both:

> The judge also views his role in terms both of what the community expects of him and what justice system agencies expect of him. This, too, brings out the best and the worst in judges. The best, as with the Midwestern juvenile court judge who refused to transfer a juvenile homicide case to the criminal court because he believed that the juvenile justice system had a greater capacity to rehabilitate this youngster. He suffered electoral defeat several years later on the political contention of permissiveness. Or the worst, as with the Southern judge who is held in high esteem in his community, in part because he believes that several nights in detention is good medicine for any child apprehended by the police, even though many of these youngsters are later dismissed without formal court proceedings.*

Role and Responsibilities of Juvenile Court Personnel

Judges. Juvenile court judges have an enormously important and difficult job. In urban areas they are administrators of the court and, unless there is a director of court services, overwhelming administrative tasks are thrust upon them. Their area of supervision encompasses the personnel of the court, which may include other judges, referees, pros-

*This excerpt from Chapter 6, "The Eye of the Juvenile Court Judge: A One-Step-Up View of the Juvenile Justice System," by H. Ted Rubin is reprinted from *The Juvenile Justice System* (Vol. V, *Sage Criminal Justice System Annuals*) M. W. Klein, Editor © 1976, p. 146 by permission of the publisher, Sage Publications, Inc.

ecuting attorneys, public defenders, social investigators, probation officers (if probation services are administered by the court, not by executive order), clerical workers, and support personnel—psychologists, psychiatrists, and physicians. Internally, financial services remain a concern of judges, especially because many face a shortage of funds. Externally, the judge may be responsible for the supervision of foster homes, detention facilities, the court clinic, and aftercare facilities.

In addition to these administrative activities, judges are expected to be kindly parents to wayward children. They must quickly dispense dosages of individualized medicine to erring children who need to be "treated" for their problems. They must also handle traffic offenses and child welfare funds and set limits on unruly children; and, of course, the dependent and neglected cases constantly demand attention.

Juvenile court judges also must be involved in public relations. If there is a citizens' advisory group of the juvenile court, it requires leadership and inspiration. The judges must constantly cultivate good relations with other criminal justice and juvenile justice agencies; and they must pacify interest groups. Boards of directors of governmental units providing financial resources want information and attention. Speaking engagements must be fulfilled. The list goes on and on.

Clearly, the job of the juvenile judge requires exceptional persons who have skills in management, finances, group leadership, human relations, public speaking, and counseling; who are knowledgeable in law, psychology, and sociology; who are truly committed to what they are doing; and who are blessed with physical endurance and emotional stability. To fill this role are approximately 3,000 judges in the United States. These judges serve in the 2,973 courts exercising jurisidiction over juvenile matters.[34]

Two recent surveys indicate that judges come from a variety of backgrounds. The National Council of Juvenile Court Judges in 1963 conducted a survey of judges performing juvenile court duties. Responses were received from 1,564, or an estimated 70 percent, of those actually involved in juvenile matters. Their average age was fifty-three, and 96.2 percent were male. Seventy-one percent of the respondents had law degrees; in contrast, 48 percent had no undergraduate degree. The average salary of full-time judges was $12,493.15 per year. Nearly 75 percent had been elected to office. Seventy-two percent of the full-time judges spent less than a quarter of their time on juvenile matters. As to court personnel, a third of the full-time judges reported that no probation officers or social workers were available to their courts; 83 percent said they did not have regularly available psychologists or psychiatrists.[35]

A 1973 survey of juvenile judges revealed that 12 percent of the

1,314 respondents were full-time judges who spent all of their working hours on juvenile matters. Eighty-six percent devoted half their time or less and 67 percent spent one-quarter or less of their time on juvenile matters. These judges averaged more than seven years in juvenile jurisdictions. Of those involved in juvenile work, 28 percent had been involved for more than ten years and 22 percent had presided in juvenile court for less than two years. In the 1973 survey, the average age was still fifty-three, and there were fewer women juvenile judges. The average salary had increased to $23,187 per year; a gain of 85.6 percent over the 1963 average. More judges in the 1973 survey had a legal education and had been admitted to the bar; they had more years of undergraduate education.[36]

In each survey, juvenile judges were given a list of problems and asked to rank them. (See Table 4-4.) Interestingly enough, they ranked the first four of their most pressing problems in the same order in both the 1963 and 1973 surveys. These problems were: inadequate or insufficient detention and shelter care, problems in foster home placement, concerns related to institutional care, and probation or social service staff matters.

Sophia Robinson categorizes five roles for juvenile judges: the parent judge, the counselor judge, the chancellor judge, the lawyer judge, and the antagonist judge. The parent judge identifies with the parent more than with the child, and he emphasizes obedience to the parents. This judge feels that, like a parent, he knows what is best for the child. The counselor judge, in contrast, emphasizes almost totally the individuality of each child. He is interested in the social history of the child and regards other court personnel as members of a professional team. The chancellor judge balances the child's rights with those of the parent and the community. He acts as the arbitrator when difficulties arise. In acting in loco parentis, this judge believes that he symbolizes the benevolent parent. The lawyer judge perceives his role primarily as that of a lawyer and regards the court as the appropriate setting for administering the law. He looks upon the court hearing as more or less an adversary trial. Finally, the antagonist judge reacts differently to each situation but generally appears to be hostile to the child.[37]

Juvenile judges not only have difficult jobs, but also wield considerable power. Power, of course, sometimes corrupts, and occasionally a judge becomes a despot or dictator in his court. David Matza, addressing himself to the abuse of power, refers to the justice of some judges as *kadi justice*. The kadi is a Moslem judge who sits in the marketplace and makes decisions without any apparent reference to rules or norms; he appears to make a completely free evaluation of the merits of each case.[38] Seemingly operating with an ability to see the whole, the kadi is

TABLE 4-4   Acute Problems of Juvenile Court Judges.
Rank-ordered, with percentage of judges responding to each item on 1973 questionnaire.

1973 Rank	Problem	1973 Percent	1963 Rank
1	Inadequate facilities for detention or shelter care pending disposition	54.3	1
2	Insufficent foster home facilities	49.5	2
3	Inadequate or insufficent training or correctional institutions	39.7	3
4	Insufficient probation or social service staff	26.6	4
5	Inadequate staff salaries	21.1	7
6	Excessive judicial workloads	16.9	8
7	Inadequate facilities for testing and psychological evaluation	15.9	5
8	Need for more knowledge of how to handle cases	15.8	6
9	Lack of community support for programs	14.0	9
10	Improvement and standardization of court procedures	10.2	10
11	Other duties preempting adequate attention to juvenile cases	7.7	13
12	Lack of specialized court or specially assigned judges	6.1	12
13	Inability to recruit qualified staff	4.7	11
14	Lack of court administrators	3.2	NA

Note: Percentages total more than 100% because each judge was asked to check three items. That is, 54.3% of all judges responding consider one of their three most pressing problems to be "Inadequate facilities for detention or shelter care pending disposition."

From: Kenneth C. Smith, "A Profile of Juvenile Court Judges in the United States," *Juvenile Justice* 25 (August 1976): 37.

not limited by rules or norms; this wise man can supposedly make an evaluation purely on the merits of each case. Applied to the juvenile court, the judge would be seen as a special kind of wise person who is able to see and know the whole. But the assumption that juvenile judges are able to discern the problem and to quickly arrive at the most desirable solution is both unrealistic and laden with potential shortcomings.

An example of marginal, if not kadi, justice was found in a small Indiana town, where the judge greeted an investigative reporter with these comments:

> Thanks for coming. I'm right honored to be in your book. Be sure to use that thingamajig (the tape recorder) so you can get in everything and not depend on your memory. Memory plays many tricks, you know. Now, you say you've been to a lot of big city courts, and I ought to warn you that it's quite different here. We don't have the money or the time for all those frills, and I don't try to put on a show. If I did, I would never get through the schedule. Can't waste time, you know, because tomorrow I have to be twenty miles away. I got twenty-six cases to hear in six hours with a twenty-minute break each hour. Just add it up and you'll see why I can't do much more than ask questions and listen less than ten minutes for each case. You'll see that most of them are easy. A boy or girl is apt to be

CERTAINLY I'm qualified to rule on this case—it's my 30th one today!!

guilty or they would not have come this far. So I just do the best I can. Just you don't be too hard on me.[39]

But many juvenile judges rise to the challenge and do remarkable jobs. Procedural safeguards and due process rights for juveniles are scrupulously observed in their courts. These judges always are seeking better means of detention and reserve the use of correctional institutions as a last resort. They somehow manage to keep up with all of the facets of their jobs. They are very committed, work long hours, and sometimes pass up promotions to more highly paid judgeships with greater prestige. The end result is that these judges usually change the quality of juvenile justice in their communities. To compare these individuals with the power-hungry, well-publicized, insensitive bureaucratic judge is not only unfair but wrong.

Director of Court Services.   Too many courts at the present time have cumbersome and archaic procedures to move cases through their several stages. One possible solution is to appoint a professional court administrator who can better manage the organization of juvenile services. Figure 4-3 is a suggested organization chart for a large juvenile court in which the professional court administrator reports directly to the chief judge.

The Court Referee.   Many juvenile courts employ the services of a referee, who has been called the "arm of the court." Referees may or may not be members of the bar, but their basic responsibility is to assist the judge in processing youths through the courts. They hear cases at the fact-finding stage and sometimes in detention hearings, but if a judicial disposition is necessary, it is usually reserved for a juvenile court judge. Referees generally have a good background in juvenile law, experience or training or both in social work, and a fundamental grasp of psychology and sociology.

Prosecutor.   Prosecutors in the juvenile court have dual roles that are somewhat contradictory. They are expected to protect society, but at the same time to ensure that those children who would harm society are provided their basic constitutional rights. One of the important tasks of the juvenile court is to clarify and define the prosecutor's responsibilities and functions, which are discharged at every stage of the court's proceedings, from intake through disposition. Large courts should employ prosecutors on a full-time basis and should provide adequate pre-service and in-service training for the prosecution staff.

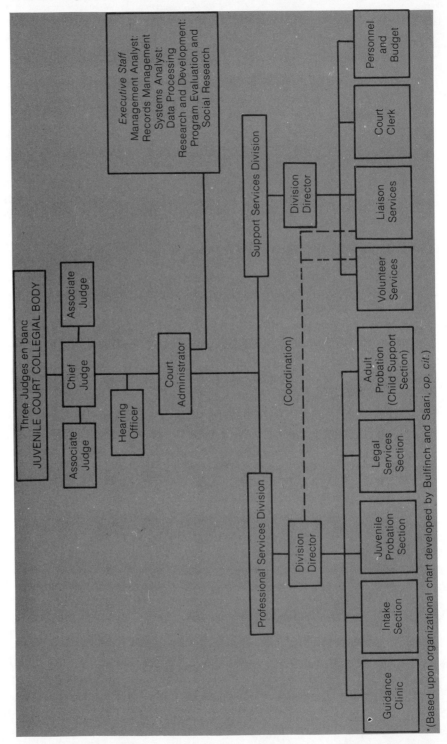

From: Richard W. Kobetz and Betty B. Bosarge, *Juvenile Justice Administration* (Gaithersburg, Md.: International Association of Chiefs of Police, Inc., 1973), p. 230.

Defense Attorney.   The number of juveniles represented by counsel has been gradually increasing since the early 1960s. But, even though more juveniles are being respresented by counsel at the present time, attorneys—especially private attorneys—are not comfortable in juvenile court.

> A private attorney in juvenile court . . . noted that there was little an attorney could contribute in this setting. "What can a lawyer say? The probation officers know better about the kids. . . . They aren't out to get them." He usually tried to get the best deal possible for a client, but this procedure had no value in a juvenile court. . . . And the lawyer's presence might even destroy the informal atmosphere, if he felt compelled to appear to earn his fee: "You have to put on a show, a presentation for the client."[40]

Attorneys also soon discover that judges expect them to be interpreters rather than advocates. If attorneys, whether private or public defenders, overact the advocate role, they risk their client's freedom. In fact, some evidence indicates that juveniles with counsel are more likely to be institutionalized than those without counsel.[41]

Director and Personnel of Intake Service Division.   The juvenile court should provide written guidelines or standards for the intake unit. This unit includes all personnel (probation officers, social workers, detention officers, psychologists, and psychiatrists) who are involved with the initial investigation of cases prior to the fact-finding proceedings.

Director and Personnel of Psychiatric and Psychological Services.   If the juvenile court provides any in-house rehabilitation services for youth, physicians, psychologists, psychiatrists, educational and vocational counselors, social workers, and supervisors of group care and foster homes become part of court services.

Innovative Court Programs   Many juvenile courts have attempted to bolster their services through one or more of the following programs.

Volunteers.   More than 600 juvenile courts are making use of community volunteers to enrich court services. (See Chapter 5.)

Improvement of Detention.   The Attention Homes in Boulder, Colorado exemplify another emerging trend: the attempt of juvenile courts across the nation to improve the detention process for children. Nonsecure detention facilities that have no fences, locked doors, or physical restraints are being constructed in a number of places. Home detention, too, is being used in St. Louis, Newport News, Norfolk, and Washington, D.C. The court pays someone to maintain close supervision of a youth in the child's home during the day when parents are away.[42] In addition, many courts are making an earnest attempt to improve the daily programs in detention centers.

Improved Coordination with Other Parts of the System.   Many judges hold weekly or monthly meetings with representatives of other agencies in the system. For example, the juvenile judge in Billings, Montana has weekly meetings with representatives of other juvenile justice agencies—the chief juvenile probation officer, the school truant officer, the deputy county attorney, sheriff's office and police juvenile-bureau chiefs, and officials of the regional mental health center. The judge also meets four times a year with school administrative personnel. In Boulder, the judge conducts weekly staff intake conferences with representatives of the welfare department, the youth service bureau, and the school. Judge Whitlatch, of the Cuyahoga County, Ohio, Juvenile Court, maintains a close relationship with the Cleveland Police Department. A liaison officer of the department is stationed at the court; the judge has frequent meetings with police-juvenile command officers; and the judge takes an active interest in the police chiefs association.[43]

ISSUES FACING THE JUVENILE COURT

The way in which several issues now facing the juvenile court are resolved will in large part determine the direction and jurisdiction of the court in the years to come.

Individualized Justice versus Standards   The Juvenile Justice Standards Project, jointly sponsored by the Institute of Judicial Administration and the American Bar Association, recommends the adoption of several guidelines that would alter juvenile justice significantly. Officially launched in 1971 by a national planning committee under the chairmanship of Judge Kaufman, comprehensive guidelines for juvenile offenders have been designed that would base sentences on the seriousness of crime rather than on the "needs" of the youth. The proposed guidelines represent radical philosophical changes and are an attempt to standardize the handling of juvenile lawbreakers.

The belief that disparity in juvenile sentencing must end is one of the fundamental thrusts of the recommended standards. To accomplish this goal, the commission is attempting to limit the discretion of juvenile judges and to make the judges accountable to the public. The plan calls for judges to submit written justifications for their decisions, which would then be subject to judicial review. Also important in the projected standards is the provision that certain court procedures would be open to the public, although the names of juveniles would still remain confidential.

There are at least twelve key points for the new juvenile justice system envisioned in the proposed standards:

1. Juvenile offenses would be divided into five classes, three for felonies, two for misdemeanors. A required sentence of two years would be imposed on juveniles who committed crimes for which adults normally would be sentenced to death, life in prison, or twenty years in prison. Juveniles could be sent to a secure or nonsecure facility. The minimum sentence for a misdemeanor or crime would be two months. In some instances, conditional freedom could be granted instead of confinement.

2. The criminal code for juvenile offenders would cover the ages from ten until a youngster's eighteenth birthday. . . .

3. The severity of sanctions for juvenile offenders would be based on the seriousness of the offense rather than on a court's view of the "needs" of the juvenile. Maximum terms for various classes of offenses would be prescribed by the legislature. The court's choice of a sentence within this maximum would be guided by the seriousness of the offense, the degree of culpability indicated by the circumstances of a particular case, and the age and prior record of the juvenile. The alternative to this approach to sentencing, the "rehabilitative ideal," has proved a failure, frequently causing needless suffering in the name of treatment. Sentencing geared to the gravity of the offense, on the other hand, reduces arbitrary sentencing disparities and prevents harsh, vindictive sanctions from being imposed in the guise of benevolence.

4. Sentences should be determinative. The practice of indeterminate sentencing, now prevalent in most states, should be abolished. Such sentences permit widely differing punishment for the same misbehavior, and create a potential for abuse that is all too often realized in practice.

5. The least drastic alternative should be utilized as a guide to intervention in the lives of juveniles and their familes. In general, the decision maker, such as an intake officer or a judge, should not impose a particular disposition unless he expressly finds that no less coercive alternatives are available to adequately further the purposes of the juvenile justice system.

6. Noncriminal misbehavior ("status offenses") and private offenses ("victimless crimes") should be removed from juvenile court jurisdiction. Possession of narcotic drugs, however, has been retained for court jurisdiction. . . .

7. Visibility and accountability of decision making should replace closed proceedings and unrestrained official discretion.

8. There should be a right to counsel for all affected interests at all crucial stages of the proceeding.

9. Juveniles should have the right to decide on actions affecting their lives and freedom, unless found incapable of making reasoned decisions.

10. The role of parents in juvenile proceedings should be redefined, with particular attention given to possible conflicts between the interests of parent and child.

11. Limitations should be imposed on detention, treatment, or other intervention prior to adjudication and disposition.

12. Strict criteria should be established for waiver of juvenile court jurisdiction to regulate transfer of juveniles to adult criminal court.[44]

Juvenile court judges are quite concerned about these proposed standards. The basic argument offered at the Third Annual Conference on Juvenile Justice in the spring of 1976 was that these standards attack the underlying philsophy and structure of the juvenile court. Judges also are concerned about how these standards would limit their authority. They see the influence of the hard-liners behind this movement toward standardization and feel that the needs of children will be neglected in the long run. Too, they challenge the idea that it is possible, much less feasible, to treat all children alike.

The adoption of these standards will be determined over the next few years. New York State was the first to act on them, through the Juvenile Justice Reform Act of 1976 that went into effect on February 1, 1977. The Act orders a determinative sentence of five years for a Class A felony, examples of which are murder; kidnapping, first degree; and arson, first degree. This initial term can be extended by at least one one-year term. The juvenile, according to the Act, should be placed in a secure facility for the first year and in a residential facility for the second year. Then, if this is approved by the director of the division, the confined youth can be placed in a nonresidential program for the remainder of the five-year term. But the youth must remain under intensive supervision for the entire five-year term.

Status Offenders
Youths can be charged with at least three different categories of offenses. First, they can be charged with a felony or misdemeanor by federal, state, and local statutes. Second, they are subject to relatively specific statutes applying exclusively to juvenile behavior: truancy, consumption of alcoholic beverages, and running away from home are examples. Third, juveniles can be prosecuted under general omnibus

statutes that include such offenses as acting beyond control of parents, engaging in immoral conduct, and being ungovernable and incorrigible. Offenses under both the second and third categories are status offenses. The status offenses statutes pertaining to behavior for which an adult could not be prosecuted have drawn increasing attention in recent years. Status offenders can be processed through the juvenile justice system along with youths who have committed criminal offenses, or they can be handled separately from felons and misdemeanants. States that pursue the latter course usually refer to status offenders as MINS (Minors in Need of Supervision), CINS (Children in Need of Supervision), PINS (Persons in Need of Supervision), FINS (Families in Need of Supervision), or JINS (Juveniles in Need of Supervision). Some jurisdictions handle these youths in a different court; others will not send them to a juvenile correctional institution.

There are at least four distinct arguments for the removal of status offenders from the jurisdiction of the juvenile court. The legal argument states that the lack of clarity of the status offender statutes makes them unconstitutionally vague in their construction; that they often are blatantly discriminatory, especially in regard to sex; and that government bodies have no legitimate interest in many of these proscribed behaviors. Second, although status offenders have not committed a criminal act, they frequently are confined with chronic or hard-core offenders. Third, in keeping with the *parens patriae* philosophy of the juvenile court, the procedure of processing and confining the status offender is not in his best interest. Some theorists, as mentioned earlier, argue that the formal intervention of the juvenile court promotes rather than inhibits unlawful behavior. Fourth, many charge that status offenders are a special class of youth who must be treated differently from hard-core or more serious offenders.[45] The Board of Directors of the National Council on Crime and Delinquency comments on these arguments:

> Whether we label children status offenders or delinquents, once introduced into the juvenile court process they become stigmatized. The benefits derived from each classification for either the child or society appear to be nonexistent. . . . The result of giving jurisdiction over noncriminal behavior to the juvenile court is that a disproportionate share of available resources is applied to youth *who pose no criminal danger to society*. (Emphasis added.)[46]

Critics decry the fact that a large proportion of institutionalized youths are status offenders. The National Assessment of Juvenile Corrections study found that 23 percent of the boys and 50 percent of the girls in institutions were status offenders. (See Table 4-5.) The Children in Custody census of 1971 revealed that 23 percent of the boys and 70 percent of the girls in public correctional settings were status offenders. Finally, another study in nineteen major cities drew the following conclusion:

1. Status offenders are more likely to be detained in detention facilities than youths who have committed criminal acts (54 percent versus 31 percent).
2. Once detained, status offenders are twice as likely to be detained for more than thirty days (51 percent versus 25 percent).
3. Status offenders are also more likely to receive harsher dispositions in juvenile court and to be sent to institutional placements (25 percent versus 23 percent), and their average length of stay is much longer.[47]

These arguments are reinforced by recent federal legislation that prohibits the assignment of status offenders to correctional facilities if

TABLE 4-5 Commitment Offense, by Program Type and Sex (in percentages)

	Status[a] Offense	Probation or Parole Violation	Misde- meanor	Drugs or Alcohol	Prop- erty	Person	(n)
Institution							
Male	23	4	2	6	46	18	(832)
Female	50	1	3	18	14	14	(349)
Community— Residential							
Male	50	3	1	10	26	10	(70)
Female	67	3	0	14	12	3	(58)
Day Treatment							
Male	45	3	4	6	30	12	(164)
Female	87	0	0	5	3	5	(37)

NOTE: Determination of commitment offense was based on youth response to the question, "Why are you here?"
[a]Status offenses include incorrigibility, dependent and neglected, truancy, running away, curfew violations, disorderly, etc.

This table from Chapter 7, "Justice for Whom? Varieties of Juvenile Correctional Approaches," by Rosemary C. Sarri and Robert D. Vinter is reprinted from *The Juvenile Justice System* (Vol. V, *Sage Criminal Justice System Annuals*) M. W. Klein, Editor © 1976, p. 181 by permission of the publisher, Sage Publications, Inc.

states receive federal monies (under Section 223 of P.L. 93–415 of the Juvenile Justice and Delinquency Prevention Act of 1974).

However, Charles Thomas challenges the notion that status offenders are merely incorrigible youths with family problems. In a randomly selected sample of 2,589 juveniles who appeared before one of two juvenile courts in Virginia between 1970 and 1974, he found that many juveniles who appeared in court for charges involving status offenses had previously appeared for more serious charges and that those juveniles whose first court appearance involved a status offense were more likely to be returned to court than either those first charged with a misdemeanor or a felony.[48]

Juvenile court judges are presently challenging the movement to strip jurisdiction over status offenders from the juvenile court. One of their most cogent arguments is that status offenders will have no one to provide for or look out for them if they are taken away from the juvenile court purview. Judge Margaret Driscoll, for example, strongly advised in a speech to the Third National Conference on Juvenile Justice in the spring of 1976 that these youths, seemingly beyond control of their parents, school, and church, need someone to provide them with guidance and structure. Driscoll maintained that status offenders, especially, need parental protection provided by the court, for this is probably the only guidance they will receive. She warned that these youths will find it considerably more difficult to survive in the modern world without the protection of the juvenile court.

This argument makes a valid point—that other agencies will have to take over if the court relinquishes jurisdiction of these offenders. Given the fragmentation of the juvenile justice system, the end result could be neglect and chaos in the lives of status offenders. Judge Bazelon responds to this line of thinking in saying:

> This situation is truly ironic. The argument for retaining beyond-control and truancy jurisdiction is that juvenile courts have to act in such cases because "if we don't act, no one else will." I submit that precisely the opposite is the case: *because* you act, no one else does. Schools and public agencies refer their problem cases to you because you have jurisdiction, because you exercise it, and because you hold out promises that you can provide solutions.[49]

Status offenders will probably remain a crucial concern of the juvenile justice system, for no evidence exists that they are decreasing in number. Neither is there any evidence that providing adequate care for "beyond control" youth will be easy. But if they are removed from the jurisdiction of the juvenile court, Bazelon and others feel that nonjudicial agencies will have to assume the work of the juvenile court. As more and more jurisdictions keep status offenders out of the court, the contention that other agencies will take over the care and guidance of these youths will be severely tested.

Morality in the Court

Court staff, according to Emerson's study, distinguish three general kinds of moral character among juveniles. Youths may be normal, which means that their behavior is basically like that of most other adolescents. Or youths may be regarded as hard-core or criminal-like offenders, who are hostile and committed to crime as a career. Finally, juveniles may be disturbed—driven to act in irrational and senseless ways by internal drives or compulsions.[50]

These three classes of moral character, in turn, provide the alternative courses of action open to the court. A normal youngster tends to receive routine handling of his case; probation is the most serious "punishment" that he will receive from the court. The hard-core youth, not surprisingly, receives incarceration in a training school or similar institution. The disturbed youth is given special care and treatment, primarily in psychiatric settings or facilities.

Emerson goes on to describe how moral character is determined in the court. The defense attorney, usually the family, and sometimes the probation officer make "pitches" to describe good moral character. The juvenile also tries to establish good moral character through use of protective strategies. However, the prosecutor, law enforcement officer, victim, and sometimes even the probation officer may become involved in denunciations of the youth's moral character. Total denunciations often come from probation officers who want to get rid of probationers who have "spoiled characters." Officials outside the court, too, use total denunciation as a necessary step in ridding caseloads of difficult youths.

Needless to say, basing "justice" on moral character can lead to extensive abuses in the juvenile court. The court has no right to be a "moral busybody." Children who come from good families, obviously, are treated very differently from those whose families are plagued by multiple problems such as divorce, conflict, abuse, and financial distress. Therefore, youths who come from troubled families have less of a chance for justice than do juveniles whose families are considered respectable. Too, when youths do not have adequate "pitches" in defense of their moral characters or are faced with vindictive complainants, the likelihood that their moral character will be effectively denounced increases significantly.

The Right to Treatment

The right to treatment has become an issue in the juvenile justice system. The right to treatment for the mentally ill was first set down in the case of *Rouse* v. *Cameron*. Since this 1968 case, the right to treatment has been upheld in several cases of juveniles whose commitment to training school was predicated on treatment. *Pena* v. *New York State Division for Youth* (1976) and *Morales* v. *Thurman* (1975) have been important in establishing this right. In the latter case, two training schools in Texas were ordered by the court to close because they did not provide a rehabilitative or therapeutic milieu.

The purpose of the right of treatment is to assure the therapeutic ideal promised by juvenile law. The right is based theoretically on the state's authority to confine for treatment under its *parens patriae* power. Not surprisingly, those who challenge the *parens patriae* doctrine and the rehabilitative ideal oppose this idea of the right to treatment. One critic believes that youths ought to have a right to punishment rather than treatment.[51]

IMPACT OF THE JUVENILE COURT UPON JUVENILES

> . . . the tragedy of the juvenile court is not that it stigmatizes so many— but that it saves so few.
>
> Robert M. Emerson

Children appearing before the juvenile court for the first time are confused and bewildered, particularly if no one is present to speak up for them. The immense structure, the archaic architecture, the well-worn corridors, and the dirty walls seem to work to make a first-timer appear very small and insignificant, very much at the mercy of the court.

Baum and Wheeler concluded from a survey of boys confined in a Massachusetts institution:

> Almost all of these youths had been in juvenile court before; indeed, over a third had been there at least three times prior to their current hearing. Yet, although no strangers to the court, many were quite unprepared for events that took place there. There seemed to be little understanding of what was going on, and for many youths the whole scene remained a blur. There were many faces, but the youths were not always sure of the relevant roles. . . . Descriptions of what the youths were told were also vague, largely because they were waiting to hear the central message— commitment or no commitment.[52]

Older youths who have been before the court on several occasions seem to have become much more sophisticated about juvenile court proceedings. They may resent the injustice of the court, may feel a mixture of boredom, impatience, and contempt, or may have learned to "play it cool."

One "experienced hand" comments:

In the children's court, I had found, there are two kinds of judges: bleeding hearts and swords of the Lord. Bleeding hearts called me son and wept over me; swords of the Lord shouted I ought to be locked up in a zoo. But I thought there was no real difference between the two. If there was room for you in the slammers, either kind sent you up. That is why I got off with a warning the twelve times before this.[53]

The evidence seems to reveal that youngsters appearing before the court for the first time are impressionable and confused; yet, those processed through the courts several times are no longer very amenable to the processes of juvenile justice. Therefore, if the juvenile court is going to have a positive impact on children, it must affect them this way on their first or second trip before the bench.

SUMMARY

The juvenile court was examined in considerable detail in this chapter. Beginning with the historical consciousness and the changing legal norms of the court, this chapter focused on the administration of the court and on several important issues related to juvenile justice. Granted that the court has fallen far short of its goals, obviously too much has been expected from it. Bureaucratic considerations continually demand top priority. The court lacks sufficient resources and community support to fulfill its mission adequately. The court has not had sufficient supervision, which has resulted in abuse on the one hand and moralistic betterment lessons on the other. Consequently, the so-called best interest of the child often consists of nothing but rhetoric banter, and too many youths suffer long-term detention because of the court's short patience.

QUESTIONS

1. Do you think the juvenile court should be changed? Why? How?
2. What are the advantages and disadvantages of basing juvenile justice on standards?
3. How should the status offender be handled by the juvenile justice system?
4. What can be done to eliminate the variance in juvenile court procedures from jurisdiction to jurisdiction?

5. How can the juvenile court become less subject to politics?
6. What can be done to raise the quality of juvenile judges?

ENDNOTES

1. 213 Pa. 48, 62 A, pp. 198–200.
2. President's Commission on Law Enforcement and Administration of Justice, *The Challenge of Crime in a Free Society* (Washington, D.C.: U.S. Government Printing Office), pp. 79–80.
3. Lisa Aversa Richette, *The Throwaway Children* (New York: J. B. Lippincott Company, 1969); Patrick Murphy, *Our Kindly Parent—The State* (New York: Viking Press, 1974); Howard James, *Children in Trouble: A National Scandal* (New York: Pocket Books, Simon and Schuster, 1971).
4. Anthony M. Platt, *The Child Savers* (Chicago: University of Chicago Press, 1969).
5. Much of the following section on the constitutional response is adapted from Frederic L. Faust and Paul J. Brantingham, eds., *Juvenile Justice Philosophy* (St. Paul, Minn.: West Publishing Company, 1974), pp. 569–575.
6. Platt, *The Child Savers,* p. 144. Quoted from *Survey 23* (February 1910): 594.
7. Ibid., p. 144.
8. Faust and Brantingham, *Juvenile Justice Philosophy,* pp. 568–569.
9. Ibid., pp. 574–575.
10. *Kent* v. *United States,* 383 U.S. 541, 86 S. Ct. 1045, 16 L ed 2d 84, (1966).
11. Ibid.
12. *In re Gault,* 387 U.S. 1, 18 L. Ed. 2d 527, 87 S. Ct. 1428 (1967).
13. Noah Weinstein, *Supreme Court Decisions and Juvenile Justice* (Reno: National Council of Juvenile Court Judges, 1973).
14. *In re Winship,* 397 U.S. 358, 90 S. Ct. 1968, 25 L. Ed. 2d 368 (1970).
15. *McKeiver* v. *Pennsylvania,* 403 U.S. 528, 535 (1971). *In re Barbara Burrus,* 275 N.C. 517, 169 S.E. 2d 879 (1969).
16. California Welfare and Institution Code, Sections 628 and 634.5.
17. Donald C. Gibbons, *Delinquent Behavior* (Englewood Cliffs, N.J.: Prentice-Hall, 1970), p. 15.
18. The thirty-three states are: Arizona, California, Colorado, Connecticut, Delaware, Florida, Georgia, Hawaii, Illinois, Indiana, Iowa, Kentucky, Louisiana, Maine, Maryland, Massachusetts, Missouri, Montana, Nebraska, Nevada, New Hampshire, New Mexico, New York, North Carolina, Oregon, Texas, Utah, Vermont, Virginia, Washington, West Virginia, Wisconsin, and the District of Columbia.
19. Law Enforcement Assistance Administration, *Report of the Advisory Committee to the Administrator on Standards for the Administration of Juvenile Justice* (Washington, D.C.: U.S. Government Printing Office, September 1976), p. 83.
20. H. William Sheridon, *Standards for Juvenile and Family Courts* (Washington, D.C.: U.S. Government Printing Office, 1966), p. 46.
21. President's Commission on Law Enforcement and Administration of Justice, *Task Force Report: Juvenile Delinquency and Youth Crime,* (Washington, D.C.: U.S. Government Printing Office, 1967), p. 15.

22. Richard W. Kobetz and Betty B. Bosarge, *Juvenile Justice Administration* (Gaithersburg, Md.: International Association of Chiefs of Police, 1973), p. 259.
23. National Advisory Commission on Criminal Justice Standards and Goals, *Corrections* (Washington, D.C.: U.S. Government Printing Office, 1973), p. 267.
24. Advisory Council of Judges of the National Council on Crime and Delinquency, *Guides for Juvenile Court Judges* (New York: National Council on Crime and Delinquency, 1963), p. 39.
25. Sanford F. Fox, *Juvenile Courts in a Nutshell* (St. Paul, Minn.: West Publishing Company, 1971), pp. 175–176.
26. Edwin M. Lemert, "The Juvenile Court—Quest and Realities," in *Juvenile Delinquency and Youth Crime,* President's Task Force Report (Washington, D.C.: U.S. Government Printing Office, 1967), p. 94.
27. Governor's Commission on Juvenile Justice, State of California, 1959.
28. Charles W. Thomas and Anthony W. Fitch, "An Inquiry into the Association between Respondents' Personal Characteristics and Juvenile Court Dispositions" (Williamsburg, Va.: Metropolitan Criminal Justice Center, College of William and Mary, 1975), p. 17.
29. H. Ted Rubin, "The Eye of the Juvenile Court Judge: A One-Step-Up View of the Juvenile Justice System," in *The Juvenile Justice System,* edited by Malcolm W. Klein (Beverly Hills, Calif.: Sage Publications, 1976), pp. 133–134.
30. Ibid., p. 134.
31. Kobetz and Bosarge, *Juvenile Justice Administration,* p. 196.
32. Ibid., p. 197.
33. Rubin, "The Eye of the Juvenile Court Judge," pp. 146–147.
34. U.S. Department of Health, Education and Welfare, *Juvenile Court Statistics, 1971* (Washington, D.C.: U.S. Government Printing Office, 1972). p. 6.
35. Kenneth C. Smith, "A Profile of Juvenile Court Judges in the United States," *Juvenile Justice* 25 (August 1974).
36. Ibid.
37. Sophia M. Robinson, *Juvenile Delinquency: Its Nature and Control* (New York: Henry Holt and Company, 1960), pp. 253–262.
38. David Matza, *Delinquency and Drift* (New York: John Wiley & Sons, 1964), p. 118.
39. Willard Heaps, *Juvenile Justice* (New York: Seabury Press, 1974).
40. Robert M. Emerson, *Judging Delinquents: Context and Process in Juvenile Court* (Chicago: Aldine Publishing Company, 1970).
41. David Duffee and Larry Siegel, "The Organization Man: Legal Counsel in the Juvenile Court," in Faust and Brantingham, *Juvenile Justice Philosophy.*
42. George Saleebey, "Hidden Closets," Special Edition (Department of the Youth Authority, State of California, February 1976), p. 67.
43. Kobetz and Bosarge, *Juvenile Justice Administration,* pp. 289–291.
44. Press Release of New York University Press and Broadcast Services, 30 November 1975.
45. Charles W. Thomas, "Are Status Offenders Really So Different: A Comparative and Longitudinal Assessment," *Crime and Delinquency* 22 (October 1976): 440–442.
46. National Council on Crime and Delinquency, "Jurisdiction over Status Offenses Should Be Removed from the Juvenile Court," *Crime and Delinquency* 21 (April, 1975): 99.

47. Statement by Allen F. Breed at the Critical Decision Making Conference, 1972.
48. Thomas, "Are Status Offenders Really So Different," p. 438.
49. Judge David L. Bazelon, "Beyond Control of the Juvenile Court," *Juvenile Court Journal* 21 (Summer 1970).
50. Emerson, *Judging Delinquents*, pp. 90–91.
51. For a review of the cases and rationale of the right to treatment see: Donna E. Renn, "The Right to Treatment and the Juvenile," *Crime and Delinquency* 14 (October 1973): 477–484.
52. Martha Baum and Stanton Wheeler, "Becoming an Inmate," in *Controlling Delinquents,* edited by Stanton Wheeler (New York: John Wiley & Sons, 1969), p. 153.
53. Matza, *Delinquency and Drift,* pp. 135–136.

REFERENCES

Emerson, Robert M. *Judging Delinquents: Context and Process in Juvenile Court.* Chicago: Aldine Publishing Company, 1969.
> *This is an excellent and easily read book on the juvenile court. It provides a case study of a court in a western city.*

Faust, Frederic, and Brantingham, Paul J., eds. *Juvenile Justice Philosophy.* St. Paul, Minn.: West Publishing Company, 1974.
> *Contains a good selection of readings and concludes with a notable essay on the history and development of the juvenile court.*

Johnson, Thomas A. *Introduction to the Juvenile Justice System.* St. Paul, Minn.: West Publishing Company, 1975.
> *A comprehensive treatment of the juvenile court; a good book for the introductory student.*

Law Enforcement Assistance Administration. *Report of the Advisory Committee to the Administrator on Standards for the Administration of Juvenile Justice.* Washington, D.C.: U.S. Government Printing Office, 1976.
> *The most up-to-date standards on the juvenile court.*

Platt, Anthony. *The Child Savers.* Chicago: University of Chicago Press, 1969.
> *A classic presentation of the juvenile court, which is must reading for the student interested in juvenile justice.*

Richette, Lisa Aversa. *The Throwaway Children.* New York: Dell, 1969.
> *This book develops the thesis that the juvenile court discards the poor to the justice system.*

5

Juvenile Probation

Probation is a judicial disposition under which youthful offenders are subject to certain conditions imposed by the juvenile court and are permitted to remain in the community under the supervision of a probation officer. The probation officer serves to assist offenders in their efforts to meet the conditions of the court. The basic goal of probation, over and above giving troublesome youths a second chance, is to provide services that will help offenders stay out of trouble with the law. Probation is the most widely used judicial disposition of the juvenile court; for example, a 1967 study revealed that 82 percent of the 348,000 youths involved with the juvenile justice system were either on probation or receiving aftercare services.[1]

The word *probation* is used in at least four ways in the juvenile justice system. It can refer to: 1) a disposition of the juvenile court in lieu of institutionalization; 2) the status of an adjudicated offender; 3) a subsystem of the juvenile justice system (the term's most common use); or 4) the activities, functions, and services that characterize this subsystem's transactions with the juvenile court, the youthful offender, and the community. The process includes the intake phase of the juvenile court's proceedings, preparation of the social investigation for the disposition stage, supervision of probationers, and obtaining or providing services for youths on probation.[2]

Probation is considered a desirable alternative to institutionalization because it allows offenders to retain their liberty but provides society with some protection against continued disregard for the law; it promotes the rehabilitation of offenders since they can maintain normal community contacts (by living at home, attending school, and participating in community activities); and it avoids the negative impact of institutional confinement. Furthermore, it costs less than incarceration.

The extent to which probation services are available varies in the counties and cities of this country. In thirty-one states, all counties have probation services, but some of these are only token services. Also, such services are often provided by persons other than paid, full-time probation officers.[3]

HISTORY OF PROBATION

John Augustus, a Boston cobbler, is considered to be the father of probation in this country. He spent considerable time in the courtroom and in 1841 accepted his first probation client, whose offense was "yielding to his appetite for strong drink."[4] Beginning with this "common drunkard," he was to devote himself to the cause of probation as he became convinced that many lawbreakers only needed the interest and concern of another to be able to straighten out their lives. Augustus worked with women and children as well as with male offenders and in fact was willing to work with all types of offenders—drunkards, petty thieves, prostitutes, and felons—as long as he met a contrite heart. Augustus instigated such services as investigation and screening, supervision of probationers, interviewing, and arranging for relief, employment, and education—all of which are still provided today.

The state of Massachusetts, very much impressed by Augustus' work, established a visiting-probation-agent system in 1869. The philosophy of this system, which was set up to assist both youths and adults, was that first offenders who showed definite promise should be released on probation. Youths would be allowed to return to their parents and to stay with them as long as they obeyed the injunction, "Go and sin no more."'[5]

Probation was regulated by statute for the first time in 1878, when the mayor of Boston was authorized to appoint a paid probation officer to the police force, to serve under the police chief. In 1880 the authority to appoint probation officers was extended to all cities and towns in Massachusetts. By 1890, probation had become statewide, with the authority to appoint resting with the courts rather than with municipal authorities. Soon thereafter, Vermont, Missouri, Illinois, Minnesota, Rhode Island, and New Jersey enacted probation statutes.

Although probation was radically extended in the wake of the juvenile court movement, probation systems varied from one jurisdiction to another. In addition, probation officers generally considered themselves servants of the juvenile court judge rather than defenders of the rights of children. Thus, they would gather relevant facts and opinions on each case to help the judge make his decision, sometimes blatantly disregarding the due process safeguards of the law. Judges, in turn, saw nothing objectionable about returning children to the care of the probation officer who had placed them at the court's mercy in the first place. Most juvenile courts relied at first upon volunteer juvenile probation officers. One observer said that their work "is the cord upon which all the pearls of the Juvenile Court are strung. It is the keynote of a beautiful harmony; without it the Juvenile Court could not exist."[6] Probation volunteers, however, largely disappeared by the second decade of the twentieth century, not to return until the late 1950s.

The spread of probation was marked by the founding in 1907 of the National Association of Probation Officers (renamed the National Probation Association in 1911). Homer Folks, one of the early advocates of probation, summarized the perception of probation in the early part of this century: "Probation provides a new kind of reformatory, without walls and without much coercion."[7] Nevertheless the idea of coercion lurked close to the surface and force was used without hesitation if the delinquent continued to disobey the law. "When sterner treatment was demanded," said one officer, "the friendly adviser became the official representative of the court with the demand that certain conditions be observed or that the probationer be returned to the court."[8]

After World War I, there was an ever-increasing demand for trained social workers to serve as probation officers. These social workers, trained under the medical model, began to treat juvenile probationers as disturbed children who needed psychiatric therapy. The philosophy and administration of probation thus retained the older concern with helping children adjust to their environment as it added a new concern with helping them resolve their emotional problems.

In addition to a greater concern for treating children's problems, twentieth-century probation theory also includes the idea of more responsibility for the delivery of services to probationers, a greater consciousness of standards, and a desire to upgrade the probation officer and restore the volunteer to probation services.

THE ADMINISTRATION OF PROBATION

The administration of juvenile probation varies both among and within states, but in the majority of states juvenile probation is under the control of the juvenile court and is funded by city or county government.

(See Table 5-1.) However, states are becoming increasingly active in providing supervision, in setting standards, and in furnishing partial subsidies to locally operated probation services.

Two questions about the organization of probation services have been debated for some time. Should probation administration be controlled by the judicial or the executive branch of government? Should this control be centralized in a state or in a local administration? Those who favor placement under the judicial branch claim that probation tends to be more responsive to court, rather than executive, direction and can provide the judiciary with automatic feedback on the effectiveness of dispositions through the reports of probation officers. Also, judges may be more likely to trust reports from their own staffs than from an outside agency. Courts have a greater awareness of needed resources and therefore are more likely to become advocates of better probation services. In addition, diversion programs would probably be used more extensively if probation were under the juvenile court, since that court might be less receptive to diversion recommendations from nonjudicial personnel.[9]

Opposing control by the court are the advocates of executive control who argue that judges are not equipped to become probation administrators and that probation staffs tend to place a higher priority on pleasing the court than on rendering services to probationers. Too,

TABLE 5-1   Administration of Juvenile and Adult Probation by Type of Agency in Fifty States and Puerto Rico, 1965

Type of Agency	Number of Jurisdictions	
	Juvenile	Adult
State:		
Corrections	5	12
Other Agencies	11	25
Local:		
Courts	32	13
Other Agencies	3	1
Total	51	51

From: President's Commission on Law Enforcement and Administration of Justice, *Task Force Report: Corrections* (Washington, D.C.: U.S. Government Printing Office, 1967), p. 35.

probation staffs could be assigned functions unrelated to probation services. Finally, under the judicial branch probation would be subservient to the court and therefore unable to develop an identity of its own.

Advocates of executive control further urge that probation should be placed under the executive branch of government because other subsystems, such as training schools, are under the executive branch. Also, the executive branch contains allied services (social and rehabilitation services, medical services, and employment and educational services), increasing the probability of coordination, cooperative endeavors, and comprehensive planning. Finally, probation under the executive branch would be more likely to receive adequate funding by the state than it would under the judicial branch, which is usually dependent on local support.

Supporters of local administration of probation believe that citizens and agencies give more support to local programs which are more open to participation by community groups and are more responsive to local needs and problems. Small operations tend to be more flexible, to adjust more quickly to change, and to be less encumbered by bureaucratic rigidity than large programs. Furthermore, in larger states the combining of all probation services could result in a very complex operation that would place a heavy burden on administration.

Those opposing local administration argue that uniformity in probation can be attained only under a state-administered probation system, in that the state-administered system can recommend and implement new programs without the approval of local political bodies. In addition, greater efficiency in the disposition of resources is assured when all staff members are state employees. These proponents also claim that a larger agency can make more effective use of funds, manpower, and other resources and can set statewide standards of service, thereby ensuring uniformity of procedures, policies, and services. Also, under state administration salaries and fringe benefits are much higher.

The National Advisory Commission on Criminal Justice Standards and Goals, after considering these arguments concerning executive and judicial control and state and local administration, recommended that probation departments be under executive control and administered by the state. However, the Commission also recommended that juvenile probation officers involved in intake be under the administrative control of the juvenile court. The Commission further stated that a written agreement specifying the relationship between the probation staff and the juvenile court should be developed and agreed to by both the judicial and correctional agencies of each state.

Although executive control and state administration of probation seem to be the best way to improve and maintain probation services, it is very unlikely that the control of juvenile probation will be removed from the juvenile court. Today, there seems to be a movement toward a combined approach to administration of both juvenile and adult probation. (See Figure 5-1.) In most states probation remains under judicial and local control and financing, but those involved are becoming more receptive to partial state subsidy. In return, the state provides training, promotes standards, and expects greater uniformity of services and practices.

Probation Subsidy   In order to bring about greater uniformity in administration of local probation, several states offer rewards of either revenue support or manpower to local systems if they comply with state standards. Michi-

FIGURE 5-1   Administration of Probation Services

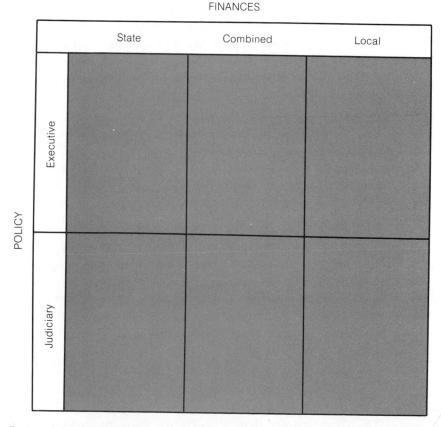

Designed for this book by Lynn Thorkildson; former Director of Probation Services Council, Springfield, Illinois.

gan, for example, assigns state-paid probation officers to work with local probation officers. But the usual practice is for the state to make direct payment to local government to defray part of the costs of probation services. In New York State, for example, a local community that is willing to meet state staffing patterns is reimbursed for up to 50 percent of its operating costs for probation services. This subsidy, which nearly doubled in a six-year period, resulted in an increase of probation staff from 1,527 in 1965 to 1,956 in 1972.[10]

Other states, such as California and Washington, have developed probation-subsidy programs that encourage a decreased rate of commitment of offenders by counties to state institutions. The money saved the state is returned to the counties. California initiated this program after a study indicated that many offenders committed to state correctional institutions could safely remain in the community under good probation supervision.

The California Probation Subsidy Program was set up in 1966 by the state's youth authority, which was authorized to pay up to $4,000 to each county for every adult and juvenile offender not committed to a state correctional institution. In turn, the counties were required to improve probation services by employing additional probation officers and reducing case loads. Additionally, it was required that each county demonstrate innovative approaches to probation, such as intensive supervision of hard-core adult offenders and certain types of juvenile offenders.

Probation Services Council of Illinois

One of the creative and exciting efforts to provide in-service training and education for adult and juvenile probation officers was initiated by the Probation Services Council of Illinois. From its inception in the fall of 1971 to the summer of 1977 the Council grew to the point where it conducted training programs nearly every month and had favorable participation and response from almost every county in the state; in fact, in 1976 the Council registered 75 percent of the 815 probation officers in Illinois. Another indicator of the growth and relevance of the Probation Services Council were the requests from Missouri and Indiana for training in Illinois for their probation officers. Indiana trained both adult and juvenile officers, but Missouri trained only juvenile probation officers.[11]

The total program, consisting of basic, advanced, and specialized levels, consists of a five-stage, 750-hour training and education experience. The first stage is the 120-hour basic training pilot project; the second through the fifth stages cover advanced and specialized training.

The 120-hour basic training pilot project is divided into three phases. Phase I is a four-day classroom training session on the campus of Sangamon State University. Upon completion of the classroom training, participants begin 14 hours of field projects in their home communities under the supervision of Probation Services Council staff. Phase II begins with two days of classroom training; the remaining 23 hours are devoted to a continuation of the field projects. Phase III also begins with two days of classroom training; it ends with 25 hours of field projects. The Council staff provides necessary assistance as much as possible to participants as they complete their projects. This innovative training program carries eight hours of undergraduate or graduate credit upon satisfactory completion of the Basic Training Pilot Project at Sangamon State University.

PROBATION SERVICES

The three basic functions of juvenile probation are intake, investigation, and supervision. At the intake stage of the court proceedings, the probation officer decides whether or not to file a petition on a child referred to the court. Investigation involves compiling a social history or study of a child judged delinquent to assist the judge in making the wisest disposition. Supervision is initiated when the judge places a youth on probation.

Intake   During the intake stage of the court proceedings (which was discussed in Chapter 4), the probation officer carefully screens the referrals to the court. Both the statutes of the state and the office of the state's attorney (prosecutor) are helpful in determining whether or not any case referred to the court actually falls under its jurisdiction. At intake, the probation officer also conducts a preliminary investigation, part of which includes an interview during which the youth is advised of his legal rights. If parents or guardians have not already been contacted, the probation department should get in touch with them to discuss the status of the child and to advise them of their right to have an attorney. The intake probation officer may need to interview the family, witnesses, victims, arresting officers, peers, or neighbors to obtain sufficient information with which to make a sound determination on the necessity for filing a court petition and for detention of the child. The probation officer also may need to contact the school and other agencies that have worked with the child. If the youth has been in court before or is already on probation, the intake officer must also familiarize himself with the previous reports.

Investigation   If a juvenile court uses the bifurcated hearing (separation of adjudicatory and disposition stages), a social study is ordered by the judge when a youth is found delinquent at the fact-finding stage of the court proceedings. Probation officers usually are given up to sixty days to make their investigation, but if the court combines the adjudicatory and disposition stages, the social study must be completed before a youth appears in front of the judge. The judge is not supposed to read this social study *until* the child is found to be delinquent.

The social study should cover the minor's personal background, information about family, educational program, present offense and previous violations of the law, and employment information. A description of the offender's neighborhood; the family's ability to pay court and institutionalization costs; the minor's physical and mental health; the attitude of the family, the police, the neighbors, and the community toward the minor; and the attitude of the minor toward the offense in question and toward himself should also be included. The social study should conclude with the probation officer's diagnosis and treatment plan for the youth. An important part of this treatment plan is the probation officer's recommended course of action. In this report the officer makes a determination of whether or not the youth should be left in the community; if the answer is yes, the conditions of probation are stated.

Supervision   Once a youth has been placed on probation, the probation officer is required to provide the best possible supervision, which includes surveillance, casework services, and counseling or guidance.

Surveillance involves careful monitoring of the adjustment the minor is making in the community. To accomplish this, the officer must establish personal contact with the minor and must learn whether the youth is attending school or is working each day, whether or not adequate guidance is being received from parents, and whether or not the probationer is obeying the terms of probation. At the same time, the probation officer must determine if the youth is continuing to break the law.

The probation officer should also provide counseling and should deliver other appropriate services to probationers. As with other practitioners in the juvenile justice system, probation officers are expected to counsel and guide the juveniles under their supervision by exposing them to various types of individual and group counseling. Probation officers use, for example, transactional analysis, reality therapy, guided group interaction, and other types of therapy in their work with clients. Crisis intervention is also a vital aspect of probation officer support of clients, for the alert and sensitive probation officer can sometimes make the difference between life and death for a troubled youth.

Delivery of services to probationers is now recognized to be as important as, or even more important than, counseling and casework. The National Advisory Commission on Criminal Justice Standards and Goals has advocated a movement away from the traditional role of the probation officer as caseworker toward that of community resource manager, or broker, to meet the goals of probation more effectively. This role requires the probation officer to mesh a probationer's identified needs with the range of available services. In helping probationers to obtain needed services, the probation officer must assess the situation, contact the appropriate available resources, assist the probationer in obtaining needed services, and follow up on the case. The probation officer, in this new role, should take the responsibility for seeing that the needed services are delivered, and then should monitor and evaluate them.

THE PROBATION OFFICER

A study by Szakos and Wice of the personal characteristics and attitudes of juvenile probation officers in Pennsylvania is helpful in identifying a typical profile of juvenile probation officers in the mid-1970s (at least in one large eastern state). Of the 390 questionnaires sent out to Pennsylvania's sixty-seven counties, 209 were completed and returned. Aside from Philadelphia, which would not participate in this research, the completed questionnaires represented fairly well all parts of the state, including the important urban, suburban, and rural areas.[12]

Table 5-2 presents the group profile of these Pennsylvania probation officers. The average respondent was "A young married man working in a small county office on a full-time basis." This sample showed

TABLE 5-2 Personal Characteristics of 209 Pennsylvania Probation Officers

Age			Married Status	
	31 and over	26.4%	Married	66.3%
	30 and under	74.6%	Single	25.1%
			Other	8.6%
Sex			Employment Status	
	Male	68.5%	Full-time	90.0%
	Female	31.5%	Part-time	10.0%

From: Joseph A. Szakos and Paul B. Wice, "Juvenile Probation Officers: Their Professional Paradox," *The Quarterly*, Vol. 34, No. 1, March 1977, pp. 21–30.

clearly that these officers were generally inexperienced; were dissatisfied with their work; were dissatisfied with their pay; had received little, if any, job training; and felt overworked. The average work span for the sample was about two and one-half years; in fact, 73 percent of the respondents had been probation officers for less than four years. Job dissatisfaction was measured by the response that 42 percent said that they planned to leave the field in the near future, and nearly 14 percent were unwilling to commit themselves on this question; only 45 percent believed that they would continue in the probation field. Nearly 80 percent of these workers either agreed or strongly agreed that they were not adequately paid: the average worker earned $10,550 a year. Few of these workers had attended more than one training session for juvenile probation officers. Finally, nearly three-quarters of these workers (73 percent) either agreed or strongly agreed that they were overworked.[13]

The profile that clearly emerges is that of an inexperienced, underpaid, and overworked employee. These general problems, in fact, probably are characteristic of most POs (probation officers) in this country. In addition, juvenile probation officers must struggle with role conflict and must satisfy conflicting pressures. They must resolve communication problems with clients, perhaps with supervisors, and certainly with other practitioners in the juvenile justice system. And, especially in small towns, they must deal with the type of moralism described in Chapter 4.

Problems of the Probation Officer   The probation officer never has an easy job, and in large departments he is expected to fulfill a variety of job responsibilities. For example, responsibilities of probation officers of the Sangamon County Department of Juvenile Court Services include intake, secure detention, the juvenile center, and caseloads of probationers released to the community. (See Figure 5-2.) With each of these diverse responsibilities, probation officers are expected to counsel and deliver services for probationers; that is, probation officers are expected to be treatment agents as well as agents of social control.

Role Conflict.   This expectation results in the creation of nearly opposite roles in law enforcement and treatment, which obviously creates problems. The police and the citizens of the community are constantly challenging the treatment role of probation officers, berating them for leaving dangerous and hard-core youths in the community. But, at the same time, probation officers encounter hostility from probationers because of their law enforcement role. Furthermore, probation officers must convince the juvenile judge that they are properly filling both roles and are doling out proper portions of treatment and control.

FIGURE 5-2   Department of Juvenile Court Services, Sangamon County

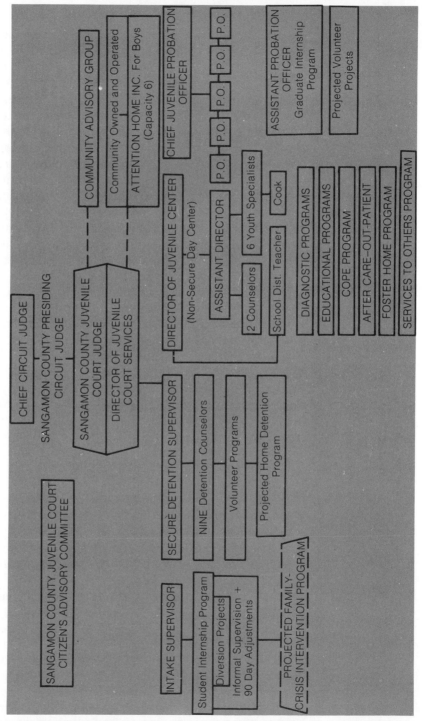

Developed by David Johnson, former Director of Court Services, Seventh Judicial Circuit, Juvenile Division.

Klockards, in developing a typology of probation officers, claims that they play one of four roles, depending on how they do their jobs.[14] Some officers play only the law enforcement role. These officers strongly feel that probation does not involve casework. They are determined to comply with the court order, and they do not intend to compromise the authority given to them by the court. Nor will they endanger society by permitting dangerous youths to remain on the streets. These probation officers, in a real sense, see themselves as policemen—"What it simmers down to is police work. We're the policemen back of the agencies."[15] The philosophy of officers who gravitate to this role dictates that firmness, authority, and abiding by the rules are essentials during the probation period.

The time servers play the second role. These probation officers are committed neither to law enforcement nor to social casework. They are merely going through the motions of the job until they retire. They also have little aspiration to do anything to improve themselves, such as attending seminars and training institutes or belonging to professional associations. Their conduct on the job tends to be rule-abiding, but they do not examine the rules and regulations. "They don't make the rules; they just work there."

The therapeutic agent is at the other end of the continuum from the law enforcer. The probation officer who fills this role tries to introduce probationers to a better way of life and to give them support and guidance as they attempt to solve their own problems. Shireman has summarized the working philosophy of the therapeutic agents:

1. We take conscious pains in our every contact with the offender to demonstrate our concern about him and our respect for him as a human being.
2. We seize every opportunity to help the offender come to understand the nature of the shared, problem-solving, helping process by actually experiencing it.
3. We recognize, bring into the open, and deal directly with the offender's negative attitudes toward us as the representatives of social authority.
4. We "partialize" the total life problem confronting the offender.
5. We help the individual perceive the degree to which his behavior has [resulted] and will result in his own unhappiness.[16]

Officers of this type frequently belong to professional associations and campaign for recognition of the professional status of probation officers.

The fourth type of probation officer recognizes the importance of both the treatment and the law enforcement components of the job. This officer attempts to combine the paternal, authoritarian, and judgmental approach with the therapeutic method. His treatment

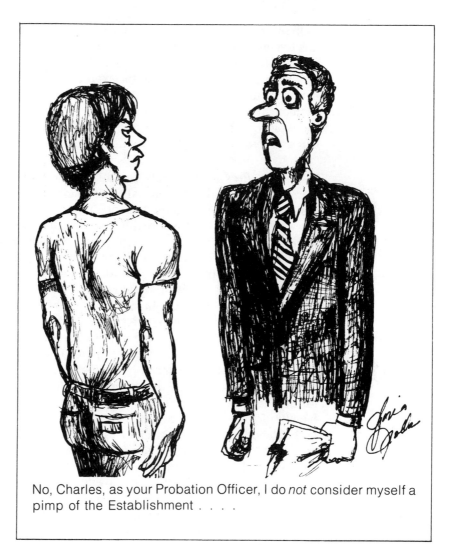

No, Charles, as your Probation Officer, I do *not* consider myself a pimp of the Establishment . . . .

orientation causes him to advise probationers to "tell all," but if a probationer does confess to a wrong (commission of a criminal act), the officer quickly assumes the law enforcement role and revocation of probation may result.

Ohlin, Piven, and Pappenfort, in exploring the role dilemmas of probation officers, found that different probation departments employ different types of workers. Some departments hire only punitive officers, those who wish to be only law enforcers. Other agencies employ officers interested solely in being protective agents, who vacillate back and forth between protecting the public and helping youth in trouble. Other departments try to engage only those who see themselves as welfare workers who are therapeutic agents for their clients.[17] Although this tendency to hire only a certain type of probation officer may reduce intradepartmental conflict, it obviously results in wide disparity among probation departments. Some, for example, are quick to penalize probationers for minor offenses, while others only penalize them as an extreme and last resort. However, the writers of this book believe that the typical probation department, particularly in large urban areas, is less and less characterized by single-role staff.

Conflicting Pressures.   Probation officers not only encounter role dilemmas, but they also must satisfy three elements—the juvenile justice system, their own ego needs, and the human needs of the client.[18] That the system comes first is a reality that probation officers face early in their careers. If the juvenile judge wants a youth's social study completed by the next Tuesday, it must be done, regardless of the needs and problems of other probationers during this week. And, in the same vein, probation officers know that the system will not tolerate too much adverse publicity; consequently, it is wise to be conservative in terms of taking chances on troublesome youths.

Probation officers, too, are human. They have ego needs and they want to feel important. They want approval and acceptance from the juvenile judge, the director of probation services, other probation officers, and clients. Granted that interest in others brought many of them to their jobs, few probation officers can function very effectively or happily if their own needs are not met. If a girl fails to respect her probation officer, she is not likely to receive much tolerance from that officer. If a boy is constantly arguing with or harassing his officer, he can expect the full weight of justice if he violates his probation terms.

The client, all too often, is considered long after the needs of the system and the officer's self have been satisfied. If the officer's initial job enthusiasm and involvement have waned and he regards the job only as one that demands much, pays little, and offers slight opportunity for advancement, his clients may indeed be shortchanged. The endless paperwork, the hours spent on the road trying to locate clients, the broken appointments, the intractable and undependable probationers, and the hostility directed toward the probation officer also make it difficult for him to maintain a close involvement with clients.

Communication Problems with Clients.   Probation officers who relate well and do an effective job with clients tend to have certain characteristics in common:

1.   They are genuine in their relationships with probationers and are not hiding behind a professional role; that is, they attempt to avoid

barriers that would isolate them from their clients. Furthermore, they try to be honest with their clients and expect them to be honest in return.

2. They respond to others with respect, kindness, and compassion. Since they are caring persons, they are able to listen and to reach out to other persons.

3. They are not gullible nor easily hoodwinked by probationers, because they know what life on the streets is like.

4. They are able to encourage others to pursue positive success experiences; they also have an uncanny knack of knowing what to say and do when others fail.

5. They have a good understanding of themselves and have a reasonable idea of their own problems, shortcomings, and needs. They know, in addition, their biases, prejudices, and pet peeves.

6. They are very committed to their jobs, for the job to them is much more than a paycheck. Moreover, their enthusiasm does not wane following the first few weeks or months as probation officers.

Probation officers who continually have problems with clients also have certain characteristics in common:

1. They do not keep their word. Either they promise more than they are capable of delivering or they simply fail to follow through on what they have said they would do.

2. They become bored with their jobs, chiefly because they see little meaning in working with youths whom they regard as losers who will always be marginal citizens.

3. They either have unreal expectations for probationers or are inflexible in interpreting the terms of probation.

4. They permit their personality problems to affect their performance on the job, which often results in a lack of warmth, a preoccupation with self, or a sharp, biting response to others. Not surprisingly, these personality traits alienate them from both probationers and other probation staff.

5. They seem to be unable to respond to lower-class youths with other than their own middle-class values, so they become judgmental and moralistic in dealing with clients.

6. They are unwilling to pay the price of changing their own lives in order to influence or alter the lives of juvenile offenders.

A basic problem for the conscientious probation officer is disciplining the violator without alienating him. For example, one probation officer:

... described the problems he had working with a boy, lamenting the fact that just as he began to get close to him he would be forced to discipline him. "I can let him go so far and then you have to snap him back. And this destroys any kind of relationship. . . . He just clams up. . . . Underneath it all, I think he's an angry boy.[19]

But, regardless of how effective and committed the probation officer may be, a number of troublesome youths will flagrantly violate their probation terms and will have to be returned to the juvenile court, which may lead to the revocation of their probation. Before punishing a youngster who has violated his terms of probation, the probation officer should make every effort to gain the compliance of the youth. An understanding of the negative impact of institutionalization should compel the probation officer to return a youth to the court only as an extreme last resort.

Paraprofessional Probation Officers

The President's Commission on Law Enforcement and the Administration of Justice and the National Advisory Commission on Criminal Justice Standards and Goals both recommended that probation services use paid subprofessional aides. Paid paraprofessionals who have had experiences similar to those of lower-class probationers can often relate better to these youths than can middle-class probation officers and volunteers in probation. As the President's Commission on Law Enforcement and the Administration of Justice explained,

> People who have themselves experienced problems and come from backgrounds like those of offenders often can help them in ways professional caseworkers cannot. Contact with a person who has overcome handicaps and is living successfully in the community can mean a great deal more to an offender than conventional advice and guidance.[20]

Ex-offenders, too, can be probation counselors; several experimental programs have found that they are effective in working with young offenders. An extensive period of pre-service training is extremely important to prepare both paraprofessionals and ex-offenders for probation responsibilities.

Volunteer Probation Officers

As mentioned earlier, throughout the last half of the nineteenth century, volunteers were widely used to provide probation services, but they largely disappeared at the beginning of this century and did not reappear until the late 1950s. Indeed, only four courts were using volunteers in 1961; but today over 2,000 court-sponsored volunteer programs are in operation in this country. The use of volunteers has become one of the most valuable ways to help offenders adjust to community life.

The National Information Center on Volunteers in Court has identified several areas in which volunteers can work effectively with juvenile offenders. A volunteer can provide a one-to-one support relationship for the youth with a trustworthy adult; can function as a child advocate with teachers, employers, and the police; can be a good role model; can set limits and teach pro-social values; can teach skills or academic subjects; and can help the youth to develop a realistic response to the environment—that is, become an extra pair of eyes and ears for him, to provide perspective.

In addition to these areas of direct contact, volunteers can assist in administrative work. They can help recruit, train, and supervise other volunteers; serve as consultants to the regular staff; become advisers to the court, especially in the policymaking area; develop good public relations with the community; and either contribute money, materials, and facilities or help to secure them from others.[21]

Volunteers can improve the morale of the regular probation staff, because they are usually positive and enthusiastic about the services they are providing. Since many volunteers are professionals (physicians, psychiatrists, psychologists, and dentists), they can provide services that the probation department may not have the financial resources to obtain. Finally, their contributions can reduce the caseload of the regular staff.

Several criticisms have been levelled at volunteer programs. They tend to attract a high ratio of middle-class persons, and they often create more work than they return in service. Volunteers cannot handle serious problems and sometimes in fact can harm their clients. Parents may resist the volunteer as an untrained worker. One of the major concerns of the chief probation officer is to ensure that each volunteer is capable of working with probationers, for misfits can clearly do a great deal of damage. But proper screening, training, and supervision can do much to ensure a high quality of probation services from volunteers.

RESPONSES OF PROBATIONERS

The delinquent's sense of injustice described by Matza in *Delinquency and Drift* seems to be less related to probation than to the police or the courts. For example, Giordano found that youths generally regarded probation merely as ineffective, although they felt somewhat positive about the individuals they had come to know within the agencies.[22] Maher and Stein concluded in a report that "the Probation Officer may be handicapped by the punitive definition of probation entertained by the delinquent himself.[23] Claude Brown's description in *Manchild in the Promised Land* of an experience he had in juvenile court seems to speak for many offenders:

> When we got in court the next morning, we went before a judge. Some people were sitting around on the sides, but there wasn't a jury. We were just standing there in front of this one judge. He said, "Do you boys know you could have hurt yourselves going into the store the way you did? That plate-glass window could have fallen down on you and broken your necks."
> The judge kept talking to us about how we had risked our lives and how we were lucky not to get hurt. He said he was going to give us another chance. We'd expected this; we'd heard that every place they could have sent us was all filled up—Warwick and Wiltwyck and Lincoln Hall. We were all under sixteen, all except Earl, and he wasn't there. They had taken him to another court.
> After the lecture, when the judge said, "I'm going to give you boys another chance," I don't know why or what happened, but I heard myself say, "Man, you not givin' us another chance. You givin' us the same chance we had before."[24]

Juvenile offenders, according to these three sources and to the personal experiences of the writers of this book, resent the conditions of probation, have positive feelings about some POs and negative feelings about others, and basically regard probation as ineffective. In short, instead of expressing a sense of outrage or injustice toward probation, youths appear to regard it as a nuisance. If the probation officer is "cool," all the better, but the law enforcement role and its threat is always apparent to the youth, because the probation officer has the power to "bust" the youth and return him to court.

THE EFFECTIVENESS OF PROBATION

A major problem in evaluating the effectiveness of probation is the wide disagreement about the definition of success. Still, a number of studies seem to indicate that probation is more effective than any other method for rehabilitating youthful offenders. England, for example, in reviewing eleven probation studies conducted in a variety of jurisdictions, reported success rates that varied between 60 and 90 percent.[25]

The best evidence concerning probation comes from a study by Scarpitti and Stephenson in which they followed 1,210 male delinquents in New Jersey for up to four years after their release from one of four programs: probation, nonresidential group center, residential group center, or state reformatory. In terms of recidivism (appearance before the juvenile court followed by a punitive disposition), only 15 percent of the probationers failed, compared to 48 and 41 percent of the boys who had been in group centers and 55 percent of the reformatory boys.[26] The survey concluded that probation appears to offer the best opportunity for juvenile offenders to avoid subsequent difficulty, providing it is granted to those who are least delinquent. The boys who failed on probation, Scarpitti and Stephenson found, presented a distinctly negative picture and their recidivism rate was much higher than that of boys in other programs.

Lipton et al. reviewed the studies of adult and juvenile probation and arrived at the following conclusions: (1) evidence exists that a larger proportion of offenders now incarcerated could be placed on probation instead without any change in the recidivism rates; (2) probationers have a significantly lower violation rate than parolees; and (3) intensive probation supervision (fifteen-ward case load) is associated with lower recidivism rates for youths under eighteen.[27] In a study published in 1977, Martinson and Wilks found that probationers have the lowest rate of recidivism.[28]

SUMMARY

Probation has more supporters than any other disposition within the justice system, for it alone can point to a positive impact on youthful and adult offenders. Yet, probation still has many problems. It is primarily under the control of the juvenile court and poorly funded by local governmental agencies. Probation officers feel overworked and underpaid; they usually are young, inexperienced, and inadequately trained. Some states and many counties have underdeveloped or no probation services, and probationers tend to perceive the law enforcement role of probation more than its counseling or supportive role. The ability of probation services to become an even more effective vehicle of juvenile corrections depends on its ability to resolve creatively these problems.

QUESTIONS

1. What do you feel is the most effective way to administer probation?
2. Do you believe that probation and parole should be administered together?
3. How can probation officers establish better relations with probationers?

4. Should more ex-offenders and paraprofessionals be employed as probation officers? What are the advantages? The disadvantages?

5. Would you like to be a probation officer? Why or why not? What major problems would you face? How would you solve them?

ENDNOTES

1. National Council on Crime and Delinquency, "Corrections in the United States," *Crime and Delinquency* 13 (January 1967): 231.
2. National Advisory Commission on Criminal Justice Standards and Goals, *Corrections* (Washington, D.C.: U.S. Government Printing Office, 1973), p. 312.
3. The President's Commission on Law Enforcement and Administration of Justice, *Task Force Report: Corrections* (Washington, D.C.: U.S. Government Printing Office, 1967), p. 28.
4. *John Augustus, First Probation Officer* (Montclair, N.J.: Patterson-Smith Company, 1972), pp. 4–5.
5. Board of State Charities of Massachusetts, *Sixth Annual Report, 1869,* p. 269.
6. Robert M. Mennel, *Thorns and Thistles* (Hanover, N.H.: University of New Hampshire Press, 1973), p. 140.
7. Homer Folks, "Juvenile Probation," *NCCD Proceedings, 1906,* pp. 117–122.
8. Mennel, *Thorns and Thistles,* p. 142.
9. The following discussion on the administration of probation is paraphrased from National Advisory Commission, *Corrections,* pp. 313–316.
10. Richard W. Kobetz and Betty B. Bosarge, *Juvenile Justice Administration* (Gaithersburg, Md.: International Association of Chiefs of Police, 1973), p. 339.
11. As of August 1, 1977, the Probation Services Council dissolved as a corporation. The Center for Legal Studies of Sangamon State University is continuing these promising programs in Illinois, but probation officers in Missouri and Indiana are no longer being trained.
12. Joseph A. Szakos and Paul B. Wice, "Juvenile Probation Officers: Their Professional Paradox," *The Quarterly,* Vol. 34, No. 1, March 1977, pp. 21–30.
13. Ibid.
14. Carl B. Klockards, Jr., "A Theory of Probation Supervision," *Journal of Criminal Law, Criminology and Police Science* 53, no. 4 (1972).
15. Diana Lewis, "What Is Probation," *Journal of Criminal Law, Criminology and Police Science* 51 (1960): 199.
16. Charles Shireman, "Casework in Probation and Parole: Some Considerations in Diagnosis and Treatment," *Federal Probation* 51 (1963): 51.
17. Lloyd E. Ohlin et al., "Major Dilemmas of the Social Worker in Probation and Parole," *National Probation and Parole Association Journal* 2 (1956): 211–225.
18. These observations were made by John Vargas, Director of Court Services, Seventh Judicial Circuit, Juvenile Division.
19. Robert Emerson, *Judging Delinquents: Context and Process in the Juvenile Court* (Chicago: Aldine Publishing Company, 1969), p. 253.
20. President's Commission, *Task Force Report: Corrections,* p. 168.

21. Ivan H. Scheier and Judith A. Berry, *Serving Youth as Volunteers,* (Boulder, Col.: National Information Center on Volunteers in Courts, February 1972), p. 14.
22. Peggy C. Giordano, "The Sense of Injustice: An Analysis of Juveniles' Reactions to the Justice System," *Criminology* 14 (May 1976): 106.
23. B. Maher, and E. Stein, "The Delinquent's Perception of Law and the Community," in *Controlling Delinquents,* edited by Stanton Wheeler (New York: John Wiley & Sons, 1968), p. 221.
24. Claude Brown, *Manchild in the Promised Land* (New York: Macmillan, 1965).
25. Ralph W. England, Jr., "What Is Responsible for Satisfactory Probation and Post-Probation Outcome?" *Journal of Criminal Law, Criminology and Police Science* 47 (1957): 667.
26. Frank F. Scarpitti and Richard M. Stephenson, "A Study of Probation Effectiveness," *Journal of Criminal Law, Criminology and Police Science* 59, no. 3 (1968): 361–369.
27. Lipton et al., *The Effectiveness of Correctional Treatment: A Survey of Evaluation Studies* (New York: Praeger Publishers, 1975), pp. 59–61.
28. Robert Martinson and Judith Wilks, "Knowledge in Criminal Justice Planning" (New York: Center for Knowledge in Criminal Justice Planning, September 1977).

REFERENCES

Emerson, Robert. *Judging Delinquents: Context and Process in the Juvenile Court.* Chicago: Aldine Publishing Company, 1969.
   Emerson's study reveals some of the pressures facing probation officers.

Bartollas, Clemens, and Miller, Stuart J. *Correctional Administration: Theory and Practice.* New York: McGraw-Hill, 1978.
   Chapter 9 describes the problems of supervision of probation managers and the leadership challenge to probation executives.

Klockards, Carl B., Jr. "A Theory of Probation Supervision." *Journal of Criminal Law, Criminology and Police Science* 53, no. 4 (1972).
   Contains an excellent discussion of the role conflicts facing probation officers.

National Advisory Commission on Criminal Justice Standards and Goals. *Corrections.* (Washington, D.C.: U.S. Government Printing Office, 1973.
   Helpful in identifying the role of probation officers as community resource managers.

Scarpitti, Frank F., and Stephenson, Richard M. "A Study of Probation Effectiveness." *Journal of Criminal Law, Criminology and Police Science* 59, no. 3 (1968): 361–369.
   The most comprehensive single study of the effectiveness of probation.

6

Community-Based Corrections

The Corrections Task Force of the President's Commission on Law Enforcement and Administration of Justice recommended that community-based corrections be used for all but the hard-core offender. The task and challenge of corrections, according to the Commission, is to keep adult and juvenile offenders in the community and to help reintegrate them into community living. The Commission also stated that:

> The advent of these programs in the postwar decades and their recent growth in numbers and prominence are perhaps the most promising developments in corrections today. These programs are by and large less costly, often far less costly, than incarceration in an institution. Evaluation has indicated that they are usually at least as effective in reducing recidivism and in some cases significantly more so. They therefore represent an important means for coping with the mounting volume of offenders that we will be pouring into corrections in the next decade.[1]

HISTORY OF COMMUNITY-BASED CORRECTIONS

Community-based juvenile corrections is part of a larger movement to keep juveniles in trouble out of training schools. Probation and parole are certainly part of this gradual movement toward deinstitutionalization. Yet, most of the community-based programs and facilities have their origins in the success of several guided-group-interaction, short-term institutional programs initiated in the 1950s and 1960s, among them the Highfields, Southfields, Essexfields, and Pinehills projects; the New Jersey centers at Oxford and Farmingdale for boys and at Turrell for girls; and the START centers established by the New York City Division for Youth.

The Highfields Project, known officially as the New Jersey Experimental Project for the Treatment of Youthful Offenders, is the most famous of these short-term programs. Established in 1950 on an estate that is the former home of General and Mrs. Charles Lindbergh, the program involved twenty delinquent boys who worked during the day at the nearby New Jersey Neuro-Psychiatric Institute and met in two guided-group-interaction units five evenings a week at the Highfields facility. Residents accompanied by staff members were permitted to go shopping and to attend movies in town. This project—short-term, small, and informally structured—became a real alternative to the typical training school.

Other residential centers of the Highfields type were created in New Jersey at Oxford and Farmingdale for boys and at Turrell for girls. The New York Division for Youth established several similar centers in the 1960s and called them START centers (Short-Term Adolescent Residential Treatment). Youths living at these START centers also worked at nearby state hospitals. Southfields, another residential group center of the Highfields type, was set up in Jefferson County near Louisville in Kentucky. Pinehills, established in 1959 in Provo, Utah, adopted the basic Highfields philosophy but abandoned the residential unit aspects (boys returned to their homes in the evenings and on weekends). Essexfields, founded in the early 1960s in Newark, was another nonresidential facility based on the Highfields philosophy.

The community-based corrections movement was further advanced by the increasing awareness of what does and does not happen to youths confined in state and private correctional centers. First, juvenile institutions often are unspeakably brutal and degrading and, as a result of the deprivations of incarceration, inmates create their own society based on violence and exploitation. Second, little evidence exists that training schools rehabilitate their residents or lower the recidivism rate. Instead, residents tend to be released with lowered self-esteem, filled with rage toward society and are well schooled in crime and committed to crime as a career. Third, training schools are prohibitively expensive to maintain. Fourth, youthful offenders need to learn how to cope with community problems and pressures: their problems began in the community, and it is in the community that they must learn how to stay out of trouble. The training school, even though it may require considerable ingenuity and resourcefulness on the part of its residents if they are to survive, still does not prepare a youth to adjust to community life. Finally, community-based corrections is vastly more humane, much more economical, and no less effective than confinement in a training school. It was easy to conclude that few, if any, youths benefited from institutionalization; many, in fact, began to believe that training schools should be closed and alternatives developed.

The most dramatic advance in this trend toward deinstitutionalization occurred when the state of Massachusetts announced that it was closing all of its training schools. This rather startling move resulted from a number of factors. First, the dynamic leadership of Jerome Miller focused public attention on the negative impact of these institutions. Miller traveled throughout the state, giving speeches on what institutionalization does to juveniles. He often took with him a juvenile offender who informed the audience of how it feels to be institutionalized. Miller stated at this time:

> Reform schools neither reform nor rehabilitate. The longer you lock up a kid in them, the less likely he is to make it when he gets out. They don't protect society. They're useless, they're futile, they're rotten.[2]

Another factor contributing to the closing was a series of scandals in and disclosures about Massachusetts juvenile institutions that had begun in 1965. Institutional staff, in particular, were attacked by the media for their brutality.

> The treatment of youths inside the institutions was at best custodial, and at worst punitive and repressive. Marching, shaved heads, and enforced periods of long silences were regular occurrences. Punitive staff used force, made recalcitrant children drink water from toilets, or scrub floors on their hands and knees for hours on end. Solitary confinement was used extensively and was rationalized as a mode of treatment for those who needed it.[3]

The refusal of the independent training schools to cooperate with the central office also prevented the Massachusetts Department of Youth Services from improving the quality of institutional services in that area. This resistance of staff members throughout the system made the central authority realize that it had little influence in setting up new programs.

Also of importance in the dissolution of the training schools was the leadership of Governor Francis Sargent, who felt that major reform in Massachusetts was imperative:

> I had been to some of the state and county [training schools], and God, I was repulsed—think that we were paying something like $10,000 a year just to keep a kid in a cage without any type of rehabilitation. It was just

really horrible. And I figured that if I didn't do any other damn thing while I was governor, I was going to [change] that system.[4]

Bridgewater was closed first. Then, in the winter of 1972, Miller closed Shirley and Lyman. When Shirley was closed, the press featured stories and pictures of Miller, members of the legislature, staff, and youth hammering down the bars and locks of the segregation cells of Cottage #9. The closing of Lyman created even more fanfare because a caravan of cars took youths from this institution to the University of Massachusetts to stay for a month while placements were arranged for them. Lancaster and two detention centers were also closed at this time and their residents, too, were taken to the University of Massachusetts. Oakdale, the last training school remaining open, was finally closed in late 1972. Jerome Miller had accomplished the remarkable feat of closing all the training schools in Massachusetts, and, outside of a few girls remaining in Shirley Training School and a few youths sent to private training schools in other states, Massachusetts had succeeded in placing all its adjudicated juvenile offenders in community-based corrections.

The idea of deinstitutionalization soon became popular in other states. The trend was so firmly entrenched by 1973 that the National Advisory Commission on Criminal Justice Standards and Goals recommended that the states should not build any more juvenile training institutions and that any existing institutions be phased out over a five-year period.[5]

It was not long before community-based corrections seemed to be the primary topic for discussion. The case appeared to be closed. The empiricist had established the futility of treatment, the reformer had documented the essential inhumanity of training schools, and the cost-benefit analyst had determined that alternatives to incarceration were effective at far less expense to the taxpayer. Many students of penology thought that the millennium was at hand. Commitment to training schools was declining, and training schools were closing down.[6]

The talk continued and some action followed. South Dakota, Minnesota, and Utah soon were assigning as many youths to community-based facilities as they were confining in correctional institutions. Oregon, North Dakota, Maryland, and Kansas also were placing nearly as many youths in community-based corrections as they were assigning to institutions.

Yet, because of the adverse publicity about youth crime and the substantial number of youthful offenders whose predatory activities represented a danger to their communities, few policymakers advocated closing all state juvenile institutions. A hard-line approach—brought on

TABLE 6-1 Youth Population in State Institutions and State Ranches and Camps

	1969	1970	1971	1973	1974
Offenders in State Institutions	40,890	38,034	33,581	24,222	25,424
Offenders in State Ranches and Camps	2,577	2,726	3,220	2,502	2,577
Total	43,467	40,760	36,801	26,724	28,001

From: Robert D. Vinter, George Downs, and John Hall, *Juvenile Corrections in the States: Residential Programs and Deinstitutionalization: A Preliminary Report* (Ann Arbor, Mich.: University of Michigan, National Assessment of Juvenile Corrections, 1975), p. 13.

by persons incensed by society's "mollycoddling" of teenage hoods and criminals—gathered momentum and had won many converts by the mid-1970s. Evidence of this approach includes the rising population of juvenile institutions and the pressure placed on judges to limit placements and enforce stricter guidelines on those youths adjudicated to community-based corrections.

Community-based corrections, nevertheless, continues to have strong public and political support as a viable solution for treating certain juvenile offenders. The most popular community placements have been foster homes, group homes (sometimes called halfway houses), and day treatment facilities. In many states, juveniles in trouble are sent to survival-training programs such as Homeward Bound and Outward Bound. The Florida Ocean Sciences Institute is another community-based program under which youngsters live at home and attend the institute eight hours a day. These programs will be discussed later in this chapter.

COMMUNITY-BASED CORRECTIONS AND THE COMMUNITY

Community-based corrections rests on a reintegration philosophy that assumes that both the offender and the receiving community must be changed. The community is as important as the client and plays a vital role in facilitating the reabsorption of offenders into its life. The task of corrections, according to this philosophy, involves the reconstruction, or construction, of ties between offenders and the community through maintenance of family bonds, employment and education, and placement in the mainstream of social life. Youths should be directed to community resources, and the community should be acquainted with the skills and needs of youthful lawbreakers.

Critics of community-based corrections challenge several of these contentions. They hold that the community deserves protection from predatory youths who intimidate and hurt the young, rape women of all ages, and victimize the elderly. They further contend that youths sent to juvenile institutions are those who have failed to benefit from a number of community placements. It is also argued that keeping lawbreaking youths in the community only reinforces their antisocial behavior; institutionalization provides the punishment they deserve.

Communities have often resisted the charge that they must assume responsibility for the problems they generate. It is much easier (and more comforting) for a community to blame the crime problem on the failure of training schools, the inefficiency of the juvenile justice system, or the personalities of offenders themselves than it is to accept responsibility for its social problems. Instead of coordination between the justice system and the community, there is all too frequently an adversary we-they relationship. Citizens often feel that the youth commission is trying to foist off a group home or a day-treatment facility on their community; correctional administrators, in turn, often tend to perceive negativism or outright hostility on the part of many citizens.

EXTENT OF COMMUNITY-BASED CORRECTIONS

The National Assessment of Juvenile Corrections (NAJC) has provided an extremely valuable analysis of community-based corrections. This study reports that the average daily population in state-related community-based residential programs during 1974 was 110 for the forty-eight reporting states, ranging from zero in six states to a high of 800 in one state. Table 6-2 shows the distribution of the 1974 average daily population.

Table 6-3 presents the average daily offender population in state-related community residential programs, reported as per capita rates (per 100,000 of total state population). Note that the variation in state use of community-based corrections is clearly evident in Table 6-3. The highest rate (20.5 per 100,000) is one hundred times larger than the lowest rate (0.2).

TABLE 6-2 1974 Average Daily Populations in State-Related Community-Based Residential Programs

	Number of States
0	6
3–49	17
50–99	11
100–149	3
150–199	5
200–399	4
400 and over	3
Total	49

Note: Mean = 110

From: Robert D. Vinter, George Downs, and John Hall, *Juvenile Corrections in the States: Residential Programs and Deinstitutionalization: A Preliminary Report* (Ann Arbor, Mich.: University of Michigan, National Assessment of Juvenile Corrections, 1975), p. 33.

This study found few associations between these rates and the basic socioeconomic characteristics of the states. No correlation exists, for example, between the use of community programs and the percentage of urbanized population. Moveover, states that make heavy use of institutions do not rely on community-based corrections or vice versa. Significantly, the researchers noted that "the *existence* or availability of community programs is neither nationwide nor of notable scale."[7]

COSTS OF COMMUNITY-BASED CORRECTIONS

The NAJC study calculated the average costs per offender-year for those states for which data were available, and found that community-based corrections is much more economical than institutionalization. Although considerable variation was found, with three states spending only $3,500 to $4,999 and several states spending over $19,000 per offender, the mean, or average, cost per offender for institutionalization was $11,657 a year.

TABLE 6-3   Ranked Distribution of 1974 per Capita Rates of Average Daily Populations in State-Related Community-Based Residential Programs (per 100,000 total state population)

Oregon	20.5	Hawaii	2.0
South Dakota	19.5	Colorado	1.9
Utah	15.8	Missouri	1.7
Massachusetts	14.1	Pennsylvania	1.5
Wyoming	13.6	Ohio	1.4
Minnesota	12.3	Oklahoma	1.4
Idaho	10.1	Delaware	1.3
Maryland	9.5	Kentucky	1.1
Kansas	9.1	Illinois	1.0
Montana	9.1	Rhode Island	1.0
North Dakota	9.1	Georgia	0.9
Nevada	6.1	Arkansas	0.8
Florida	5.5	South Carolina	0.8
Vermont	5.4	Maine	0.5
Arizona	4.9	California	0.4
Virginia	3.2	Nebraska	0.2
Tennessee	2.9	Texas	0.2
New Jersey	2.8	New York	0.2
Michigan	2.7	Alaska	0
West Virginia	2.6	Indiana	0
Iowa	2.5	Louisiana	0
Mississippi	2.5	New Hampshire	0
Alabama	2.3	New Mexico	0
Wisconsin	2.2	North Carolina	0
Connecticut	2.1		

Note: Mean = 4.3 per 100,000

From: Robert D. Vinter, George Downs, and John Hall, *Juvenile Corrections in the States: Residential Programs and Deinstitutionalization: A Preliminary Report* (Ann Arbor, Mich.: University of Michigan, National Assessment of Juvenile Corrections, 1975), p. 35.

Table 6-5 shows the average cost per year for offenders in community programs; the modal category is in the $2,000 to $3,999 range with few states spending above $10,000 per offender. Whereas confining youths in an institution costs states about $11,600 per year, keeping them in community residential facilities costs about $5,500 per year on the average. The savings are clearly greater per offender per year. But the NAJC study found that the costs in most states remained just as high or higher because more youngsters were being processed through

TABLE 6-4 1974 Average Costs per Offender-Year for State Institutions, Camps, and Ranches

	Number of States
$ 3,500– 4,999	3
$ 5,000– 7,999	11
$ 8,000–10,999	15
$11,000–13,999	4
$14,000–18,999	10
$19,000 and over	4
Total	47

Note: Mean = $11,657

From: Robert D. Vinter, George Downs, and John Hall, *Juvenile Corrections in the States: Residential Programs and Deinstitutionalization: A Preliminary Report* (Ann Arbor, Mich.: University of Michigan, National Assessment of Juvenile Corrections, 1975), p. 25.

community-based correctional systems. At the same time, states maintained their established institutions and staffing, the costs of which were basically fixed. The study concluded that savings would indeed be meaningful if states were to increase deinstitutionalization substantially rather than modestly and if they were to fund community-based corrections rather than maintain corrections at the state level.

MAJOR TYPES OF COMMUNITY-BASED PROGRAMS

The major community-based programs are foster care, group homes, and several other types of community-based treatment programs, including Outward Bound and Homeward Bound.

Foster Care   A foster home shelters one or two neglected, abused, or delinquent youths with a single family, usually for a short period of time. The state or local government pays board to a husband and a wife who serve as surrogate parents, usually in a state-licensed home. Approximately 7,100 youthful offenders were assigned to foster homes in this country on an average day in 1974. This figure is considerably larger than the

TABLE 6-5   1974 Average Costs per Offender-Year for State-Related Community-Based Residential Programs

	Number of States
$ 210– 1,999	5
$ 2,000– 3,999	10
$ 4,000– 5,999	7
$ 6,000– 7,999	6
$ 8,000– 9,999	4
$10,000–17,800	4
Total	36

Note: Mean = $5,501

From: Robert D. Vinter, George Downs, and John Hall, *Juvenile Corrections in the States: Residential Programs and Deinstitutionalization: A Preliminary Report* (Ann Arbor, Mich.: University of Michigan, National Assessment of Juvenile Corrections, 1975), p. 40.

5,663 reportedly assigned each day to community-based correctional facilities.[8] The reason for this is that foster home placements are often made by a department of social services rather than by the juvenile court; therefore, foster care is neither administratively nor fiscally within the framework of state juvenile corrections policy, and the juvenile corrections agency is unable to monitor these placements.

The NAJC study stated that foster home placements "have not been an intentional component of states' deinstitutionalization policies," but the average cost of less than $2,500 a year recommends their "inclusion in juvenile corrections policy" and they "constitute a promising direction for extending community corrections at significantly lower cost levels."[9]

Offenders who need a close relationship with an adult model and who are capable of responding to affection and individual attention are probably the best candidates for foster home placements. However, offenders whose attitudes and behavior make them a threat to others in the community generally do not function well in a foster care setting.

To manage a foster home well is not an easy task. The neglect and rejection previously experienced by most foster children often generate either overdependency or acting-out behavior. These children are frequently passed from one home to another, for they continually have problems adjusting to their new environment. Runaway behavior is also common, and many foster children are regularly involved in law-violating behavior. Finally, it should be noted that foster parents, who often go from one crisis to another, are usually poorly compensated for the care of their foster children.

The ideal foster home possesses most of the following characteristics:

1. The foster father has a high degree of participation in the minor's care.
2. The foster parents accept the natural parents as significant persons in the minor's life.
3. The foster family is well-accepted in the neighborhood and the community.
4. The foster parents' own children seem secure and well-adjusted.
5. Relationships within the family are characterized by mutual respect.
6. The foster parents help the minor understand that he can be loved.
7. The foster parents give affection without expecting immediate returns.
8. The foster family has a clear set of ground rules for behavior but a teenager's need for privacy and group activities is recognized.[10]

Group Homes   The group home, the group residence, and the group foster home are all used in juvenile corrections in this country. The term *group home* generally refers to a single dwelling owned or rented by an organization or agency. Although it is not part of an institutional campus, this facility provides care for a group of about four to twelve children and staff are viewed as houseparents or counselors rather than foster parents. The administrative, supervisory, and service responsibility for the group home rests with the parent agency or organization. Usually indistinguishable from nearby homes or apartments, the group home reaches out to the community for resources and service.[11]

The terms *group residence* or *halfway house* are used in some parts of the country to identify a small facility serving about thirteen to twenty-five youths. It usually houses two or more groups of youths, each with its own child-care staff. This residence tends to use agency rather than community services, and its architecture and large size differentiate it from nearby homes and apartments.

Group foster homes also shelter youthful offenders. These homes sometimes are effective for those youngsters who are unable to tolerate a close one-to-one relationship with foster parents. Group-care foster homes have become increasingly popular in the Midwest, chiefly in

Minnesota, Wisconsin, Ohio, Iowa, and Michigan. Group homes fulfill several purposes in juvenile corrections. First, they provide an alternative to institutionalization. Dependent, neglected, and other noncriminal youths, especially, are referred to them. Group homes also provide situational offenders with an alternative to institutionalization, thereby avoiding their confinement with chronic offenders. Second, group homes may be used as short-term residences, whereas community resources deal with youths' community problems, such as family differences. Third, group homes can be used either as a "halfway in" setting for offenders who are having difficulty keeping to the conditions of probation or as a "halfway out" setting for juvenile offenders who are returning to the community but do not have adequate home placement.

Group home programs tend to vary from home to home because they have been developed to meet varying needs for different populations and communities and standard guidelines do not exist. Consequently, group homes often reflect the personal philosophies of their founders or directors. "It became apparent," states a report on the role of halfway houses in corrections, "that each particular program is practically an entity in itself, arrived at by people willing to experiment in a field where total confusion and ambiguity reign regarding concept and theory."[12] Intake criteria, length of stay, treatment goals, target population serviced, quantity and quality of staffing, services offered, physical facilities, location in relation to the rest of the city, and house rules are extremely diverse in group homes in this country.

Many group homes are very treatment oriented. They have a social work director and use group therapy. These group sessions are largely supportive; they do not probe very deeply and discussion is usually limited to problems as they arise. Guided Group Interaction (GGI) is probably the most popular treatment method; the members of the group are expected to support, confront, and be honest with one another to the end that they may be helped in dealing with their own problems. The role of the therapist in GGI is to help the members develop a more positive and prosocial group culture. Some group homes, however, deliberately avoid a comfortable climate, and staff may even try to arouse anxiety. One director put it this way: "It seems to me the aim is to create a degree of discomfort and uncertainty in order to foster self-examination."[13] Without a relaxed atmosphere, youths may become unsettled and thereby more receptive to personality change.

Florida has developed a fairly extensive network of group homes. Of the seventeen community-based treatment centers serving 400 youngsters, nine are halfway houses, or group homes, developed on the Criswell House model. The first Criswell House in Florida was established in 1958; it housed twenty-five youths on probation and parole and used guided group interaction. In addition to these larger halfway houses, Florida has three START centers—small group homes located in rural settings with their own schools on the grounds—and five group homes for emotionally disturbed children, administered by husband-and-wife teams.

Probationed Offenders Rehabilitation Training (PORT) and the Silverlake Experiment are two widely publicized group homes for juvenile offenders. PORT was established in 1969 in southern Minnesota as a live-in, community-based treatment program for both adult and juvenile offenders. The PORT facility is a former nurses' residence leased by the state from the community. Some of the unique features of this project are the combination of adult and juvenile offenders, the use of college students instead of the guard/counselor staff members, and the heavy involvement of community resources. Group treatment and behavior modification are the chief treatment methods. Although no comprehensive evaluation is yet available, mixing adults and juveniles seems to be working well, college students have satisfactorily replaced custodial staff, and local resources have been a key to the success of the program.[14]

The Silverlake Experiment in Los Angeles was a very ambitious group program, in which up to twenty delinquent boys at a time, ages sixteen to eighteen, were assigned to a large family house in a middle-class neighborhood. Offenders lived at the house during the week, attended school daily, and went home on weekends. In this Highfields-like project, a group session was held each day for the purpose of developing a more positive social system and involving peers in decision making.

Day Treatment Facilities Day treatment facilities have begun to multiply around the country. A strong case can be made for the nonresidential center inasmuch as many youngsters are not suited to a residential program, as evidenced by the large number of runaways from residential centers—sometimes 50 percent.

Empey, Newland, and Lubeck note a positive characteristic of these settings:

> It seems logical to assume that, even though a delinquent may be subjected to many controls and some pressures, the chance to return home each night rather than having to live twenty-four hours each day with those pressures, and the people who generate them, may have a salutary effect.[15]

Nonresidential programs also make parental participation easier. Too, such programs are obviously more economical, since it is not necessary to provide living and sleeping quarters. Meals can be arranged for through tickets to local restaurants, contracts with catering services, or participation in school lunch programs. Fewer staff members are needed: a director, an assistant, a work supervisor, and a secretary may be the only required staff.

The nonresidential centers typically serve young male offenders, although California operates two for girls and several coeducational programs. The California Community Treatment Project includes a few youths placed in foster homes, but it is essentially nonresidential in nature. The New York Division for Youth has established several nonresidential (STAY) programs under which young people go to work or school during the day and return to their homes at night. The STAY program, similar to many of the other nonresidential programs, exposes youths to a guided-group interaction experience.

Probably the most glamorous nonresidential program is the one conducted by the Associated Marine Institutes (AMI) in Florida. This privately operated corrections program, funded jointly by state, federal, and private donations, uses the sea to stimulate productive behavior in juvenile offenders. Most of the 130 trainees, boys between fifteen and eighteen, live at home; a few live in foster homes. They attend one of the five centers of AMI (Deerfield Beach–Florida Ocean Sciences Institute, Jacksonville, Tampa, Miami, and St. Petersburg) for eight hours a day for up to nine months. In addition to basic education classes, they receive training in seamanship, diving, and other nautical skills. The youths, who are referred to the program either by the courts or the Division of Youth Services, must undergo a thirty-day evaluation period before they are accepted as regular trainees. The major incentive for boys in this program is the opportunity to earn official certification as scuba divers.[16]

But in spite of these and other programs, day treatment facilities still are used more for diversionary programs than for community-based corrections. Runaway centers, drug drop-in centers, and alternative schools are examples of day treatment facilities outside of the juvenile justice system. These three will receive brief attention in the next chapter.

Outward Bound and Homeward Bound

Two exciting alternatives to institutionalization are the Outward Bound and Homeward Bound programs. Outward Bound programs were first used in England during World War II. The first Outward Bound school in the United States was the Colorado Outward Bound School, which was established in 1962 and accepted its first delinquents in 1964. This program, situated in the Rocky Mountains at an altitude of 8,800 feet, consists of mountain walking, backpacking, high altitude camping, solo survival, rappelling, and rock climbing. Other

Outward Bound programs soon followed in Minnesota, Maine, Oregon, North Carolina, and Texas. A Homeward Bound school was opened in 1970 in Massachusetts. Several community-based wilderness programs that begin and end in the community but include sessions in a nearby wilderness area are also in operation.

Outward Bound schools and other adventure-centered programs have used the challenge of wilderness training to develop a success experience. The "overcoming of a seemingly impossible task" provides "an opportunity to gain self-reliance, to prove one's worth, to define one's personhood." Over five hundred youthful offenders, including some females, have participated in the program since 1964. This wilderness experience, lasting approximately three weeks, has four phases: training in basic skills, a long expedition, a solo, and a final testing period. The skills necessary to survive and travel in a wilderness environment are taught in basic training. The locations of these programs include forests, high mountains, canoe country, the sea, and the desert.[17]

The Massachusetts Department of Youth Services, which had been one of the strongest supporters of Outward Bound, decided to begin its own program in the early 1970s. Employing some of the best elements of the Outward Bound model, a series of pilot programs were initiated that evolved into the two-phase, six-week program called Homeward Bound.

When they arrive at the Homeward Bound lodges, the youths selected for this program receive from the assistant superintendent and a counselor an overview of what is in store for them. They are told that the program is very rugged, has limited openings, is voluntary, must be completed once it is begun, and once completed allows the youth to be paroled directly to home. These two staff members then explain a few basic rules to each new enrollee. They inform him that there are no locks, no fences, and no secure rooms in this program. During Phase I, visiting is permitted, mail is not censored, phone calls may be made and received, and personal clothing may be worn. But visiting or phone calls are not permitted during Phase II, which takes place either on the Appalachian Trail or at sea.[18]

Thirty-two youths are assembled for Phase I and divided into brigades of eight each. This phase lasts two weeks. The days are spent working in community service projects, developing physical fitness, and working with a counselor toward developing a realistic plan for release. Classes are conducted in the evenings on ecology, orientation, survival, search and rescue, ropes and knots, overnight expeditions, and seamanship.

Phase II, from the first day, requires youths to put into practice what they learned in Phase I. The "quiet walk" comes in the first few days and is a real eye opener of what is in store for participants. Neither quiet nor a walk, it requires the youths to run at a cross-country trot for five or six hours over forest trails, through swamps, across rivers, and into nearly impenetrable woodlands. Each youth is asked to step forward and sign a pledge following the quiet walk, reiterating his desire to continue in and complete the Homeward Bound Program.

One demanding and frightening experience follows another. The overnight training expedition is followed by the three-day expedition; this is followed by the ten-day mobile course across the Appalachian Trail, often in several feet of snow. Next, such experiences as the one hundred-foot rappell, rock-climbing expeditions and circuit training, and a three-day solo await all enrollees. The brigade returns to the "homeplace" after each youth has completed his three-day solo. The final event in the program is the awarding to each youth of his certificate and emblem.

The most important staff member in Outward Bound or Homeward Bound is the person who works directly with youths. These counselors literally have the lives of youths in their hands; several boys, in fact, have lost their lives in Outward Bound programs. Enrollees may be experts on how to survive in the streets, but they usually are experiencing a new and frightening world in the wilderness. Participants must be motivated to give their best, supported while they are struggling with the difficulty and fear of the tasks, and responded to with praise and reinforcement when they successfully complete each experience. The job of the counselor is to make certain that the program is a success experience for as many as possible. He has to be a master psychologist, knowing how to push and when to quit. He must be able to encourage those who are ready to drop out and to alert those whose carelessness may cost them their own lives or the lives of others.

RESPONSE OF OFFENDERS TO
COMMUNITY-BASED PROGRAMS

Youthful offenders prize their freedom. Therefore, it is to be expected that they would prefer community-based programs to institutional confinement and that they would prefer nonresidential to residential programs. The available studies seem to confirm this.

The National Assessment of Juvenile Corrections questioned youths about whether or not they thought that other people had labeled them as criminal. Of the national sample, 56 percent of institutionalized youth thought others had labeled them criminal, while only 36 percent in day treatment or community residential programs thought so.[19]

The Center for Criminal Justice of the Harvard Law School, in its study of deinstitutionalization in Massachusetts, found that the type of placement affects the way youthful offenders feel about staff members. Coates et al. summarized the research on staff-resident relationships (communicating, decision making, providing help, and punishing or rewarding behavior): "Nonresidential programs and foster care consistently received more favorable assessments than did group homes or secure care." For example, in terms of involvement in actual decision making, 47 percent in nonresidential care and 44 percent in foster care indicated that they were able to participate in making choices, while only 33 percent of juveniles in group homes and 26 percent in secure care had been given this ability to make choices.[20]

Institutionalized youths, in contrast, seem to be very negative about their former foster care placements. Accusations of institutional residents include the charges that foster parents, especially foster fathers, want them there only as workhands and expect an inordinate amount of work from them; that foster children are treated much differently from the foster parents' own children; that unduly restrictive rules are placed on foster children; that foster parents provide little warmth and genuine affection for other foster children; and that foster parents are punitive. But, in view of the fact that many of these institutionalized offenders were youths who had failed in foster-home placements, these certainly are not unbiased statements.

EFFECTIVENESS OF COMMUNITY-BASED PROGRAMS

Research has been done on the Silverlake Project, Provo Project, the California Youth Authority Department's Community Treatment Project (CTP), the deinstitutionalized services for youth in Massachusetts, and the Outward Bound programs.

A study of the impact of the Silverlake project indicated that boys freely shared information about problem behavior and that the effectiveness of the peer culture as a social control measure increased as time went by. However, very little difference was found after one year between the Silverlake project youths and those in the control group; yet, the cost for the Silverlake program was one-third of what the cost would have been for institutionalizing these youths.[21]

The Pinehills Project in Provo set up an experimental design to assess the effectiveness of the program. Youths assigned to this program were compared with a group placed on probation and another group committed to an institution. Although there is some question about the research design, only 16 percent of the Pinehills youths who completed the program had been arrested within six months after release, in comparison with 23 percent of the probation controls and 58 percent of the institutional controls.[22]

The California Youth Authority's Community Treatment Project (CTP) consistently found that the overall success rate of project participants was higher than that of youths in the regular Youth Authority program. During the twenty-four-month follow-up in phase II, for example, 43 percent of the male experimentals had violated parole compared to 63 percent of regular Youth Authority releasees.[23] These findings, nevertheless, have been challenged by James Robinson, Paul Lerman, and others who claim among other things that decision making by the authorities altered the experimental results.

In Massachusetts, the Harvard Center for Criminal Justice has completed its second annual comparison of recidivism rates of youth formerly confined in the training schools of Massachusetts with the rates of youth in the network of community-based services. Comparing a sample of offenders paroled by the Youth Service Board from the training schools during the fiscal year 1967–1968 with a comparable sample of youth released from the department's regional programs in 1973 and 1974, Coates et al. discovered that no significant differences in recidivism rates were evident in regions I, II, III, and IV. However, further analysis revealed that "youth placed in secure care facilities had much higher recidivism rates than youth placed in group homes, foster care, or nonresidential programs."[24]

Kelly and Baer presented the results of a two-year demonstration project conducted by the Massachusetts Department of Youth Services that involved sixty boys who attended Outward Bound schools and sixty boys who were treated routinely by juvenile corrections authorities. Effectiveness was measured primarily by comparing the recidivism rates between the two matched groups twelve months after parole. Recidivism among the experimental group was much lower after the first year: 42 percent of the control group had failed, compared to 20 percent of the experimental group. However, the differences between the two groups had nearly disappeared after five years.[25]

In October of 1976, Martinson and Wilks published a preliminary report that summarized all relevant research. They found that "reduced-custody residential establishments (halfway houses, group homes) appear to have a high recidivism rate (41.6 percent) when introduced *prior* to a sentence of imprisonment, but a lower rate when introduced following incarceration."[26]

Certainly the evidence of these programs and others is conflicting. Even in those studies in which recidivism rates are lower for youths left in the community, the criticism is often made that juveniles who were more likely to succeed were selected for the experimental group and that authorities altered the results by giving the experimentals more chances than they gave controls before returning them to the juvenile court. Thus, it is very difficult to substantiate the widespread conclusion that community-based corrections lowers the recidivism rate. But, on the other hand, a very good case can be made for the assumption that community-based corrections is at least as successful as institutionalization, with far less trauma to youngsters and less cost to the state. If three weeks in a wilderness program, for example, is as effective as months or even years of confinement in training schools, then it would behoove society to place a major emphasis on community-based corrections when establishing social policy and planning.

ISSUES IN COMMUNITY-BASED CORRECTIONS

Some of the important issues in community-based corrections center around securing greater community involvement in corrections; the wisdom and practicality of following the Massachusetts policy elsewhere; and an examination of the policy implications of supplementary corrections versus expansion of community-based corrections.

Community Involvement in Community-Based Corrections

To break down community resistance and to obtain greater citizen involvement in juvenile corrections, especially during the ascendency of the hard-liners, departments of juvenile corrections must develop and implement certain plans and strategies. At least three components must be present: (1) a strategy for improving community attitudes; (2) a strategy for citizen involvement; and (3) a strategy for deciding who will be placed in community facilities. Unfortunately, there is no agreement on how to implement any of these three plans.

Careful planning is obviously necessary to gain greater public support for community-based programs. A department should mount a massive public education effort through the communications media, should seek support for the project from the various subcommunities of the community—ethnic, racial, and special interest groups—and should develop a sophisticated understanding of the decision-making processes in society.[27] But should this be done before or after a program has been initiated in the community?

Supporters who advocate keeping the community informed as soon as a site for a program is chosen claim that to do otherwise is dishonest. But opponents of this approach argue that advance information will permit the community to mobilize to resist the proposed community program. They claim that the community is more likely to accept an already established and successful program than one that exists only on the drawing board.

No one disagrees that citizen involvement is imperative. A citizen can serve in the important role of policymaker through membership on an advisory committee of a community facility or with a voluntary association interested in corrections. A citizen can become part of a group working for penal reform. As an advocate, a citizen can provide direct services to offenders and intercede for them when necessary. However, disagreement enters the picture when planning for citizen involvement.

There is widespread controversy over the selection of youths to be placed in community-based programs. One approach is conservative: if the wrong youth is put in the wrong place at the wrong time and commits a serious or violent crime, such as rape or murder, the adverse publicity may destroy the best-planned and implemented program. Therefore, to preserve the viability of community-based programs, only juveniles most likely to be helped should be kept in the community. The opposing approach argues that all but the hard-core recidivist should be retained in the community, for it is there that the youth's problems began in the first place. Advocates of this position feel that in-stitutionalization will only make better criminals out of confined youths. Some of these supporters even propose leaving many of the hard-core or difficult-to-handle youths in the community.

The Feasibility of Training Schools

The strongest support for doing away with juvenile correctional institutions is probably found in Massachusetts, where all training schools have been closed. In this state, about 425 juveniles are placed in group homes or in other residential facilities, such as private boarding schools and YMCAs; about 75 are in residential facilities in neighboring states; about 200 are in foster homes; and another 700 are in nonresidential day programs. Although 50 juveniles on any given day are in secure detention and another 85 or so are in secure "intensive care" facilities, officials of the Department of Youth Services deny that these small facilities can be compared to traditional correctional institutions. Contrary to rumor, no evidence exists that youth crime in Massachusetts has risen dramatically or that more juveniles are being transferred to adult courts. In short, Massachusetts seems to be successful in its program of deinstitutionalization. It has problems, but nearly all policymakers in this state feel that the problems are less severe than those they would encounter in operating a system of corrections institutions. Joseph Leavey, former director of Youth Services, states this point very aptly:

> We've got problems, but we always had problems. When we had Lyman School, the problem was what about the race wars, what about the fact that the roof's falling down, what about the tremendous number of

runaways, what about brutality by staff. Now we've got problems like what are we going to do about the contract with Catholic Charities, or what are we going to do about [getting more] purchase-of-service money, or about evaluation. They're healthier problems.[28]

The mood of the country, as stated throughout this book, is much less receptive to total deinstitutionalization now than it was in the late 1960s and early 1970s. But, a great majority of the public and in justice practitioners still believe that community-based programs are desirable for at least some youthful offenders. In a survey of the top juvenile correctional administrators across the country, the staff of *Corrections Magazine* asked the following question: "Do you think that community programs are more effective at rehabilitating offenders than institutional programs?" Of the forty-eight respondents, twenty-three answered yes; two, no; seven didn't know; and sixteen felt they were effective for some offenders. Less than 20 percent of this sample challenged the efficacy of community programs for selected youths.[29] Nevertheless, it is unlikely that many of these administrators or any other policymakers at this time would agree to a policy of total deinstitutionalization.

Impact of Supplementary Programs on Community-Based Corrections

Some concern has been expressed that the use of community programs will tend to supplement rather than replace institutions, thereby leading to an expansion of the juvenile correctional system. In examining this issue, Vinter et al. noted that state institutions, camps, and ranches confined nearly 10,000 fewer youths in 1974 than in 1969, because states were confining fewer status offenders.[30] They additionally pointed out, however, that no connection exists between the per capita average daily populations in institutions and those in community-based programs. The increased use of community programs does not imply less use of institutions. Of the two available means of arriving at a high level of deinstitutionalization—increasing the number of offenders in community settings or reducing institutional populations—these NAJC researchers found that deinstitutionalization was usually achieved through the first approach. For example, the average rate of institutionalization for the ten most deinstitutionalized states was less than the fifty-state average (13.3 compared to 17.8), but the assignment of offenders to community-based programs resulted in a higher-than-average *combined* rate of assignment to both types of programs (25.6 compared to 22.5). Vinter et al. therefore concluded that the concern of those who fear that the development of community-based corrections can lead to an expansion of the correctional system as a whole appears to be justified.[31] Rutherford and Bengur also found that community-based corrections was widening the net of juvenile corrections.[32]

SUMMARY

Community-based corrections is an important dimension of juvenile corrections. But support for community programs is considerably less than it was in the early 1970s, for even the most avid supporters of community correctional programs now speak more of the importance of the selection process and less of the necessity for closing all juvenile institutions. Little new evidence is being introduced that validates juvenile institutionalization, yet it continues to be far more widely used than community-based corrections. Part of the problem, of course, lies in the recent origin of community-based corrections. There are few community-based corrections facilities in most states and they are under considerable attack by community-control proponents. The decision in Massachusetts to close all of its training schools is an example of correctional policy undergoing a dramatic change. But, instead of storming the ramparts, community-based programs seem to be in the position of holding the fort or perhaps even retreating a step or two.

QUESTIONS

1. Do you feel that combining juveniles and adults, as PORT does, is a direction in which community-based programs ought to move?
2. What are the advantages and disadvantages of coeducational programs in the community?
3. Of the programs discussed in this chapter, which do you feel is the most ideal for helping offenders reintegrate into the community?
4. What specific strategies can departments of juvenile corrections pursue to enlist greater support from the community for community programs?
5. Why has the Massachusetts decision to deinstitutionalize totally not been duplicated elsewhere?

ENDNOTES

1. President's Commission on Law Enforcement and Administration of Justice, *Task Force Report: Corrections* (Washington, D.C.: U.S. Government Printing Office, 1967), p. 38.
2. Sid Ross and Herbert Kupferberg, "Shut Down Reform School?" *Parade* (September 1972), p. 4.
3. Yitzhak Bakal, *Closing Correctional Institutions* (Lexington, Mass.: D. C. Heath and Company, 1973), p. 154.
4. Statement by Governor Sargent, quoted in *Corrections* 2 (November–December 1975): 30–31.
5. National Advisory Commission on Criminal Justice Standards and Goals, *Corrections* (Washington, D.C.: U.S. Government Printing Office, 1973), p. 360.
6. John P. Conrad, "We Should Never Have Promised a Hospital," *Federal Probation* 39 (December 1975): 4.
7. Robert D. Vinter, George Downs, and John Hall, *Juvenile Corrections in the States: Residential Programs and Deinstitutionalization: A Preliminary Report* (Ann Arbor, Mich.: University of Michigan, National Assessment of Juvenile Corrections, November, 1975), p. 51.
8. Vinter, Downs, and Hall, *Juvenile Corrections,* p. 62.
9. Ibid., p. 65.
10. Edward Eldefonso and Walter Hartinger, *Control, Treatment, and Rehabilitation of Juvenile Offenders* (Beverly Hills, Calif.: Glencoe Press, 1976), p. 183.
11. Martin Gula, *Agency Operated Group Homes* (Washington, D.C.: U.S. Government Printing Office, 1964), p. 33.
12. Oliver J. Keller, Jr., and Benedict S. Alper, *Halfway Houses: Community-Centered Correction and Treatment* (Lexington, Mass.: D. C. Heath and Company, 1970), p. 114.
13. Letter from Richard Rachin, Resident Director, J. Stanley Sheppard Youth Center, New York, 16 May 1967, in Keller and Alper, *Halfway Houses,* p. 20.
14. Nora Klapmuts, "Community Alternatives to Prison," in *A Nation without Prisons,* edited by Calvert R. Dodge (Lexington, Mass.: D. C. Heath and Company, 1975), pp. 122–123.
15. LaMar T. Empey, George E. Newland, and Stephen G. Lubeck, *The Silverlake Experiment: A Community Study in Delinquency Rehabilitation, Progress Report No. 2* (Los Angeles: Youth Studies Center, University of Southern California, 1965), p. 130.
16. "Can Delinquents Be Saved by the Sea?" *Corrections* 1 (September 1974): 77–88.
17. Joseph Nold and Mary Wilpers, "Wilderness Training as an Alternative to Incarceration," in Dodge, *A Nation without Prisons,* p. 155.
18. Herb C. Willman, Jr., and Ron Y. F. Chun, "Homeward Bound: An Alternative to the Institutionalization of Adjudicated Juvenile Offenders," in George G. Killinger and Paul F. Cromwell, Jr., eds., *Alternatives to Imprisonment: Corrections in the Community* (St. Paul, Minn.: West Publishing Company, 1974).
19. Rosemary C. Sarri and Robert D. Vinter, "Justice for Whom? Varieties of Juvenile Correctional Approaches," in *The Juvenile Justice System,* edited

by Malcolm W. Klein (Beverly Hills, Calif.: Sage Publications, 1976), pp. 186–189.

20. Robert B. Coates et al., "Exploratory Analysis of Recidivism and Cohort Data on the Massachusetts Youth Correctional System" (Cambridge, Mass.: Center for Criminal Justice, Harvard Law School, July 1975), pp. 40–45.

21. William T. Pink and Mervin F. White, "Delinquency Prevention: The State of the Art," in Klein, *Juvenile Justice System*, p. 21.

22. LaMar T. Empey, Maynard Erickson, and Max Scott, "The Provo Experiment: Evaluation of a Community Program," *Correction in the Community: Alternatives to Incarceration* (Sacramento: California Department of Corrections, 1964), pp. 29–38.

23. Klapmuts, "Community Alternatives to Prison," p. 115.

24. Coates et al., "Exploratory Analysis," pp. 1–2.

25. Nold and Wilpers, "Wilderness Training," pp. 157–158.

26. Robert Martinson and Judith Wilks, "Knowledge in Criminal Justice Planning" (New York: Center for Knowledge in Criminal Justice Planning, 1976), p. 2.

27. National Advisory Commission, *Corrections*.

28. "Officials Say Juvenile System Works," *Corrections* 1 (June 1975): 33.

29. "National Survey on the Value of Rehabilitation Programs," *Corrections* 1 (June 1975): 5.

30. Vinter, Downs, and Hall, *Juvenile Corrections*, p. 14.

31. Ibid., pp. 76–78.

32. Andrew Rutherford and Osman Bengur, "Community-Based Alternatives to Juvenile Incarceration," Law Enforcement Assistance Administration Phase 1 Report (Washington, D.C.: U.S. Government Printing Office, n.d.), p. 15.

REFERENCES

Keller, Oliver J., Jr., and Alper, Benedict S. *Halfway Houses: Community-Centered Correction and Treatment.* Lexington, Mass.: D. C. Heath and Company, 1970.
    An excellent book including the history, characteristics, and profile of halfway houses.

Killinger, George G., and Cromwell, Paul F., Jr., eds. *Alternatives to Imprisonment: Corrections in the Community.* St. Paul, Minn.: West Publishing Company, 1974.
    This reader is a very helpful source book on community-based corrections.

Ohlin, Lloyd E.; Miller, Alden D.; and Coates, Robert B. *A Preliminary Report of the Center for Criminal Justice of the Harvard Law School.* Washington, D.C.: U.S. Government Printing Office, n.d.
    Contains several important studies of the process and impact of the closing in Massachusetts of all training schools.

Rutherford, Andrew, and Bengur, Oscar. *Community-Based Alternatives: Na-*

tional Evaluation Program, Phase I Summary Report. Washington, D.C.: U.S. Government Printing Office, October 1976.

 A good evaluation of the effectiveness of community-based corrections.

Vinter, Robert D.; Downs, George; and Hall, John. *Juvenile Corrections in the States: Residential Programs and Deinstitutionalization: A Preliminary Report.* Ann Arbor, Mich.: National Assessment of Juvenile Corrections, the University of Michigan, 1975.

 An outstanding monograph on community-based corrections, which appraises the present status and gives policy recommendations.

7

Diversion

The prevention of youth crime is the ultimate goal of the juvenile justice system. Many authorities feel the most effective strategy is diversion, or turning juveniles away from further processing by the juvenile justice system. They believe that contact with the system is harmful to youth and, therefore, alternative programs should be used. The passage of the Juvenile Justice and Delinquency Prevention Act of 1974, in fact, should result in a sharp increase in diversionary programs since one condition it set for the funding of local and state juvenile programs was the establishment of diversionary alternatives. However, conceptual, operational, and empirical problems pervade these efforts to divert juveniles from the justice system.

HISTORY OF DIVERSION

Diversion is as old as the juvenile justice system. Yet, the emphasis on diversionary programming began only in 1967 when the President's Commission on Law Enforcement and Administration of Justice recommended the establishment of alternatives to the juvenile justice system:

> The formal sanctioning system and pronouncement of delinquency should be used only as a last resort.
> In place of the formal system, dispositional alternatives to adjudica-

173

tion must be developed for dealing with juveniles, including agencies to provide and coordinate services and procedures to achieve necessary control without unnecessary stigma. Alternatives already available, such as those related to court intake, should be more fully explored.

The range of conduct for which court intervention is authorized should be narrowed, with greater emphasis upon consensual and informal means of meeting the problems of difficult children.[1]

Two theoretical notions provided the gunpowder for this explosive recommendation. First, a major influence on the rise of diversionary agencies was the mounting belief throughout the 1960s that adolescents tagged as delinquents by social control agencies are likely to live up to their label. Merton described this process as a self-fulfilling prophecy.[2] Lemert argued that society's reaction is critical in determining whether juvenile lawbreaking remains situational or develops into a consistent pattern of law-violating behavior.[3] Labeling was seen as a "process of tagging, describing, emphasizing, making conscious and self-conscious; it becomes a way of stimulating, suggesting, emphasizing, and evolving the very traits that are complained of."[4] More recent theorists have developed this argument further and placed even greater emphasis upon labeling as the critical factor leading to a deviant career.

The most direct statement tying labeling theory to diversion is found in the work done by the National Strategy for Youth Development and Delinquency Prevention. The approach to delinquency prevention is this study identified three processes that block youth from satisfactory maturation and growth and weaken their ties to societal norms: the entrapment of negative labeling; the limited access to acceptable social roles; and the resulting process of rejection, alienation, and estrangement. Figure 7-1 is a diagram of this theoretical scheme.

The differential association theory provided a second theoretical justification for diversion. As developed by Sutherland, Ohlin, Cohen, and others, this theory holds that individuals learn delinquent or criminal behavior from others, especially if they are in intimate contact with them.[5] This theory had sufficient impact that policymakers became concerned about placing noncriminal youths with hard-core or career delinquents because they were afraid that these juveniles would learn criminogenic motives, techniques, and rationalizations from these offenders.

Supporters of diversionary programs cited other values to be derived from these programs, such as the reduction of case loads, the more efficient administration of the justice system, the freeing of the juvenile court to handle the more difficult cases, the development of an advocate role apart from the formal justice system, and the provision of more therapeutic settings in which youths and parents can resolve problems.[6]

FIGURE 7-1

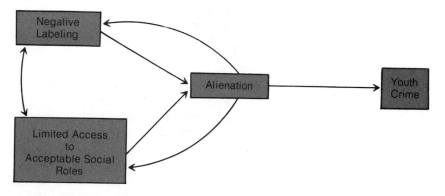

Adapted by permission from *Phase I Assessment of Youth Service Bureaus, Summary Report of Youth Service Bureau Research Group for LEAA* (Boston: Boston University, 1975), pp. 17–18.

Diversion projects, supported by these rationales and advocated by the President's Crime Commission, required only a funding base to be put into operation as a viable alternative to the juvenile justice system. The first stages of funding were established when Congress passed the Omnibus Crime Control and Safe Streets Act of 1968 and the Juvenile Delinquency Prevention and Control Act of 1968. These acts were intended to help state and local communities establish new agencies or to make existing agencies more effective in dealing with youth. In 1970, Congress amended the Safe Streets Act to require that a portion of the funds received under the Law Enforcement Assistance Administration block grant program be allocated to community-based correctional programs and facilities, both juvenile and adult. The Juvenile Delinquency Act of 1972 directed the focus of its activities to the creation of new and the maintenance of old diversionary programs in the community. Finally, the Juvenile Justice and Delinquency Prevention Act of 1974, as previously mentioned, continued to provide a funding base for diversionary programs.

DEFINITIONAL PROBLEMS

Presently, considerable confusion exists about the meaning of *diversion*. Part of this results from the rapid development of diversionary programs in so short a period of time. Much of the confusion also can be traced to the variety of forms and definitions of diversion. There are numerous types of diversion, each with certain practices commonly associated with it:[7]

Traditional diversion refers to the discretionary judgments by juvenile justice personnel on whether or not to process offenders, to process them informally, or to refer them to nonspecialized community programs. As previous chapters have indicated, discretion and informal processing are widely used in juvenile corrections.

Screening refers to removal from the system, generally without referral, which takes place especially at the intake stage in the juvenile court. This does involve the process of turning youths away from the justice system, but it does nothing to correct the behavior that brought them into the system originally.

Minimization of penetration involves informal intervention or processing and/or referral to programs inside the juvenile justice system. The emphasis here is on preventing offenders from becoming more deeply involved in the juvenile justice system.

True diversion is the termination of official processing and/or referral to a program outside of the juvenile justice system. The criteria for true diversion include the following: First, true diversion presupposes a receiving agency that offers youth services or prevention programs. This supposition suggests a distinction between screening and diversion because screening does not involve referral, service, or follow-up. In comparison, true diversion implies all three. Second, the diversionary referral must replace further official processing in the juvenile justice system. Third, the receiving agency should lie outside the formal jurisdiction of the justice system; that is, this agency should be independent of the system. Fourth, diversion must occur between apprehension and adjudication. And last, diversion should not be coercive; offenders must be able to choose whether or not to participate in these programs.[8]

New diversion relates to the post-1967 emphasis on developing new programs for keeping juveniles out of the system. These programs may include both traditional and true diversion.

DIVERSIONARY PROGRAMS

Juvenile diversion, broadly defined, is initiated either through the police, the courts or probation services, or agencies outside the juvenile justice system. The first two practice traditional diversion, while the third involves true diversion.

The Police   Police discretion, it will be remembered, may account for as much as 90 percent of all diversion. The patrol officer, who becomes an on-the-spot prosecutor, judge, and correctional system, typically warns and releases the youth without formal processing. Juvenile police officers frequently view their task as one of diverting juveniles from probation (minimization of penetration). They may thus counsel, warn, release, place on informal probation, or refer to a private agency or program. Some departments have school resource officers, police officers assigned to a particular school who are to prevent youths from coming into contact with the system or to divert juveniles from more intensive contact with the system.

Police diversionary programs have multiplied rapidly in the 1970s. For example, California alone has more than 150 police diversionary programs. Police programs include predelinquent intervention as well as the diversion of actual offenders.

Community Predelinquent Programs.   The Los Angeles County Sheriff's Department teaches several courses in high school and junior high settings for interested students. In a program conducted jointly by the Flint Police Department and the Mott Program of the Flint Board of Education, 650 boys in sixteen elementary schools meet weekly to learn about school safety, juvenile delinquency, community relations, city government, court procedures, bicycle safety, and crime and detention.[9]

The city of Miami has developed a program in which two officers in uniform—one black and one white—tour all the elementary schools within the city in order to instill respect for authority and the police department among younger children. The Officer Friendly Program, which exists throughout the country, is also used to develop better relations with younger children.

The Police Department of St. Petersburg, Florida recently hired a ventriloquist to represent the police department with Yabby, her dummy. The name "Yabby" was taken from the initials of the department's Youth Aid Bureau. Appearing on television and in person at the various elementary schools, "Policewoman Pat" and her dummy have had nearly an electrifying effect upon children. Similar programs are being set up in other communities.

Kentucky State Police set up an island camp for the purpose of working with predelinquent and underpriviledged boys aged ten to fourteen years. Established in 1965 and staffed by volunteer troopers who are off-duty or on vacation, this recreation program has gained momentum through the years. Both the Kentucky State Police and citizens involved with the program feel that it has been an unqualified success in building better relations between the troopers and the youthful campers.

Other predelinquent programs include the law enforcement Explorer posts jointly sponsored by the Boy Scouts of America and police departments and the ride-along program. This program, in which juveniles are permitted to ride in police cars, has been so successful that it has spread like wildfire. High school students, school dropouts, youths on probation, and college students have all become involved in this program designed to improve relations between juveniles and police.

Police Diversion of Juveniles.   The police refer many juveniles to such social agencies as youth service bureaus, mental health clinics, child welfare departments, the Big Brother and Big Sister associations, YMCAs and YWCAs, boys clubs, religious groups, and recreational groups. Youth service bureaus, in particular, are becoming more popular with law enforcement officers as they now often have staff on duty twenty-four hours a day.

The New York City Police Department has developed a program of weekend dialogues between police officers and sixteen- to nineteen-year-old teenage gang leaders at a country house on Long Island. In an informal atmosphere where everybody is on first-name basis, all participate in the preparation of meals, clean-up chores, group activities, and they share common facilities. It is hoped that increased communication developed by this program between the police and gangs will help to divert these youths from antisocial behavior.

The Pleasant Hill, California Police Department was the first local enforcement agency to initiate a police youth service bureau. Like other youth service bureaus, this police youth service bureau offers a variety of counseling programs, tutoring, job assistance, and classes in drug education. But unlike nonpolice youth service bureaus, this agency is staffed by three police officers, as well as two civilians, and it focuses on police-youth rap sessions. Two of the major emphases of this police bureau are to curb truancy and to decrease the number of runaways.

The Richmond, California Police Department's Juvenile Diversion Program, initially funded by LEAA and subsequently aided by the California Youth Authority, provides direct helping and counseling services to those youths who come in contact with the law. Crisis intervention, behavior management training for parents, counseling, tutorial services, and employment assistance are some of the basic elements of this program. The police hope that this twenty-four-hour service will deter misbehaving juveniles from becoming further involved in the juvenile justice system.

The Graduate School of Social Work of the University of Illinois initiated pilot projects with the Wheaton and Niles Police Departments in Illinois. These programs provide diversionary counseling services that are beyond the expertise of the patrol or youth officer. Over half of the first referrals to these police social agencies were juveniles. Encouraged by the success of this program, other Illinois cities—Maywood, Champaign-Urbana, and Springfield—soon followed with programs of this nature. Although the other programs chose individuals with a

Master of Social Work (MSW) as directors, the Springfield Police Department appointed a line police officer to this position.

Probation and Courts   Misbehaving juveniles who penetrate as far as the court system can still be diverted. At this stage, the probation intake officer can dismiss the youth, can warn the youth and release him, can refer him to a program outside of the system, can place him on informal probation, or can file a petition on the juvenile. Filing a petition is the most extreme alternative, for it involves further processing within the system. Placing youths on informal probation minimizes their penetration because the youth is kept within the system without any official sanctions. Warning and releasing and referring to an agency are true diversion.

If a petition is filed, the case moves on to the investigation officer, who is responsible for writing a probation recommendation for the juvenile court. This probation officer, too, may choose to divert the youth because of the discovery of new facts, a change in the youth's attitude, or the program services available.

Court and Probation Programs.   The juvenile judge, in turn, may choose to divert the youth to a crisis intervention program consisting of several sessions of intensive counseling or to a long-term counseling and treatment program. For example, the 601 Project of the Sacramento Probation Department provides short-term family crisis counseling instead of juvenile court processing for status offenders, truants, runaways, and incorrigible youngsters. Youths and their parents meet with 601 Project counselors, generally within two hours of referral, to work out problems together. This program has been expanded and now includes other cases, such as petty theft, possession of drugs, drunk and disorderly conduct, or receiving stolen property. In October 1976, the 601 Project was relocated to Neighborhood Alternative Centers, where it is staffed by graduate student volunteers as well as regular probation officers.[10]

The court may also divert youthful drug abusers to drug clinics. The Santa Clara County Juvenile Probation Department has a program of this nature. Santa Clara uses three different intervention alternatives: education-counseling, transactional analysis, and psychodrama. Parents often must attend these clinics with their children. Failure of a youth to participate usually means his return to the court.

Diversion Outside the Juvenile Justice System   As the juvenile code changes, the handling of specific offense categories is sometimes transferred to alternative legal structures such as departments of welfare or children's services. For example, in Illinois status offenders are referred to the Department of Children and Family

Service. In such cases, the youths are no longer in the jurisdiction of the justice system. However, these alternative legal structures may develop all of the trappings of legal authority usually found in the juvenile justice system, with the result that youths may suffer all the ill consequences of the traditional correctional system.

Alternative Programs. Youths in trouble can be diverted to social agencies, including private or public mental health agencies; private family counseling programs; community action agencies; youth advocate agencies, such as Big Brother and Big Sister; recreational programs such as boys clubs, the YMCA, and the YWCA; and drug programs.

Alternative schools provide a meaningful educational experience for pupils with attendance or other school-related problems. These schools are designed for students who are not motivated, who are bored by the traditional academic classroom, or who are behind in their work. Within the alternative school, sessions often are shorter than in regular schools, attendance may not be compulsory, and juveniles sometimes can work or train for a job. It is hoped that after three to six months pupils will be ready to reenter their own public school. According to Lemert:

> The "600" and "700" schools of New York City are the best known examples of special schools for student deviants. They provide intensive services for "disruptive" and delinquent children. The 600 schools concentrate on those with severe behavior problems, the 700 schools service children with "consistent" problems, especially those with court records. Actually these schools are a "system within a system" and have fairly elaborate procedures for referrals and admissions. Altogether in 1959 there were twenty-two units and annexes ranging from day schools to special units for children within psychiatric hospitals. Chicago's two special schools, Montefiore and Mosely, are less differentiated than those in New York, and in the case of Montefiore seem to be tied closely with the Family Court. Direct referrals come from school transfer or from welfare agencies.[11]

Shelters for runaways are temporary homes for runaway children. Runaways either find these homes themselves or are referred to them by parents, police, schools, courts, or other agencies. They eat and sleep in the center until the staff is able to reconcile a youth and family or find other permanent living arrangements. Treatment typically includes individual and group counseling, referral to other agencies, follow-up family counseling, and sometimes job placement and vocational rehabilitation.

The first youth service bureaus were established in Chicago and in Pontiac, Michigan in 1958. Several more were organized in the early

1960s, but the major impetus to these community agencies came in 1967, when the President's Commission on Law Enforcement and Administration of Justice recommended the establishment of youth service bureaus to work with youthful offenders outside the justice system. They are organized under a variety of names, such as youth resource bureau, youth assistance program, Listening Post, and Focus on Youth, but the youth service bureau is the name most often used.

Sherwood Norman's analysis of youth service bureaus has been influential in shaping the conception of YSB objectives and functions. He identified three possible functions of this diversionary agency: service brokerage, resource development, and system modifications. First, the youth service bureau acts as an advocate for youths to ensure that they receive the services they need. Specifically, this means that the YSB coordinates youth services in the local community; that it defines youth problems and develops plans or strategies for addressing those needs; that it identifies gaps in services; and that it defines the role of local service agencies concerning community needs. Norman, in this regard, proposed that the YSB serve all the community youth while focusing on diverting offenders from the justice system. Second, the youth service bureau is responsible for working with citizens in developing new resources that are presently unavailable. It does this by contracting for needed services or when such services cannot be purchased, by encouraging existing agencies to expand their programs or to develop these specialized services. Finally, when the attitudes and practices of established institutions are found to be contributing to antisocial behavior in juveniles, system modification becomes an important function of the YSB. The YSB is also charged to challenge, to educate, to consult, and to resort when necessary to political pressure to see that resources and institutions are responsive to the needs of children.[12]

In his study, Norman observed five different models of youth service bureaus used in various communities:

> A *cooperating agencies model,* in which several community agencies each donate the full-time paid services of one worker to the Youth Service Bureau. Working as a team with a coordinator, these workers accept individual referrals and involve citizens, youth, and professionals in solving problems related to acting-out behavior in youngsters.
>
> A *community organization model,* in which neighborhood citizens, under the direction of a coordinator, mobilize to form a board, develop services, and meet crises as circumstances in the neighborhood indicate urgency.
>
> A *citizen action model,* in which the YSB citizen committee has many subcommittees active in developing a great variety of youth services, while staff receive direct referrals and use case conference techniques and community resources to resolve individual problems. (This program originated in Pontiac, Michigan, where it has been in operation over ten years.)
>
> A *street outreach model,* which grew out of the New York City Youth Board and uses storefront neighborhood service centers as bases for therapeutic group activities including administration of the neighborhood youth corps.
>
> A *system modification model,* which focuses on helping schools, institutions, programs, agencies, etc., become more sensitive and responsive to the needs of young people and thus contribute less to their behavior problems. Demonstration projects encourage new approaches to old problems, diverting offenders into positive, community-based efforts.[13]

An LEAA report found that in 1975 a majority of YSB programs were located in communities of 10,000 or less. The majority served 500 or fewer clients per year, and only 14 percent served more than 1,000 persons annually. Most projects had multiple sources of funds. Total funding was $100,000 or less for most of the projects. Only 7 percent had budgets of $500,000 or more. The clients of these YSBs were predominantly white and male. Over half of the programs' client populations included only 30 percent or fewer minority group members and only 40 percent or fewer females. The most common source of referral was the juvenile justice system. Schools were the second important source of referral; and parents and self-referral came third. Other community agencies were much less important referral sources. The vast majority of YSB programs sent a client back to the juvenile justice system as a consequence of nonparticipation.[14]

Youth service bureaus across the country offer a variety of programs. Drop-in centers have been established where youths can find recreational and social activity. YSB hotlines, where volunteers counsel troubled youth over the phone, are quite common. Figure 7-2 is a typical announcement of a YSB hotline. YSB truancy programs receive referrals from school, work with juveniles concerning school problems, and provide tutoring, counseling, and other needed services. Some YSBs make arrangements for temporary care for runaways and other adolescents who need temporary homes. A twenty-four-hour crisis intervention program is sometimes available to distraught young people. Programs for pregnant teenagers provide counseling and referral to local agencies, prenatal instruction and care, family planning information, and whatever else is needed to help the youth and her family deal with the situation.[15]

In La Puente, California, the Bassett YSB provides a free medical clinic, which is oriented to dealing with drugs, venereal disease, pregnancy, and other youth health problems. The La Puente YSB also has a human relations service to deal with problems of discrimination and racial unrest. The Springfield, Illinois YSB has a youth advocacy program through which college students are trained to serve as volunteers to help troubled youth. The Springfield YSB also visits community rock concerts to assist young people who are experiencing bad drug trips. The youth service bureau in New York City sponsors an educational incentive program to help disadvantaged youth gain admission to college and technical schools. In San Diego, California, the youth service bureau provides a series of public education programs to inform the community about youth and youth services.

Supporters of YSBs contend that they provide services to a variety of groups:

> For the *court,* the YSB provides a reduction in "nuisance cases" and a source of follow-up services for nonadjudicated children.
> For *probation officers,* the YSB provides a reduction in time-consuming "informal adjustment" cases, which are more effectively resolved outside an authoritative framework.
> For *police officers,* the YSB provides an alternative to detention and court referral when, in the officer's judgment, release with warning is insufficient but filing a petition is not imperative.
> For the *public schools,* the YSB provides a link with the social work

FIGURE 7-2 Y.S.B. Hotline

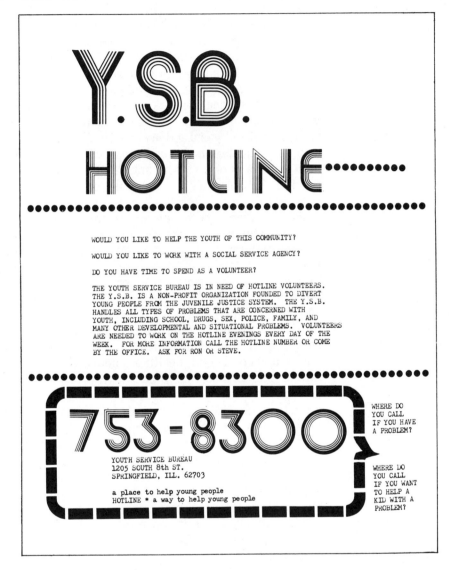

community so that truancy and other school behavior difficulties can be handled through cooperative problem solving with other agencies.

For *citizen volunteers,* the YSB provides a chance to turn from frustration over juvenile delinquency to constructive efforts on behalf of youth and youth-serving agencies.

For *private social agencies,* the YSB provides an extension of youth services through citizen action.

For the *welfare department,* the YSB provides an advocate for troubled youth and support for protective services available to young children.

For *youth,* the YSB provides the listening ear of someone who can cut establishment "red tape" in an effort to solve their problems.

For the *community* as a whole, the YSB provides an opportunity to accept responsibility for assisting its troubled and troubling youth by coordinating services on their behalf rather than relying on court authority.[16] (Italics added.)

In 1975, the Youth Service Bureau Research Group conducted a national evaluation of youth service bureaus. The *Phase I Assessment* of YSBs was designed to answer the question: What contributions do YSBs make to preventing or correcting youth crime? A major finding of this study was that YSBs contribute relatively little in any community to solving the problem of youth crime.

Other findings include the following:

1. Most YSBs provide direct services, especially counseling. They are no different in this respect from other local youth-serving agencies that receive referrals from juvenile justice system agencies.

2. In the process of providing direct services, a variety of pressures push YSBs into questionable types of involvement with juvenile justice system agencies, and the consequences tend to be coercive and stigmatizing practices.

3. YSBs, nevertheless, are among the few existing helping services for youth and as such fill a large gap in such services in various size communities.

4. The informal and formal conditions attached to YSB referrals seem to reinforce the operational connections between YSBs and the juvenile court. They therefore function as a form of probation agency.

5. Most referrals to YSBs from court intake or pre-trial hearing processes are made as informal dispositions without the advantage of due process safeguards.

6. The role and effectiveness of YSBs in initiating and coordinating efforts to change local justice systems and nonsystem agencies remain a matter of speculation because of the paucity of process evaluation studies.

7. Most YSBs devote a great deal of their limited time, energy, and staff resources to obtaining the funding for survival. At the same time, YSBs must deal with diverse pressures that operate to reduce their credibility and effectiveness as agencies serving youthful offenders.[17]

This evaluation of youth service bureaus pointed out the dangers of coercion when youths must cooperate with YSB staff or be returned to the juvenile court. Another problem is that YSBs are so dependent on the juvenile justice system for support that it is difficult for these bureaus to challenge or bring change to the system. And finally, the precarious state of the existence of YSBs, in that they must receive funding from state and local agencies when their federal grants terminate, makes it difficult for them to obtain permanent local support.

EVALUATION OF DIVERSIONARY PROGRAMS

In general, empirical studies of diversion have not demonstrated that doing something (treatment, services) is necessarily better than doing nothing. Several studies have indicated that diversionary programs do tend to reduce recidivism; yet, other researchers warn that the unanticipated consequences of diversion challenge the viability of this concept. Some of these consequences are: widening the net by increasing the number of youths contacted by the system; increasing the size of the system (budget and staff); creating new legal entities; altering traditional programs (e.g., abandoning screening in favor of diversion into the system); increasing the influence of legal authorities within private programs; and ignoring clients' due process rights.[18]

PREVENTION

Given this sobering evidence about the fad of diversion, the problem of correcting and controlling delinquent behavior remains a real one. We believe that the most effective answer to the youth crime problem is to eradicate the need for after-the-fact solutions. Local communities must take care of more of their misbehaving youngsters, rather than permit the justice system to handle them.

The Chicago Area Project provides a model of a community dealing with its own problems. Of the various delinquency prevention programs, the Chicago Area Project has the most impressive evidence of success. The project was initiated by Shaw and McKay in the 1920s in Chicago and has since spread throughout Illinois. Local neighborhoods—supported by their own organizations and agencies—intervene when problems arise in the lives of their children.

To become effective in preventing and controlling delinquency, individuals in these communities must become advocates for children, and a widely supported, grass-roots organization that is indigenous to the community must be established. The effective advocate can have a profound impact on juveniles. The following characteristics typify the effective advocate:

1. This person has the ability to care intensely about others and to give and receive love. This ability implies a concern for the total well-being of the juvenile as well as the wisdom of knowing not to do too much.

2. This person has the gift of self-acceptance—looking upon oneself as a person of real worth.

3. This person is able to be genuine with others and does not hide behind a false front. As a result, he is able to establish a deep relationship with troubled juveniles.

4. This person is a good listener and can hear both words and nonverbal messages.

5. This person has the ability to empathize because he is able to recall his own feelings as a teenager.

6. This person is willing to become involved and to take risks. He is not afraid to change old systems or ideas that no longer are effective.

7. This person has a good blend of realism while still retaining a healthy amount of optimism and idealism.

8. This person is a nourishing person and has a great deal to offer. As a result, he is able to boost the self-concept of juveniles and make them feel better about themselves.

9. Finally, this effective advocate has the ability to accept failures, does not claim to have all the answers, and does not try to solve all the problems. He is aware of "burn out" and, therefore, is able to take a break and to be renewed when the need arises.[19]

The individual with the right motivations for becoming an advocate believes he has something to offer, feels that people care about him, desires to help others, and both enjoys doing so and finds it meaningful. An individual with the wrong motivations believes that he has all the answers and must share them with others; feels some guilt that he is trying to work off, is searching for purpose and meaning in his life, or needs to be needed.

The Streetside Boosters of Springfield, Illinois are one example of the community organizing itself to deal with youth problems. This grassroots organization, set up in the mid-1970s, first announced itself to the community with this statement left at each door:

There's a New Gang in the Neighborhood

We call ourselves the "Streetside Boosters." But we're not your ordinary type of gang. We are a group of Sangamon State students who are interested in the problems of children and youth. For the past several months most of us have been meeting in the basement of an old school on the East Side looking into the problems of kids growing up in Springfield. Police and court statistics show that kids living in an area from Carpenter to South Grand and from 11th to 19th Streets face a much greater chance of getting picked up by the police and sent to juvenile court than kids from most other sections of town. Now, we all know that kids from all over the city get involved in delinquent behavior, but kids from *this area* are five times as likely to end up in court.

As we became aware of these facts in our studies we naturally started talking about how things could be changed. We know that a number of different social agencies are doing things in this area but that doesn't seem to be keeping kids out of trouble. We looked at what some other cities are doing and found that one of the best ways of helping kids with problems is to get people living *in the neighborhood* to work together in reaching out to them. This is done by encouraging activities that will benefit all children growing up in the neighborhood. No one knows these kids any better than you do.

That's the reason why we're putting this leaflet in your door and in the doors of all the other homes and apartments in this area. We believe that you can help keep kids out of trouble.

FIGURE 7-3   There Is a New Gang in the Neighborhood

In the ensuing months, this "gang in the neighborhood" gathered momentum and received considerable support from Chicago Area Project staff throughout the state. The Booster philosophy slowly emerged during this time. See Figure 7-4.

The Streetside Boosters are both experiencing community acceptance and developing indigenous leadership within the East Side. They also have effectively diverted juveniles in trouble away from the justice system. In one particular situation, a number of people from the neighborhood attended juvenile court and persuaded the juvenile judge to return a youth to the neighborhood, rather than send him to the department of corrections.

SUMMARY

Turning juveniles away from further processing by the juvenile justice system is an important social goal. Diversion has become somewhat of a fad and is looked upon by many as a panacea for youth crime. Diversion, in its broad sense, is found in programs sponsored by the police, the juvenile court and probation, and agencies outside the justice system. The youth service bureau, especially, has gained popularity in working with youthful offenders. However, mounting evidence challenges the efficacy of diversionary programs; the most serious criticism is that they result in more youngsters getting caught in the net of the juvenile justice system.

From police to community-based corrections, little evidence exists that the system works or that it effectively discharges its mission of keeping kids from coming back. Diversionary programming, as this chapter noted, also has questionable effectiveness and may in the long run do more damage than it does good, for diversion is after the fact and results in more youths becoming involved with the justice system. Although delinquency prevention too has generally fallen far short of stemming or controlling youth crime, community organization appears to be a promising method of dealing with youth law-violating behavior. The Chicago Area Project generally and local incorporation of the philosophy of this project specifically are recommended as ways for communities to deal more effectively with juveniles in trouble.

FIGURE 7-4

THE BOOSTER PHILOSOPHY

1. The neighborhood is the unit of operation.

2. Most parents in high delinquency areas are concerned about their children and their welfare and are distressed at the prospect of their getting into trouble with the law.

3. People living in high delinquency areas possess a largely untapped abundance of intelligence, skills, talents, leadership abilities, interests, concerns, and potentials.

4. These people are quite capable of designing, funding, operating, and evaluating neighborhood based programs for the welfare of their own children.

5. Such programs can be successful because they provide the neighborhood and its people with real opportunities of earning and exercising pride, self-respect, autonomy, independence, personal involvement, self-responsibility, self-confidence and self-fulfillment.

...ness because of their "outside" nature and their inability to thereby satisfy the personal and neighborhood needs listed above. In addition, we assume that any method which attempts to treat in individualistic terms those persons whose life organization is the product of a whole set of community forces is subject to very serious limitations. Such persons can respond to a program of social treatment to the extent that the program addresses itself to and embraces the whole social world in which the individual is immersed.

7. All neighborhood residents are welcome to participate in the area project program regardless of their past activities or record. The only requirement is a sincere interest in the welfare of neighborhood children. Local residents are not regarded as clients or beneficiaries, but as indispensible agents through which community betterment programs can be effectively administered.

8. No child, regardless of how disruptive his behavior, is excluded from the program. Special efforts are made to deal with the hardest to reach kids.

9. When a child or adult from the neighborhood is incarcerated, the neighborhood committee remains in contact with him/her and paves the way back into the neighborhood and a more desirable role in it.

10. When paid staff are utilized as neighborhood workers or streetworkers, they are to be local residents. Trained staff are utilized to serve as catalysts to initiate area projects in new neighborhood areas and to train the new resident leaders until the program becomes autonomous.

11. The area project seeks to utilize to the maximum established neighborhood institutions.

12. The activities program is regarded primarily as a device for enlisting the active participation of local residents in a constructive community enterprise and creating and crystalizing neighborhood sentiment with regard to the task of promoting the welfare of children and the social and physical improvement of the neighborhood as a whole.

13. All activities are carried on with a view to aiding the neighborhood to become conscious of the problem of delinquency, collectively interested in the welfare of its children, and active in promoting programs for such improvements of the community environment as will develop in the children interests and habits of a constructive and socially desirable character.

14. WE NEVER GIVE UP ON A KID!

QUESTIONS

1. What is your evaluation of diversion?

2. How frequently does true diversion take place in the juvenile justice system?

3. Why is the charge that diversion widens the net of the juvenile justice system so serious?

4. Why has true diversion failed to live up to the expectations of its supporters?

5. Do you believe that the Streetside Boosters could serve as a model for other communities? What are the shortcomings of this model?

ENDNOTES

1. President's Commission on Law Enforcement and Administration of Justice, *Task Force Report: Juvenile Delinquency and Youth Crime* (Washington, D.C.: U.S. Government Printing Office, 1967), p. 2.

2. Robert K. Merton, *Social Theory and Social Structure,* 2d ed. (New York: Free Press, 1957), pp. 421–426.

3. Edwin M. Lemert, *Social Pathology* (New York: McGraw-Hill Book Company, 1951).

4. Frank Tannenbaum, *Crime in the Community* (Boston: Ginn and Company, 1938), p. 31.

5. Edwin H. Sutherland and Donald R. Cressey, *Criminology* (Philadelphia: J. B. Lippincott Company, 1974).

6. Andrew Rutherford and Robert McDermott, *National Evaluation Program Phase I Summary Report: Juvenile Diversion* (Washington, D.C.: U.S. Government Printing Office, September 1976), pp. 2–3.

7. Ibid., pp. 3–4.

8. *Phase I Assessment of Youth Service Bureaus, Summary Report of Youth Service Bureau Research Group for LEAA* (Boston: Boston University, 1975), pp. 104–106.

9. Several of the following programs are discussed in: Dan Pursuit et al., *Police Programs for Preventing Crime and Delinquency* (Springfield, Ill.: Charles C Thomas Publishers, 1972).

10. Roger Baron and Floyd Feeney, *Juvenile Diversion through Family Counseling: A Program for the Diversion of Status Offenders in Sacramento County, California* (Washington, D.C.: U.S. Government Printing Office, February 1976).

11. Edwin Lemert, *Instead of Court: Diversion in Juvenile Justice* (Washington, D.C.: U.S. Government Printing Office, 1971), pp. 27–28.

12. Sherwood Norman, *Youth Service Bureau: A Key to Prevention* (Paramus, N.J.: National Council on Crime and Delinquency, 1972), pp. 12–13.

13. Sherwood Norman, *The Youth Service Bureau: A Brief Description of Five Programs* (Paramus, N.J.: National Council on Crime and Delinquency, 1970), pp. 1–15.

14. *Phase I Assessment of Youth Service Bureaus,* pp. 45–46.

15. Daniel Katkin, Drew Hyman, and John Kramer, *Juvenile Delinquency and the Juvenile Justice System* (North Scituate, Mass.: Duxbury Press, 1976), pp. 422–423.
16. Norman, *The Youth Service Bureau,* pp. 11–12.
17. *Phase I Assessment of Youth Service Bureaus,* pp. iv–vii.
18. Rutherford and McDermott, *Juvenile Diversion,* p. 5.
19. Mike Brown, a former staff member of the Springfield, Illinois Youth Service Bureau, contributed these characteristics of the effective advocate.

REFERENCES

Carter, Robert M., and Klein, Malcolm W. *Back on the Streets.* Englewood Cliffs, N.J.: Prentice-Hall, 1976.
> *Has a number of good readings on diversion.*

Gibbons, Don C., and Blake, Gerald F. "Evaluating the Impact of Juvenile Diversion Programs." *Crime and Delinquency* 22 (October 1976): 411–420.
> *Does a good job in evaluating the present effectiveness of diversionary programming.*

Lemert, Edwin M. *Instead of Court: Diversion in Juvenile Justice.* Chevy Chase, Md.: National Institute of Mental Health, 1971.
> *Although it is now dated, Lemert's monograph remains an important resource in the study of juvenile diversion.*

Phase I Assessment of Youth Service Bureaus, Summary Report of Youth Service Bureau Research Group for LEAA. Boston: Boston University, 1975.
> *A really first-rate study of the youth service bureau.*

Rutherford, Andrew, and McDermott, Robert. *National Evaluation Program Phase I Summary Report: Juvenile Diversion.* Washington, D.C.: U.S. Government Printing Office, September 1976.
> *This brief pamphlet provides a good overview of diversion and clearly presents its major shortcomings.*

part II

INSTITUTIONALIZATION

8

Closed Juvenile Facilities

Some juveniles break the law again and again. The juvenile justice system is lenient up to a point, but confinement is imminent if youths are believed to be dangerous to themselves or to others or if they show little sign of mending their ways. Some youths, however, are placed in detention although they have not broken the law. Children as young as three years old occasionally are found in jail, and children who have no families are put in training schools and detention homes. Other noncriminal youths who are misplaced into various corrective institutions include status offenders, the mentally ill, the mentally retarded, the epileptic, the handicapped, and the chronically disordered.

Detention homes, shelters, reception or diagnostic centers, training schools, ranches, forestry camps, and farms are all considered corrective elements of the juvenile justice system. In addition, so many youths are confined in county jails and police lockups that these, too, must be considered part of the juvenile justice system; to ignore these facilities is to do a great injustice to the youths who are confined in them.

This chapter examines these institutions and their history and general functions. Special attention is paid to training schools, because they hold youths for the longest periods of time.

THE HISTORY OF JUVENILE CORRECTIONAL INSTITUTIONS

The Beginnings

At the time of the American Revolution, the penal system in the colonies was modeled after that in England. The larger urban jails,

"Spare the rod and spoil the child."

county jails, and prisons contained men, women, and juveniles who were felons, misdemeanants, insane, and sane—sometimes without any separation. Smaller rural counties, on the other hand, had less need for these larger jails and prisons of the cities.

In neither city nor county were youths expected to get into trouble, but if they did, they were subject to the same punishments as adults. Beyond that, normal community processes were thought sufficient to keep them in line. Community norms were enforced through gossip, ridicule, and other informal social pressures, and little formal social control was needed. Watchmen, magistrates, and sheriffs were the local enforcers, and those caught, including youths, received fines, beatings, and floggings; were put in stocks; were driven through town in carts to be ridiculed by the citizenry; and, in extreme cases, were hanged, burned, mutilated, or banished from the community. After punishment, some youths were apprenticed to local craftsmen; others were sent, until about the middle of the 1800s, on extended whaling voyages; and still others were placed with relatives or farm families.[1]

In the late 1700s and early 1800s, the United States was in a period of transition. The rural way of life was threatened, and the changes were having an irreversible effect on the structure of society. There was increasing concern about what to do with the growing numbers of juveniles who were abandoned, were runaways, or had run afoul of community norms. The young nation was caught in a dilemma. On the one hand, thinkers reasoned that the natural depravity of man made attempts at rehabilitation useless and that banishing the guilty was simpler than either punishment or rehabilitation. On the other hand, some hoped to find specific causes for deviancy, and the family often was believed to be the source. Common sense and the examination of case histories indicated that older offenders usually had been problem children. The idea emerged that if institutions were to be set up for children, perhaps the well-adjusted family could provide the model. Similar models had long been used for the poor; why not for children who had problems?[2]

Regardless of the source of the problem, the situation demanded a solution. The increasing numbers of delinquents and of children running in the streets of larger cities, the increase in population, and the changing character of society in the United States were all putting increased pressure on existing facilities. Conditions in the jails and prisons were deplorable. Troubled youths were sentenced for fixed periods of time and were confined with the worst society had to offer. Some youths died of disease, and morals were corrupted as children ten to eighteen years old were confined with adult felons.

The First Homes.   When citizens and reformers became concerned about these inhumane conditions, their solution was the house of refuge. These houses were for all children, not just delinquents. Benevolence and compassion, along with concern over the degrading conditions in the jails and prisons, motivated the development of the homes.

New York started the first school for males in 1825, followed by Boston in 1826 and Philadelphia in 1828. Other cities, including Bangor, Richmond, Mobile, Cincinnati, and Chicago, all followed suit over the years. Twenty-three schools were built in the 1830s and thirty more in the 1840s. Of these, the vast majority were for males, with an occasional institution reserved for females. Their capacity ranged from 90 at Lancaster, Massachusetts to 1,000 at the New York House of Refuge, with a median number of 210. The promise of these institutions seemed so great that youths with every type of problem were placed in them. The New York Reformatory accepted children adjudicated guilty of committing crimes as well as those who simply were in danger of getting into trouble. The poor, destitute, incorrigible, and orphaned were all confined. Admissions policies were obviously quite flexible, and little concern was shown for due process; some youths were simply kidnapped off the streets. Not until later did institutions begin to limit their rosters to those who had committed crimes.

The children generally were confined for periods ranging from less than six weeks to about twenty-four months, although some stayed longer. In some institutions the youths were taught trades, such as manufacturing shoes, brushes, and chairs, or were readied for apprenticeships to local craftsmen. Sentences were indeterminate and superintendents of the institutions made the decision as to whether the apprenticed youths would be released or returned to the institution.

The first of these early reformatories set aside for females was chartered in New York in 1824. Some schools were biracial, but many, especially those in the southern states, were segregated. Even in the North, blacks were often sent to the state prisons and county jails rather than to the new houses of refuge.

These juvenile institutions accepted the family model wholeheartedly, for it was designed to implant the order, discipline, and care of the family into institutional life. The institution, in effect, would become the home, peers become the family, and staff become the parents. The central thrust of the schools was to separate youths from the degradations and temptations of the vice-ridden and disorganized cities. Orphanages and houses of refuge offered such separation, but they were marked by a rigorous system of control and discipline. The ordered life of the house of refuge was to be substituted for the disordered life of the community.

Discipline would be severe if rules were disobeyed, but the reformers believed that once the authority of the superintendents was established, they would be looked upon admiringly and as friends. Belief in these principles was so great that parents for the first time had to surrender their authority to superintendents and could not participate in the upbringing of their unruly children.

The first houses of refuge did not differ greatly from the existing state prisons and county jails. Built to hold inmates securely, some were surrounded by walls, and their interiors were designed to implant the notions of order and rationality in their charges:

> The buildings were usually four stories high, with two long hallways running along either side of a row of cells. The rooms, following one after another, were all five by eight feet wide, seven feet high, windowless, with an iron-lattice slab for a door and flues for ventilation near the ceiling.

Each group of eleven cells could be locked or unlocked simultaneously with one master key; every aperture within an inmate's reach was guarded by iron. On the first floor of each wing was a huge tub for bathing, sizeable enough to hold fifteen to twenty boys; on the fourth floor were ten special punishment cells.[3]

These institutions were based on the congregate system, with large numbers of clients sharing a single room or cell. Some later facilities, especially those built after 1850, were based on the cottage system, which will be discussed later.

Treatment of the youths paralleled the sameness of the facility's physical plant. When the youths entered, they were dressed in identical clothing and given identical hair cuts. If they caused trouble, they were punished. Placing offenders on a diet of bread and water or depriving them of meals altogether were milder forms of punishment. A bread-and-water diet was often coupled with solitary confinement if a severe punishment was deemed necessary. Corporal punishment, used by itself or in combination with other punishment, consisted of whipping with a cat-o-nine-tails or manacling with a ball and chain. The worst offenders were shipped off to sea.

The rules were devised to inculcate order, obedience, and discipline; hence, the school, the workshop, and the church were all brought into the house of refuge. Routines were established, schedules were organized, and the homes began to resemble military organizations rather than families. Youths were awakened by bells and their days were partitioned by the ringing of bells. They awoke at sunrise, were marched to washrooms, paraded in ranks for inspection, marched to chapel, attended school for an hour, and went to breakfast when the bells rang again at seven o'clock. From seven-thirty until noon the boys worked in the shops, making nails and other needed items of the day, and the girls sewed, did laundry, cooked, and cleaned. The lunch hour was from noon until one o'clock, and then work was continued until five o'clock. A half-hour was allowed for washing and eating, following which there were two-and-a-half hours of evening classes. After the evening prayer, youths were marched back to their cells, were locked in, and were expected to be quiet for the night until the routine began again.[4]

The specific order of daily events varied from institution to institution, but all followed the same basic schedule and routine. In some, youths were counted frequently to make sure that none had escaped, and in many facilities, silence was maintained at all times, even during the recreation and exercise periods. Eating at any time other than regularly scheduled meals was forbidden, and youths who wanted more food at lunch or dinner had to raise a hand to request it. In school, everyone answered questions by reciting in unison.

As the use of these houses continued into the 1840s and 1850s, some of the institutions were called industrial schools, and states began to set up their own training schools. Many of these schools also began to segregate the delinquent from the nondelinquent. Concern over the stigmatizing effects of confinement led some reformers to change the names of the schools. Some were named after individuals and others after their locations, such as the George Junior Republic and Sleighton Farms. By 1857 seventeen of the existing institutions for children were primarily for delinquents, with a combined population of 20,000 youths.

The Cottage System. Introduced in 1854, the cottage system spread throughout the country. Reformers had succeeded in placing the industrial schools outside cities, their rationale being that youths on farms would be reformed when exposed to the rural virtues, the simple way of life, and the bounty of Mother Nature. With the new cottage system, the process of individual reform could be furthered, as residents were housed in separate buildings, usually no more than twenty to forty per cottage. The training schools were no longer supposed to be fortress-like in either physical design or in the relationships within them. The first cottages were log cabins; later ones were of brick or stone. This form of organization was widely accepted and is the basic design for many juvenile facilities even today.

The rural way of life also permitted the youths to help support themselves. With good management, the institution not only could raise its own food but also might realize a profit. Youths worked the fields and took care of the livestock, thereby learning responsibility and new work skills.

Three major changes began to affect juvenile institutions in the final decades of the nineteenth century—the increasing size of their populations, a decrease in funds from state legislatures, and the admission of more dangerous offenders. As a result, the industrial school became custodial, and superintendents had to accept custodianship as an adequate goal. The industrial school was still better than the jails, reformers reasoned, and the dangerous classes were at least being isolated from society. Faith in the industrial school continued into the twentieth century. Youths were generally confined for less than two years, and very few remained confined for over four years.

The Present   Only minor modifications have taken place in the way society has dealt with institutionalized juveniles throughout the twentieth century. The most impressive modification is the evolution of treatment. Case histories had been used since the founding of the very first homes, but by the 1920s they had become a fundamental element of juvenile corrections, though used more in arriving at parole decisions than in

FIGURE 8-1   St. Charles Training School, one of the old cottage systems. Courtesy Illinois Department of Corrections.

treatment. They are still available if therapists want to use them. Juvenile corrections has moved toward the scientific handling of clients as they are classified into fine gradations in many facilities. A growing emphasis is now placed on individualized diagnosis and treatment, including individual psychotherapy and group therapy. Guided group interaction and positive peer culture, in particular, have become popular therapies.

Juveniles now are able to graduate from state-accredited high school programs while confined in training schools. Some youths are permitted home furloughs; some even are allowed to work in the community during the day. Recreational programs in the institution have become more diverse, as have vocational programs; printing, barbering, welding, and painting are among the courses offered in a well-equipped training school.

Finally, the structure of juvenile institutions has changed somewhat during this century. The types of juvenile institutions have multiplied to include ranches and forestry camps (minimum security), educational and vocational training schools (medium security), and end-of-the-line institutions (maximum security). Some of the larger training schools have abandoned the cottage system and have returned to incorporating the entire facility under one roof. Cottage parents are being replaced in many groups by staff members who work eight-hour shifts.

THE PROCESSING OF JUVENILES

After youths are picked up by the police and referred to the courts, a decision is made as to whether they can remain with their families or must be placed in detention. If they are placed in detention, they end up in a jail, a detention home, a juvenile hall, or a reception or diagnostic center of the juvenile court. The juvenile court, as noted in Chapter 4, may also assign these youths to a shelter or to a foster home.

The primary concern in this chapter is the youth who is placed in an institution. In many states such youths are briefly detained in a diagnostic or reception center before being assigned to some other facility. These reception and diagnostic centers are sometimes found in specific institutions rather than in a centralized state or regional coordinating agency whose sole function is diagnosis.

After diagnosis and classification, the youth is remanded to the institution believed to be most appropriate for him. Again, since many states do not have reception and diagnostic centers, youths are simply thrown in wherever space exists. Some states do make an effort to segregate youths on some basis such as age, previous criminal history, or behavioral characteristics, but few make any really serious effort at accurate classification. (This will be examined in greater detail in Chapter 11.)

The institutions are divided into two general categories: temporary care facilities and correctional facilities. Detention homes, shelters, reception or diagnostic centers, and jails are temporary care facilities; training schools, ranches, forestry camps, and farms are correctional facilities. A primary difference between these two types of facilities is the absence of correctional programs in temporary care facilities. Another difference lies in the much shorter length of stay required in temporary care facilities. Also, most temporary care facilities house both females and males in the same general location, whereas correctional facilities generally separate them.

THE NATURE OF SECURITY

Security in the temporary care and correctional facilities varies considerably; it may be minimum, medium, or maximum. Generally, though, shelters, camps, ranches, and farms are minimum or medium security, whereas detention homes, training schools, and jails are maximum security. With the exception of the occasional out-patient diagnostic centers, most diagnostic and reception centers are maximum or medium security, especially since many are connected with training schools.

Maximum security institutions for juveniles do not quite parallel those for adults. Training schools are generally surrounded by fences but rarely have the walls or guards characteristic of the adult prison. These fences are fairly high and are sometimes electrified or consist of two fences, one inside the other. The interiors of juvenile maximum security facilities suggest totality more than do their exteriors. Hallways are often bleak, and doors to rooms, cells, and institutional areas are usually locked. The staff, who wear street clothes, carry large rings of keys for the locked doors, which are often of heavy steel. Windows are so small that a youth could not escape even if the thick glass or plexiglass could be broken and they are covered by heavy screens or bars. Exits to the outside may be both chained and locked. On the brighter side, many of today's modern institutions have individual rooms and small dormitories, but security and control are still the basic concern of staff.

Medium security institutions do not differ much from the maximum security facilities. Custody and control are still a prime concern of staff, and head counts still are occasionally made. Probably the main difference between the two is that the atmosphere is slightly more relaxed and residents can move about more freely, are trusted a little more, and are permitted more off-campus visits than in maximum security facilities. But life still centers about the institution, with the youth's relationship to the community almost nonexistent.

Minimum security facilities continue the trend toward relaxed relations between the residents and staff. Residents may have keys to their rooms, be permitted to move freely on the grounds, and realize that the absence of a fence makes escape possible practically any time they wish. Staff still supervise residents fairly closely, but with nothing of the rigorousness of the maximum security institutions. Youths are permitted to have home visits more frequently than in the other types of institutions and may hold jobs in the community. In some cases, residents of training schools and detention homes are allowed to attend community schools.

THE EXTENT OF JUVENILE FACILITIES

By the 1970s approximately 722 juvenile facilities were in operation in the United States; of these, about half were state and half locally operated.[5] Table 8-1 shows the number of children held on one day by

TABLE 8-1   Number of Juvenile Facilities and Number of Children Held on June 30, 1971

Type of Facility	Number of Facilities	Number of Children Held on June 30, 1971		
		Total	Male	Female
All facilities in the U.S.	722	57,239	44,140	13,099
Dentention centers	303	11,748	7,912	3,836
Shelters	18	363	237	126
Reception or diagnostic centers	17	2,486	1,988	498
Training schools	192	35,931	27,839	8,092
Ranches, forestry camps, and farms	114	5,666	5,376	290
Halfway houses and group homes	78	1,045	788	257

From: U.S. Department of Justice, *Children in Custody: A Report on the Juvenile Detention and Correctional Facility Census of 1971* (Washington, D.C.: U.S. Government Printing Office), p. 1.

each type of facility. It is immediately obvious that detention centers, training schools, and ranches, camps, and farms outnumber other facilities. The bulk of the population remains in training schools and detention centers. It is also important to note that the population of jails is not included in these figures, even though it is estimated that jails receive over 100,000 youths each year. Thus, jails also are a very important part of the juvenile justice system. The impact on youths, then, of training schools, detention homes, and jails is considerable. When the number of youths in detention homes is added to that of youths in training schools, we find a total of 47,700 out of 57,239 in these two types of facilities.

Table 8-2 shows the number of clients held in all juvenile facilities. Detention homes, it should be noted, usually hold both males and females, whereas training schools most frequently house males and females in totally separate facilities. Ranches, camps, and farms are oriented primarily toward males, as are halfway houses and group

TABLE 8-2   Number and Percent of Juvenile Facilities by Sex of Inmates, June 30, 1971

	TOTAL FACILITIES		FACILITIES HOLDING MALES ONLY		FACILITIES HOLDING FEMALES ONLY		FACILITIES HOLDING MALES AND FEMALES	
	Number	Percent	Number	Percent	Number	Percent	Number	Percent
All Facilities	722	100	278	38	86	12	358	50
Detention centers	303	100	7	2	5	2	291	96
Shelters	18	100	3	17	1	5	14	78
Reception or diag-nostic centers	17	100	3	18	2	12	12	70
Training schools	192	100	106	55	51	27	35	18
Ranches, forestry camps, and farms	114	100	103	90	8	7	3	3
Halfway houses and groups homes	78	100	56	72	19	24	3	4

Adapted from U.S. Department of Justice, *Children in Custody: A Report on the Juvenile Detention and Correctional Facility Census of 1971* (Washington, D.C.: U.S. Government Printing Office), p. 4.

homes. The number of training schools for females is about half those for males, since males are processed for crimes more frequently than are females.

Table 8-3 shows the length of sentences being served by clients in the different types of facilities. Stays in temporary care facilities are fairly brief; youths assigned to reception and diagnostic centers have longer stays, of slightly over one-and-one-third months. Detention center residents have the shortest stays—eleven days on the average. Confinement in correctional facilities is considerably longer. Youths are kept in training schools an average of 8.7 months, receive slightly shorter stays that average 7.2 months in ranches, forestry camps, and farms, and average 6.6 months in halfway houses and group homes. The training school, then, holds youths for the longest periods of time. The significance of this fact will become apparent in the next several chapters.

Examination of Table 8-4 shows that detention centers and train-ing schools have the highest capacity of any of the institutions. Any institution with a capacity of more than 150 spaces is considered by many to be a large institution. Examination of Table 8-4 shows that a striking number of the 116 training schools have a capacity of 150 or more. Detention homes have the next largest capacities, with 15 hold-

TABLE 8-3   Estimated Average Length of Inmate Stay for Fiscal 1971, by Type of Facility

Type of Facility	Average Length of Stay
All temporary care facilities	14 days
Detention centers	11 days
Shelters	20 days
Reception or diagnostic centers	51 days
All correctional facilities	7.8 months
Training schools	8.7 months
Ranches, forestry camps, and farms	6.6 months
Halfway houses and group homes	7.2 months

Adapted from U.S. Department of Justice, *Children in Custody: A Report on the Juvenile Detention and Correctional Facility Census of 1971* (Washington, D.C.: U.S. Government Printing Office), p. 4.

ing 150 or more clients. Significantly, slightly fewer than half of the detention homes hold fewer than 25 residents, with 79 holding fewer than 50, as the halfway houses and group homes are almost all designed for fairly small populations.

The facilities do differ in the type of juvenile they house, but Table 8-5 shows that all categories of juveniles, including adjudicated delinquents, juveniles awaiting court disposition, dependent and neglected children, and juveniles awaiting transfer to other jurisdictions, are put in all types of facilities, with the exception of the ranches, forestry camps, and farms.

Another surprising fact is that the vast majority of institutions do not provide separate facilities for different categories of clients. For example, of detention homes holding both adjudicated delinquents and juveniles awaiting court disposition, 279 mix the youths and only 13, or 5 percent, separate them. That pattern holds for just about all the facilities and all of the categories. This is significant because dependent and neglected youths and juveniles who are awaiting court disposition have not been proven to have committed any crime; yet they are confined with hard-core juvenile offenders. Add to these figures the many thousands of similar youths who are confined in jails and police lockups each year, and the story is grim indeed.

TABLE 8-4 Number of Juvenile Facilities by Designed Capacity by Type of Facility, June 30, 1971

Type of Facility	Total Number of Facilities	Fewer Than 25 Inmates	25–49	50–99	100–149	200–299	300–399	400–499	500 or More
All Facilities	722	238	134	148	61	55	28	8	12
Detention centers	303	142	79	50	17	4	4	1	1
Shelters	18	14	2	—	1	—	—	—	—
Reception or diagnostic centers	17	—	3	3	3	4	3	—	—
Training schools	192	11	6	31	28	47	21	7	11
Ranches, forestry camps, and farms	114	4	34	64	11	—	—	—	—
Halfway houses and group homes	78	67	10	—	1	—	—	—	—

Designed Capacity of Facilities

From: U.S. Department of Justice, *Children in Custody: A Report on the Juvenile Detention and Correctional Facility Census of 1971* (Washington, D.C.: U.S. Government Printing Office), p. 5.

TABLE 8-5 Juvenile Facilities by Type of Inmate Holding Patterns by Type of Facility, Fiscal Year 1971

Type of Facility	Total Facilities	Adjudicated Delinquents and Juveniles Awaiting Court Disposition			Adjudicated Delinquents and Dependent and Neglected Children			Juveniles Awaiting Court Disposition and Dependent and Neglected Children			Dependent and Neglected children and Juveniles Awaiting Transfer to Another Jurisdiction		
		Total Facilities	FACILITIES That Hold Separately		Total Facilities	FACILITIES That Hold Separately		Total Facilities	FACILITIES That Hold Separately		Total Facilities	FACILITIES That Hold Separately	
			Number	Per cent		Number	Per cent		Number	Per cent		Number	Per cent
All Types of Facilities	722	317	26	8	157	33	21	150	33	22	148	35	24
Detention centers	303	279	13	5	124	30	24	132	32	24	130	33	25
Shelters	18	12	3	25	8	2	25	10	1	10	10	1	10
Reception or diagnostic centers	17	2	—	—	4	—	—	2	—	—	2	1	50
Training schools	192	20	10	50	11	—	—	4	—	—	4	—	—
Ranches, forestry camps and farms	114	2	—	—	1	1	100	—	—	—	—	—	—
Halfway houses and group homes	78	2	—	—	9	—	—	2	—	—	2	—	—

FACILITIES HOLDING

From: U.S. Department of Justice, *Children in Custody: A Report on the Juvenile Detention and Correctional Facility Census of 1971* (Washington, D.C.: U.S. Government Printing Office), p. 13.

Finally, some mention should be made of the costs of these facilities. Table 8-6, from the National Assessment of Juvenile Corrections, shows the 1974 average costs for a year's stay in state institutions, camps, and ranches. In twenty-six states the average yearly cost per offender is between $5,000 and $11,000. The cost in ten states is between $14,000 and $19,000, with a mean of $11,657. These figures are no doubt higher today because of inflation. In addition, the 1971 *Children in Custody* survey found that the correctional facilities cost less than the temporary care facilities. If temporary care facility costs were calculated as well, the costs per offender per year undoubtedly would rise even higher.

These costs are significant, since considerable controversy now exists over justifying the relative costs of confining youths in correctional institutions or putting them in community-based programs. According to figures from the NAJC study, halfway houses and group homes are the cheapest and reception or diagnostic centers are the most costly. The latter, no doubt, cost more because of the number of professionals and the special testing services needed in their operation. Nevertheless, the argument for community treatment because it is cheaper holds some merit.

TABLE 8-6   1974 Average Costs per Offender-Year for State Institutions, Camps, and Ranches

	Number of States
$ 3,500– 4,999	3
5,000– 7,999	11
8,000–10,999	15
11,000–13,999	4
14,000–18,999	10
19,000 and over	4
Total	47

Note: Mean = $11,657.

From: Vinter, et al., *National Assessment of Juvenile Corrections* (Ann Arbor: University of Michigan, 1975), p. 25.

JAILS AND DETENTION HOMES

The dependent and neglected in some jurisdictions are placed in foster homes and under shelter care, but in many parts of the country they end up in jails and detention homes. They are, then, confined either with youths being held for disposition by the court or with incarcerated adult offenders.

Jails

Jails have changed very little in the past 200 years. Many of the earliest jails, in fact, are still in use today, and about 44 percent of the cells are at least twenty-five years old. The federal government has rated only 20 percent of all jails as suitable for federal offenders. Goldfarb comments on his impressions of one jail:

> I was shocked to discover conditions so horrible I could not believe them. The jail was far worse than the state prisons I had just seen. Inside a relatively modern exterior in a modest, busy part of town was a cramped, dark, dank interior. Large four-sided cages each held sixteen men, with disheveled beds and an open toilet. Inmates are kept inside these cages twenty-four hours a day throughout their often prolonged stays at the Atlanta jail. There is no privacy and no activity at all, artificial air and light, and nothing at all to do day and night. A dismal atmosphere, a constant din and a wretched stench pervaded the place.[6]

Later, in discussing the abuse of juveniles by detention staff and in prisons, Goldfarb reiterates a common theme. Most of the children in these jails have done nothing, yet they are subjected to the cruelest of abuses. They are confined in overcrowded facilities, forced to perform brutal exercise routines, punished by beatings by staff and peers, put in isolation, and whipped. They have their heads held under water in toilets. They are raped by both staff and peers, gassed in their cells, and sometimes stomped or beaten to death by adult prisoners. A number of youths not killed by others end up killing themselves.[7] Even if these youths were guilty of something, few people would condone this type of treatment.

Given the character of these facilities, the fact that only five states actually prohibit jailing youths under any circumstance is appalling. Table 8-7 shows the conditions under which states permit the jailing of juveniles.

Probably the most distressing fact brought out by Table 8-7 is that juveniles can be jailed at all. However, they not only can be jailed, but also can be so confined without court orders, purely at the discretion of the police. Some of the youths who are jailed are merely dependent and neglected, and more than half of them are only status offenders. Other

TABLE 8-7   Statutory Provisions Governing Jailing of Juveniles

Statutory Provision	Number of States
Under no circumstances	5
If approved by Department of Social Services	1
With a court order	11
Without a court order if 15–16	2
Without a court order if 12–14	11
Without a court order if a "menace"	4
In separate sections	15
Any time, any place	2

Table from Rosemary C. Sarri, "The Detention of Youth in Jails and Juvenile Detention Facilities." Reprinted from *Juvenile Justice* (November 1973), Journal of the National Council of Juvenile Court Judges.

youths are convicted and awaiting further legal action and some are serving sentences of varying lengths. For example, of the youths listed as jailed in the *1960 Census, Special Report, Inmates of Institutions*, 4 percent had been jailed for periods ranging from one to two-and-a-half years; another 4 percent for between two-and-a-half and five years; over 3 percent for between five and ten years; and nearly 4 percent—505 children—had been jailed more than ten years.[8]

The larger counties and cities of this nation apparently do not feel they have to place youths in detention. Yet, when problems do arise, they must put these youths somewhere; they, therefore, continue to place their neglected or delinquent children in jails or lockups. Of the 100,000 or so children placed in these facilities, 66 percent have not been found guilty of anything. Only three states claim that jails are never used for children. Even in the nine states that forbid by law the placing of juveniles in jails, some local administrators obviously do not comply. Other states prohibit the placement of juveniles with adults, but these laws, too, are often violated. Shocking too is the fact that children under seven years old have been confined in substandard county jails for lack of shelter care or foster homes. The practice of jailing juveniles is considered so harmful that it has been objected to by virtually all professionals, including psychologists, psychiatrists, sociologists, penologists, the International Association of Chiefs of Police, the National Sheriff's Association, the U.S. Children's Bureau, and the National Council on Crime and Delinquency.

Training of jail personnel is a universal need. Jails are sadly lacking in any organized programs. The National Jail Census found that

FIGURE 8-2 Juvenile Wing of the Sangamon Secure Juvenile Detention Facility, Springfield, Illinois. Courtesy of Larry Gruff.

86 percent of the jails in the nation do not have recreational programs; 90 percent lack educational facilities; and only slightly over 50 percent have medical services.[9] Considering the possibility of rehabilitation in this context borders on the absurd.

The use of jails is, unfortunately, an important part of our juvenile corrections philosophy. Not only do jails hold large numbers of youths, but the conditions under which they are held have considerable adverse impact on the residents. Clearly, youths should never be confined in a jail; but the alternative believed necessary by many states, the detention home, is often not much of an improvement.

Detention Homes

The horrible conditions of early jails and prisons led reformers to look for alternative placements for children. The training school was one early answer, but these houses of refuge were generally looked upon as longer-term facilities. Something else was needed, not only in recognition of the belief that children were different from adults, but also as an alternative to the extremely degrading conditions found in the jails and prisons. The juvenile court was viewed as part of the answer to treating children, but it did not supply a place to put these juveniles. The detention home soon emerged and was so well accepted that these homes spread all over the nation to the present day; 66 percent of the population is now served by close to 300 detention homes. Still, by the late 1960s eleven states did not have any homes, nor did 93 percent of the counties. Reuterman's nationwide survey in 1970 identified 288 detention homes in the United States, which handled approximately 488,800 youths per year, an increase over the 317,860 found in a national study done in the mid-sixties. The average daily population of these homes was estimated at 13,567, with an average of 61 youths per home. The figures also indicated that 26.5 percent were almost always overcrowded and another 28.5 percent were occasionally overcrowded. Thus, 55 percent of the detention homes in the United States were operating above capacity, with larger homes operating above capacity more often than the smaller ones.[10]

The detention facilities are run by the city or county government, the welfare department, state agencies, or the court. These homes are as varied as the agencies running them. Some are converted dwellings made secure, while others are fortress-like additions to local jails and courthouses. Some differences in security practices exist, but most are considered medium to maximum security with a definite custodial emphasis. For example, when administrators in the Reuterman study were asked what the goals of their detention homes were, their responses fell into four categories:

> *Custody* as stressing the provision of a secure, restricted, short-term environment; *rehabilitation* as stressing improved adjustment in any way, or the provision of an opportunity for study or observation; *humanitarian* as stressing the provision of a pleasant homelike atmosphere; and *punishment* as stressing showing them they must pay for their behavior or similar responses.[11]

A more detailed breakdown of the orientation of detention home administration is shown in Table 8-8.

A further perspective was gained by comparing the size of a home with its orientation. Table 8-9 gives the information that Reuterman obtained on the size and orientation of seventy homes. The figures show that fully 60 percent of the superintendents considered custody to be their primary orientation. These findings run counter to the orientation of most professionals, who believe that rehabilitation and helping children should be the desired goals of detention homes. That many improvements are needed is indicated by the next set of data.

When programs offered by the homes were examined, they were found to be woefully inadequate. (See Table 8-10.) The three most popular programs were schooling, which usually was carried on in conjunction with the public school system; recreation, which no doubt consisted primarily of playing cards and Ping-Pong or reading old

TABLE 8-8   Orientations of Detention Home Administrators* (N = 83)

Primary		Number	Percent
Custody		25	30.12
Rehabilitation		22	26.50
Humanitarian		7	8.43
Punishment		2	2.40
Custody	Rehabilitation	15	18.07
Custody	Humanitarian	2	2.40
Rehabilitation	Custody	7	8.43
Rehabilitation	Punishment	1	1.20
Humanitarian	Rehabilitation	1	1.20
Punishment	Rehabilitation	1	1.20

*Data was missing or could not be classified in nine homes.

Table from Nicholas Reuterman, *A National Study of Juvenile Detention Facilities* (Edwardsville, Ill.: Delinquency Study and Youth Development Project, Southern Illinois University, 1970), p. 32.

magazines; and work, which frequently meant such chores as keeping toilets and floors clean. Because many homes are understaffed, and those staff are undertrained and undereducated, two questions emerge: What is the quality of these programs? How effective are they?

The President's Commission on Law Enforcement and Administration of Justice stated that 82 percent of the homes had medical services. That report may have been accurate for the sample studied (242 homes), but it does not mean that youths in most homes have immediate access to a doctor; it merely means that 82 percent of the facilities made arrangements for medical services. Somewhat surprising too is the fact that less than 50 percent of the detention homes had caseworkers and psychologists. Considering that the purpose of detention is to provide temporary care for juveniles in trouble, these figures seem extremely low, especially since many youths are confined because they have problems that require professional care. Moreover, the care that is available is often of low quality. Only 35 percent of the facilities required their superintendents to have a bachelor's degree; only 16 percent required them to have a graduate degree; and about 50 percent

TABLE 8-9   Capacity of Detention Home and Primary Orientation* (N = 70)

Capacity	Custody	Rehabilitation	Total
20	12	4	16
20–50	15	14	29
51–100	7	5	12
101–200	6	3	9
200	2	2	4
Total	42	28	70

*Data on size of home was missing for two homes.

Table from Nicholas Reuterman, *A National Study of Juvenile Detention Facilities* (Edwardsville, Ill.: Delinquency Study and Youth Development Project, Southern Illinois University, 1970), p. 35.

TABLE 8-10   Number and Percent of Homes Offering Various Types of Programs (N = 167)

Program	Number	Percent
Use of volunteers	109	65.3
School	125	74.3
College personnel involved in programs	46	27.5
Work program	136	81.4
Recreation program	151	90.4
Group treatment methods	35	20.9
Public relations using detention home personnel	115	68.9
Other (religion, individual counseling, token economy)	92	55.1

Table adapted from Nicholas Reuterman, *A National Study of Juvenile Detention Facilities* (Edwardsville, Ill.: Delinquency Study and Youth Development Project, Southern Illinois University, 1970), p. 111.

did not require a bachelor's degree for staff supervisors.[12] No claim is made that a college degree is necessary for staff to care adequately for residents. However, since children in detention are upset upon finding themselves in such a situation, extreme skill and care must be exercised by the staff, and a degree, hopefully, should assure that personnel in the homes have some knowledge of and exposure to new methods of treatment and rehabilitation.

Not only, then, do detention facilities lack the full complement of services necessary for the comprehensive handling of juveniles, but the extreme variation in services—from none to adequate—that are offered from state to state means that many youths receive no care at all and are put in local jails or lockups, in training schools, or in reformatories. Some states have taken over the detention function from local jurisdictions, but the services still vary from the use of local jails and local detention centers to various forms of diagnostic and correctional programs. Many states simply reimburse counties and municipalities for providing detention services.

Another recent trend is the development of regional detention centers. In several states the regional detention center is actually a training school; in other states it is a separate facility. Yet, even if a separate facility is available, not all youths from all parts of the state are confined in the regional facilities and some are still kept in local jails, at least overnight. Fairly adequate clinical testing is available in some states, but in most, the youths are simply confined pending further legal action.

The foregoing statistics and information about the operation of the homes, unfortunately, do not tell the whole story; life on the inside is far more complex than is suggested by the statistics. Some homes, for example, are run by sensitive staff who genuinely try to be of benefit to the children; in others, residents receive inadequate diets, are beaten by staff and peers, are raped by peers and occasionally by staff, and, in general, are subjected to terrifying experiences. The extreme pressures put on some youths produce mental anguish, psychiatric illnesses, and physical disease. In addition, the fact of being in detention generates such hopelessness in some youths that they come to feel the only way out is suicide.

PUBLIC AND PRIVATE TRAINING SCHOOLS

Public Training Schools   The report of the President's Commission on Law Enforcement and Administration of Justice covered 220 state-operated facilities, which comprised 86 percent of the juvenile training facilities in the

United States. The remaining 14 percent were private or locally run operations and three institutions run by the federal government.[13] Six states had nine or more facilities, and eight had only one. (See Table 8-11.) Those with only two schools allotted one to boys and one to girls. Over half the states had three or fewer facilities.

The above figures would seem to indicate that institutions must be considerably overcrowded in those states that have few facilities, but they were not necessarily so. In seventeen jurisdictions the number of confined youths was 10 percent below capacity, and only eleven jurisdictions were 10 percent above capacity.

Although the NAJC study showed a drop in the population of the training schools by the mid-seventies, another trend was emerging. Experts report that so far in the last half of the seventies training school populations are increasing, caused apparently by the public's reaction to the seeming rise in youth crime. If this is indeed the case, the majority of the states may have considerable difficulty in providing adequate space for these increasing numbers in the juvenile justice system—if they choose institutional care. The likelihood is, unfortunately, that facilities in most states will have a fairly large number of residents, a factor that is a definite handicap in effective treatment. Because of the increase in commitments to the training schools, it is also extremely likely that many states may find it necessary to reduce the length of stays.

TABLE 8-11   Distribution of Training Schools by States

No. of Jurisdictions	No. of Facilities	Total facilities
6	9 or more	69
18	4 to 8	97
6	3	18
14	2	28
8	1	8
52		220

From: President's Commission on Law Enforcement and Administration of Justice, *Task Force Report: Corrections* (Washington, D.C.: U.S. Government Printing Office, 1967), p. 144.

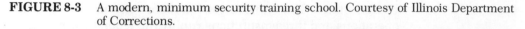

FIGURE 8-3   A modern, minimum security training school. Courtesy of Illinois Department of Corrections.

Medical and Dental Services.   At first glance, the services available to residents of training schools appear adequate. The President's Commission on Law Enforcement and the Administration of Justice reported that medical, recreational, dental, and other services are available in over 70 percent of all training schools. (See Table 8-12.) For example, confined youths often receive extensive dental care to rectify a lifetime of neglect, and special services, such as the removal of tattoos, are sometimes available if offenders desire them. To provide these specialized and routine services, many institutions have a full-time nurse on duty and a physician who visits one or more days a week. But these figures do not tell the whole story. In some training schools, youths are locked in their rooms all night and cannot get out, which can be dangerous if an illness develops during the night. Too, insensitive staff often ignore complaints, believing that the youths are either faking illness or just want some attention. Doctors and sometimes nurses are available only at certain times or are merely on call. Youths who become ill may have to wait hours for treatment. Nevertheless, it is unquestionably true that most institutionalized youths are provided with better medical and dental care than they have had before.

TABLE 8-12 Services Available in State-operated Juvenile Institutions by Number of Institutions*

Service	Number of Institutions (Total: 220)	%
Medical	221	96
Recreation	208	95
Dental	206	94
Education	193	88
Casework	190	86
Social work service	173	79
Psychological	165	75
Psychiatric	156	71

From: President's Commission on Law Enforcement and Administration of Justice, *Task Force Report: Corrections* (Washington, D.C.: U.S. Government Printing Office, 1967), p. 144.

Education.   Academic education usually is reserved for certain training schools in each state. These institutions normally are middle-of-the-line facilities that are more confining than camps and ranches but are less stringent in security and control features than the end-of-the-line schools. Accredited by the state for granting high school diplomas, these academic schools are run for eleven months of the year, five days a week. Classes are usually small, with ten or fewer pupils. Remedial mathematics and English are frequently taught. Programmed instruction is becoming popular, and students are usually allowed to progress at the rate most satisfactory to them.

When the educational facilities of the schools were examined in the 1960s, they looked somewhat better than other types of programs. For example, the teacher ratio was better than the ratio in any other area of staffing. The recommended ratio is 1:15, one teacher to fifteen students, whereas the national average is 1:17. Thirty-six states are over the 1:20 ratio, but twenty-four do better than the recommended 1:15 ratio. One interesting aspect of the teacher situation is that public schools are responsible for the education of about 5 percent of all confined youths, with about 36 percent of them engaged in remedial work. Probably the basic reason for this generally optimistic teaching situation is that education is better structured than is counseling. Not

FIGURE 8-4   Biology Class in a Training School. Courtesy of Illinois Department of Corrections

only do most administrators recognize the necessity for education, but teaching methods are also well developed.

A visit to juvenile institutions, however, does not provide a very favorable impression of the academic programs themselves. Classroom instruction is at best sluggish, and many students are either asleep or totally bored. Moreover, residents are also quick to inform the visitor that they do not want to attend school and feel that it is a waste of time. But many residents are able to earn a high school diploma and others progress to the level of admission to higher education.

Vocational Training.   Medium and maximum security juvenile institutions usually offer vocational training to residents. The well-equipped training school for boys provides vocational programs in automobile repair, welding, printing, woodworking, carpentry, barbering, machine shop, drafting, and food service. The well-equipped training school for girls offers training programs in sewing, food service, secretarial skills, beauty care, and, in some, computer programming.

In addition to attending vocational classes, residents also perform a number of maintenance tasks in the institution. As one mimeographed youth commission publication put it:

FIGURE 8-5 College Intern Instructs Resident in the Operation of a Thermal Forming Machine. Courtesy Illinois Department of Corrections.

It is felt that many boys can profit from engaging in necessary chores which must be done. We expect each boy to share in these tasks on a rotating basis. However some are assigned to work details for a specific period of time. It is hoped in this way good work habits and skills may be offered on a half-time daily basis, receiving school credits as occupational training courses. Some of these jobs include janitoring, painting, storeroom control, and general maintenance.[14]

But of far more significance than vocational training is the help that vocation rehabilitation counselors provide in getting jobs in the community for the offenders.

Treatment Programs. In 1965, treatment personnel totaled 1,154 out of 21,247 staff employed by state institutions. The recommended ratio of treatment staff to clients is 1:21, but thirty-five states exceeded this figure. These treatment personnel were psychiatrists, psychologists, and social caseworkers. The President's Commission found that four states were able to meet a recommended 1:150 ratio of psychiatrist to offenders, but the equivalent of only 46 psychiatrists were found for all 220 facilities polled. One-half of the psychiatrists were found in five states and one state had the equivalent of ten full-time pyschiatrists. At the time of the report, 236 additional psychiatrists were needed nationally and 282 more were required if the average daily population of the facilities were to be adequately treated.[15]

About the same situation applied to psychologists. Almost 60 percent of all psychologists were found in nine states; twenty-one states each had the equivalent of one psychologist; and only twelve states met the recommended standards of 1:150. Against these figures, the nation's juvenile institutions needed 100 more psychologists than they employed.

The number of caseworkers was also inadequate. Institutions employed only 66 percent of the needed total on the basis of the recommended standards of a ratio of 1:30. To meet national requirements, another 487 caseworkers were needed in the United States in 1967. Potential caseworkers may be surprised to learn that only about 40 percent of their time will be spent in contact with children. The remaining time is spent in "evaluation conferences, administration and staff consultation, and arranging referrals and placements."[16]

Too often treatment personnel are put in administrative positions. They become paper pushers rather than people changers, and the time they can spend with residents decreases. Even when institutions have psychologists and psychiatrists, most of these professionals are too busy to see residents except on a happenstance schedule, despite the fact that many therapy programs require extensive contact with the individual. Social workers, too, are often not very happy in their jobs in training schools. For many, the job is their first, and they can hardly wait to get a little experience so that they can get out of the institution.

Religious Instruction. Most states still give lip service to religious instruction, an important aspect of juvenile training schools since their inception. However, in 1967 twelve states had no chaplains in their facilities and thirty-two had less than one chaplain for each institution.

In the nation as a whole, the ratio of chaplains to inmates is 1:268, whereas the recommended ratio is 1:150; in only one-half of the states is the ratio 1:150.

The state training schools usually have a full-time Protestant chaplain and a part-time Roman Catholic priest. Religious chapels customarily are part of the physical structure of these facilities. Moreover, many of the private institutions were founded and are funded by a Protestant or Roman Catholic group. The Roman Catholic Church has been involved with dependent, neglected, and delinquent youth for many years and has spent enormous sums in building, staffing, and maintaining institutions for these youth.

However, in spite of the purported contribution religion has made to troubled youth in the past, in the present, Protestantism and Catholicism are having little impact. The religious programs offered are at best impotent and at worst coercive and demanding—some institutions still compel residents to attend chapel one or more times a week. Residents then rebel by talking or sleeping throughout the services. All too often the chaplain is considered part of the Establishment because he serves on institutional-release and other important decision-making committees. Furthermore, these chaplains have been known to threaten their inattentive resident congregations with adverse release reports.

It is beyond the purview of these comments to explore the importance of religion in the lives of juvenile lawbreakers. Certainly, organized religion is seen by them as part of the society that labeled them as deviant and outsiders, thereby often making it unpalatable in any form. If any religion were acceptable, it would no doubt be of the sect and store-front church variety, but institutional administrators tend to be adamant in their insistence on employing middle-class chaplains to minister to primarily lower-class offenders.

Recreation. The President's Commission on Law Enforcement and the Administration of Justice reported that 95 percent of the facilities surveyed had recreational programs. Recreation has received a heavy emphasis in the past century, both as a preventive of delinquency and as an element of institutional care. Juveniles like to play, and it is thought that teaching them a competitive sport can build self-respect and self-confidence. Even though community studies of the impact of recreation on the prevention of delinquency have been less than favorable, most institutional administrators do put a major emphasis on recreation.[17]

Residents participate in such active sports as flag football, softball, volleyball, basketball, and occasionally boxing. Cottages often compete against each other in these sports, and sometimes the institution competes in a community or a police league. Activities for more passive youths include building model cars, painting, decorating the cottages (especially at Christmas), checkers, ping-pong, and pool. The techniques of drawing, squiggle game, costume play, and mutual storytelling are useful for younger children.

Recreation departments in some institutions take selected residents to special community events, such as athletic contests, rock concerts, and auto races, and sometimes on canoe trips and overnight or weekend campouts. Often, work at state and county fairs, under the supervision of the recreation department of their facility, provides both recreation and learning for residents.

Dancing, music, and drama are also part of the recreational plan. Coeducational facilities stage dances for residents, and residents of male institutions frequently invite residents of female facilities to dances. Many training schools also have a music group that performs for the student body and plays concerts in the community. If a teacher is interested in drama, plays are put on several times a year.

The Volunteer. Volunteers are important adjuncts to institutional programs. Confined offenders frequently are more receptive to services rendered by unpaid volunteers, who can present the needs of incarcer-

FIGURE 8-6 Recreation in a Training School. Courtesy of Illinois Department of Corrections.

ated youth and can become their advocates in the community as adequately, or more so, than paid staff. Among the many services that volunteers provide for institutionalized youth are: education (tutoring and supplying books); entertainment (choral programs and other types of entertainment presented by community groups); chaperoning (escorting selected youths to community events); counseling (one-to-one contact with offenders); self-improvement (encouraging youths to have a better self-image through positive reinforcement); family service (contacting and reassuring parents on special problems); financial aid (providing money for a youth's canteen account); gifts (supplying Christmas and birthday remembrances); job-finding (assisting youths to find community jobs while they wait to be released or to find permanent jobs after release); letter writing (many youths need help in writing letters to family and friends); religious activities (outside groups present religious services and music); and recreation (playing basketball, softball, and other sports with residents).

Some states, needless to say, have better-developed volunteer programs than others. For example, the Ohio Youth Commission has appointed volunteer coordinators who are able to generate interest in most of the foregoing activities. An institution that has an active volunteer program can greatly enrich the stay of its residents.

Prerelease Programs. These juvenile institutions have two types of prerelease programs. Under the first, residents are transferred to another cottage or to another location to begin a formal program of community reintegration, including exposure to experiences designed to prepare them for a full return to the community. Techniques of interviewing for a job, instruction on how to read the help wanted section of a newspaper, and assistance in money management are important elements of the program. The second type of prerelease program provides more privileges for residents but expects more responsible behavior from them in return.

Home furloughs, afternoon trips off campus, and permission to work in the community are typical of the privileges given to residents of prerelease cottages or to those who are just a step or two away from release. Home furloughs are probably the most widely used. Some staff believe that permitting youth to be reintegrated gradually to the community after an absence of perhaps several years will help ease the shock of release. Home visits also provide opportunities for youths to interview for jobs and to visit with family members. Trips off campus for several hours with parents are sometimes permitted by some training schools. This enables parents and child to spend time together away from the institution and possibly to shop for a wanted item of clothing or to eat in a restaurant. Community jobs generally are reserved for those youths who are only two or three months from release and who need financial resources before they return to community living, and staff are very careful in choosing the residents who are permitted to work in the community. Unfortunately, juveniles often fail on outside jobs because of their own immaturity and because minor infringements are not overlooked. Administrators of juvenile institutions are also quite concerned about whether or not their charges will return after a home visit; in fact, they do have a high percentage of runaways on these occasions.

Private Training Schools

The private training schools should not be overlooked, because of the number of youths they hold. Pappenfort and Kilpatrick, in a national study of all types of institutions, reported that private facilities constituted about 34 percent of the institutions for delinquents, holding about three in twenty of known delinquents.[18] Moreover, the 1974 *Children in Custody* report indicates there are 1,337 private institutions in the United States.[19] Furthermore, their numbers are probably increasing since federal and state funds are now set aside for such institutions. Children are now a big business in the United States, and there is some evidence that a number of operators are jumping on the monetary bandwagon.[20]

The problem in attempting to deal with private institutions is that no sure way exists of determining just how many do hold juvenile lawbreakers. Some are concerned primarily with the retarded, the sick, the mentally ill, the handicapped, and the hard to handle. Of these youths, some are delinquent but ostensibly are confined for other reasons. In addition, some institutions that supposedly admit only youths with a specific type of problem will bend their rules and accept those with other problems, including delinquency.

Most citizens are probably more familiar with these private institutions than with other juvenile facilities. The long history of private training schools, which developed from the early houses of refuge, has worked to keep them in the public eye—as has their continuing need for funds from many sources. Soliciting such funds requires considerable advertising, and the public has been bombarded for years by pleas from various homes that describe in appealing detail the quality of their programs, the good they do, and the success, as adults, of their former residents. The fact that many are religiously supported adds to the public's knowledge of their existence, since requests in their behalf sometimes come from the pulpit.

The claims made by these institutions make them appear to be very attractive. Their sentimental appeals are as eye-catching and heart-tugging as are the reasons given for their success: a limited intake; expert professional staff; and better staff-client ratio than that of the public training schools.

Proponents of private institutions also argue that their smaller size makes them more effective. They do seem to be smaller in general, since less than one-half of the children are housed in institutions of 100 or more. The Protestant institutions tend to be smaller and the Catholic, larger. The religious institutions probably are better than other institutions, but any facility with over 100 clients is unlikely to maintain any distinctiveness from the public training schools.

Many claim too that the private schools are more flexible and innovative than the public schools. This is probably accurate, although private school administrators are frequently beset by the pet theories and therapies of influential board members. The result is often a flitting from one pet project to another in attempting to satisfy the whims of board members rather than the needs of the youths. The argument is somewhat overstated, for the public training schools also vacillate considerably in programming. But private schools generally do have the advantage of being free from political pressures.

These general claims are accurate to a degree since, for example, some schools do limit their intake, but many, especially those dealing in the interstate commerce of children, take as many as they can get. As was noted earlier, the availability of federal and state funds has sometimes led to the establishment of schools by those who simply want to make money. Their primary goal is to warehouse the children as cheaply as possible and thereby reap good profits, and they are aided in this quest by the inadequate licensing procedures of the states.[21] Some homes limit their clientele to particular religious groups, but accept all categories of youths from that group, thereby ending up with as great a hodgepodge as any of the public institutions. Public training school directors are especially critical of the intake policies. They believe that these policies allow the private schools to avoid dealing with the worst offenders, who could profit most from the supposedly beneficial programs of the private schools. Further, these offenders then end up in public schools and multiply the schools' problems by giving them a bad image when violence occurs or their recidivism rates are high. Finally, "statistics show that approximately 70 percent of private institutions employ such [treatment] professionals as part of their full-time staff, while only 60 percent of public institutions can offer these services to the juveniles,"[22] but since 30 percent of these homes do not have professional staff, such as psychiatrists, clinical psychologists, and psychiatric caseworkers, their general overall effectiveness is questionable.

One of the most definitive studies of a private institution is Polsky's *Cottage Six*. Polsky's underlying explanation of the dynamics of the clique structure in the cottage does not differ greatly from the study of Bartollas et al. of a public training school. The varieties of aggression, the ranking of residents, the nature of status, threat gestures, and scapegoating were surprisingly similar in both. The only difference between the two, in fact, is the foci of the studies. Street et al., in *Organization for Treatment,* studied both private and public facilities. Some of the small private as well as large public institutions covered in this study emphasized treatment, but other institutions, small and large, had no treatment; small as well as large emphasized discipline and hard work. Presumably, being public or private has little to do with whether an institution is custodially or treatment oriented.

SUMMARY

Jails, detention homes, and training schools were criticized severely in this chapter. The jails are of ancient vintage, are poorly staffed by less-than-qualified personnel, and lack programs. The detention homes are newer, but they also are poorly staffed and lack needed programs. The training schools are both old and new, but they, too, need more trained staff and more comprehensive programs. All in all, none of these facilities is adequate for the placement of children.

Contemporary experts radically disagree on social policy for juvenile detention. Some argue for an increase in the numbers of these facilities, but others claim that they all should be closed down. Some believe that with proper staff-resident ratios and improved programs these facilities can provide well for juveniles in trouble, and others assert that these settings are violent, inhumane, and damaging to all children. Some feel that these facilities should be constructed in the community, while still others recommend isolating them in rural areas. But beyond the disagreement is the reality: More and more juveniles are being sent to these institutions.

In implementing a confinement policy, a number of factors should be taken into consideration. If at all possible, youths should be kept in their home communities. If confinement is necessary, the detention home or training school (jails should never be used for children) should be in or very near the home community. The facilities should remain small, with detention home populations not exceeding thirty and training school populations not exceeding fifty, housed in at least four separate living units. The facilities should be pleasantly furnished and security features provided only after adequate staffing, programming, and a satisfactory, safe physical plant have been developed. If such facilities are absolutely necessary, they should be coeducational, completely committed to full use of community resources, and, wherever possible, should integrate residents into community programs.

QUESTIONS

1. Discuss the nature of the changes in American society at the time of the Revolution and immediately afterward.

2. How were delinquents to be improved in early institutions? What was the philosophy of the houses of refuge?

3. Name the various facilities used to house delinquent youths.

4. What are the criteria used for confining youths in institutions?

5. Discuss the role of the jail in confining youths.

6. What is the primary emphasis of those who run detention houses?

7. From this discussion of training schools, what are their greatest problems?

ENDNOTES

1. David J. Rothman, *The Discovery of the Asylum* (Boston: Little, Brown and Company, 1971).
2. Ibid., pp. 53–54.
3. Ibid., p. 226.
4. Ibid., pp. 225–227.
5. A new *Children in Custody* report has been released recently. This new report showed that the number of juvenile correctional facilities had risen from 722 to 829, an increase of 15 percent, by June 30, 1974. The report also indicated ". . . the 829 public facilities were divided into 396 state-administered and 433 locally administered places. Distributed by type of facility, there were 331 detention centers; 21 shelters; 19 reception or diagnostic centers; 185 training schools; 107 ranches, forestry camps, and farms; and 166 halfway houses and group homes." U.S. Department of Justice, *Children in Custody: Advance Report on the Juvenile Detention and Correctional Facility Census of 1974*, Law Enforcement Assistance Administration. Washington, D.C.: U.S. Government Printing Office (February 1977), p. 2. Readers desiring an update on tables 8-1, 8-2, 8-3, 8-4 and 8-5 are urged to consult the final report for the *Children in Custody* study for 1974. Generally, the number of children in training schools and shelters decreased between 1971 and 1974, while the numbers of those in halfway houses and group homes increased. See the *Advance Report for Children in Custody, 1974*, p. 3.
6. Ronald Goldfarb, *Jails: The Ultimate Ghetto* (Garden City, N.J.: Anchor Press, 1975), p. 5.

7. Ibid., pp. 286–344.
8. Ibid., p. 296.
9. Law Enforcement Assistance Administration, *National Jail Census, Report on the Nation's Local Jail and Types of Inmates* (Washington, D.C.: U.S. Government Printing Office, 1970).
10. Nicholas Reuterman, *A National Study of Juvenile Detention Facilities* (Edwardsville, Ill.: Delinquency Study and Youth Development Project, Southern Illinois University, 1970), p. 39.
11. Ibid., p. 53.
12. President's Commission on Law Enforcement and Administration of Justice, *Task Force Report: Corrections* (Washington, D.C.: U.S. Government Printing Office, 1967), p. 112.
13. Ibid., p. 143. Interestingly enough, the federal government plans to close its juvenile facilities. Also these figures must be modified in light of the 1974 *Children in Custody* study. See note 5 above.
14. Clemens Bartollas, Stuart J. Miller and Simon Dinitz, *Juvenile Victimization* (New York: Halsted Press, A Sage Publication, 1976), p. 22.
15. President's Commission, *Task Force Report: Corrections,* p. 143.
16. Ibid., p. 145.
17. Lloyd E. Ohlin, "Institutions for Predelinquent or Delinquent Children," in *Child Caring: Social Policy and the Institution,* edited by Donnel M. Pappenfort, Morgan Dee Kilpatrick, and Robert W. Roberts (Chicago: Aldine Publishing Company, 1973), p. 193.
18. Donnel M. Pappenfort, Morgan Dee Kilpatrick, and Robert W. Roberts, eds., *Child Caring: Social Policy and the Institution* (Chicago: Aldine Publishing Company, 1973).
19. The advance report for *Children in Custody, 1974* indicates that of the 1337 private facilities, 805 were halfway houses and group homes and 395 were ranches, forestry camps and farms. The remainder ". . . were distributed as follows: 4 detention centers, 67 shelters, 5 reception or diagnostic centers, and 61 training schools." U.S. Department of Justice, *Children in Custody: Advance Report on the Juvenile Detention and Correctional Facility Census of 1974,* Law Enforcement Assistance Administration. Washington, D.C.: U.S. Government Printing Office (February 1977), p. 2. Of the 31,749 youths in these facilities 70 percent were males; 16,955 of the 31,749 youths were in ranches, camps and farms; 9,919 were in halfway houses and group homes; 4,078 were in private training schools; and the remaining 797 were in short term facilities. *Children in Custody, 1974* advance report, pp. 3–4.
20. Kenneth Wooden, *Weeping in the Playtime of Others* (New York: McGraw-Hill, 1976).
21. Ibid.
22. Ohlin, "Institutions," p. 191.

REFERENCES

Reuterman, Nicholas. *A National Study of Juvenile Detention Facilities.* Edwardsville, Ill.: Delinquency Study and Youth Development Project, Southern Illinois University, 1970.
   This is the most comprehensive study of juvenile detention facilities.

Rothman, David J. *The Discovery of the Asylum.* Boston: Little, Brown and Company, 1971.

> *Rothman's study is a fascinating and informative account of the beginning of the various types of institutions.*

Pappenfort, Donnel M.; Kilpatrick, Morgan Dee; and Roberts, Robert W., eds. *Child Caring: Social Policy and the Institution.* Chicago: Aldine Publishing Company, 1973.

> *This selection of readings provides an excellent overview of juvenile institutionalization.*

9

The Inmate World

What is it like to be an inmate in a juvenile institution? Obviously, this question can be answered literally only by a juvenile who spends time in a correctional setting, but this chapter will attempt to capture a glimpse of what institutionalization is like for some juveniles. Focusing upon a male situational offender and his response to a maximum security training school, the chapter will also consider, in passing, the prowess of the chronic and the plight of the noncriminal offender. Granted that life for a youth in a camp or a ranch is less severe than that portrayed here and that the institutional experience for a girl is different from that for a boy, this chapter should disclose the impact of institutionalization on some youths.[1]

INITIAL RESPONSE

Frightened and bewildered, Johnny sat handcuffed to another youth in the back seat of a state car as the officials of one state training school transported him to an end-of-the-line maximum security facility in a midwestern state. He could not help reflecting with great trepidation on the various rumors he had heard about his upcoming placement. He had been told, for example, that the institution was underground, that staff beat boys with hoses, that black inmates were huge and victimized all whites, that a long stay would be forthcoming, and that it was nearly impossible to escape from this setting. Johnny's time for reflection was

234

short, for much more quickly than he expected, the state vehicle reached its destination. Supervised carefully and still handcuffed, the two youths were taken into the institution.[2]

As soon as the official transfer process was completed, their orientation to this institution began. Johnny first met the intake cottage staff members and then, escorted by one of the staff members, he was taken around to meet the superintendent, the chaplain, the nurse, and his social worker. He also received his room assignment, customary haircut, and clothes allotment. A good deal of the first day was spent in listening to various intake staff members explain cottage and institutional rules. Johnny, however, was so frightened that he merely went through the motions of listening to what was said.

Therefore, very much in a daze, this new youth attempted anxiously, almost desperately, to gain control over his new social world. He was concerned, of course, with how he could best cope with it. In general, Johnny—a composite case history of the situational offender —decided to stay by himself for the first few days and to be suspicious of peers. He knew that it would be during the few first days that peers would place the most pressure on him. Fortunately, he had not been sexually victimized in other institutions, because peers would be able to use such a fact to place relentless pressure on him. He also kept his distance from staff, primarily because staff members gave the bigger boys power over the smaller ones in the training school he had just come from and he, like many of his peers, got pushed around as a result.

VICTIMIZATION

In the meantime, cottage peers studied the newcomer carefully. In fact, most of their interaction with him was geared specifically to see how far the newcomer could be pushed. When the new youth walked into the cottage on that first day, his peers attempted to answer four basic questions about him: How is he holding himself? How much does he have? Will he defend himself? and Is he a punk? These questions are concerned with how fearful he is, what can be exploited from him (food, clothes, cigarettes, or sex), whether he will resist, and whether he has been sexually exploited in the past.

Being white, Johnny was approached by another white, who walked up to him asking his name, where he was from, and what he was confined for. After feeling him out with these questions, this "new friend" asked him for a pack of cigarettes, promising to pay him back in the near future. But more than exploiting Johnny for a few cigarettes, the purpose of this initial contact was to set the newcomer up for later victimization and to see where he would fit in the pecking order of the cottage. Johnny gave this "new friend" several cigarettes, but he refused to give him a whole pack, saying, "Man, they got to last me all week."

The approach of the black youths was quite different. Engaged in a politics of scarcity because they usually have little or no money in the canteen account, they have greater need to exploit for cigarettes and food. Consequently, they were more direct and forceful than whites about extorting scarce items from this newcomer. The sexual exploiters in the cottage will follow any possible avenue to sexually victimize newcomers. As Johnny watched these sexual exploiters work on other neophytes, he could see that they were subtle, constantly harassing passive youths, and then waiting for a moment of weakness. Eventually, a newcomer who demonstrates strength will be left alone, but he must battle for some time with both sexual and nonsexual aggressors.

In his early days in the institution, Johnny was exposed to numerous types of exploitation. He was sitting down for lunch one day when another youth walked up to him, picked up his dessert, and said, "You don't want this, do you?" Johnny started to rise and to take his dessert back, but then he glanced at the piece of cake and said "No, take it." He realized that this was a mistake because this same peer walked up later and demanded a cigarette: "Give me a square." Johnny looked him right in the eye and said, "Go get your own squares."

On the following Saturday morning, after Johnny had been to the weekly canteen, he returned to the cottage and was accosted by several peers as he walked in the door. He had seen how the weak and the new lose all they have as item after item disappears. He refused to have his burden lifted, although he did give a pie and a bottle of pop to one of the tough kids in the cottage.

A dude in another cottage had "accidentally" bumped him two times. Johnny let it go the first time, but he pushed him back the second time. The officer had to separate them because they were "starting to get down to it." Johnny, like almost every new youth, also had heard such comments as, "You're a punk, aren't you?" "We heard what happened to you at Camp. . . . We all know you're a punk. You'd better give in, or we're going to hurt you."

Johnny quickly became aware that there was a ranking of exploited items in the cottage. He realized that the best clue to the value of an item is the ease with which peers will give it up. Some items, for example, are given up easily while youths fight viciously to retain others. The ranking in his particular cottage is shown in Figure 9-1.

Johnny decided that he would go as far as item 4. If a strong peer put enough pressure on him, he would give up his institutional dessert, institutional favorite food, at least some of his canteen pop and candy, and some of the soft drinks and candy that his parents brought from home. But he refused to go any further. Allowing sex, of course, was out of the question because it literally meant giving up his manhood. It also meant being isolated from the group and being considered a social outcast.

Johnny liked to watch others. It did not take him long to observe how various peers reacted to the pressure put on them. For example, the youth who had come to the institution with him had been assigned to the same cottage, and it was obvious that he was "getting over" for anyone who was interested. Johnny said to him one day, "Man, what are you giving up your ass for? We heard what happened last night in the dorm." He received this response:

> . . . If you're a punk and you've been a punk for a long time and you want to stop, it's very hard because you've got so many desires in you. If you enjoy what you was doing before and then after you do it, you get a guilty feeling—you don't know where to turn. Like you say, I want to stop and then you get to the point where it's just like you need a woman, you get horny or something like that. It gets to the point where you want to do it again, and you don't know what to do. You say you want to stop, but there's something in you that wants to keep going.

Another peer in Johnny's cottage was handling his pressure in a different way. He was small, was unable to fight, and had feminine characteristics. He clearly had decided to develop an "exchange relationship" with one of the more aggressive youths in the cottage. He did everything for this peer—shined his shoes, gave him the cigarettes he got from the canteen, gave him the candy and pop that his parents brought to him every other week, and provided sexual privileges. In exchange, his new "friend" offered protection from other peers.

A third youth responded to the physical and psychological pres-

FIGURE 9-1   Ranking of Material and Sexual Exploitation

Institutional dessert	Institutional favorite food	Canteen pop and candy	Parents' pop and candy	
1	2	3	4	
Institutional clothing	Toilet articles	Cigarettes	Personal clothing	
5	6	7	8	
Radios	Physical beating	Anal sodomy[3]	Masturbation of others	Oral sodomy
9	10	11	12	13

sures of exploitation by trying to take his own life. He drank metal polish and nearly died before they pumped his stomach out at the hospital. When he returned, Johnny asked him why he had tried to kill himself and received this answer:

> The first day I came in the institution I was sitting in the nurse's office and these guys came up from Pine Cottage. . . . They said, "the boogey man is going to get you" and all that kind of stuff. They were pretty big guys, and they got me a little shook up inside. I didn't think nothing of it, so I went up to the cottage. The first day I got up in the cottage, I got in a fight. I was pushed for homosexuality, and I got in a fight. The "man" [cottage supervisor] blamed me for it and made me do some work and all that. So as it went on, I was down in the school area, and I got approached homosexually and I had to fight through that. I was approached about four or five times, and I had to fight myself out of these situations. Well anyhow, after I had to fight myself out of these situations, it really messed me up mentally, you know. I was really bothered by it. It was really affecting me. . . . So then they started bothering me so much and everything kept on building up, so I drank some metal polish.

A fourth youth handled his pressure differently. He was small, and the youngest in the cottage, and he looked as if he would be an easy pushover. He was approached by several large youths who wanted to sexually exploit him in a music class. When the teacher left the classroom, they had their opportunity. The attempted exploitation was initiated by one youth who said, "I want some ass"; that prompted three other youths to approach the victim. However, this youth immediately picked up a chair, broke off a leg, and swung it at one of the approaching boys. Three of the four aggressors retreated at this point, and watched the two circle each other. Although the strong youth was able to wrestle the leg away from the uncompliant victim, he was unable to subdue him sexually. The teacher finally returned, and the altercation was ended. This inmate's response had warned other peers not to "mess" with him, and he was never sexually approached again.

As Johnny thought about exploitation in the training school, it seemed clear that there were several different groups. One very small group did not become involved in exploitation; these youths obviously only wanted to do their time and get out. They were strong and highly respected by peers and staff alike, but simply wanted to stay out of trouble. Johnny heard one of these youths say one day, "I don't want to get involved in kid's stuff. I just want to get out of this place." A second group was made up of the inmate leaders and their lieutenants. They took whatever they wanted from others and were not exploited by anyone. They ruled the cottage and made everyone their victims. A third group consisted of those youths who exploited some peers and, in turn, were victimized by others. They both gave up material items and took from others. Those in another group never exploited anyone, but were sometimes exploited by others. Finally, some youths were the chronic victims in the cottage. They seemed incapable of protecting themselves and were constantly being exploited. All of their valuable material items were taken, they were used as "punching bags" by aggressive peers, and they supplied sexual favors for anyone who was interested. Indeed, they were the cottage scapegoats.

As Johnny continued to reflect on this aspect of institutionalization, it seemed to him that the exploiters and victims handled themselves differently. Aggressors usually were boys who knew how to protect themselves, who had been in institutions before, and who had committed serious crimes on the streets. Consequently, they were "cool," and their entire bearing warned others not to mess with them. In contrast, scapegoats and sometimes-victimized youth usually were those who had committed minor crimes in the community or were actually noncriminal. They had run away from home, had gotten "busted" on a drunk charge, or could not get along with their parents. Once institutionalized, they ran away from one placement after another, and finally ended up in this maximum security setting. They did not belong there. They knew it, and so did their peers. Johnny heard one of them say one day, "All there is is a bunch of animals in here." In contrast to the "coolness" of exploiters, these residents looked and acted scared to death.

THE SOCIAL HIERARCHY

Johnny knew, as did all his peers, that each cottage had a well-defined pecking order. In his particular cottage, the youth at the top was called a heavy. He was very strong and more or less was chosen by inmates to be their leader. Johnny found it interesting that this youth did not have to fight for this leadership position as inmate leaders did in his previous placement. Nor would a youth vie for this leadership position until the present heavy was released. But once the heavy position became vacant, several of the strongest youths in the cottage would attempt to gain the support of peers. A nonphysical power struggle would go on until one youth won the privileges and the power of cottage leadership.

One of the biggest prizes of the heavy was the favoritism he was shown by cottage supervisors. Even the social worker went out of his way to be nice to the heavy. This inmate leader was permitted to go to more cottage dances than other peers, he had a better work detail, he was permitted to carry matches, and, most importantly, he received more home visits and a shorter stay than other cottage youth. In turn, staff expected this heavy to keep the other residents in line. Johnny saw how Craig, the heavy when Johnny first arrived, was always going around warning his peers not to create any problems. Craig, especially, would report anything he had heard via the grapevine concerning potential runaways.

The heavy usually had two or three lieutenants to support him and to carry out his wishes. The lieutenants made certain that the heavy got a second cereal when he did not like his breakfast. The heavy, of course, always had cigarettes supplied to him. He was given second portions of favorite food. He had more than enough "goodies" from the canteen, and he always received first choice on special treats brought by parents from home. The lieutenants were constantly with the heavy, and they were given respect from other peers because of their relationship with the cottage inmate leader. As already stated, they generally did not try to challenge the heavy, but they did attempt to build support so that they could assume the leadership of the cottage when the heavy was released.

Next in the pecking order were the youths known as slicks. These youths were sophisticated and mature. They had been in institutions several times, were strong and deserved respect, but generally were not involved in the power struggles in the cottage. Their basic goal was to do their time and get out. To achieve this goal, they avoided problems in all areas of the institution. They did not "rat" on peers, but they did go out of their way to cooperate with cottage staff. They ran errands for staff, would "rap" with them in the office, and did everything possible to convince staff that they did not belong in the training school.

The booty bandits occupied the fourth position in the cottage hierarchy. They seemed to have but one intent—to sexually exploit weaker peers. Johnny often wondered why they got so involved in sexual exploitation; he knew that it usually resulted in their staying longer in the institution. Even though staff often were not certain about their predatory activities, they still held it against these youths. Perhaps, Johnny reasoned, it was a matter of power, for by making a boy into a girl, they were asserting their power over him.

Merchants made up the fifth position. Johnny knew only one merchant well, a youth who had an uncanny ability to find sought-after items. He did this not only for peers, but also for staff. Johnny remembered one time when a favorite staff member was looking for floor wax. This cottage supervisor had called his supervisor and been informed that no one in the institution had any wax. The staff member reported his problem to the merchant and somehow the merchant located a can of wax. The merchant also traded radios, clothes, and other stolen items to those who could pay with cigarettes. He sometimes was able to smuggle contraband into the cottage, such as money, pornography, drugs, and hacksaw blades. He was continually peddling one item for another and seemed to profit from these transactions.

The mess-up was further down the social ladder of the cottage. This youth never seemed to do anything right. He was always involved in trouble—breaking the rules, disobeying staff, and creating conflict with peers. His inability to make an adequate institutional adjustment lengthened his stay. Johnny met one of these mess-ups and could not understand why he created the problems he did. This youth was in constant fights with peers—most of which he lost. In fact, he appeared to challenge those whom he did not have a chance of beating. He went out of his way to irritate staff, and he always lost his privileges right before something good was about to happen. For example, he had been waiting for a home visit for over two years and had talked about it constantly, but the day before he was going home, he made sexual advances to a female teacher.

The thief also occupied a lowly rung on the social ladder. This youth was despised because he was always stealing items from rooms. The honor that existed among thieves in this training school decreed that no one take anything from anybody else's room. The thief, however, did not follow this norm, and once he was caught, both staff and peers kept constant watch on him. Still, he continued to steal cigarettes and other small items.

Scapegoats were clearly on the bottom. In the sixteen months that Johnny spent at this training school, he got to know several of these youths. Isolated from the group and considered total outsiders, these sexual victims were treated as if they did not exist. They were not permitted to handle food and were considered to be so unclean that peers often would not even smoke their cigarettes. Yet, these youths were called upon when other inmates wanted sexual release. Scapegoats were on the bottom and it seemed as if everyone wanted them to stay there.

Johnny's response to this social order was to stay away from these social positions or roles. He attempted to keep others from "messing" with him, but he, in turn, did not "mess" with anybody else. He particularly did not want to be engulfed in the lower roles in the cottage; therefore, he attempted to avoid "messing" up or getting into conflicts with staff. In terms of exploitation, he was a giver and taker, but he made certain that he was not victimized for anything that would plunge him to the bottom of the inmate society. He tried to get along with both whites and blacks in the cottage. As a result of his efforts, he was considered to be all right by peers and was given some respect.

THE INMATE CODE

Social roles were not new to Johnny, for they had been present at his previous placement. But the inmate code was new. At his last training school, inmates were not organized enough or did not have the solidarity to develop extensive inmate norms. At this institution, the code was taught to residents as soon as they arrived, and they opened themselves to harassment from peers if they violated tenets of the code. One of the strongest norms was not to "rat" on peers. Obviously, residents wanted the hidden aspects of inmate life to remain hidden. Youths who violated this tenet sometimes were physically beaten by peers or, at the least, isolated from normal interaction.

"Be cool" was another inmate norm. In this training school for older youths, whining, complaining, or acting childish when things did not go your way were not living up to the strength tenets of the code. A youth was expected to handle his own battles, to be a man, to do his time without complaining, and not to run from fights.

"Don't get involved in other inmates' affairs" was a similar norm. Everyone was expected to stand on his own two feet and to take care of himself. If he was not strong enough to protect himself, then he deserved what he got. Thus, residents were admonished not to interfere with the affairs of others. Even if a resident heard that someone was going to attempt suicide or that peers were going to gang up on a friend, he was not to run to the staff with the information or warn the target of the impending aggression.

"Don't buy the people-changing" was highly supported by residents. They had another way of putting it, but the meaning was clear—don't sell out to staff and don't take seriously their treatment efforts. Of course, it was necessary to pretend in order to be released, but down deep, residents must remain the same. Staff, according to this norm, ultimately are the enemy. The most socially approved way to approach staff is to manipulate, or "to run game," on them.

Other norms were found in the code, but they lacked the universal recognition and acceptance of the aforementioned ones. Johnny, like his peers, tried to follow these norms for several months, but eventually abandoned them to some degree in order to be released. He followed them as long as he did because it was important for him to attain peer approval. All he lost from his compliance was a few months of time, but others were not so fortunate, as the norms were used by stronger peers to make the existence of the weaker more miserable.

TRAINING SCHOOL LIFE

Johnny found the average day quite boring. Inmates were awakened by cottage supervisors, were rushed by staff, had a little breakfast thrown at them, were given a couple of minutes for a smoke break, and then were marched to school in twos. Johnny had academic classes in the morning, and the first two were dreadful. He slept through most of these classes. But the third class was different. The teacher seemed to take a real interest in students. This was a class in remedial reading, and the teacher and her assistant made a special attempt to work with each student. Johnny had never liked school, but he halfway tried in this class. He liked the teacher, and he wanted to impress her that he was learning. After class, she would occasionally ask him how things were going. She took an interest in him, and he felt that she was concerned.

After this class the inmates were marched back to the cottage for the noon meal. Johnny had problems with a few youths in another cottage, and verbal conflict always seemed to break out with them as they were lining up to return to the cottage. Unless lunch was hamburgers, bean soup, or chili, Johnny did not like these meals at all; often, they were cold and tasteless. After the meal was over, the boys were marched back to school for the afternoon session. Johnny looked forward to his afternoons, for he was in welding class all afternoon. If you did your work and stayed out of trouble, the instructor would not bother you. Johnny was very much interested in learning all he could about welding. He had a cousin who worked as a welder in a steel mill and made good money. He liked working by himself on a project. He especially enjoyed the privacy because there was so little privacy in this training school. But the time passed all too swiftly, and it was time to return to the cottage.

Evenings were never good. First, there was a group meeting, a transactional analysis group that met nearly every day and lasted until supper. If the food was ribs or chicken, then suppers were all right; otherwise, Johnny quickly gobbled down his food without thinking much about what he was eating. He surely did miss his mother's cooking. Following the evening meal, during nice weather, the boys put on their gym shorts and were taken to the outside athletic field. Generally, everyone in the entire institution was on the field and staff members were stationed so that they could stop anyone who made a run to the fence. This was a drag, for Johnny had never liked sports. He particularly detested calisthenics. The director of recreation seemed big on calisthenics, and they did them several times a week. Then, they would run several times around the field. The superintendent was fond of telling his charges that a worn-out boy stays out of trouble. Johnny thought all of this was bullshit. The period following calisthenics was usually open recreation; that is, residents did whatever they liked. Johnny usually stood around talking with a friend, but sometimes they had to watch a softball or football game between cottages.

The youths then were taken back to the cottage and showered; Johnny felt as if they were run through the showers like cattle. When the cottage supervisor did not watch carefully, weak youths were sometimes sexually exploited during this shower period. An hour or so of television followed. This was all right, but Johnny rarely got to watch what he wanted. The strong youths in the cottage always got to choose the programs and generally he did not care for their choices. However, since he wanted peer approval, he did not want to alienate anyone, so, he just sat there and watched the programs. Boys had to be in their rooms at nine and lights were turned out by staff at ten. In Johnny's cottage, there were sixteen single rooms and two dormitories, each holding four youths. Johnny had a single room. He would lie there at night, thinking how much he wished he were home. It was at night that he realized how painful the training school experience was for him. He sometimes tossed for hours before he was able to fall asleep.

The weekends seemed worse than the other five days. So much of the time he was totally bored. Recreation was increased on weekends to take the place of school. Church was required on Sunday mornings. Johnny had never been interested in church, and he was particularly galled by the pompous protestant chaplain. Johnny was not certain what bothered him about this chaplain, but he could not stand him. Johnny felt that the only good things about the weekend were the canteen on Saturday morning, the movie on Sunday night, and that monthly visit from his parents. How he looked forward to their visit. Some of the unfortunate inmates had no one to visit them, or their parents only came once or twice a year. But Johnny's came faithfully once a month. They usually brought a bucket of chicken, a couple of pies from home, a carton of cigarettes, and several bottles of pop. The Sunday night following the monthly visit was the worst time for Johnny. It was then that he would plan his escape, although he had promised his parents that he would not run away.

RELATIONSHIPS WITH STAFF

Johnny felt that most cottage supervisors were indifferent to residents. They acted as if their position was only a job and not a very good one at that. A good part of the time, Johnny felt that most of the cottage supervisors took advantage of inmates. They slept on the job. They did not police the shower area as much as they were supposed to. They stayed in their offices and watched television programs on a set that one staff member had brought from home. They did not seem very interested in talking with residents, and at times told residents to leave them alone. In short, they did not do what they were supposed to do.

One cottage supervisor was really hated. He had beaten a youth with a flashlight one night for no reason. He had struck a couple of other inmates. Furthermore, he was unreasonable at cottage reviews and was known to be instrumental in having youths turned down for release because of very minor violations, such as a dirty room or a day or two of

Relax, Johnny—This is really not so bad. Just memorize those rules, listen to staff, relate to your peers, report any suspicious behavior, remember society is your friend—and have a good day.

poor performance on a work detail. More than one resident promised to "get him" following release.

In contrast, another cottage supervisor was understanding and fair and seemed interested in all the residents. Contrary to the code, peers spent hours talking with him. Johnny overheard one youth respond to the question, "Do you like Mr. Roberts?" by saying, "I'll tell you the truth, I love him. He's just like a father to me. He'd do anything for me, in reason." What was so surprising about this response is that this youth had just finished putting down every other cottage supervisor. "I will never forget how upset Mr. Roberts was that morning when they found Ron after he killed himself."

It took a long time, but Johnny found himself not only talking with this cottage supervisor, but also sharing deep concerns with him. This staff member informed Johnny that peers were his problem. He advised Johnny that he needed to learn to stand on his own two feet and not to be so dependent on his peers. Mr. Roberts also informed Johnny that he had a good mind and that he should learn to use it. Supported by this encouragement, Johnny prepared for and received his G.E.D. He also acquired all possible skills in the welding shop.

Manipulation of staff[3]   Inmates resented the power the staff had over them. Their freedom literally was in the hands of the cottage supervisors, and the whims of staff could keep them in the institution month after month. However, it was risky to physically challenge or threaten staff; it was much safer to approach them with sham, intrigue, and manipulation. If a resident could manipulate staff, he not only got what he was after but had the pleasure of "getting over" the keepers who made them toe the institutional line.

Of the variety of manipulating games played on staff, four were Johnny's favorites:

"If Not That One, How about This One?"

Con: This is a trick used by many youths, especially those who are known to lose their temper or act-out violently. Knowing that staff fear them to some extent, these residents capitalize on this fear to manipulate staff.

Hook: If a resident can put staff members into a situation in which staff fear the youth will lose his temper and become violent, the fear can be used to the resident's advantage.

Processing of Game: The resident approaches the staff member with a request. The request is considered extreme, and even the youth knows that it will be turned down. When it is turned down, the youth is ready, for he comes back immediately with another, more reasonable request.

Payoff: The staff member, not wanting to incur the youth's wrath, quickly grants the second request—the one actually wanted in the first place. As a result, the youth achieves a slightly higher standard of living or a little more freedom of action.[4]

"Give Me a Chance To Prove That I'll Come Back"

Con: In the custodial setting, it was very difficult to escape. Therefore, some youths developed a good program so that they would be eligible for a home visit.

Hook: The trick is for the inmate to convince staff to let him have a home visit. Thus, he continually badgers staff: "Trust me! Give me a chance to prove that I'll come back."

Processing of Game: Some residents simply do everything the cottage supervisors and social worker want in order to convince the keepers of their readiness for a home visit.

Payoff: The coup is complete when the youth departs the facility with a bus ticket in his hand and a smile on his face.

"You've Really Helped Me"

Con: A youth tells a staff member how helpful he has been "in turning him around." He proceeds to illustrate this by some new insight (which actually has been gleaned from other staff).

Hook: Residents know that staff want them to improve, and they soon learn to put on a "front." Although experienced staff are wise to this game, newer and more naive cottage supervisors or social workers are easily impressed and have their egos highly inflated by such statements.

Processing of Game: Residents act like model inmates anytime this staff member is around.

Payoff: Youths win the game if this one particular staff member supports them so strongly at their review that they are released.

"I Will Get You"

Con: The objective of this game is to physically intimidate a social worker.

Hook: Social workers are often from middle-class backgrounds and hold values of nonviolence and nonaggression. They do not know how to handle threats on their lives by an aggressive inmate, especially if this youth has crimes of violence in his criminal record.

Processing of Game: The youths use their own superior physical strength, acts of defiance, and other games of psychological one-up-manship to reinforce their dangerousness. They may angrily tell staff, "I will get you when I get out of here." After threatening them once or twice and forcing the concerned social worker to wonder what can be done to get back on the residents' good side, youths then become friendly. The social worker frequently jumps at the opportunity to reinforce this positive response and may even speed up their release.

Payoff: Residents who are convincing earn extra privileges and sometimes even receive an early release.

TREATMENT

Johnny was not impressed by the institution's efforts to treat him. The social worker, for example, always wanted to talk about inmates' problems. Johnny and most of his peers in the cottage were not interested in talking to the social worker about their problems. They did not feel very close to the worker and did not believe that their past was any of his business. The worker asked such questions as: Do you love your mother? How do you feel about your brothers and sisters? What is the earliest experience you can remember? The second social worker Johnny had in that cottage had each resident write a life story, draw pictures of people, and make up stories from pictures. Johnny did not feel close to either of these men. He did not feel that they had anything in common with him nor could they understand the experiences he had had in life. Neither knew how to communicate with him the way Mr. Roberts did.

In Johnny's transactional analysis group, he was taught such things as the three ego states—the child, the parent, and the adult. Perhaps he was influenced by his peers, but he never did take this very seriously. He knew that the aggressive youths in the cottage, such as lieutenants and booty bandits, warned their passive peers not to tell of their victimizations. Peers wanted to keep as much from staff as possible, for they did not want staff to know what was really going on in the cottage.

However, two youths in Johnny's cottage took transactional analysis seriously. They read books on it, had the group leader do life scripts on them, talked about it even when staff were not around, and felt that it was making a difference in their lives. One of these youths told Johnny that he was trying to find himself; he said that one needs a strong mind to make it in life and that he was using TA to give him that strong mind.

COPING WITH INSTITUTIONALIZATION

Johnny spotted several different coping responses to institutional life. Open rebellion was one possibility. Few youths pursued this, but those who did tried to take on the staff and the institution whenever possible. They disobeyed orders, sneered at staff, became involved in confrontations with staff, and did everything possible to show their toughness. More typically, residents decided to take advantage of whatever amenities the institution had to offer. They did not want to stay in the institution, but, as long as they were there, they decided to make the best of it. They were always trying to get extra food, to escape unpleas-

Okay Punk—Dis here's group therapy—Smile, rap with the man—Look sincere and don't spill your guts about last night.

ant tasks, and to get undeserved privileges. The heavy was the youth who derived the most material benefit from his institutional stay. Conforming oneself to the staff's norms and values was a third possible adaptation. But this was one response that few residents pursued. Playing it cool was the coping response of the "slick." This youth did his time without getting into trouble with peers but yet stayed free of serious involvement with cottage supervisors. As youths became impatient to be released, more decided to follow this response simply to be released. The final response was withdrawal. This could range from physical escape from the institution, to escape into drugs (grass, glue, paint thinner, or gasoline), to escape into mental illness, and finally, to suicide. During Johnny's stay at this facility, he saw each one of these coping mechanisms.[5]

IMPACT OF INSTITUTIONALIZATION

Johnny knew that institutionalization created various emotional reactions. These feelings, for the most part, had to be suppressed, since expressing them might lead cottage supervisors and social workers to consider youths to be acting-out. But Johnny knew that peers felt a variety of strong feelings generated by their institutional stay. These included righteous indignation, rage, fear and anxiety, shame and humiliation, and hopelessness and despair.

Righteous indignation is expressed by those who feel they should not be confined. They are upset over what they perceive to be injustice, for they believe that they were "set up" by the police, the judges, and the community officials. Any possible positive effects of the institution are negated because these youths do not feel that they did anything to warrant being confined in the first place. Clearly, there really is not anything the institution can do for them.

Youths who express rage go even further than do the righteously indignant. They act-out continually, feeling that they have been "messed over" by the institution and staff. A hatred for the green walls and bars grows into a consuming passion. Thus, they are willing to attack anyone and anything they believe to be standing in their way. Staff who try to control them become the objects of their anger and are sometimes attacked in a fit of rage; peers who get in their way are pushed around or attacked. Enraged youths justify their behavior by saying that peers have been "messing over them."

The pressure on youths, especially weaker ones, leads them to considerable fear and anxiety. To them, the juvenile facility is an alien world, filled with strong aggressive peers who are constantly trying to exploit them. The slightest gesture is interpreted as a serious threat. Feeling powerless against what they perceive as overwhelming odds, they do not know whom to turn to for help; if they run to staff, they know that they will be told to stand up and fight—a tactic of which they are incapable, both physically and psychologically. Nervous tics, stuttering, weight loss, and inappropriate actions begin to be seen in their behavior.

Some youths feel shame and humiliation because of their institutional experience. The exploited become shameful of their actions and feel humiliated before peers and staff. Those whom others use as a punching bag become depressed and desperate, trying to deny that others have the upper hand over them. Yet, they are willing to admit, when pushed, that they are patsies for strong youths. Although they abhor what they are forced into, they are neither strong nor aggressive enough to protect themselves. They resent strong residents, but they simply cannot stand up to them. They have intense feelings of shame and humiliation and hope that this dreadful experience will soon be over.

The youth who is pushed too far may end up in despair, feeling total hopelessness. Johnny overheard this conversation between a youth and his social worker:

Social Worker: "When we pulled you out of your room last night, I thought you were a goner."

Inmate: "I don't care. I wish I would have died."

Social Worker: "You've a lot to live for. You have your whole life in front of you."

Inmate: "I just can't make it in here anymore. I just can't make it. Life is no good. I'm miserable. I would like to be nothing."

Social Worker: "Don't you have people who care for you? How about your aunt? She's always writing. How about Pam [girlfriend]?"

Inmate: "I'm weak. I'm kind-hearted. Take, for instance, my cigarettes. People keep coming up and asking for one and I say, 'Yeah, take one.' But they take the whole pack. And then I began to give up sex. I'm always tense and nervous. I've always been degraded. I would rather be dead than continue to suffer in this hellhole."

Johnny himself felt righteous indignation about his confinement. Except for his G.E.D., welding skills, and his relationship with Mr. Roberts, he did not feel that he had derived any positive benefits from his stay. If anything, he felt degraded, deprived, and stigmitized by this experience. Indeed, he thought to himself, "I have learned more about crime in the past year and a half. I didn't know shit when I came here." He could not wait to get back on the streets. He was going to make up for lost time.

RELEASE

His release day finally came. He knew he was free as soon as he got out of the institutional station wagon at the bus station and the driver drove off. It felt so good to be back on the streets again. He went inside the station to buy a Coke and to wait for his bus. He discovered, much to his amazement when he began to drink the Coke, that his hands were shaking. He realized that he was frightened. Johnny could not believe it. Why should he be frightened? Where was that old self-confidence? What had the institution done to him?

QUESTIONS

1. What factors seem to contribute the most to resident social organization?

2. What is victimization? What are its causes in the institutional setting? What can be done to make our institutions safer?

3. What parts of the inmate code do you believe have the most serious consequences for cottage living?

4. What are some of the games played by juveniles in institutional settings?

5. Why did one staff member get such a good response from inmates?

6. How can we make our training schools more humane and positive settings for juveniles in trouble?

ENDNOTES

1. This chapter is adapted from Clemens Bartollas, Stuart J. Miller, and Simon Dinitz, *Juvenile Victimization: The Institutional Paradox* (New York: Halsted Press, A Sage Publication, 1976). The questions youths ask of newcomers are found on page 55 of *Juvenile Victimization*. Figure 9-1 is found on page 75. The games are a paraphrase of the games found in Chapter 11, and the modes of adaptation are paraphrased from Chapter 10. The interview with the hopeless youth is quoted from page 173.

2. This section on Initial Response is paraphrased from Clemens Bartollas, "Institutionalization: Trauma and Deliverance," *Faith and Reason* 1 (Spring 1975): 29–30.

3. Adapted by permission of the publisher, from *Victimology: A New Focus*, Volume V, edited by Israel Drapkin and Emilio Viano. (Lexington, Mass.: Lexington Books, D.C. Heath and Company, 1975.)

4. Eric Berne has popularized game transactions in human behavior. The games described here do not fully utilize the concept of the switch, the crossup, or the payoff.

5. These adjustments to institutionalization are derived from those found in Erving Goffman, *Asylums* (Garden City, N.Y.: Doubleday Anchor, 1961).

REFERENCES

Bartollas, Clemens; Miller, Stuart J.; and Dinitz, Simon. *Juvenile Victimization: The Institutional Paradox*. New York: Halsted Press, A Sage Publication, 1976.

This book is the first to focus directly on institutional exploitation.

Davis, Alan J. "Sexual Assaults in the Philadelphia Prison System and Sheriff's Vans." *Trans-action* 6 (December 1968): 9–17.

Contains startling accounts of the sexual victimization of juveniles as they were being transported in vans to the Philadelphia Jail.

Fisher, Sethard. "Social Organization in a Correctional Residence." *Pacific Sociological Review* 4 (Fall 1961): 87–93.
Parallels many of the findings of the Bartollas, Miller and Dinitz study.

Giallombardo, Rose. *The Social World of Imprisoned Girls.* New York: John Wiley & Sons, 1967.
Giallombardo compares the cottage life of three training schools for girls. This study provides a good understanding of what institutionalization is like for the juvenile girl.

Polsky, Howard. *Cottage Six—The Social System of Delinquent Boys in Residential Treatment.* New York: Russell Sage Foundation, 1962.
This is an important study because it examines the social hierarchy of a cottage in a private training school.

10

The Staff Response

Clearly defined skills, interest in young people, and on-the-job training are needed to work effectively with institutionalized juveniles. This chapter will examine why some staff members excel and leave a permanent, positive impression on residents, while other staff do irreparable harm to the youths who cross their paths. Specifically, the positions of superintendent, teacher, social worker, and cottage supervisor are given close attention.

It is not easy to work in a juvenile institution. The resentment of some residents, the testing of staff by these residents, the complaining of fellow staff, and the conflict among different levels of staff create problems for all institutional personnel. Neither do the punishment-oriented climate of some training schools nor the dearth of positive rewards encourage staff involvement.

STAFF LEVELS

At least five categories of staff are employed in large juvenile correctional facilities: top administrators, treatment personnel, academic and vocational teachers, custodial staff, and those who provide indirect services. The specific responsibilities and titles of personnel vary from one institution to the next, largely depending on the size and purpose of each training school.

Top administrators usually include a superintendent, a deputy superintendent in charge of programs, a deputy superintendent for indirect services, a social services director, a cottage-life supervisor, and a director of education. The cottage-life supervisor is in charge of control and security and supervises all the cottage parents or the staff who have replaced cottage parents in many training schools. He often reports directly to the superintendent. The social services director is in charge of treatment programs, supervises all the treatment staff, and usually reports to the direct services superintendent. Figure 10-1 illustrates the less complex organization of small training schools, ranches, and camps.

Academic and vocational teachers make up the second staff category. Large training schools often have a principal, a vice-principal, two or more guidance counselors, a librarian, and many academic and vocational teachers. The principal generally reports to the direct-services superintendent. On the other hand, many forestry camps do not even have an education department.

Treatment staff comprise a third category. Large training schools employ social workers, group leaders, recreational leaders, one or more psychiatrists, one or more psychologists, a physician, a dentist, one or more nurses, one or more chaplains, and, sometimes, a volunteer coordinator and a vocational rehabilitation counselor. The psychologist, the psychiatrist, the dentist, and the physician are usually part-time employees. If the institution has a full-time chaplain, he is usually a Protestant; a Roman Catholic chaplain is recruited from the community to say Mass and to hear the confessions of Catholic youths on Sundays. Social workers, recreational leaders, and group leaders report directly to their supervisors; the chaplain, the nurse, the physician, the psychiatrist, and the volunteer coordinator usually report to the social service director, the deputy in charge of direct services, or perhaps the superintendent.

Nonprofessional staff, who have more contact with residents than any other staff members, are still another category. Although placing a husband and wife in charge of a cottage has traditionally been the most popular policy in training schools, the trend today is to employ nonprofessional staff to work eight-hour shifts and to live in the community. The latter are referred to by different titles—youth leader, youth supervisor, youth counselor, group supervisor, cottage supervisor, cottage counselor, correctional officer—but, whatever the title, their main tasks are to provide twenty-four-hour care of residents and to maintain a secure cottage. This group also contains several different levels, who generally work under the supervisor of cottage life.

The last category is made up of personnel in indirect services: the personnel director, the business manager, the superintendent of buildings and grounds and staff, the secretaries, the food service staff (if food

FIGURE 10-1   Organization of Illinois Youth Center

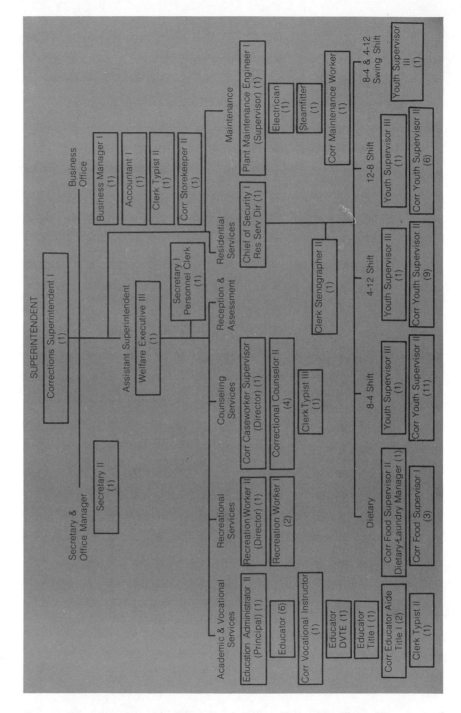

Reprinted by permission of the Illinois Youth Center, Hanna City, Illinois Department of Corrections.

is prepared in the facility), and the janitors. Indirect staff are usually not involved with residents, unless maintenance, food service, and janitorial staff happen to have youths assigned to them.

STAFF CHARACTERISTICS

The survey of juvenile correctional institutions by the National Assessment of Juvenile Corrections revealed that most staff members are relatively young, male, white, and married, and have been involved in work with confined youth for a number of years. (See Table 10-1.) Overall, their educational background indicates that they are probably better prepared than are correctional personnel in adult institutions (at least according to a 1966 national survey).[1]

Since more than 50 percent of the juveniles institutionalized are nonwhite, it is evident that a 27 percent minority-group representation among staff is relatively low. It is true that minority-group representation has increased in recent years, but this improvement is less marked at the executive staff level, which is still 80 percent white and male. Significantly, male administrators predominate even in coeducational and female programs.[2]

Institutional personnel tend to be slightly older, to be less educated, and to have more seniority in their jobs than staff of community-

TABLE 10-1   Staff Statistics by Occupational Subgroups

						Percentage with 5 Years in			
	Me-dian Age	Male (%)	White (%)	Mar-ried (%)	With Degree (%)	Pro-gram	Correc-tions	Work with Children	(n)
Executive	34	80	84	61	63	35	53	85	(48)
Treatment	30	68	68	55	72	21	25	44	(213)
Teaching	35	56	70	66	73	25	26	56	(196)
Living Unit	34	52	68	59	29	18	22	33	(260)
Clerical and maintenance	39	43	76	73	19	26	30	47	(162)
Aggregate	35	60	73	63	51	25	32	53	(879)

This table from Chapter 7, "Justice for Whom? Varieties of Juvenile Correctional Approaches," by Rosemary C. Sarri and Robert D. Vinter is reprinted from *The Juvenile Justice System* (Vol. V, *Sage Criminal Justice System Annuals*) M. W. Klein, Editor © 1976, p. 182 by permission of the publisher, Sage Publications, Inc.

based facilities. In fact, 50 percent of institutional staff in an average unit have five years experience in their current program.[3]

The National Assessment of Juvenile Corrections did a national survey of institutional staff in the mid-1970s, and the 1,175 respondents indicated the following categories as their most important concerns: treatment aspects of the program, local community interaction, staff working conditions, custodial elements of the program, and interorganizational contacts. Staff also were asked to differentiate between actual goals (actual practice in the program) and ideal goals (what "you yourself think . . . should be"). Significantly, the treatment of offenders was perceived by staff groups to be the most important goal. Custodial considerations ranked second in importance for all groups except the executive, who viewed the custody emphasis as next to the lowest. Except by clerical and maintenance personnel, who ranked them in the middle, interorganizational contacts were perceived as least important.[4]

SUPERINTENDENTS

The superintendency of a training school is a much sought-after position. The pay is good, and the position frequently has several attractive fringe benefits, such as the use of a state vehicle and a home on the institutional grounds. The superintendent has high status in the local community and great authority in the institution. But, in spite of these inducements, many superintendents keep their jobs for only a short period of time. Staff-management problems, excessive numbers of runaways, and changes in the political administration of the state cause some superintendents to be relieved of their jobs. Superintendents in large, problem-oriented training schools also may simply burn out after two or more years. Too, good administrators are sometimes promoted to other positions or receive good job offers from the private sector.

Fortunately, political appointments to superintendencies seem to be declining in juvenile corrections because the spoils system's payoffs for political support no longer include these jobs. Institutions have been crippled by these appointments, for such appointees are often inexperienced and come from a variety of unsuitable backgrounds. These appointees frequently lack administrative experience and do not know how to perform the delicate task of people-changing. They just keep the institution functioning until the next political election, at which time they may find themselves replaced by a new political appointee.

But many superintendents do introduce new programs and policies into their institutions: Residents may be placed in groups, or intake cottages may be established; an open-door policy, in which staff of all levels are urged to bring their concerns to the superintendent, may be initiated; or outside consultants may be brought into the institution

Not now—Hendricks—Why must you staff members complain so? Remember—the Governor has confidence in me—and so must you if we're to whip this place into shape.

to teach staff how to run groups, how to set up a management by objectives program, or how to use zero-based budgeting. However, these and other innovations usually need the approval of the director's office.

Staff response to administrative changes can vary from enthusiastic endorsement of these programs to active resistance or even sabotage. In addition to the feasibility of specific innovations in a particular institution, many other factors affect staff response. The most important is the management policy of the superintendent—participatory or dictatorial, his rapport with staff, the past history of change in the institution, and the ability of the superintendent to be an effective change agent.

In a national survey of juvenile correctional administrators in 1975, one question was: "What should be the primary goal of your institution?" Rehabilitation received twenty-four (51 percent) of the responses; punishment, ten (22 percent); public protection, nine (19 percent); rehabilitation and public protection equally, eleven (23 percent); and other goals, two (4 percent). In addition, only ten respondents (21 percent) agreed while thirty-one (65 percent) disagreed with the research evidence that treatment programs have no effect on the rate of recidivism.[5] Thus, the majority of these administrators feel that rehabilitation programs should be the goal of their institutions and the vast majority believe that these programs are having positive impact on youths.

The effective superintendents generally come from jurisdictions strongly committed to serving juveniles in trouble. The tradition of professional child care is better developed in some states than in others. The agencies supervising youths in these states have enough political clout and legal authority to bring in trained professionals, who should have the following qualifications:

> The superintendent should have the training and experience that will command the respect of the entire staff, particularly the various professional persons who make up the core of the institutional treatment program. He should have demonstrated in his experience his ability as an administrator, his understanding of the treatment function, and his capacity to make effective use of all professional personnel. He should be selected from leaders in social work, clinical or social psychology, psychiatry, education, education-related fields in child development, and should have a record of understanding and successful work with children. The superintendency requires administrative skills of the highest order, particularly those which will effectively coordinate the specialized efforts and talents of the professional people heading up the various departments in the institution. Graduation from college and the completion of graduate training in one of the fields indicated above are educational requirements. In addition to the thorough knowledge of the principles and practices of institutional management, he should have five or more years of successful supervisory or administrative experience, at least two of which should have been in institutions or agencies dealing primarily with youths on a twenty-four-hour basis.[6]

Problems   The superintendent is faced with a variety of problems from the day he assumes his position. Runaways create a major problem for most superintendents; youths flee from confinement in great numbers because ranches, camps, farms, and some training schools have few security features. Moreover, when a fleeing youth commits a rape or a murder, or when too many youths escape, the community is likely to become incensed, which results in adverse publicity in the media and irate letters to public officials.

Superintendents also must prove themselves to the central office, for they actually have much less authority than their subordinates believe they have. In fact, some inexperienced institutional heads are given little authority and must continually request permission to act from the department of corrections or the youth commission. However, if they are able to forestall numerous runaways, riots, violence, and suicides, the top executives should be given authority and freedom in which to act.

The task of the superintendent is often complicated by problems with labor unions, civilian review boards, and the informal power of staff. Labor unions can harass administrators and polarize line staff. Civilian review boards sometimes overrule important disciplinary decisions, such as those affecting termination and long-term suspensions. A minor technical point or a threat of legal action, for example, may be used by the union to reinstate a person who brutalizes residents. As might be expected, top executives feel immobilized by these decisions. Line staff also have considerable informal power in the institution, for they are a large and cohesive group. If they are alienated from the superintendent, they can create countless headaches by challenging and even sabotaging his policy.

In addition to these general problems, top administrators may be faced with fiscal constraints, high turnover of competent staff, chronic absenteeism and tardiness, staff brutality and perhaps even sexual victimization by staff of residents, smuggling of contraband into the institution, staff resistance to change, deteriorating facilities, vacant positions "frozen" by the political administration, and other adverse conditions.

The combined pressures of these problems, especially in large training schools, frequently result in harassed, fear-ridden, and bone-weary top executives, who can respond in several ways. First, they can withdraw into less demanding employment in the public or private sectors. Second, they can withdraw into their offices and let the staff run the institution. This approach to management creates a great deal of power for, and a loss of control over, staff. Third, superintendents can demand that all personnel maintain a secure institution that is free of problems, disregarding how it is done. Under this mandate, staff are harshly punished for not preventing runaways and for any institutional problems. This punishment-oriented managerial approach, not suprisingly, can result in questionable and even brutal treatment of troublesome youths.

But top executives can also exert strong and positive leadership if they are able to rise above these problems. Effective superintendents tend to be forceful, charismatic, hard-working individuals who win the respect and the support of all personnel. They are interested in relating to staff, but at the same time they maintain some social distance from subordinates. They are receptive to staff at all levels, but they refuse to be controlled by any one group. They are ready to go the second mile with a staff member troubled by a personal problem, but woe to the chronically negligent or irresponsible individual. They have confidence in themselves and at the same time trust staff enough to share leadership with them. In short, they are fair with all, but, in return, expect first-rate work and cooperation.

ACADEMIC AND VOCATIONAL TEACHERS

Glaser found that vocational teachers in prisons formed better relationships with inmates than did any other staff.[7] Although this may not always be true in the training school, they certainly seem to receive more favorable responses from residents and fellow staff than do the academic teachers. Because vocational courses are usually in demand, a troublesome youth can be easily removed from the shop and replaced by someone more compliant. Confined juveniles know this, just as they know that being taken out of the shop area probably means being returned full-time to the academic area, which few residents find desirable. Many residents are genuinely intent on learning beauty culture, automobile repair, welding, or food service skills since they anticipate that this training will help them find jobs when they are released. Finally, vocational instructors are often older than academic teachers and are seemingly more in command when working with delinquent youths.

Academic teachers, in contrast, seem to have more problems with residents than do any other staff members. This is particularly true in maximum security training schools that house older delinquent boys, such as Indian River in Ohio; Preston Boys School in California; and St. Charles in Illinois. Residents, who usually resent being compelled to attend school, are often difficult to control. Moreover, the middle-class backgrounds of many teachers clearly do not prepare them to teach hostile, street-wise, lower-class offenders.

Bartollas, Miller, and Dinitz found in a study conducted in an Ohio maximum security juvenile institution for males that both male and female academic teachers were vulnerable to exploitation by the residents. Male teachers were threatened, and female teachers were exposed to lewd and suggestive remarks. Indeed, on several occasions helpless teachers stood by while one student was sexually assaulted by others. So desperate do the academic teachers become that they buy cigarettes, candy, and soft drinks for residents in an attempt to win their friendship and cooperation.[8]

Academic teachers seem to be in conflict with staff at all levels, as well, even with social workers who are fellow treatment staff, with the result that in some institutions they end up as outsiders. Line staff fail to respect them because they have difficulty in controlling troublesome youths. Social workers tend to blame teachers for school problems of the youths on their caseloads.[9]

Because of this lack of respect and these conflicts, many academic teachers find it impossible to maintain a positive attitude toward the job. In contrast to the high anticipation they first felt, they begin to see the days creep by tediously as the job becomes no more than a source of income. They begin to envy teachers in community schools as they begin to deprecate their own jobs. Teachers do, of course, find an occasional student who is interested in learning, but all too often residents come to class either to sleep or to create problems.

Still, some academic teachers overcome these difficulties and do remarkable jobs with confined youths. The most effective teachers often come from lower-class backgrounds. Older teachers also seem to do a better job and to gain more respect from students than do younger teachers. Female teachers in their early twenties, in particular, often have a difficult time adjusting to the institutional setting. The effective female teacher is likely to fulfill the role of the firm mother—willing to give, but demanding respect and obedience. The effective male teacher generally is able to handle himself physically. One noted, "If they give me any shit, I'll beat their asses." Yet, one of the most effective male teachers the writers have had the privilege of knowing was confined to a wheelchair.

Predictably, staff turnover is high, as ineffective teachers come and go very quickly, but there are always some teachers who are truly committed to teaching youthful offenders and who remain for long periods of time.

THE SOCIAL WORKER

Usually designated as the basic treatment agent in most institutions, the social worker has varied and extensive duties. Social workers generally use social casework in their therapeutic intervention with residents, which is that phase of social work that deals directly with maladjusted persons. Thus, the goal is to determine the kind of help these persons need and to assist them in coping with life.[10]

Social workers who engage in casework see themselves in a variety of roles. Some perceive themselves as psychotherapists and actually practice psychotherapy. Others adopt a treatment modality, such as reality therapy or milieu therapy, and view themselves as practitioners of it. Still others use an eclectic approach to therapy, choosing here and there until they have designed what is for them an effective way to communicate with offenders. Finally, some do no more than collect social histories or backgrounds of clients.

In addition to maintaining regular contact with those who comprise their case load, social workers are expected to write evaluation reports every month or two on each youth's progress, copies of which are often sent to the supervisor, to the central office of the youth commission, and to the youth's aftercare officer. When the institutional release procedure has determined that a resident is ready to go home, the social worker is further expected to do all the paperwork required for release. Although various jurisdictions require different reports from institutional social workers, only the well-organized worker does not feel overwhelmed by the never-ending reports, regardless of the type of institution he serves.

Social workers are expected to perform many services for residents: check their canteen balances, find out why parents have not written, set up enrollments in vocational programs, obtain social security cards for those who do not have them, call aftercare officers, talk with teachers about class problems, protect residents from aggressive peers, intervene in staff-resident problems, and accompany inmates on shopping trips prior to release or a home visit. Additionally, if an institution permits home furloughs, social workers generally are expected to make many of the arrangements. If an institution permits selected youths to work in the community, the social workers must justify this privilege for a resident to the institutional administrators and often may have to find the jobs as well. If a girl is pregnant, her social worker may be required to make many of the arrangements for childbirth and perhaps carry out adoption procedures.

The degree of authority given social workers varies considerably. Generally, private institutions accord them greater authority than that given in state training schools; they also have more authority in female than in male institutions. But authority tends to decrease as an institution becomes more custodial in emphasis; thus, camps and ranches typically give social workers more authority than do end-of-the-line institutions.

The organizational structure of the institution also determines the degree of authority of the social worker. In some institutions, for example, social workers are in charge of and supervise the staff in a cottage unit. They become, then, middle managers responsible for both the treatment and custodial concerns of the unit. They, of course, delegate most of the custodial tasks, but they are ultimately responsible for seeing that these tasks are done.

In the usual organizational structure, the social worker has an office in either the administration building or in the cottage unit itself. The social worker is expected to be a treatment specialist and an adviser to institutional personnel about ways to work most productively with juveniles in trouble. But the caseworker, although a professional staff member, has no delegated authority to act for the client: When a cottage supervisor or cottage parent and the social worker disagree on how to handle a particular youth, the desires of the custodial staff usually prevail over those of the social worker.

Problems   Forming a trusting and caring relationship with clients is usually a difficult task for the social worker. A white social worker, especially, often does not find it easy to communicate with a lower-class black or a Mexican-American youth. Not only does the social worker have little in common with the youth, but also the juvenile probably is not interested in developing such a relationship. Rather, the resident only wants the social worker to speak up for him in review meetings, to comply with his requests, and to avoid interfering with the inmate world. In contrast, a middle-class white or black youth may be very interested in forming a friendship and even a counseling relationship with the social worker. In fact, the middle-class youth may want to depend upon the social worker to protect him from predatory peers.

Not infrequently, social workers have communication problems with other cottage staff. Nonprofessional staff sometimes feel that social workers are full of book knowledge but lack experience, cannot understand what it is like to be a delinquent from the ghetto, are easily manipulated, and make poor decisions about residents.[11] Furthermore, line staff frequently feel, and may even tell the social worker, that he will not be around for more than a year or two because he only looks upon his job as a steppingstone to a better one.

New social workers, in an attempt to become effective treatment agents, typically work fifty to sixty hours a week. They are involved in and very enthusiastic about their jobs, for they probably perceive of themselves as advocates for youth in a rigid and punitive system. Too, they often are shocked by the dehumanizing and sometimes brutal way residents are treated by that kindly parent, the state.

But it is not long before new social workers realize that they need the approval and acceptance of cottage staff. To gain such approval, social workers are often tempted to compromise their own values and to accept the values and norms of nonprofessional staff, which tend to differ slightly from institution to institution. In one maximum security institution, the social workers found themselves accepting the attitudes of line staff, first by viewing juveniles as hostile manipulators attempting to avoid responsibility, and second, by assuming that institutional administrators were doing everything possible to make their jobs more difficult. This resulted in the abandonment of their roles as advocates for innocent clients and their acceptance of the view that the administration is an enemy to be resisted in every way. Next, these social workers accepted the idea that they should cut every corner possible, for they began to look upon their work as no more than a poorly paying job. The climax came when social workers began to justify the striking of youths by saying "they got what they deserved."[12]

Finally, social workers must deal with the custodial climate of the institutional setting. Obviously, the climate in an honor camp is much different from that in a maximum security institution reserved for the hard-core offender. But, in most training schools, social workers find the custodial emphasis of the facility disturbing, if not actually oppressive. For example, administrators expect social workers to maintain good security practices, to assure that residents conform to institutional regulations, and to reserve the privilege of home visits and community jobs to the most trusted residents. Custodial staff must approve of home visits in many institutions, and social workers usually are terribly frustrated when their treatment decisions are overruled by custodial personnel. Too, social workers, particularly males, often are expected to join the chase when an escape occurs. Walking through the woods looking for a runaway is an experience most social workers will long remember for at least two reasons: It is not only a dangerous task because the social worker may suddenly be attacked by the escapee, but it is also clear and decisive testimony to both residents and the social worker that the social worker is, ultimately, a custodial agent.

One institutional social worker said that he felt like Sisyphus—the legendary king who was condemned throughout eternity to push a heavy stone up a steep hill, only to have it roll back to the bottom time after time, The stone, representing the social worker's efforts, was heavy because there were so many reasons why residents in institutions failed. The hill comprised all the debilitating factors pitted against the youth—institutional rules and procedures, lack of home support, established patterns of failure, antisocial friends, and inconsistent and sometimes brutal treatment from staff members. The total impact was impotence and frustration, which the social worker felt was the chief reason why his co-workers stayed such a short time in juvenile institutions.[13]

In short, social workers do not have an easy job in juvenile institutions. Some are overwhelmed by the institutional environment and leave as soon as possible; others overcome the problems (or should we

say mountains?) and become influential policymakers. Effective social workers have clearly observable traits. First, they are highly committed to the role of helping the cottage team to design beneficial programs; they become, in effect, the catalyst behind the cottage team. Second, they are hardworking, perceptive, and skillful, traits that win the respect of line staff. Third, effective social workers are able to communicate with residents and refuse to be intimidated or controlled by them. Fourth, they place a high priority on involving offenders' families in therapy, particularly if the home community and the institution are close to each other. Finally, they are usually successful in getting residents to accept or commit themselves to a treatment plan that the resident, the social worker, and cottage staff jointly develop. The plan is sometimes called a contract and has short- and long-range treatment goals.

THE YOUTH LEADER OR COTTAGE PARENT

Cottage parents, or youth leaders, fulfill the important role of providing twenty-four-hour care to residents. They wake the youths in the morning, see to it that they dress and wash for breakfast, supervise the serving of breakfast, and conduct a brief room inspection. Next, they make certain that those students enrolled in the academic and vocational programs go to school and that those who work in the kitchen, on the grounds, or in the community arrive at their job. In the more secure training schools, students are escorted to their particular assignments, but in many minimum security facilities, they are permitted movement without staff supervision.

The cottage parent generally remains in the cottage to prepare lunch and to take care of other cottage work. Cottage supervisors or youth leaders are usually assigned duties that keep them busy until they pick up the residents for lunch. These duties usually include school patrol one week, inspection of the rooms of boys on restriction the next, and outside patrol of the recreation fields the third (though not always in this order).

Residents are picked up from school and brought back to the cottage for lunch, after which they are returned to school or to other assigned details, and the youth leaders return to their assigned duties. The shift usually changes at 3 p.m., before school is out. The afternoon shift generally picks up the school youths and brings them back to the cottage. If the institution has an active group program, the cottage supervisors may then hold group meetings with residents. Guided group interaction, positive peer culture, or transactional analysis (see Chapter 11 for discussion of these group methods) may be used. Otherwise, the period from the end of school until the evening meal is free time.

Following the evening meal, especially during good weather, residents are permitted to go outside. They may participate in organized sports or merely do as they choose. Staff at this time have to be particularly watchful because runaways frequently take place during these outdoor activities. An hour or so of television follows this sports activity, and then residents are sent to their rooms around 9 p.m. to prepare for bed. Lights are usually out around 10 p.m., and the afternoon shift is then off duty and leaves the institution at 11 p.m.

The night shift then takes over, generally, with only one staff person in each cottage from 11 p.m. to 7 a.m. This person's job basically is to make certain that there are no runaways during the night and to be available should a problem arise or an illness occur. He often spends the greater part of the eight-hour shift sitting at a desk in the staff office and responding to the every-thirty-minutes or so phone check on cottage security.

The youth leader is a key figure in the handling of confined youths. On one hand, some youths become very close to their cottage leaders and a few even come to regard them as father or mother figures. Many residents stay in touch with their favorite youth counselor following their release; some even return to the institution to visit. Cottage parents and youth leaders who are interested and very much involved in their charges' lives are the ones who receive a warm response from residents. Some of these staff become remarkable treatment agents and have a permanent impact on youths.

On the other hand, many residents regard their cottage supervisors with real animosity and disgust. They feel that cottage staff are not interested in them. One youth said to a cottage staff, "You don't care if I live or die." Indeed, residents are often correct with such accusations, for some staff display little warmth and concern for residents. Unfortunately, a few staff even exploit them in every conceivable way.

A number of researchers have pointed out that treatment-oriented juvenile institutions seem to generate more trusting relationships with staff, less suspicion, and more cooperation among inmates.[14] In comparison, custodially oriented prisons and maximum security training schools generate hostility, suspicion, and fearfulness among staff and inmates.[15]

That the basic organizational goal, treatment or custody, affects the quality of institutional life is not surprising. In custodially oriented settings, staff are reminded again and again that custody is king and are suspended when they make a mistake and forget that fact. In time, they tend to perceive themselves as correctional officers only. But in treatment-oriented institutions, cottage staff are likely to be involved in the treatment process. They may be group leaders and may conduct groups several times a week. They may be responsible for contact with parents who visit when the social worker is not on duty. They may, if the need arises, make some of the arrangements for residents' home visits. They may be asked to find a job for a resident approved for work in the community. They probably will be faced a number of times by desperate youths who need to be talked out of killing themselves, or of escaping, or of permitting themselves to be sexually victimized. They will be asked to give oral or written evaluations of each youth at his periodic review, and they are usually asked to be present and to be part of the decision-making process at the time of review. These experiences, of course, have a positive impact on staff, and the result is that many begin to perceive themselves more as helpers than as mere controllers or custodians.

Staff Conflict   However, the number of juvenile institutions in which cottage staff fulfill treatment roles and functions is still quite small. In most of the training schools, camps, and ranches across the country, considerable staff conflict is present because various levels of staff have different expectations as to their own and others' duties, values, roles, and behaviors. One of the greatest sources of conflict stems from the gap in education levels of professional and nonprofessional staff. Prestige, power, and higher salaries often accrue to those who have achieved higher educational levels. Lower-level staff resent the disparities and become bitter. Since they are in more direct continuous contact with youths than are any of the other staff, line staff feel that they should be rewarded commensurately. They also feel that they understand the youths better and are more realistic about how they should be handled than are professional staff.

Weber's study of five public and private institutions stressed the value orientations, conceptions of status and role, perceptions of delinquency and treatment, and the results of the conflicts among professional and nonprofessional staff. In this study, professionals were found to be more positive toward "book learning" than nonprofessionals. They favored an analytic approach to problems and emphasized the discussion of problems with other professionals. At the same time, they were split in their attitudes toward lower-level personnel. Some lower-level staff were perceived to be kind, caring, sincere, and hardworking in their relations with youths, whereas others were thought to be rigid and insensitive authoritarians. In addition to the attitudes toward professionals that have already been discussed, nonprofessionals tended to see professionals as too impractical, too inexperienced, and too naive to understand the total operation. Many actually were looked upon as inept and as manipulators of the system. Finally, nonprofessional personnel felt that much of the behavior of professional staff was a disguise to cover up their hostilities.[16]

These conflicts had important effects on the five institutions in Weber's study. Nonprofessionals did not attend meetings at which they were expected, and each group ignored the other. The groups were split both within and between, and dissension permeated the ranks of each. Wherever possible, both professionals and nonprofessionals tried to escape their routine duties and to engage in activities that took them away from daily problems. Professional staff engaged in research and ignored problems. Nonprofessional staff ignored problems, slept instead of working, gave evidence of being maladjusted, left work early, or withdrew into their own world and "did their own thing."[17]

Staff Code   Informal codes sometimes determine group behavior much more than formal bureaucratic rules do. Similar to the inmate code discussed in the last chapter are the unwritten values and norms of the line staff in many institutions. These norms are part of the oral tradition of the institution and provide staff with guidelines on how to approach their fellow workers, their jobs, and the residents. The newcomer who chooses to ignore the informal code and to go his own way may find his stay made quite uncomfortable by experienced staff. In fact, the prestige accorded cottage staff in some institutions depends upon their allegiance to the code.

In the Bartollas et al. study, the line staff of this end-of-the-line male juvenile institution had developed an informal code that spelled out acceptable and nonacceptable behavior. Part of the strength and cohesiveness of line staff in this institution lay in their ability to turn to their own reference group for acceptance and reinforcement. Youth leaders who did not follow the code were punished by other staff, and these guidelines, stating right and wrong, were taught to new staff during their first months on the job.[18]

The real losers in this particular institution were the residents. Some of the norms contributed to negligence; the formal rules stated the duties of the staff, but the informal rules permitted staff to go their own way. This negligence occasionally led to great exploitation of the residents; for example, the staff member who failed to supervise showers increased the chances of sexual victimization of weaker residents. The informal code also permitted staff to give privileges or rewards to resident leaders if they kept the cottage quiet. The staff member said, in effect, "Keep the cottage quiet, and you can do what you want." Obviously, this benefited those at the top of the social order, but those at the bottom sometimes experienced real hell.

One-to-One   Cottage staff, thus, form relationships with residents that vary
Relationships   from "significant other" to indifference and exploitation. Empirical evidence to date seems to indicate that youth leaders or nonprofessional staff are able to form deeper and more positive relationships with residents than are professional staff.[19] Many line staff, as adolescents, had experience on the streets and struggled in a lower-class environment, which gives them the edge over professional staff who come mainly from middle-class backgrounds.

Weber, in describing the characteristics of the effective institutional staff, made the following observations:

> These determinants indicate that irrespective of technical or professional training, rehabilitative work with delinquents in institutions requires people who have genuine interest in children, who are emotionally mature and stable, and will react to problems with a high degree of adaptability and versatility; who will make a sincere attempt to understand human maladjustments and will react with personal warmth when dealing with personality problems of children; who can work agreeably with associates, and who can act with initiative, perseverance and leadership; who are sufficiently intelligent to learn quickly and deal constructively with the difficult problems arising in institutional rehabilitative work; who have the ability for critical abstract thinking yet can apply themselves to concrete problems; and who are free from social and religious prejudices.[20]

Other characteristics effective institutional staff tend to have are:

1. They generally are at least in their late 30s, are mature, have stable personal lives, and are law-abiding citizens.
2. They are caring, concerned, and genuine. Consequently, they communicate that they can be trusted and that they are concerned about what happens to confined youths.
3. They have had several years of experience in working with confined juveniles.
4. They have the ability to see beneath the "fronts" of their charges, are street-wise, and cannot be manipulated easily.
5. They provide a role model that nearly all residents respect.
6. They are dedicated to the task of providing a safe environment for residents. Even though exploitation is often a serious problem in juvenile institutions, these staff are almost uncanny in their ability to spot the residents that are likely targets for exploitation and to know what is needed to support these youths as they serve their time.
7. They are able to respond to residents in a fair and consistent way. This creates a more stable and secure living environment, one in which residents know that they will be treated fairly.
8. They usually believe that increasing the freedom of offenders to make decisions is important. They feel that growth comes from giving freedom to persons when they are ready to accept more responsibility.
9. They generally place a major emphasis on positive experiences for offenders, believing that this is the best way to improve their self-esteem.

10. These line staff consistently remind offenders that they are re-- sponsible for their own behavior; that is, incarcerated youths must face up to their negative and disruptive behavior.

CAREERS IN JUVENILE INSTITUTIONS

The disadvantages of a correctional career loom large in the minds of many people. First, there is the poor public image of jobs in corrections:

> The Harris survey of public attitudes toward corrections shows that correctional workers rank in the middle of a group of occupations in terms of public confidence. However, youthful respondents expressed less confidence in correctional rehabilitative work than in all other vocations except businessmen. Also, there was a high rate of "not sure" responses among the adults which would indicate a lack of familiarity with the correctional field. And, among teenagers, the level of confidence in various corrections-related occupations drops as the youth's educational level rises. It is apparent that this low confidence is not a disparagement of the attitudes or attributes of correctional workers, but a reflection of the lack of demonstrable success in the eyes of the respondents. Further, only 13 percent of the adult respondents would recommend correctional rehabilitation as a career for a young person close to them; the percentage was slightly smaller among those with college educations. Correctional rehabilitation was the lowest rank of all career interests by the teenagers themselves, with only 1 percent saying they would give serious consideration to the field.[21]

Other factors that militate against correctional careers include the general disenchantment with training schools, the racial conflicts and violence in training schools, and the lack of competitive salaries.

To overcome these negative features, salaries must continually be upgraded in juvenile corrections, modern management principles should be used more fully, more manageable work loads should be designed for all levels of staff, and continuous in-service education should be made available to all personnel.

Educational Criteria for Correctional Professionals   Certain educational qualifications are necessary for the professional staff member in a juvenile institution. As a result, many academic institutions have introduced programs devoted to the study of juvenile and adult corrections. In January 1974, more than 300 academic institutions offered basic training and degree programs in corrections. Today's correctional worker is much better educated and trained than ever before. Minimum academic standards for institutional social work-

TABLE 10-2   A Guide to Educational Levels for Corrections

Academic Level	Potential Contribution to Corrections
Doctoral	Acts largely independently; conducts research, provides consultation; acts as 'change agent' . . . is seldom on full-time payroll.
Master's	Research and consultation skills, often at maximum level; minimally, is assigned a special case load; generally serves client indirectly.
Bachelor's	Probably the lowest level of preparation for direct service to client in the field; carries case load, is a therapist, and performs quite independently.
Associate in Arts (community college)	Probably entry level for the line worker; after thoughtful and extensive orientation, becomes agent for direct service to client.
High School Diploma	With well-designed preentry and postentry training will supply all services otherwise not supplied; needs career motivation.

From: Joint Commission on Correctional Manpower and Training, *Staff Report: Perspectives on Correctional Manpower and Training* (Washington, D.C.: U.S. Government Printing Office, 1970), p. 42.

ers usually include a bachelor's degree in liberal arts. The master's degree is preferred in social work, with supervised field work in a correctional agency. In some jurisdictions youth leaders are required to have at least two years of college work in liberal arts, but the preferred applicant in these jurisdictions is the person with a bachelor's degree in liberal arts.[22]

Staff Development

Recognition of the need for on-the-job training for both professional and nonprofessional staff is becoming widespread in juvenile corrections. In some states, staff development is achieved through attendance at a state training academy or through participation in seminars conducted by a staff-development unit of the correctional system or attendance at in-house staff development seminars.

Training academies exist in several states. The Correctional Training Academy in Illinois was begun in 1973 with a small planning grant

FIGURE 10-2   Staff Development Unit

STAFF DEVELOPMENT UNIT

GROUP WORK ASSIGNMENT   DATE _____

                                               INST. _____

1. Construct an organization chart containing your job area supervised. Indicate on the chart the structure areas above you as well as below you.
   a. Are the relations, as you know them, clearly defined with those above you and those below you?
   b. What is your specific responsibility and authority?
   c. Are your objectives and programs coordinated laterally with your co-equal supervisors as well as vertically with top management?
2. What type of an informal organization system is in effect within your institution?
   a. Does it have a status and communication system?
   b. Is there a self-appointed leader?
   c. Is this informal system receptive to changes by the formal organization (top management)?
   d. What changes are necessary, if any, to balance the two systems into a harmonious working unit?

from the Law Enforcement Assistance Administration, and it now trains all levels of correctional staff. This academy offers a four-day pre-service training course for youth supervisors and in-service training for senior youth supervisors. Training begins on a Monday morning in the Academy in Chicago and ends Thursday evening.

Some correctional systems also have a staff development unit that conducts training programs in participating institutions. In a course taught to top and middle managers, the Staff Development Unit of the Ohio Youth Commission trained the group in decision making and problem solving. Figure 10-2 is a typical exercise for such a group.

In-house staff development is a third approach to training institutional personnel. Managers, for example, can be taught how to become integrators, team builders, catalysts for improving intergroup relationships, job enrichers, and conveners of organizational confrontation meetings. (All these will be discussed in Chapter 12.)

The effectiveness of staff development training programs is heavily dependent on the ability of the trainers or leaders to establish rapport, communication, and credibility with the institutional staff. A leader known to the writers who was particularly effective with line staff was able to establish a warm and open learning environment, was well prepared for each session, and related the theoretical to his many years of experience as a youth leader and a youth leader supervisor.

SUMMARY

The emergence of therapies and educational and rehabilitative programs has created problems in juvenile facilities. Professionals normally command higher rewards than those with less education, which generates resentment among those lower on the scale of benefits, status, and compensation. Since the beginning of this century, at least, administrators have had to mediate the ensuing conflict. Differences in status and pay have split institutions into competing and often hostile factions. The problem is compounded by the fact that seldom is there enough money to run programs as they should be run. Corners are cut and both programs and staff suffer. Another complicating factor is that the inadequate resources available to administrators often mean that less-than-qualified staff must be hired, especially in the lower ranks. Administrators find they must operate with staff who proceed on the basis of folklore rather than solid therapeutic and rehabilitative principles. The result is the sometimes unnecessary use of force and brutality and the consequent resistance of residents to worthwhile programs.

This is not to deprecate the vast number of lower-level and professional staff in our juvenile facilities who are kind, sensitive, caring, and committed and who are dedicated to doing all they can to help these youths. Such staff, who are found at all levels, care deeply about the youths under their care. They make personal sacrifices to help the kids, go out of their way to get decent homes and jobs for them, enter into involved discussions with other staff to determine how best to help a troubled youngster, and then shed tears when a favorite "troublemaker" leaves. They then wait anxiously, hoping to hear that all has gone well and that the youth has "made it" on the outside. All too often, they never know. Their frustrations increase. Everyone in such a milieu then becomes a victim. They have been given the job of making an imperfect institution function, but they have not been given the resources or moral support to accomplish the assignment. The ideal is that they will perform miracles; the reality is that they must keep the youths quiet and out of sight.

QUESTIONS

1. What are the administrative staff categories in juvenile correction facilities? Whom do they supervise?
2. What are the basic problems faced by superintendents? How do they solve these problems?
3. What are the problems of teachers in juvenile facilities?
4. What are the problems of social workers in juvenile facilities?
5. What are the problems of youth leaders or line staff?
6. Would you be interested in working in a juvenile institution? Why or why not?

ENDNOTES

1. Rosemary C. Sarri and Robert D. Vinter, "Justice for Whom? Varieties of Juvenile Correctional Approaches," in *The Juvenile Justice System*, edited by Malcolm W. Klein (Beverly Hills, Calif.: Sage Publications, 1976), p. 181.
2. Ibid., p. 182.
3. Ibid., p. 182.
4. Ibid., pp. 182–183.
5. "National Survey on the Value of Rehabilitation Programs," *Corrections* 1 (May/June 1975): 5.
6. Richard M. Carter, Richard A. McGee, and E. Kim Nelson, *Corrections in America* (Philadelphia: J. B. Lippincott Company, 1975), p. 52.
7. Daniel Glaser, *The Effectiveness of a Prison and Parole System* (Indianapolis: Bobbs-Merrill, 1964), pp. 90–91.
8. Clemens Bartollas, Stuart Miller, and Simon Dinitz, *Juvenile Victimization: The Institutional Paradox* (New York: Halsted Press, A Sage Publication, 1976), pp. 183–195.
9. George H. Weber, "Conflict between Professional and Non-Professional Personnel in Institutional Delinquency Development," *Journal of Criminal Law, Criminology and Police Science* 48, no. 1 (May/June 1957).
10. Paul W. Tappan, *Juvenile Delinquency* (New York: McGraw-Hill Book Company, 1949), p. 362.
11. Clemens Bartollas, "Sisyphus in a Juvenile Institution," *Social Work* 20 (September 1975): 365–366.
12. Ibid., p. 366.
13. Ibid., p. 366.
14. Street et al., *Organization for Treatment: A Comparative Study of Institutions for Delinquents* (New York: Free Press, 1966); Bernard B. Berk, "Organizational Goals and Inmate Organization," *American Journal of*

Sociology 71 (March 1966): 522–534; Oscar Grusky, "Organization Goals and the Behavior of Informal Leaders," *American Journal of Sociology* 62 (July 1959): 59–67.

15. Donald Clemmer, *The Prison Community* (New York: Holt, Rinehart and Winston, 1958); Lloyd W. McCorkle, "Social Structure in a Prison," *Welfare Reporter* 8 (December 1956): 5–15; Gresham Sykes, *Society of Captives* (Princeton, N.J.: Princeton University Press, 1958); Richard McCleery, "Policy Change in Prison Management," in *Complex Organization: A Sociological Reader,* edited by Amitai Etzioni (New York: Holt, Rinehart and Winston, 1961), pp. 376–400.
16. Weber, "Conflict," pp. 27–37.
17. Ibid., p. 37.
18. Bartollas, Miller, and Dinitz, *Juvenile Victimization,* 197–215.
19. Glaser, *Effectiveness;* Bartollas, Miller, and Dinitz, *Juvenile Victimization;* Stuart J. Miller, "Post-Institutional Adjustment of 443 Consecutive TICO Releases", (Ph.D. dissertation, Ohio State University, 1971); Carl F. Jesness et al., *The Youth Center Research Project* (Sacramento, Calif.: American Justice Institute, 1972).
20. Weber, "Conflict," p. 165.
21. B. F. Mitchell, "Recruiting Ideas That Get Results," *Public Personnel Association* (Chicago, n.d.), p. 121.
22. Edward Eldefonso and Walter Hartinger, *Control, Treatment, and Rehabilitation of Juvenile Offenders* (Beverly Hills, Calif.: Glencoe Press, 1976), pp. 233–234.

REFERENCES

Bartollas, Clemens; Miller, Stuart J.; and Dinitz, Simon. *Juvenile Victimization: The Institutional Paradox.* New York: Halsted Press, A Sage Publication, 1976.

> *Chapter 12 of this book describes the normative code of youth leaders in a juvenile institution.*

Bartollas, Clemens. "Sisyphus in a Juvenile Institution." *Social Work* 20 (September 1975): 365–366.

> *Contains both a description of a social worker's job in a juvenile institution and hints on how social workers can become effective treatment agents.*

Sarri, Rosemary, and Vinter, Robert D. "Justice for Whom? Varieties of Juvenile Correctional Approaches." In *The Juvenile Justice System,* edited by Malcolm W. Klein. Beverly Hills, Calif.: Sage Publications, 1976.

> *Derived from the National Assessment of Juvenile Corrections Research Project, this article is an excellent study of institutional staff.*

Weber, George H. "Conflict between Professional and Non-Professional Personnel in Institutional Delinquency Development." *Journal of Criminal Law, Criminology and Police Science* 48 (May/June 1957).

> *Weber's article is extremely helpful in understanding the conflicts between treatment and custodial staff in many juvenile institutions.*

11

Treatment Technologies

Juvenile offenders are confronted and almost overwhelmed by the various methods used to treat, save, rehabilitate, remodel, remake, or otherwise "recycle" them. Juvenile corrections, far more than adult corrections, has as its guiding premise the rehabilitation of individuals before they become hardened criminals. To that end, researchers from every discipline have looked for the key that will modify the behavior of offenders.

Punishment was believed to be the answer for a long period of time. But in the 1700s, the founding fathers of our country substituted a religious orientation as the proper way to work with wayward children. This moral and religious emphasis slowly gave way by the second half of the nineteenth century to firm discipline and rigorous work training. The study of the character and mental condition of individual lawbreakers was the accepted treatment during the first four decades of the twentieth century. Sociology began to dominate treatment efforts in the 1950s and 1960s with the use of predelinquency community programs, detached workers with juvenile gangs, group interaction, job training, and community reorganization. Psychology has continued to vie with sociology for supremacy in juvenile corrections. The current state of corrections seems to be that a new idea springs up each day, each heralded as the panacea for youth crime.

Approaches to treatment range from individual to group methods. This chapter presents a general discussion of treatment in juvenile institutions and describes and evaluates the treatment modalities that are most popular today.

PROBLEMS OF THERAPY

Psychiatrists, psychologists, social workers, and nonprofessional line staff are responsible for therapy in institutions. While psychiatrists and psychologists are chiefly administrators in private facilities, they primarily serve as consultants in public institutions; that is, they are brought in when emergencies occur or when residents must be evaluated before release. Thus, day-to-day rehabilitation methods are generally left to the two other categories of workers—nonprofessional staff and social workers.

Several factors militate against a positive impact of treatment in both community- and institutionally based settings. First, treatment efforts in juvenile corrections frequently lack the sophistication to deal with the complexity of the human personality. This lack of sophistication stems from the fact that these methods are often used either by untrained staff who are not really committed to what they are doing or by middle-class professional staff who lack the ability to communicate with street-wise juvenile offenders. Furthermore, counties, states, and the federal government differ widely in the financial commitment they make to treatment both in institutional and community-based corrections. Significantly, only a few "showplace" programs are given the financial support needed to conduct effective treatment methods and programs. The inmate peer culture, too, has unquestionably more clout with residents than the norms and values of their keepers; this inmate subculture, therefore, usually counteracts the efforts of staff to resocialize the inmates. Staff conflicts and jealousies also tend to attenuate consistent and unified approaches to treating confined offenders. Finally, the coercive nature of these settings makes the formation of open and trusting relationships of staff with offenders very difficult.

It is not surprising that once youths become committed to criminal careers and delinquent subcultures, most of the treatment efforts of private, county, state, and federal agencies fail to affect them. Wheeler and Cottrell note, "There are no demonstrable and proven methods for reducing the incidence of serious delinquent acts through preventative or rehabilitative procedures".[1] Ohmart has added, "There appears to be a growing consensus that most correctional institutions probably deter the rehabilitation process in most offenders more than they assist it."[2]

Allen Breed, the Director of the California Youth Authority, adds a pessimistic note:

> We don't kid ourselves that we treat kids. They treat themselves and rehabilitate themselves if they want to. . . . In the last few years we've been trying to work more toward a justice model than a treatment model. If there is an example of unfairness in the system, it's probably in

how discipline is handled in correctional institutions, particularly with juveniles, because we're supposed to take on the parent role. Whether the most elementary elements of due process are provided is entirely accidental.[3]

Hood concluded from his review of criminological research that lengthy institutional sentences are no more successful than shorter ones; that fines are more successful than probation or incarceration with both first offenders and recidivists in all age groups; and that open institutions seem to be at least as effective as closed ones for the "better type of offender." He also found that various treatment modalities had little or no impact on subsequent criminal behavior.[4] Lipton, Martinson, and Wilks, too, have challenged the belief that rehabilitation of offenders is an achievable goal.[5] In view of this research, it is easy to succumb to the growing consensus in adult corrections that rehabilitation is dead. Indeed, some feel that rehabilitation should no longer be a goal of juvenile corrections. A predominant attitude is, "If we have learned anything at all about treatment, it is that nothing works."

Proponents of the medical and adjustment models, not surprisingly, strongly reject this conclusion. They are quick to defend institutional and community-based treatment. They argue that juveniles have a legal right to treatment and that through therapy some lawbreakers gain the strength to avoid further unlawful activities. This change would not occur, according to this line of thinking, without therapeutic intervention and treatment.

Mann, in examining clinical psychoanalysis, group work, and education and vocational training, found that each of these approaches had some success with youthful offenders convicted of serious crimes. Morover, he found that the content of successful programs gave the offender freedom to enter the program of his choice and to decide how long to stay in it; maximized the involvement of youths in the program; contained clearly defined tasks; sought to install responsible, fair, consistent, and thoughtful behavior; reinforced positive behavior with significant rewards; and simulated the real world in which the new behavior was to be lived. Thus, Mann contends that some youngsters do receive benefit from institutional programs.[6]

Another study that supports this viewpoint is the Fricot Ranch Study. In an evaluation of two treatment programs for delinquent boys, an analysis of parole violation rates for all residents showed that boys in the more intensive program did better. The findings suggest that positive treatment outcomes are demonstrated only when a total commitment is made to treatment. Also, any subprograms must be evaluated with sophisticated research designs that take into account variations in subject, milieu, and treatment.[7]

CLASSIFICATION OF OFFENDERS

An assumption formed early in the twentieth century is that the first step of treatment is to diagnose and classify. Thus, psychiatric evaluations and psychological workups are usually administered to youths soon after their adjudication, even if they have been tested previously in the community. This testing frequently takes place at a diagnostic center, and institutional staff, armed with these evaluations, then decide where to transfer the youth.

Until recently, offenders were classified according to their personality dynamics. The Ohio Youth Commission, for instance, classified adjudicated youth as mentally retarded, psychoneurotic, personality disordered, antisocial, passive-aggressive, passive-dependent, adolescent adjustment reaction, behavior disordered, group delinquent, and unsocialized. Another popular classification system is the Jesness Inventory. This test uses eleven scales to classify adolescents into personality types and to evaluate personality change: social maladjustment, value orientation, immaturity, autism, alienation, manifest aggression, withdrawal-depression, social anxiety, repression, denial, and asocial index.

But in the 1960s, the theory of differential treatment began in California and spread across the country. This theory contends that the impact of treatment varies according to the type of violator. Hence, what works with one youthful offender may have no effect whatever, or a definitely negative impact, on another.

I-Level   The first major effort to implement differential treatment was that which evolved from the Preston Typology Study. The basic assumption of this modality was that the failure of many institutional treatment programs was related to the absence of specific differential treatment goals and techniques. The major goal of the modality was to develop an efficient procedure for classifying residents according to the Interpersonal Maturity Level Classification System developed by Warren. Additional goals were to assign residents to staff whose treatment philosophy matched the resident's needs and interests; to train staff in the classification system; to stimulate the development of differential treatment strategies for each subtype of offender; and to evaluate the impact of differential treatment.[8]

Adopted by the California Youth Authority in the 1960s and other states in the 1970s, the I-Level Classification System proposes that personality integration follows a certain sequence in normal adolescent development. Therefore, this classification system attempts to discover the world view of offenders by focusing on their perception of self, others, and the world. According to Warren and others responsible for developing this system, the I-Level of a person is directly related to his ability to identify and involve himself with others. This seven-point classification ranges from I_1 (infantile in interpersonal maturity) to I_7 (Christ-like). Most offenders are found to be at the I_2, I_3, and I_4 levels and are further subdivided into nine delinquent subtypes.[9]

The I_2 youths generally perceive living in the world as extremely difficult, since they believe themselves to be the whole world; consequently, they feel that all desires must be immediately fulfilled without contributing anything themselves. This egocentrism leads the youth to view the world as either taking or giving, and other people are evaluated purely on the basis of whether they satisfy the youths' wants or whether they withhold desired goals. These youths blame others when something goes wrong and their desires are left unfulfilled. When they blow up, they often revert to infantile behavior.

The I_3s understand that their own behavior is related to whether or not they get what they want, but they have difficulty understanding the feelings, needs, and motives of those around them. They try to encourage others to make "giving" rather than "denying" responses. Because they lack an idealized value system, they seek out an external structure made up of rules and formulas; the world is perceived in terms of power relationships. These youths blame others for problems experienced in the past and minimize their own culpability. As a result, they are unable to predict accurately the responses of others.

The I_4s perceive the world according to an internalized system of values that, if not fulfilled, leaves them feeling upset and guilty. These youths see themselves as unique and better than others, and they try to live up to their perceptions by achieving recognition. In fact, they often model themselves after persons recognized as having accomplished important goals, even if those goals are antisocial. Considerably advanced beyond the two types already discussed, the I_4s understand some of the forces impinging upon them from the outside. They realize to some extent why others act as they do, and they have some insight into the feelings and actions of others. Because they are achievers and goal-oriented, they plan and worry about the future, aware that things may change.

The Quay System

The I-Level Classification System has avid critics as well as disciples. Some of the most vocal criticism comes from institutional staff who feel that offenders ought to be evaluated solely on the basis of their behavior. This point of view persuaded administrators of the Robert F. Kennedy Youth Center in Morgantown, West Virginia to use a system designed by Hubert C. Quay that evaluates behavior rather than world view. The Quay System divides delinquent behavior into four types: inadequate-immature; neurotic-conflicted; unsocialized-aggressive or psychopathic; and socialized or subcultural. The inadequate-immature type consists of those youth who behave childishly and irresponsibly; the neurotic-conflict type is made up of anxious, insecure juveniles whose internal conflicts create problems for themselves and others; the unsocialized type is composed of those who adhere to the values of their delinquent peer group; and the subcultural type consists of adolescents who are involved in gang delinquency.[10]

Offenders are classified even more specifically within these categories by means of three instruments: a checklist of behavioral problems, completed by staff who have observed the youth; a true-false questionnaire filled out by the offender himself; and a checklist of his life history, based on presentence reports. The purpose of these and other measuring devices is not only to match youths with the most effective treatment, but also to match staff to the cottage program in which they can be most effective.[11]

Classification Schemes Compared

Of these various classificatory systems, the psychiatric categories seem the least helpful. First, knowing that a youth is passive-aggressive or has an adolescent adjustment reaction is not very helpful in designing a treatment plan for him; that is, translating these broad categories into concrete treatment plans is difficult. A second problem is related to the adverse effect of labeling. Emotionally disturbed youths, for example, are acutely aware of their psychiatric diagnosis. Third, juveniles generally are distrustful of psychiatrists and psychologists and try to conceal as much as possible from them. Children in trouble are very much aware that the results of interviews and tests may prolong their stay and therefore they attempt to give the best "presentation of self" they can. This, of course, raises serious questions about the validity of psychiatric interviews and psychological tests.

The Quay classification system has not proved very effective at the Robert F. Kennedy Training School. The staff of this modern federal institution have questioned whether or not the behavior of youths in each of the four categories is really differentiated. They feel that this process of classifying offenders actually creates more behavior problems than it solves. The peer population, for example, became increasingly unmanageable and had a higher rate of escape after the scheme was initiated. Additionally, the lack of specific guidelines for staff who work with each type of youth is frustrating.[12]

However, the I-Level Classification System remained extremely popular until the mid-1970s, partly because it provided a manual that offered instructions on how to work with each type of youth. Thus, once a person was I-leveled by a person trained in this modality, staff could find the suggested treatment in the manual. Another advantage is that the I-Level scheme does provide some protection for passive institutional residents because it tends to separate them from aggressive peers. The I-Level System, too, discriminates between offenders more amenable to institutional treatment and those who have a better chance of succeeding if left in the community. It was found, for example, that only those classified as the I₃Cfc were aided in their community adjustment (less recidivism) by a period of institutionalization. Finally, proponents claim that I-Level classification reduces the number of institutional management problems. The Preston Typology Study reported a reduction in the number of rule infractions, peer problems, and the use of restriction in the six experimental living units studied.[13]

On the other hand, serious questions are being raised concerning the validity of I-Level theory. Its utility is questioned because of the limited number of staff trained to apply it. Another weakness disturbing to institutional staff is that I-Level classification tends to produce racially homogeneous groups or cottages; consequently, an I₄ cottage will have almost all white boys, while an I₃MP cottage will have almost all black residents. A third criticism relates to labeling. Considered "sickies" in the institution, I₄s often come to see themselves as emotionally disturbed and therefore begin to play the role. As one I₄ youth so poignantly put it, "They think I'm sick; therefore, why shouldn't I act that way?" Staff also claim that the treatment guidelines are still too general to be applied to specific cases. An additional objection is that this system recommends matching offenders with staff, which is not possible in many institutions because unions challenge the movement of staff from one cottage to another. Also not to be ignored is the frequent lack of commitment of line staff to this system of differential treatment. These criticisms, especially that having to do with racial groupings, have resulted in the I-Level System rapidly losing popularity. Significantly, California—where I-Level originated and has received much of its support—has now dropped the use of this system in its juvenile institutions.

INSIGHT THERAPY

Psychotherapy   Psychotherapy can be defined as the use of psychiatry in treating emotional problems. Psychiatrists, clinical psychologists, and psychiatric social workers have used psychotherapy to treat delinquents for years. The basic technique of this therapeutic approach is to encourage offenders to explore their past so that they can learn to handle present emotional problems presently expressed in aggressive behavior.

Youthful offenders, according to this approach, are sick and need to be treated by a properly trained therapist. Because of a lack of love and emotional warmth in their homes, youths develop conflicts and unconscious needs. These needs may manifest themselves as a need for punishment, a propensity for aggressive behavior, a desire to prove masculinity, a need to punish parents, and a denial of the need for nurture.[14]

One of the important consequences of the therapeutic relationship is transference, in which the therapist comes to represent an authoritative figure from the youth's past. But, quite different from the youth's rejecting and punitive parents, the therapist is accepting and sympathetic to the offender. Aichhorn suggests:

> If delinquency is to be cured and the asocial youth made fit again for life in society, the training school must provide him with new ties and induce him to attach himself to persons of his environment. We try to bring about such attachments by the kindly manner in which we treat our pupils.[15]

In other words, it is hoped that upon discovering that all adults are not like their rejecting parents, youths will terminate their acting-out behavior. The therapist must also help the offender acquire a new sense of dignity and worth. However, the trusting therapeutic relationship should be developed over a period of time and should be coupled with firmness and justice. The intended consequence of this relationship is that the youth will begin to identify with the values of the therapist and to acquire a new sense of self-worth and self-respect.[16]

Insight and acceptance of the therapist are crucial for successful psychotherapy. The therapist encourages the youth to reflect on his past life and, as the patient describes painful experiences from his early years, the therapist can hopefully discover the emotional experiences that are shaping the present behavior of the troubled youth. Once the therapist has this information, his job is to lead the youth gently toward this same insight. The therapist does not tell the youth, but instead leads him to work through his mental blocks. Finally, the youth discovers how "the inner child of the past" is affecting the present.

The final step occurs where a youth is able to use this insight to alter his behavior. The offenders ultimately must be responsible for their own actions, for their growth process is dependent upon overcoming negative and self-defeating behavior. Institutionalized youths must learn to comply with the rules and norms of their social environment if they are to stay out of trouble with the law when they return to the community.

The research findings on the effectiveness of psychotherapy in preventing recidivism are mixed. Several studies found that certain types of youths seem to benefit from this type of treatment. Yet, the effectiveness of psychotherapy is called into question by several other studies that found that treated and untreated youths did not differ significantly at the time of release from the institution, in the seriousness of parole violation, or in the opinion of parole officers who evaluated them. After evaluating the various studies, Lipton et al. formulated the following hypothesis:

> Amenability to individual psychotherapy can be ascertained more readily and has greater predictive relevance for older (eighteen to twenty) than for younger male inmates (thirteen to sixteen); pragmatically oriented individual psychotherapy, that is, focused on personal, vocational, and social issues, is more effective in reducing recidivism than psychoanalytically oriented individual psychotherapy for both younger and older youthful male inmates; a combined program of individual and group psychotherapy is associated with a lower rate of recidivism than no treatment, but it is less successful than either individual psychotherapy alone or group psychotherapy alone; under conditions where individual psychotherapy is effective in reducing recidivism, its effectiveness will be enhanced if the treatment staff are enthusiastic about the program and show personal interest in the offender.[17]

One of the great limitations of the psychotherapy administered in state institutions is that there invariably is not enough time for either a psychiatrist or a clinical psychologist, or both, to conduct weekly or more frequent psychotherapy sessions. Indeed, these psychiatrists, who usually work part-time on an hourly rate, must spend nearly all of their time holding emergency interviews with confined adolescents.

Transactional Analysis   Transactional analysis (TA) focuses upon interpreting and evaluating interpersonal relationships. Used by several state and federal agencies, mostly in California and Ohio, this treatment modality tries to teach youthful lawbreakers to relate to others in an adult, mature way. Eric Berne, founder of TA, felt that it can overcome the typical resistance to psychotherapy:

> Since the majority of teenage patients are sent or brought to treatment, the relationship to the therapist is not an autonomous one so that there is a strong temptation to rebellion, withdrawal, or sabotage. In effect, the therapist becomes a delegate of their parents which under the usual contract puts him in a great disadvantage from the beginning. The sought-for "cure" too often resembles a prescription written by the parents, who visualize the therapeutic relationship as a Parent-Child one, and the patient tends to do the same. The situation can be decisively altered at the social level by explicitly setting up an Adult-Adult contract, whereby the therapist offers to teach the patient transactional analysis,

with the provision that the patient can do as he pleases with what he learns.[18]

Thus, the youthful offender is taught an approach to human relationships that he can apply to his life in the way he feels is most helpful.

In applying this modality, the TA leader usually first does a script analysis, which is an attempt to understand how the "tapes" of the past are influencing the behavior of the juvenile in the present. This concept of script analysis is based on the premise that human memory acts as a three-track tape that records the events individuals experienced during their first years of life, the meaning attached to those events, and the emotions they experienced when these events occurred. Each person often replays his tape when similar situations are encountered later in life. The consequence of negative script replay is that many individuals become "losers," failing to attain their goals and becoming involved in self-defeating behavior. The TA leader seeks to discover the youth's script by diagnosing his voice, vocabulary, demeanor, gestures, and answers to questions. TA is based on the belief that persons can change their scripts, and the function of the TA leader is to help individuals make this change. For example, if a mother has told her daughter that she will never succeed at anything and if this has become a self-fulfilling prophecy, the therapist tries to communicate to the daughter that she can succeed in achieving her goals.

One of the hopeful outcomes of the life-script interview is that residents are willing to negotiate a treatment contract; that is, the youths will state how they wish to change. This treatment contract normally has both short- and long-range goals, project group goals, academic goals, and social behavior goals. Once his goals are set, the youth is considered to be in treatment. Throughout the treatment period these goals and progress toward them are constantly reviewed by staff.

As soon as the offenders are placed in groups, they learn that one of the first objects of TA is to make them become aware of the different kinds of social interaction they use in dealing with others. TA conceptualizes three ego states—the "child" (relic of one's past), the "parent" (internalization of the teaching and values of one's parental figures), and the "adult" (the mature and responsible adult). The TA therapist then tries to help the residents to recognize when they are emerging from each state, so that they are able to function more often in the "adult" ego state. Since the adult can turn off the not-OK feelings of the "child" tape, the TA leader tries to free the "adult" state so that it can deal objectively with the other two states.[19]

The youthful offender is also taught the four life positions that constitute the relationship perceived between the self and others.

1. I'm OK—You're OK: the position of the normal healthy individual who starts on the assumption that he and others are emotionally well-adjusted to life.
2. I'm not OK—You're OK: this position reflects a neurotic, depressed outlook on life—others are emotionally healthy but he is not.
3. I'm not OK—You're not OK: this position, which is that of autistic children and schizophrenics, produces severe individual problems in relating to the world and people around him.
4. I'm OK—You're not OK: this position, often observed in the delinquent and the sociopath, means the individual believes that he is justified in gratifying his own immediate impulses, regardless of the consequences.[20]

A further function of the TA leader is to teach the games that group members play in their interactions. According to TA, a *game* is a series of transactions that moves toward a predictable, well-defined outcome. Berne describes game behavior as "a series of moves with a snare or 'gimmick.'"[21] Games serve to keep a person from intimacy with others, and they usually involve those offenders who are "coming out" of their impulsive, immature-child states.

Transactional analysis has explored the games both treatment staff and offenders play that hinder the treatment process. These games are the means by which youthful offenders keep their emotional distance from staff. Such game behavior no doubt began with juveniles' feelings of powerlessness at the hands of the police and judges and continued throughout their stint in the system. This type of behavior obviously is intended to circumvent the control and power of the system.

Thus, the TA leader, whether psychotherapist, psychiatric social worker, or paraprofessional, not only is a dispenser of information about the basic tenets of TA, but also helps offenders become better aware of their social interactions. In addition to helping offenders individually, the TA leader observes group interactions among offenders and, when these interactions are taped on audiovisual equipment, studies in greater depth each youth's interpersonal relationships.

A real problem in implementing this modality is staff resistance. In the Youth Center Research Project at the O.H. Close School for Boys in California, these comments were made by staff at the end of the first year of the project:

> The trouble with TA is that we have had this training course and are now supposed to go out and act like junior psychologists. I think we need more training. I don't feel competent to work with TA. It bothers me. I've been holding small groups. Now I've been told I can't have small groups. I've

got to have TA. Bullshit. I don't know what TA is. I had good small groups. Administration expects miracles. I don't see TA making any more difference with kids than anything else we've ever done.[22]

There are, however, several advantages in using TA for treating juveniles. The first is that TA is easy to learn. Offenders, for instance, readily understand gaming behavior. One TA leader altered TA terminology further to make it even more comprehensible to offenders. The Parent ego state became "the man"; the Adult was changed to "cool head"; and the Child was altered to "the kid."[23]

Another advantage of TA is that it has real appeal to some offenders. In the Close Training School in California, residents printed wall posters with the following games:

Try and Help Me.
"My problems are 'out there,' not in here."
Stupid
"Nobody told me. How was I supposed to know."
You Can't Trust Anybody
"My parents turned me in."
Why Don't You _____ ? Yes, But . . .
"No matter what you say to me, I will find some excuse not to change."
I'm Just a Typical Teenager
"Everybody my age gets into trouble sometime."[24]

Data from Close Training School reflected, further, that residents exposed to TA tend to have higher morale, develop more positive attitudes toward staff members, become more hopeful and optimistic about the future, and establish greater feelings of self-esteem and well-being. Discipline problems also are reduced because residents become much more positive about the living units. Offenders confined at Close Training School reported that they believed their program encouraged autonomy, facilitated the learning of insight, helped solve personal problems, and helped them set practical goals. An additional advantage of TA is that staff can use it to understand their own behavior, thereby experiencing themselves the treatment applied to their charges. Finally, subjects paroled from Close School did significantly better during their first twelve months following release than had offenders released in prior years. The parole violation rates were also significantly lower than those of comparable age groups released from other California juvenile institutions.[25]

In spite of the popularity and success of TA, its most glaring limitation is the difficulty in applying the technique to youths who are evading personal change, who have gross behavior problems, and/or who are not motivated to examine their own problems. The mature are the most likely to profit; the immature and sociopathic usually withdraw, and the manipulator tries to "game" staff and the other inmates. Youthful offenders with borderline intelligence are also limited in their ability to examine their behavior through such an intellectual exercise. As one youth said, in a statement rather representative of the way many offenders feel, "I think TA is a bunch of bullshit."

Nevertheless, transactional analysis is a treatment method that appears to be increasing in popularity in both institutional and community-based corrections.

BEHAVIOR TREATMENT

Reality Therapy   A very popular treatment modality, reality therapy, was developed by two Los Angeles psychiatrists, William Glasser and G. L. Harrington. This modality assumes that irresponsible behavior arises when persons are unable to fulfill their basic needs. According to this approach, the basic human needs are relatedness and respect, and one satisfies these needs by doing what is realistic, responsible, and right.[26]

The three Rs of reality therapy are reality, responsibility, and right-and-wrong. In using this approach with older delinquent girls at the Ventura School in California, Glasser always made each adolescent face the reality of her behavior in the present; he refused to accept any reason for irresponsible behavior, and he expected the girls to maintain a satisfactory standard of behavior.

Glasser defines the major differences between conventional and reality therapy as follows:

1. Because we do not accept the concept of mental illness, the patient cannot become involved with us as a mentally ill person who has no responsibility for his behavior.
2. Working in the present and toward the future, we do not get involved with the patient's history because we can neither change what happened to him nor accept the fact that he is limited by his past.
3. We relate to patients as ourselves, not as transference figures.
4. We do not look for unconscious conflicts or the reasons for them. A patient cannot become involved with us by excusing his behavior on the basis of unconscious motivations.
5. We emphasize the morality of behavior. We face the issue of right and wrong which we believe solidifies the involvement, in contrast

to conventional psychiatrists who do not make the distinction between right and wrong, feeling it would be detrimental to attaining
the transference relationship they seek.

6. We teach patients better ways to fulfill their needs. The proper
   involvement will not be maintained unless the patient is helped to
   find more satisfactory patterns of behavior. Conventional therapists
   do not feel that teaching better behavior is part of therapy.[27]

Reality therapy involves three phases: first, the offender forms an
honest personal relationship with the therapist; second, the therapist
indicates that the negative behavior is understood but not condoned
(but although irresponsible behavior is rejected, the youth is accepted);
third, the therapist teaches offenders better ways to fulfill their needs
within their social reality.

Glasser emphasizes consistent discipline and warm acceptance
and believes that offenders should be given increased responsibilities:

> We firmly believe that an institutional training school, or a mental hospi-
> tal, can produce better results when warm relationships along with in-
> creasing responsibilities are stressed by an undivided staff. The girl who
> comes to Ventura has spent her life excusing her behavior in a world
> where people were not consistent, where one person told her one thing,
> someone else told her another, and most told her different things from day
> to day. Every effort must be maintained to provide a unified philosophy of
> treatment where the staff provides both consistent discipline and warmth
> and affection. But warmth never supersedes discipline, nor discipline
> warmth.[28]

Reality therapy has not been sufficiently studied to permit any
definite statements about its effectiveness. Glasser estimates that it has
succeeded with about 80 percent of the girls at Ventura School. He cites
as proof of his case the statistic that only 43 out of 370 girls at the school
were returnees while he was a therapist there. Another reality therapy
program was developed for the treatment of adult and youthful sexual
offenders at Western State Hospital in Washington. When offenders
demonstrated consistent and responsible behavior, they were recommended for conditional release. Although an in-depth follow-up of this
program has not been made, hospital records show that only 8.9 percent
of these ex-offenders were rearrested from 1958 to 1968.[29]

There are several advantages in using this modality with
juveniles. The first is that paraprofessionals can occupy a great role in
working with clients because the basic tenets are easily learned. Second, paraprofessionals are much more attracted to the basic assumptions of reality therapy than to other treatment modalities. For example,
they like its emphasis on responsibility, its negation of extenuating

circumstances, and its focus on the present. Third, it seems to be easier to achieve consistent treatment with this modality.

Criticisms of this modality center around its oversimplification of the dynamics of the human personality. Critics feel, in this regard, that insight is helpful to certain offenders in dealing with their antisocial behavior. They believe that an exploration of the past is sometimes necessary to deal adequately with the present. Reality therapy is further criticized for its tendency to encourage paternalistic and authoritarian attitudes in therapeutic interaction. Similarly, others suggest that this modality attracts rigid and inflexible persons who use it as a shield to hide their own authoritarian attitudes. The proponents of reality therapy are also accused of moralism and of oversimplifying the definition of what is right and wrong.

Despite these criticisms, reality therapy is pervasive and influential in juvenile corrections. Because so many of its assumptions are agreeable to line staff, the popularity of this modality will endure long after most of the other methods have been forgotten.

Behavior Modification   Behavior modification refers to the application of instrumental learning theory to problems of human behavior. It is based on the assumption that all behavior is under the control of its consequences in the external environment. If a behavior is reinforced immediately and systematically in a positive way, the frequency and rate of that behavior should increase, but if a behavior does not receive a positive reinforcement, the frequency should decrease.

A wide variety of techniques are used to reinforce positive and extinguish negative behavior. They include systematic desensitization, extinction of undesirable responses, training in assertiveness, counter-conditioning, conditioning against avoidance responses, and the use of tokens. Behavior modification uses environmental contingencies to alter the offender's response.[30]

Behavior modification does not employ such terms as *repressed desires, self-concept, unconscious needs,* and *superego,* because they refer to unnecessary inferences about internal psychological characteristics. Behavior, rather than self-awareness or self-knowledge, is important in behavior modification. Attending primarily to the observable stimulus and the observable response, the behavior modification therapist tries to change behavior by determining the desired result, the stimuli that can control it, and the reinforcements that are to be contingent upon the response.

Reinforcers are both positive and negative: attention, praise, money, food, and privileges are positive reinforcers; threats, confinement, punishment and ridicule are negative reinforcers. Positive reinforcers produce the more effective and enduring behavior changes.[31]

The behavior modification therapist attempts to reduce gradually the antisocial behavior of youthful offenders. The expectation is that each reduction will lead to greater accomplishments and that eventually the youth will be able to live within the law. Consistency is a crucial component of behavior modification therapy; therefore, each staff member must systematically provide the positive and negative reinforcers.

Behavior modification therapy also cautions against the use of punishment unless youths are dangerous to themselves or to others. When punishment is needed, swift and consistent action should follow the undesirable behavior. Instead of punishment, behavioral therapy recommends the use of brief time-out periods during which no reinforcement of any kind is available. For example, standardized fines provide this consistent and immediate application when tokens are used as reinforcers.

The Robert F. Kennedy Youth Center has employed behavioral modification therapy since it was built in the 1960s. At this youth center, reinforcement strategies are built into every inmate activity and are designed around the class-level system and a token economy:

> The class-level system has proved to be one of the institution's most highly effective motivators of good behavior. By achieving progressively higher goals set by the cottage committee, youths can earn advancement from trainee to apprentice to honor student. Living accommodations, work assignments, pay, clothing, and recreation improve with each class level.
>
> Students usually progress from trainee to apprentice in three to five months and reach honor status in from five to eight months. They usually are ready for release in ten to twelve months.
>
> Another major reinforcer of positive behavior is the token system. While this approach to retraining has been used successfully in other areas (mental health, retardation, emotional disturbance), its application in corrections has been limited. Consequently, its institution-wide use at the Center represents one of the most ambitious undertakings in the field of corrections to date. Under the token economy, students earn points (one point equals one cent) as they meet goals set in each program area (school, work, cottage life). The students use the points to "buy" a wide variety of goods and services available at the institution. Each youth receives a weekly paycheck, in points, based on staff ratings of his daily performance. The paycheck again reflects the distinction made between class levels. Apprentices earn points at a rate higher than trainees, and honor students earn at a rate higher than apprentices. A student also may earn bonus points, awarded on the spot for certain kinds of positive behavior. A student's institution expenses, including room rent, are deducted from his pay check. Trainees pay the least and apprentices and honor students pay more for their more desirable quarters. Fines, which are few, are also deducted from the paycheck. Here, again, discipline is

differentiated. . . . A fine for an honor student may be up to three times that assessed a trainee.

Students also can use their points to buy commissary items, snack bar goods, and civilian clothing and to participate in recreational activities. Points are not transferable from one student to another; a student can spend only what he earns himself. In effect, the point system teaches youths that if they want something, they must work for it.[32]

The Karl Holton School in California also has a behavior modification program designed around an elaborate token economy. If a youth is scheduled for parole in six months, he must earn 8,288 points to be recommended for parole. This is 85 percent of the possible point total; if he earns more than 85 percent, he will have an earlier referral to the parole board. Nearly everything a resident does in this training school is covered by a contract drawn up by him and his treatment team. Contracts usually cover seven days and include such items as being more courteous to peers or staff, completing a school assignment, and avoiding incidents in the academic area. Youths are awarded a specific number of points and a specific number of tokens for the completion of each contract. Points cannot be taken away, but misbehavior is punished by a fine that reduces the youth's ability to purchase special privileges.

One of the great strengths of behavior modification therapy is that it has had a greater impact on the sociopathic offender than has any other treatment modality. A major reason for this is that behavior modification techniques can immediately reinforce target behaviors. A study by Bernard and Eisenman reported that sociopathic offenders are easier to condition than normal subjects by either social or monetary reinforcement once the behavior therapist discovers what is rewarding for the youth he is treating.[33] In addition to helping the sociopath, behavior modification also appears to have a greater impact on the manipulator than more traditional therapies. Furthermore, behavior modification is specific and is often effective in short-term intervention. Finally, behavior modification is one of the most flexible of the treatment methods.

The critics of behavior modification have levelled several major criticisms against it. One of the most frequent attacks states that treating only the offender's overt symptoms is too superficial to be effective. Many critics also charge that this treatment method is not lasting. Humanists feel that the human being is too unique and complicated to be treated only according to his overt behavior. It is also feared that behavior denoting even greater disturbance may take the place of the eliminated symptom. Another criticism states that the principles of behavior modification require considerable consistency and continuity, if not sophistication, which is atypical of institutional treatment. Finally, critics feel that it is very difficult to apply behavior modification to those youths who do not manifest overt behavioral problems.

In spite of these shortcomings, behavior modification will no doubt continue to be a popular treatment modality for working with juvenile offenders.

GROUP THERAPY

A number of techniques are currently being used to work with groups in juvenile corrections. These include group psychotherapy, psychodrama, social group work, guided group interaction, positive peer culture, and milieu therapy. A drawback of these techniques is that they often are used interchangeably and have considerable ambiguity.

Group Psychotherapy

Group psychotherapy differs from the approaches that follow because the therapist, usually a psychiatrist or a clinical psychologist, is very much in control and directs the group process. The therapist uses the group context to focus on the problems of juvenile lawbreakers. Since it follows the same philosophy as psychotherapy, group psychotherapy attempts to achieve the goals of insight development. Extensive probing is therefore characteristic of this type of group work.

Empirical findings on group psychotherapy are mixed but generally positive. Roy Persons found that males exposed simultaneously to group psychotherapy and individual therapy did considerably better on parole than untreateds did on the variables of reincarceration, new-offense rates, and parole violation rates.[34] Truax et al. found that counselors who were chosen carefully for a series of twice-weekly meetings over three months apparently had effectively influenced young girls. This psychotherapy program resulted in the experimentals spending less time in incarceration than girls who had not gone through the experimental program.[35]

However, several other studies showed no difference in the recidivism rate of experimentals and controls. Clearly, further research is needed, but the improvement in recidivism rates in some studies and the improved behavior that resulted from group psychotherapy in other studies suggests that the method has possibilities.

A major problem that must be overcome is that offenders often see this modality as a "total assault on the self" and are reluctant to open up before these "headshrinkers." Reinforced by the values of their delinquent peer subculture, juveniles find it easy to play games or con the professional staff. Nevertheless, some groups are led by caring people who overcome these obstacles and effectively communicate with group members.

Psychodrama   In the 1930s, J. L. Moreno began to experiment with group methods in which patients are directed to act out their emotions. A patient does this on a stage or in a specially designated area and is led to become involved with members of the group who perform counter-roles. By using various techniques, such as role reversal, psychodrama helps patients to develop new insights into their behavior and role performance.

The popularity of psychodrama in juvenile corrections has waned through the years, chiefly because institutions usually lack the economic resources to attract appropriately trained therapists. However, psychodrama has influenced the development of role play, theater games, and improvisation theater, all of which are used in working with youth in trouble.

In 1974, Ma Goose, Inc. began a twice-weekly improvisational theater workshop series at the San Francisco Juvenile Court's Hidden Valley Ranch for youthful offenders (fourteen to sixteen years old). By using various improvisational structures, residents were able to focus on their relationships, take on new roles, switch roles, and develop particular characteristics. Role play is used more often in institutional treatment. In this technique, participants take on the role of another person, perhaps a parent, law enforcement officer, girlfriend, or teacher, and attempt to perceive life in this person's role. If youths feel comfortable with each other and are not inhibited by the role-playing process, this technique can be helpful in giving offenders insight into how they feel and react. It is hoped, of course, that residents will carry the insights over into community life.

Whether role playing arises as an actual skit or is suggested spontaneously by members of the group or staff, it is one way in which child-caring therapists are facilitating growth in interpersonal relationships. Indeed, role play, theater games, and improvisation theater are valuable techniques that are presently underused.

Social Group Work   Professional social workers learn in their graduate training how to lead groups. Different versions of social group work exist, but they all focus on the individual group member in an effort to help him function more effectively and to derive greater satisfaction from group participation.[36]

Konopka, a leading authority on social group work, lists some of the principles of this approach:

1. The worker's main function is helping and this helping is perpetuated to establish purposeful relationships with group members.
2. The worker must be warm, understanding, and spontaneous, but yet be able to maintain and enhance group direction.

3. The worker has to accept group members without accepting their behavior and often "limits" have to be utilized but in a constructive manner.
4. The worker has to manage the group while at the same time not forgetting the uniqueness of the individual.[37]

Social group work, like psychotherapy, does not have the popularity it once had in juvenile corrections. Only in private institutions, in fact, are social workers still involved in group work. Social workers generally have too much paperwork and other related duties in state institutions to do group work; in addition, few of them have had the necessary graduate training or feel comfortable in leading groups.

Guided Group Interaction

Guided group interaction is probably the most widely used treatment modality, as this approach to group work is found in at least eleven states: New Jersey, South Dakota, Minnesota, West Virginia, Illinois, Georgia, Florida, New Hampshire, Maryland, Michigan, and Kentucky. According to this philosophy of youth work, peers must be honest with each other in order to help all group participants become more aware of their problems. Since the 1940s, when this modality was first used, it has been the assumption of guided group interaction (GGI) that peers could confront other peers and force them to face the reality of their behavior more effectively than could staff.

The guided group interaction approach is characterized by a nonauthoritarian atmosphere, intensity of interaction, group homogeneity, and an emphasis on group structure. Of these, the most important characteristic, which pervades every part of the cottage program, is the nonauthoritarian atmosphere. Residents in many residential GGI programs, for example, are given considerable say in when a group member will be released, granted a home furlough, or be approved for off-campus visits; in how a group member will be punished; and whether the outside door will be locked or left open at night.

Giving residents responsibility for decision making, of course, is a different approach to child care from that followed in most correctional settings. The adult leader is responsible for seeing that a delinquent subculture is not established in the cottage and that negative peer leaders do not seize control of the GGI groups. The adult leader constantly refers the decision making back to the group. When informed that a fellow group member planned to run away, for example, one staff member retorted: "What do you want me to do? He's your buddy; he's part of your group. You can talk to him; sit on him if you have to; but it's up to all of you to help one another."[38]

Youthful offenders usually go through several stages in becoming involved in guided group interaction. Youths initially are guarded in their responses, but as their defenses begin to weaken, they learn to give up their games and defenses because of the encouragement received from peers and the group leader. In the second stage, the residents' interpersonal problems are brought into the open. They are encouraged to talk about themselves and to have their values scrutinized and challenged by the group. In the third stage, the offenders begin to examine the difficulties they have had with their environment. The group members, who begin to develop real trust among themselves, probe the problems of institutional and street living. The fourth stage is that in which the offenders feel secure and accept reeducation. When they see that their problems are not unique and that dealing with them is possible, they feel less antagonistic toward the group and become more receptive to what is said. In the final stage the residents set up an outline of a plan for change. Using his own and the group's evaluation of him, each youth makes a conscious decision about the way he wants to behave in the future.[39]

Guided group interaction was first used with juvenile offenders in the Highfields Project in New Jersey in the early 1950s. As described in Chapter 6, in this short-term facility sixteen and seventeen-year-old boys worked during the day at a nearby mental health facility and lived at the project at night; residents were permitted to go into town with a staff member and to live as normal a life as possible. The most important part of this experience was that residents met five times a week with their guided group interaction leader. In this group experience they were expected to be honest with each other to enable each participant to face the reality of his behavior.

The philosophy of group work developed in the Highfields Project led other agencies to adopt this approach to treating youthful offenders. Scott and Hissong describe the way GGI was implemented in a juvenile institution in Kentucky. In this setting, groups met five times a week for ninety-minute sessions. Members of a group were from the same cottage and were together at least half a day, either in work assignments or in vocational classes. Every attempt was made to form groups that were homogenous in sex, delinquent sophistication, and physical and emotional maturity. The group leaders, who were usually social workers or psychologists, held the sessions just before or after the evening meal. The therapist was instructed to stay on top of the social interaction among peers. This involved being not only cognizant of the social organization among residents, but also aware of the exploitation-victimization patterns in the cottage. The group therapist checked daily with cottage parents, work supervisors, and other staff to determine the problems that were being manifested by various group members. If a negative leader was dominating the group, the therapist sought to control the youth in one way or another. Often the therapist accomplished this by requesting another strong youth more amenable to treatment to vie for leadership with the disruptive resident. Each meeting focused on the problems of a single youth. Although several residents might request a specific meeting, the group itself decided who would "get" the meeting. Residents were encouraged to disclose their problems as long as their acting-out did not harm others. Group members sometimes put tremendous pressure on the youth who had the chair to be honest about himself. Group members were further expected to "rat" on any cottage youth involved in negative behavior. In return for their commitment to the prosocial values of the group process, group members had some say about when each member was ready for release.[40]

The research findings on guided group interaction have been mixed. Some studies challenge the premise that GGI in nonresidential settings is more effective than incarceration. For example, when youths released from the Highfields Project were compared with youths who were sent to Annadale Reformatory, GGI was found to be effective in reducing the recidivism of blacks but not of whites. The general picture that emerges, however, is that a GGI experience in a nonresidential program is at least as effective as and much less costly than confinement in a state facility.

A great strength of guided group interaction is its determination to circumvent the values of the delinquent-peer subculture. This modality, in urging residents to be honest and open with each other, attempts to move group participants to a more positive, prosocial stance. Another advantage is that it represents a comprehensive strategy for dealing with troubled youth. It is, in effect, a total system for mitigating the impact of a delinquent subculture. A third advantage is that guided group interaction seems to gain acceptance on the state level; it has done so in several states. Also important is the fact that guided group interaction can be led by line staff, thereby increasing staff involvement in the treatment process. A final advantage of guided group interaction is that responsibility is thrown back onto offenders; thus, in interacting with peers, offenders become aware of their problems and are directed toward their resolution.

A major problem in using guided group interaction is the shortage of trained group leaders. Too, since this approach to group work lacks a single spokesman, a number of versions and designs of the basic principles have emerged. In consequence, no clear and consistent philosophy guides the process of working with offenders in groups. The emphasis of GGI on peer group norms and values further tends to slight the importance of individualism. Extreme care must be taken to ensure that peer group norms established and monitored by institutional staff do not repress the youthful offenders' needs for self-identity and autonomy. Finally, peer group norms created by guided group interaction may not always be transferable to actual life situations that will be encountered upon release.

Although guided group interaction has more critics in the 1970s than it did in the 1960s, and its followers are becoming more aware of its shortcomings, it continues to have a profound impact upon the treatment of confined juveniles.

Positive Peer Culture

The concepts of positive peer culture have generated considerable excitement in juvenile corrections. Developed by Harry Vorrath and associates as an outgrowth of guided group interaction, positive peer culture (PPC) has been implemented in all of the juvenile state institutions in West Virginia, Michigan, and Missouri.

Vorrath believes that PPC "is a total system for building positive youth subcultures."[41] He condenses a great deal of the philosophy of this approach to troubled youth when he says:

> Built around groups of nine youths under the guidance of an adult leader, Positive Peer Culture is designed to "turn around" a negative youth subculture and mobilize the power of the peer group in a productive manner. Youth in PPC groups learn how to identify problems and how to work toward their resolution. In group sessions and in day-to-day activities the goal is to fully involve young people in the helping process.
>
> In contrast to traditional treatment approaches PPC does not ask whether a person wants to receive help but whether he is willing to give help. As the person gives and becomes of value to others he increases his own feelings of worthiness and builds a positive self-concept.
>
> PPC does not avoid the challenge of troublesome youth; rebellious and strong-willed individuals, when redirected, have much to contribute. Those who have encountered many difficulties in their own lives are often in the best position to understand the problems of others. Positive peer culture does not seek to impose specific rules but to teach basic values. If there were one rule, it would be that people must care for one another. Caring means wanting what is best for a person. Unfortunately, positive caring behavior is not always popular among youth. In fact, negative, harmful behavior frequently is more acceptable. Therefore, PPC uses specific procedures to foster caring behavior. Once caring becomes fashionable, hurting goes out of style.

Vorrath acknowledges the pervasiveness of peer influence and feels that winning over its subculture is necessary if its influence is to be positively rechanneled. Young people, according to Vorrath, can become experts in dealing with the problems of other young people. However, the group meetings sponsored by PPC must break through the antisocial values of young offenders if such meetings are to be positive.

Positive peer culture is developed through ninety-minute meet-

FIGURE 11-1   Positive Peer Culture Group Meeting. Courtesy Illinois Department of Corrections.

ings five times a week. Characterized by trust and openness, PPC focuses on the direct and immediate problems of the lawbreaking youth. Believing that groups function most effectively when they are homogeneous, leaders try to include youths who are similar in age, sex, maturity, and sophistication. Coeducational groups are believed to be counterproductive.

Groups are made up of nine youths who sit in a circle; the leader is part of the circle but sits at a desk. The meeting is usually opened by each youth in turn talking about the particular problems encountered that day. Then the group decides, largely based on what has been said, who will "have" the meeting. Instead of this person being on the "hot seat," as might be the case in some encounter groups, PPC provides a context in which help is received from other group members. The group leader, a line staff member who works directly with residents, concludes the meeting by an eight- or ten-minute summary of what has taken place.

Participants in this group modality are taught to refer to positive behavior as great, intelligent, independent, improving, and winning and to refer to negative behavior as childish, unintelligent, helpless, destructive, copping out, and losing. Caring is presented as a strong and masculine trait.

There are generally four distinctive stages of group development:

1. *Casing.*   In the first stage students and staff are not comfortable with one another, since no discernible group structure exists. At this point students usually attempt to seek information about one another and the staff but avoid showing themselves. During this highly defensive stage they may seek out a scapegoat in a weak member or in the adult staff.

2. *Limit testing.*   As the students begin to reveal their basic personalities and true behavior, they gravitate into cliques. Individual members begin to experiment with techniques of participating in group meetings (perhaps even to mouthing the right words), but their ties to previous negative values continue, and thus considerable negativism can be expected. A great deal of tension is generated around revealing oneself and one's feelings about other members. Although students start to recognize their own distinctive problems, they cannot yet function as a truly positive group.

3. *Polarization of values.*   As the students discover alternatives to their previous values and behavior, they are brought to the point where they must decide whether or not they really want to change. Cliques and subgroups become more tenuous and crumble away, producing much anxiety. At this stage hostility may be prevalent within the group or directed toward the leader by factions of the group. Gradually a common sense of purpose develops among some of the group members. Those who have started to adopt a new value system now are bound with a strong sense of mutual solidarity and a beginning group identification. Those who are unable or unwilling to accept new nondelinquent roles may react antagonistically, struggling to retain negative influence; when they fail they may withdraw, even to the point of running away.

4. *A positive peer culture.*   This is the final stage, when the students have formed a strong, cohesive, clique-free group that embodies a value system of mutual care and concern. The group relies less and less on adult leadership and places considerable demands on its members to face their problems, to help one another, and to work eagerly on the problems of the more defensive new students in the group. At this stage the old members become virtual social workers on a twenty-four-hour basis. These youths are nearing readiness to return to the broader culture.

The group leader in this modality is not a therapist in the traditional sense, but more like a special teacher or coach who instructs, guides, redirects, and motivates the group to work on problems. The leader must be both an effective limit setter and a sympathetic listener; he also needs to have a kind of mystique. Since part of the leader's responsibility is to build a degree of anxiety into the group, group members must be kept from being able to understand and predict the leader's behavior. But the primary basis of this mystique rests in the leader's knowledge of what is taking place in the group. All interactions and the functioning of each group member must be understood. The leader can keep the group off balance by perceiving what takes place "back stage."

To fulfill this demanding leadership role, the leader must be able to detect rigged meetings, read nonverbal behavior, protect weaker members from being hurt by the group process, discover what the basic problem of each resident actually is, and neutralize negative, controlling leadership in the group. Two major tasks in overcoming the peer subculture are detecting rigged meetings and neutralizing the strong, negative peer leader. Peers, as Vorrath recognizes, are quick to con staff members. Thus, he provides these hints to alert the group leader that a rigged meeting may be in process:

1. A student in the meeting suddenly becomes verbal after a long period of little or no interest in the group.
2. The attention of the group is directed to one or two scapegoats, and other students do not bring up their problems.
3. A student who has been "bad" for several months suddenly becomes "good." (A youth may feel that if he puts on a bad act for awhile and then follows with a good act, he will appear to have changed.)
4. Students are playing up to either the group leader or other staff.
5. A student attempts to give information about other students on an individual basis rather than in a group.
6. Group members play it safe in the meeting, trying to keep anyone from getting angry.

The negative indigenous leader (NIL) can pose an even greater problem. Usually operating with assistants, this strong peer leader normally is adept in handling staff and good at playing roles. Because the NIL "cases the situation, plans moves in advance, and keeps cool under stress," he is a real threat to a positive, caring group. To reclaim this negative leader, Vorrath suggests that the most effective strategy is to undercut any foundations of peer support, which can be accomplished by capturing the lieutenants. But, according to PPC, the lieutenants must be captured outside of the group or the negative indigenous leader will come to their defense.

This capture can be effected by making the lieutenants responsible for both their own behavior and that of the NIL. The group leader is advised to push this a step further and to accuse the lieutenants of disloyalty to the NIL. If they really cared, the rationale states, they would want to help their leader. Once the lieutenants are captured, Vorrath recommends that new roles be given to them so that they can use their strength positively.

Vorrath also feels that the group has to be involved in decision-making processes, such as whether or not to give a youth a home visit or when to release a resident. Although he acknowledges that institutional staff ultimately must make these decisions, he feels that the recommendations initially should come from the group. The group, in discussing the possibility of releasing a member, concerns itself with both the member's present problems and those he will experience when he returns to the community.

The Minnesota Department of Corrections examination of the parole statistics of the Red Wing Training School, which used PPC, is the only follow-up research on this modality. This facility had a recidivism rate in excess of 50 percent before it used PPC, and an 18.5 percent rate three years after this program was implemented. But in *Children in Trouble: A National Scandal,* Howard James provides a qualitative statement on the impact of PPC:

> Mr. Vorrath was given the opportunity to prove that his ideas worked with small groups in Kentucky, Washington, D.C., and in scattered spots across the country. The projects were successful. He was able to turn small groups of tough delinquents around. But Mr. Vorrath wanted to try his program at a large institution. He got his chance in 1968 after things fell apart at a rather average reform school at Red Wing, Minnesota. Youngsters rioted and ran. Mr. Vorrath was called in.
>
> Using a technique that might be described as building a culture of caring, Mr. Vorrath divides the boys into groups, with each member responsible for all the boys in his group.
>
> His program is built on love—"not the sweet, sugar-coated kind," he adds. "I'm talking about the unselfish love that makes a Marine crawl on his belly into enemy lines to save a wounded buddy." There can be little doubt that the program works. At Red Wing, I talked to boys sprawled on the lawn playing chess on a warm Sunday afternoon. Others batted a baseball around—all without supervision. The boys learn to help each other stay out of trouble.[42]

There are certain problems implicit in the use of PPC at the present time. First, where does PPC expect to find these "ideal" leaders? The authors have met relatively few staff in juvenile corrections who come anywhere near to filling these high expectations. Also, Vorrath seems to underestimate the ingenuity and resourcefulness of peer subcultures. This modality suggests, for example, that staff must remain beyond the understanding and predictability of their charges. When it is remembered how intensively residents study staff, this presents an almost impossible obstacle to the average person. And, even if staff members could build a high enough wall around themselves to avoid disclosing "where they are coming from," this wall might be so high that their caring and love could not break through. Too, is it possible to teach caring relationships to youths who have experienced exploitation and deprivation all their lives and who, in fact, see life as "dog eat dog"? There is the additional problem of neutralizing lieutenants and, ultimately, the negative inmate leader. It would appear that PPC is underestimating the resourcefulness and power of an inmate leader, for it is not likely that he will give up as easily as Vorrath suggests. Finally, although Vorrath believes that the basic assumptions of these youths can be changed, few people change many of their background assumptions over the period of a lifetime—much less when they are stripped of their freedom and in therapy.

For this exciting modality to be properly evaluated and for these and other questions to be answered, more research is obviously needed. But its initial successes should remind both followers and critics that PPC remains one of the most promising ways to treat, change, correct, and rehabilitate juvenile offenders.

Milieu Therapy   The basic purposes of milieu therapy are to create an environment in which offenders can find support and strength and to so shape that environment that its components will contribute to eliminating antisocial behavior. A major emphasis in this modality is the development of unified staff teams to work with residents. Usually found in a controlled environment, milieu therapy originates from both the influence of the therapeutic community and the efforts of professional social workers to treat the total environment.

The therapeutic community concept evolved from the contributions of Maxwell Jones and other behavioral scientists. This approach strives to overcome patients' passivity toward therapy by providing them with a degree of authority in the operation of the therapeutic unit. Jones found that "people living together in a hospital, whether patients or staff, derived great benefit from examining, in daily community meetings, what they were doing and why they were doing it."[43] By reducing the role differences between the keepers and the kept, the therapeutic community gives patients every opportunity to analyze their own behavior. A "living learning" experience, according to Jones, requires that patients face interpersonal problems directly and subject themselves to feedback from the group.[44]

Milieu therapy is eclectic in its approach, as evidenced by two programs that were formulated in an institution for older male juvenile offenders. Each was carried out in a cottage setting. The first program took place in a cottage that housed the most severely disturbed boys in an end-of-the-line state institution. The social worker and the line staff decided to use a number of treatment strategies that would make the total environment therapeutic.

Casework.   Because of the disturbed nature of the residents, each staff member agreed to talk to and counsel them in those areas in which the team anticipated problems in the community. The social worker also helped residents to develop short- and long-term goals.

Group Work.   Each boy was placed in a group that met and was led by either the social worker or a youth leader. A meeting to resolve conflicts was held once a month, during which time staff members dealt with any problems that had emerged.

Family Intervention.   Both youth leaders and the social worker initiated interaction with families; for example, they telephoned parents, urging them to visit their boys and to talk with a staff member.

Juvenile Victimization.   In an effort to avoid sexual and material exploitation, team members supported the inmate leader as long as he provided information on exploitation.

Educational and Vocational Training.   Boys were urged either to graduate from the institution's fully accredited high school or to enter a program of vocational training in such areas as welding, painting, barbering, or printing.

Self-concept Therapy.   Team members attempted to create experiences that enabled residents to feel better about themselves. One technique involved a weekly cottage meeting conducted by the social worker who used films, group discussion, and specific exercises for the boys to carry out during the week.

Community Exposure.   Team members found jobs for those youths who would profit from a work experience in the community. Home visits and off-campus jobs were also widely used.

The second program was carried on in a cottage populated by boys who had been involved in serious crimes against persons or who had histories of creating behavioral problems in other institutions. This cottage also was served by a strongly cohesive team. For example, team members faithfully kept a daily log of relevant information on residents, which made youth leaders on the afternoon shift aware of what had taken place during the morning shift. The social workers coordinated the weekly team meetings, one interesting result of which was that all decisions derived from group consensus. Among the methods used were:

Contractual Agreement.   On the day that a boy entered the cottage, he was assured that his past was forgotten and that he would be held responsible only for what happened from that point on. Staff, in addition, carefully explained what constituted acceptable and unacceptable behavior. Residents were then expected to set goals for themselves, and their progress toward release depended on the fulfillment of those goals.

Guided Group Interaction.   The group was expected to circumvent any negative interaction among residents, such as exploitation or fighting.

Reward System.   The team set up three groups, each of which had successively greater institutional privileges; when a youth met certain goals, he was promoted to the next higher group.

Vocational Training.   The social worker strove to place boys in vocational training programs; he also used the contacts given by vocational instructors to aid in his search for permanent jobs for youths when they were released.

Home Visits for Job Interviews.   Shortly before their release residents were sent home on a seven-day visit for the specific purpose of being interviewed for a permanent job arranged for by either the social worker or the parole officer.

Finally, everything in the program of this cottage was designed to help residents become responsible for their behavior and to plan for their futures realistically.[45]

Findings of empirical studies on the effectiveness of milieu therapy are mixed. The most outstanding strength of milieu therapy lies in its focus on the entire living unit. The necessary teamwork among staff members also requires that treatment and custodial staff learn to work together. Furthermore, milieu therapy provides more opportunities for individual decision making than do many other methods. The communication problems among social workers and line staff reduce the possibility of using this approach in many settings, for only an unusually capable social worker will be accepted by other staff as part of the team. Staff, too, tend to get "burned out" by the high degree of commitment and its constant demands. Staff members, at the same time, often are taunted by other staff in the institution—"We don't get paid for treatment. What are you trying to do—be a social worker?" Finally, it is difficult, in the coercive atmosphere of most training schools, to create a therapeutic environment.

THE INSTITUTIONALLY BASED COUNSELING
CONTINUUM PROGRAM

The basic thrust of the institutionally based counseling continuum program, a pre-parole reintegration program based at the Valley View Illinois Youth Center, is to send out institutionalized youth into the community for five or more days a week and to have them return to the institution for a day or more of intensive counseling.

Youths who participate in the institutionally based counseling continuum (IBCC) program are referred to the program by their cottage team when the team concludes that they are nearing release. Reasons for referring residents usually are of three types: they can benefit from weekly assistance in the development and implementation of a community program; they have requested this assignment; or their families need assistance in supporting their return to the community. If a referred youth chooses not to participate, he simply remains in the regular institutional program and is paroled through the normal process.

To be eligible for this program, residents also must be able to return to the institution for the weekly counseling session, must either be in school or hold a full-time job, and must have an adequate home environment. During their time away from the institution, the residents' behavior is monitored and evaluated through visits to their homes, schools, jobs, or other program placements. The results of these visits are recorded by the youths' counselors and are discussed when the youths return to the institution on the weekend.

The purpose of the return to the institution is to hold the youth accountable for his community performance. This is accomplished through program agreements, performance contracts, and counseling sessions. Program agreements enable the youth and his counselor to establish specific goals when he enters into the program. These long-term goals are written as program agreements for a parole hearing. They are further formalized into weekly performance contracts. Weekend counseling sessions generally are conducted on a one-to-one basis as the youth and his counselor review the past week, discuss his evaluations, and establish performance contracts for the coming week. Other pertinent issues relating to the reintegration of the youth into the community are also discussed.

The institutionally based counseling continuum program has been in operation since 1972. The first evaluation indicated a significant reduction in recidivism for those youths who had successfully completed the program as compared to those who had been paroled directly from an institution. The National Clearinghouse stated in the *Illinois*

TABLE 11-1   Treatment Technologies

Type	Treatment Goal	Qualifications of Therapist	Length of Treatment Period	Frequency of Treatment	Expected Response from Offenders
Individual or Group Psychotherapy	Lead youths to insight	Psychiatrist, psychologist, psychiatric social worker	frequently extensive or long term	several times a week if possible	Will examine individual problems with therapist
Transactional Analysis	Lead youths to insight	Psychiatrist, psychologist, trained nonprofessional staff	usually several months	once or more a week	Will examine individual problems in a group context and will learn a new approach to interpersonal relationships
Reality Therapy	Help youths to fulfill basic needs	Psychiatrist, psychologist, trained nonprofessional staff	short period of time	once or more a week	To learn reality, responsible behavior, and right from wrong
Behavior Modification	Help youths to react positively	Anyone who can assume role of therapist	usually long term	tends to be continuous rather than interwoven with nontreatment	To continue their reinforced, positive behavior
Psychodrama	Insight into individual behavior	Psychiatrist	extensive or long term	at least once a week if possible	Examine behavior through role reversal

Social Group Work	More effective functioning	Professional social worker	several months	at least once a week	Will be honest with the group and will be receptive to insights of the group
Guided Group Interaction	Develop prosocial norms and values	Anyone trained in GGI	several months	four or five times a week	Will become responsible for others in the group
Positive Peer Culture	Develop prosocial norms and values	Anyone trained in PPC	several months	four or five times a week	Will genuinely care for other group members
Milieu Therapy	Develop new behavioral norms	Anyone	extensive or long term, may extend over several years	tends to be continuous rather than interwoven	Will participate in changing the total environment through treatment
Institutionally-Based Counseling Continuum Program	Help youths adjust to parole	Counselor or social worker	three or four months	once a week	Will remain trouble-free during the five or six days a week they are in the community

Corrections, Master Plan, Juvenile Corrections, Report 1, "Probably the most significant program utilizing community resources is the IBCC Program."

SUMMARY

This chapter discussed and evaluated the basic treatment technologies in juvenile corrections. These therapies are grouped under insight (psychotherapy and transactional analysis), behavior treatment (reality therapy and behavior modification), group therapy (group psychotherapy, psychodrama, social group work, guided group interaction, positive peer culture, and milieu therapy), and reintegration (institutionally based counseling continuum program). See Table 11-1 for the relationships of these modalities to each other.

Other treatment modalities, such as gestalt therapy, rational-emotive psychotherapy, and methods to overcome learning disabilities, could have been included in this chapter. Although the first two are rarely used in juvenile corrections, learning disability therapy is a "fad" at the present time, and some interest is beginning to be expressed in working on learning disabilities of institutionalized juveniles. The Indiana Boys School, for example, places a heavy emphasis on programs dealing with learning problems of residents.

The courts state that youths being processed by the juvenile justice system have the right to treatment, but in reality, these treatment programs are usually less than sophisticated. Psychiatrists and psychologists are seldom seen by residents, social workers are too involved in paper work, and the responsibility for treatment tends to be left to the line staff. However, in spite of the widespread pessimism concerning the effectiveness of treatment programs, many institutionalized youths claim that one or more of these methods are helpful to them.

QUESTIONS

1. Do you agree with the statement that no treatment is effective for juvenile offenders?

2. If you were superintendent of a training school, which treatment methods would you use? Why?

3. What type of staff member would be effective in carrying out the treatment method you have chosen? Why?

4. Would you hire ex-offenders to work in your institution? Why or why not?

5. Do you feel that the goals of positive peer culture are realistic?

6. How would you treat those youths who do not respond to the rules of your prescribed treatment method?

ENDNOTES

1. Stanton S. Wheeler and Leonard S. Cottrell, Jr., *Juvenile Delinquency: Its Prevention and Control* (New York: Russell Sage Foundation, 1966).

2. H. Ohmart, "The Challenge of Crime in a Free Society," *Youth Authority Quarterly* 21 (Fall 1968).

3. *Corrections Magazine* 1 (September 1974): 48.

4. R. G. Hood, "Research on the Effectiveness of Punishments and Treatments," *Collected Studies in Criminological Research I* (Strasburg: Council of Europe, 1967).

5. Douglas Lipton et al., *The Effectiveness of Correctional Treatment: A Survey of Treatment Evaluation Studies* (New York: Praeger Publishers, 1975).

6. D. Mann, *Intervening with Convicted Serious Juvenile Offenders* (Santa Monica, Calif.: Rand Corporation, July 1976).

7. Carl F. Jesness, "The Fricot Ranch Study: Outcomes with Small versus Large Living Groups in the Rehabilitation of Delinquents," Research Report No. 47 (Sacramento, Calif.: California Youth Authority, 1965), p. 2.

8. Carl F. Jesness et al., *The Youth Center Research Project* (Sacramento, Calif.: American Justice Institute, 1972), p. 3.

9. The following materials on I-Level are taken from Marguerite Q. Warren, "The Community Treatment Project: History and Prospects," in *Law Enforcement Science and Technology,* edited by S. A. Yefsky (Washington, D.C.: Thompson Book Company, 1972), pp. 193–195.

10. Roy Gerard, "Institutional Innovations in Juvenile Corrections," *Federal Probation* 34, (December 1970), pp. 38–40.

11. Ibid.

12. Ibid.

13. Jesness et al., *Youth Center Research Project,* pp. 3–4.

14. Melton F. Shore, "Psychological Theories of the Causes of Antisocial Behavior," in *Contemporary Corrections: A Concept in Search of Content,* edited by Benjamin Frank (Reston, Va.: Reston Publishing Company, 1971), p. 293.

15. August Aichhorn, *Wayward Youth* (New York: Viking Press, 1963).

16. S. A. Szurek, "Some Impressions from Clinical Experiences with Delinquents," in *The Antisocial Child: His Family and His Community,* edited by S. A. Szurek and I. N. Berlin (Palo Alto, Calif.: Science and Behavior Books, 1969), pp. 80–81.

17. Lipton, *Effectiveness,* p. 210

18. Eric Berne, *Transactional Analysis in Psychotherapy* (New York: Grove Press), p. 355.
19. Robert J. Wicks, *Correctional Psychology* (San Francisco: Canfield Press, 1974), p. 26.
20. Thomas A. Harris, *I'm OK—You're OK* (New York: Harper & Row, 1967), pp. 37–53.
21. Eric Berne, *Games People Play* (New York: Grove Press, 1964), p. 48.
22. Jesness, "Fricot Ranch Study."
23. Lois Johnson, "TA with Juvenile Delinquents," *Transactional Analysis Bulletin* 3 (1969): 31.
24. Jesness, "Fricot Ranch Study," pp. 89–90.
25. Ibid., p. 313.
26. William Glasser, *Reality Therapy* (New York: Harper & Row, 1965), p. xii.
27. Ibid., excerpts from pp. 44–45.
28. Ibid., p. 70.
29. George J. MacDonald et al., "Treatment of the Sex Offender," (Fort Steilbacoon, Wash.: Western State Hospital, 1968).
30. Jesness, "Fricot Ranch Study," p. 7.
31. Robert C. Trojanowicz, *Juvenile Delinquency: Concepts and Control* (Englewood Cliffs, N.J.: Prentice-Hall, 1973), p. 246.
32. Gerard, "Institutional Innovations."
33. J. L. Bernard and R. Eisenman, "Verbal Conditioning in Sociopaths with Spiral and Monetary Reinforcement," *Journal of Personality and Social Psychology* 6 (1976): 203–206.
34. Roy W. Persons, "Psychological and Behavioral Change in Delinquents Following Psychotherapy," *Journal of Clinical Psychology* 22 (1966): 337–340.
35. Charles B. Truax et al., "Effects of Group Psychotherapy with High Accurate Empathy and Nonpossession Warmth upon Female Delinquents," *Journal of Abnormal Psychology* 71 (1966): 267–274.
36. Elizabeth A. Ferguson, *Social Work: An Introduction* (Philadelphia: J. B. Lippincott Company, 1963), p. 13.
37. Gisela Konopka, "The Social Group Work Method: Its Use in the Correctional Field," *Federal Probation* 20 (July 1956): 26–27.
38. Interview with Harry Vorrath quoted in Oliver J. Keller, Jr., and Benedict S. Alper, *Halfway Houses: Community Centered Correction and Treatment* (Lexington, Mass.: D. C. Heath and Company, 1970), p. 55.
39. Wicks, *Correctional Psychology,* pp. 50–51.
40. Joseph W. Scott and Jerry B. Hissong, "Changing the Delinquent Subculture: A Sociological Approach," in *Readings in Juvenile Delinquency,* edited by Ruth Shonle Cavan (Philadelphia: J. B. Lippincott Company, 1975), pp. 486–488.
41. The following materials are found in Harry H. Vorrath and Larry K. Brendtro, *Positive Peer Culture* (Chicago: Aldine Publishing Company, 1974).
42. Howard James, *Children in Trouble: A National Scandal* (New York: Simon & Schuster, 1971), pp. 150–151.
43. Maxwell Jones, *Social Psychiatry in Practice* (Baltimore: Penguin Books, 1968), pp. 16–17.
44. Wicks, *Correctional Psychology,* p. 39.
45. Bartollas, Clemens, "Sisyphus in a Juvenile Institution," *Social Work,* Vol. 20, No. 5 (September 1975), pp. 364–368. Reproduced with permission of the National Association of Social Workers.

REFERENCES

Berne, Eric. *Games People Play*. New York: Grove Press, 1964.
  This book is the classic on interpersonal games.

Harris, Thomas A. *I'm OK—You're OK*. New York: Harper & Row, 1967.
  Presents the basic tenets of transactional analysis in an interesting and readable way.

Lipton, Douglas; Martinson, Robert; and Wilks, Judith. *The Effectiveness of Correctional Treatment*. New York: Praeger Publishers, 1975.
  A comprehensive study of what works in rehabilitation programs in both the institution and in the community.

Trojanowicz, Robert C. *Juvenile Delinquency: Concepts and Control*. Englewood Cliffs, N.J.: Prentice-Hall, 1973.
  A good review of the treatment modalities found in this chapter.

Vorrath, Harry H., and Brendtro, Larry K. *Positive Peer Culture*. Chicago: Aldine Publishing Company, 1974.
  This book is a must for those interested in positive peer culture.

Wicks, Robert J. *Correctional Psychology*. San Francisco: Canfield Press, 1974.
  Wicks has done a good job of reviewing all the important areas of correctional psychology.

12

Management Principles
for Juvenile Facilities

Inadequate staffing, the nature of organizational processing, and the degrading character of the inmate world prevent most residents in juvenile facilities from benefitting from their confinement. For these and other reasons many experts argue for deinstitutionalization; that is, reducing the populations of institutions and keeping youth out of contact with the formal system wherever possible. Yet, trends toward deinstitutionalization simply are not strong enough to protect youths from confinement; nearly every state is still using correctional facilities for youths believed to need institutional care.

The question then becomes, "Considering that there is no headlong rush to abandon institutions, what can be done to improve them?" One answer is to improve the quality of management. Jails, detention homes, and training schools usually are operated on a military model; some practitioners call them punishment-centered bureaucracies because harsh techniques are used to maintain order, control, and discipline.

A moment's reflection suggests that correctional facilities are run this way because correctional personnel and administrators feel that they must be run this way. Punitive control methods, in other words, are a philosophy or ideology of management. But is this the only way to run such institutions? Many experts think not, especially as many new concepts have evolved out of general institutional management. Authoritarian administrators, of course, are found everywhere. Their management method helps only to solve their personal needs, and

316

management philosophy has supported that style for a number of decades. However, research is showing that other techniques are very effective, especially those in which residents as well as staff are able to provide their unique input to the management of their facility.

In the last chapter a number of therapeutic techniques were discussed that usually are almost impossible to administer under traditional management. Therapy simply cannot be dictated, for trust and rapport are the essential ingredients of the various individual and group methods. These two elements are very seldom found in traditionally managed facilities. Therapeutic techniques are in fact based upon the therapist-client and client-client acceptance of each other. Interestingly enough, new concepts of management are also based on similar premises and consequently hold much promise for the field of juvenile corrections.

In this chapter, then, a number of general management principles that can wean correctional facilities away from the typically harsh, discipline-oriented models are presented. Although much research remains to be done to determine the best way of implementing these general theories on juvenile (and adult) corrections, those presented herein appear to offer the only way to salvage treatment and to create a more benign milieu for our correctional system. But first, a look at some of the assumptions made by classical managers.

CLASSICAL MANAGEMENT ASSUMPTIONS

Since the beginning of the industrial revolution, society has used bureaucracies to organize much of human life. The idea that gave birth to bureaucracy was that if the ordered, controlled thought of the scientific revolution could be used to master the physical environment, it could also be used to master human behavior.[1] Subsequently, the same principles that allowed for detailed analysis of the physical universe were applied to the management of human affairs.

Bureaucracy was developed to help society reach goals. Each organization was assumed to have a goal, and the entire organization was then structured to guarantee that that goal would be achieved. For example, each detail, from the size and shape of windows to the layout of halls and rooms, was carefully taken into consideration in the construction of many of our early houses of refuge. To keep residents in line and to prevent mischievous behavior, administrators generally ruled with considerable harshness and brutality. One early administrator who had an opposite reputation played with his charges and cared for them. He made his board of directors very nervous with this "permissiveness," and, not surprisingly, another administrator was soon given control.

Although this occurred in the second quarter of the 1800s, the theme is still familiar. Early administrators had a rigid, stern, and harsh orientation in the belief that residents would come to love and respect them as a result of such treatment.

A basic, then, of the classical style of management is the formulation of rules and structures to reach goals. Classically oriented administrators believe in keeping the authority at the top and controlling through countless regulations. Thus, they acquire power, establish the rules, and then command others to do their bidding. Classically oriented administrators thereby make certain that middle manager and line staff realize who has the formal authority in the organization.

Top administrators also often believe that lower-level personnel can be controlled and motivated to perform their jobs solely through monetary rewards. Many place a major emphasis on this form of control and assume that once it is implemented, the organization will run without problems. If problems do arise, the second half of the power equation, coercion, comes into play. If someone is perceived to be stepping out of line, classically oriented administrators typically have two responses: either they exercise their authority to threaten or punish the violator, or they tell the violator that he can leave if he does not like the organization.

Many classically oriented administrators also mistrust everyone below them. McGregor has classified this somewhat paranoid, cynical approach to people as Theory X.[2] In corrections, the Theory X manager believes that lower-level staff are basically lazy and are trying to avoid work. Rules to keep the staff working are assembled in a handbook of rules and regulations that are to govern both professional and non-professional staff. Strong punishment is inflicted on violators of these rules.

This style of management creates alienation among both staff and residents.[3] Unfortunately, administrators who use this style are not much concerned about alienation and low morale because they believe these are basic characteristics of all people. The result is that suspicion develops at all levels of the organization. The continual need for rule enforcement requires that superintendents be on the watch for infractions, and subordinates must tread softly and constantly look over their shoulders for rule enforcers. No one trusts anyone and suspicion grows.

Under Theory X, promotions depend upon the ability to follow and implement rules. Personnel must perform according to the prescribed policy and hide infractions carefully to give the impression they are enabling the organization to reach its goals effectively and efficiently. At the same time, if others can be made to look as though they are not doing their jobs, the possibilities for promotion are even better.

The key to effective and efficient job performance is information, but in classically managed organizations, information flow must follow the authority and communication channels, which are set up hierarchically. Information, therefore, has to travel along these duly constituted channels, regardless of whether it is coming from the bottom or from the top. Obviously, difficulties are created by forcing an organization to operate in this manner. Since information must flow only up or down, individuals can withhold information fairly easily, to the detriment of others on the staff. For example, when information is withheld, competitors for promotions may be deprived of information that is necessary for making decisions. When differences in philosophy exist, as happens often when treatment and custodial personnel are both within the organization, the withholding of information may occur in epidemic proportions. Furthermore, not only is information withheld, but also persons often refuse to cooperate with their peers. Line staff, for example, sometimes refuse to give caseworkers information needed for evaluating youths. The end result is that jobs defined as legitimate by the organization end up being performed poorly or not at all.

The consequence of classical management is that administrators often feel that whenever anything happens, someone is deliberately causing trouble. Riots, violence, and strikes are prime examples of happenings that administrators are quick to say were caused by outsiders or troublemakers. Yet, as we have implied, such problems actually may be caused by the structure of the organization and the attitudes of management. The use of force and coercion against inmates may bring about compliance, but it also brings resentment, suspicion, and distrust. The result may be disastrous. The situation in correctional facilities is bad to start with, and to increase the pressures through harsh, authoritarian discipline severely aggravates the problem.

To reiterate, administrators of many facilities cause many of their own problems. Their philosophy tells them not only that they are correct but also that there is only one correct way to run the organization. The expertise and experience of those down the line is ignored or derided, and lower-level personnel are made to feel that they do not count. Residents, of course, know exactly where they stand and have no illusions as to the amount of confidence placed in them by their keepers; their experiences lead them to resignation and alienation.

As alienation increases, outbreaks of violence become more and more probable. Each time a resident speaks up, the degree of punishment is increased. An ever-increasing spiral is created, one in which repression begets more alienation, and resentment begets more repression. The cycle continues until youths can stand it no longer and take out their revenge on whomever is nearest. Frustrated residents may beat one another or they may turn their wrath on staff or on the institution. Although this cycle occurs far more frequently in adult than in juvenile facilities, youths do occasionally rebel. Staff have been killed and institutions have been burned or otherwise destroyed. It is probable that most of these events could have been prevented by the use of sophisticated management principles.

GENERAL GOALS IN THE MANAGEMENT OF JUVENILE FACILITIES

Goals in correctional facilities are usually in conflict. The public expects institutions to provide retribution, protection, and rehabilitation, together with the deterrence of potential offenders. The goals or combinations of goals that citizens expect for our facilities are largely determined by citizen interest groups. The person caught in the middle is the superintendent. Citizens' interest groups, residents, and treatment and custodial personnel push for conflicting goals, leaving the superintendents in clearly untenable positions, for they must mediate among the conflicting parties and yet try to achieve their own goals.

The choice generally is obvious. The community desires protection above all else and therefore the superintendent, if he wants to keep his job, must keep the institution quiet. Consequently, as Street, Vinter, and Perrow pointed out, most juvenile correctional facilities are primarily custodially oriented, even when treatment is purported to be the primary goal.[4]

The proponents of treatment find, fortunately, that the situation is not quite so bad in juvenile corrections as in adult corrections. American citizens have long accepted that some effort should be made to rehabilitate juveniles, whereas they are not quite so sure about dealing with adults. However, even though the public is amenable to treatment for juveniles, the conflict among goals not only remains but also reaches far into the ranks of both the treatment and custodial personnel and the residents.

When an administrator first assumes control, he generally attempts to impose his own philosophy on the organizational structure. He may or may not be successful, depending partly on the orientations of the staff who hold power. But the acceptance of a particular philosophy also depends to a certain extent on the residents. Change of any kind brings about a restructuring of relationships, and few—staff or residents—want their world changed.

One way out of the dilemma is for the administrator to make a distinction between official goals and actual goals. Official statements are created for public consumption and released to the media. In the meantime, life in the organization either goes on as usual or changes are attempted and the ensuing conflicts mediated. Official respectability is maintained and the administrator is free to pursue his goals. Needless to say, conflict continues between those who want punishment and those who want rehabilitation. Therefore, an important task of the administrator is to bring these conflicting groups together.

Participants also bring personal goals with them. These goals affect them sometimes as individuals, sometimes as members of informal groups. When studies of organizational life were first begun, researchers assumed that employees' working conditions contributed greatly to their satisfaction on the job. These assumptions were modified greatly in the 1930s as it became clear that employees had other reasons for working in organizations.[5]

Maslow gave tremendous impetus to research on human motivation. He suggested that human beings act in particular ways because they have certain basic needs that range from physiological, safety, social, and ego needs to developmental needs. Maslow's contention was that the first needs, the physiological, must be fulfilled before a person could go on to satisfy the next, or safety, needs. Then, as these were fulfilled, the social and other needs could be met, with self-development fulfilled last.[6] When this concept is applied to juvenile correctional institutions, it becomes apparent that superintendents, business managers, social workers, line staff, and residents all have unfulfilled needs. These needs, of course, affect how institutional staff do their jobs and how they respond to their charges.

Residents, caseworkers, and all others also have a variety of social goals ranging from desires for a job they like, a stable family situation, and a steady income to desires to go bowling on Tuesday night or to date a certain coworker. People want to improve themselves, want work of a particular kind, and desire recognition and advancement. At the same time, most are not happy in jobs with poor administrators, where they are excessively supervised, where there is not enough work, and/or where working conditions and salaries are poor.[7] The persons who hold these goals, whether they be employees or residents, also group themselves informally. These groups then become a crucial part of all correctional settings and affect the way the facilities are operated. For example, when Massachusetts decided to close its training schools, custodial personnel with friends in high places got together to influence those friends to keep them open. When Street, Vinter, and Perrow studied the change of administrators in one facility, they found that custodial staff had successfully resisted the change, thereby demonstrating that informal groups can sometimes thwart the best efforts of administrators.[8] Classical managers ignore such groups; modern managers work with them, and the key to working with them is information.

INFORMATION FLOW

Information is important for many reasons. Classical managers who operate on the basis of a vertical flow of information assume that the only legitimate information is that which goes up and down the prescribed communication channels; we know in fact that information goes in all directions.

Those who know best the value of informal communication are probably the line staff and the residents. In fact, without some tie-in to the resident grapevine, most staff would find the administration of their living units impossible. Many potential suicides, escapes, beatings, and rapes can be discovered if the staff go behind the scenes and develop contacts with residents they can trust. Indeed, corrections probably has never operated without the use of this grapevine. Although informal communications do not always follow prescribed communication channels, their flow is often at least as important as the information that flows vertically. Today, good managers make sure they are plugged into this informal flow.

They must, however, study the institution carefully. A new superintendent, manager, or social worker, for example, will try to learn all he can about the informal groups, including their membership. He determines who the most influential members are and why they are so important. He will do the same with the resident groups—who is in them, and what are their goals? A very good administrator will discover which staff have access to which kinds of residents and to what types of information. This knowledge is critical to the safe and effective operation of the facility.

Operational information is of the utmost importance. Everyone needs information to do his job, but the sources are sometimes limited, inaccurate, or incomplete. A modern solution to this problem is to make sure that each person has access to all the information he needs. The number of potential incoming residents, the number of residents per living unit, and the problems of relationships are all necessary information. So too are such specifics as details of supplies and housekeeping. Also mandatory is the availability of information on social services, on testing services, and on explanations of various types of therapy and their relationship to particular residents. The data often can be computerized and print-outs distributed, or the information can be sent in the form of hand-outs and memoranda, to ensure that everyone who needs information receives it.

This may sound like the classical way of dispensing information, but there are several basic differences. The first is that this system provides everyone with all the information needed to do his job; information cannot be withheld from others to make the withholder look better. The second basic difference is that the information flow through the organization is lateral as well as vertical. Everyone at the same level of authority receives the same information. All line staff, social workers, and maintenance people receive what they need for their particular level.

Conflict between line staff and social workers in a juvenile correctional facility can be reduced by giving both groups the same information. It is also important to inform all residents of the reasons for the rules. To do so will provide them with an understanding of why the more important rules are necessary. An even more positive approach would be for line staff, social workers, and administrators to sit down with resident groups and formulate a complete set of new rules. All groups would then be able to provide input based on organizational and personal goals, and everyone would have a better understanding of one another. When everyone participates in rule formulation, each has a stake in following these rules.

The above process is called organization development (OD). The integration of personal with organizational goals and the development of new methods of getting job information to everyone lead to a general improvement in the organization. With everyone involved, the total organization becomes more actively involved in making sure that the structure functions. However, several other factors must be considered before such organizational development can be most effective.

CONTEMPORARY MANAGERS

Important factors in organizational improvement are the way managers operate and the methods they use in planning. Managers have always made decisions, organized and staffed positions, planned and controlled activities, and led groups toward objectives.[9] They continue to perform these functions today, but the role of the manager has become increasingly complex with the emerging new systems of knowledge, the more highly educated staffs, and the new and sophisticated equipment.

Today, when the requirements of modern managerial positions are examined, it is apparent that coordinating work flow and making decisions, rather than control and direction, are the chief components of the manager's job. Most of his time is spent with others at a comparable level of the organization.[10] Managers also provide leadership in ways to work more effectively with organized groups. Team building and improving intergroup relations are considered vital functions of the contemporary manager. Management by objectives (MBO), a deliberate attempt to state organizational goals more explicitly and to integrate them with personal goals, has become an important tool for the modern manager. Obviously, the manager as described here is not the commanding, authoritarian type; he is a data collector, a planner, an implementor of action, and a predictor of events.[11] Human relations become the focus of attention, and the manager who takes on the role of integrator is well aware of this.

Improving Intergroup Relations

The manager as integrator, then, must bring together the diverse elements in his organization. If hostility between line staff and residents prevents open discussion, the manager brings together a staff member who speaks for line staff and an inmate leader who speaks for residents. The two individuals are asked to determine how conflict began and to state each group's perception of the other. Consideration of how the problems should be solved then follows. Once this is done, the line staff member and the resident leader are asked to report back to their respective groups. Each group can then be asked to put in writing what it thinks of the other and the written comments exchanged for further discussion. Then, as those within each group begin to respond to each other's assumptions, the leaders may meet again or the two groups can be brought together for open discussions. This method brings the two groups closer together and the manager can begin working toward an understanding of the goals of both the facility and the personnel. This is a well-known approach in management-labor relations.

These meetings should not be judgmental; that is, the manager should steer participants away from condemning and blaming each other and should focus on each group's perceptions and what caused them. Eventually the stereotypes held by members of the groups will begin to break down as they become more realistic in their appraisal of each other.

Team Building

Once group members begin to understand and to talk with each other, additional steps can be taken. If achieving organizational goals is the task, teams may be set up to discuss what those goals should be and how they should be implemented. Such teams are composed of participants from all levels of the facility—residents, maintenance people, line staff, teachers, secretaries, and administrators are all represented. As might be expected, these people have varying perceptions of one another; hence, their stereotypes of each other may have to be broken down before they will be able to communicate among themselves.

The manager who is integrating this diverse mass of individuals into solid small groups must be well aware of their feelings, attitudes, and perceptions before the groups meet. Roles can be analyzed both before and during the group meetings; communication processes can be studied during the group meeting and feedback given to the group's members. By further analyzing the degree of trust, the work, the effectiveness, and the nature and the extent of participation and, especially, by noting whether or not members are growing personally and intellectually on the job, the manager as integrator can contribute to each person's job effectiveness and happiness. The integrator who is capable of instigating this activity must have certain characteristics:

1. Integrators need to be seen as contributing to important discussions on the basis of their competences and knowledge, rather than on positional authority.
2. Integrators must have balanced orientations and behavior patterns.
3. Integrators need to feel that they are being rewarded for their total product responsibility, not solely on the basis of their performances as individuals.
4. Integrators must have a capacity for resolving interdepartmental conflict and dropouts.[12]

MANAGEMENT BY OBJECTIVES (MBO)

One of the major advantages of MBO is that it brings all levels of staff into the decision-making process. The concept was first used in the 1950s and was more fully developed during the 1960s. The MBO technique recognizes that everyone has his own goals and tries to use these goals to the organization's advantage. Input from the entire organization is received and, through group discussion, everyone comes to understand the position of everyone else. Hopefully, employees will then not only understand but also contribute to the achievement of organizational goals. The supervisor, in turn, is able to understand and to become supportive of subordinates in achieving their desires.

Probably the best way to initiate MBO is to recognize that hostilities, conflicts, suspicion, and mistrust have built up in any organization over the years. Managers then use team-building techniques for improving intergroup relations that will reduce these problems and break down barriers. Juveniles, line staff, social workers, teachers, and administrators all have stereotyped views of one another, and these must be changed or modified.

The manager simply cannot walk into a meeting and expect change to occur. He must learn about employee goals through talking with all personnel. He can then become an integrator, mediating the differing viewpoints. The several levels at which change can take place and the extent of any potential change must be understood. Completely open discussions begin when the time is ripe to move the process forward.

The goal is to plan the desired results. Each member of the organization is looking for certain results in his job, and plans must be structured to permit each person and the organization to reach those goals. If organizational participants are solicited for their opinions, most will rise to the challenge, offer their insights, and help considerably in coordinating their phase of the operations with the total operation.

Once an organization's general goals have been agreed upon, the next step is to implement these goals. Meetings again are set up, as in reaching the general goals, and participants attack goal-implementation problems. Their perceptions of how the facility is running are put in writing and are discussed, as are possible solutions for specific problems. Again, the purpose is to break down barriers so that people will begin to trust one another and eventually to bring everyone to the point where there is understanding of how the organization can be run. The manager's objective is to encourage employees to become more innovative, imaginative, and ingenious, more willing to accept responsiblity, and more willing to exercise their intellect in achieving objectives. Ability to carry out these processes provides the basis on which employees are evaluated for promotion.

MBO is, then, people-centered—it places great confidence in the ability of people to exercise their individual talents. Care is taken to ensure that employees know what results are to be achieved and, if they have participated in making the decision, that they are able to exercise considerable latitude in promoting good organizational functioning. Once they have fullfilled their functions, managers are responsible for seeing that feedback about progress reaches all employees. The success of MBO is dependent upon feedback; only by ensuring feedback can improvement be made or problems be recognized for solution. Shared knowledge of desired results, the feasibility of the results, the length of time in which the results will be achieved, and their effect on basic goals will emerge as the organization begins to function smoothly. Undesirable consequences can be reduced by following this approach. All personnel know the role they are to play in achieving the objectives. MBO consists of five elements: the mission, the goals, the objectives, the preparation of planning statements, and the progress review.

Mission

The achievement of the mission is the broadest and most general goal of an organization. For example:

The mission of the Department of Corrections is to promote the public safety by assisting communities in the prevention of juvenile delinquency, administering sections of the law in a just and humane manner, providing opportunities for the offender to develop alternatives to unlawful behavior, and facilitating his reintegration into a free society; thereby contributing to an effective, efficient and equitable system of justice in Illinois.[13]

This is a clear statement of the purpose of an organization and its function as it relates to public expectations: the public is apprised of the benefits of the program; that is, that delinquency will be prevented and that offenders will be made fit to reenter society.

Goals   Goals are the ends desired: in general terms they are the results, conditions, or aims the organization hopes to achieve. Goals are stated in definite terms and identify precise results. Thus, measurement is possible, and the organization is able to determine exactly whether or not its purpose is being achieved.

The goals, then, indicate the direction the organization must take and the limits within which results are to be achieved. Goals are also the specifics of the mission. When they have been delineated, a good start can be made toward understanding the functions of the several parts of the organization and identifying the alternatives.

Objectives   Examples of objectives in juvenile corrections include the exact characteristics of a program to be implemented or the nature of a parole system that will reduce recidivism by a certain percent. Whenever possible, dates for program completion should be established. For example, if October 31 is the completion date for five group therapy sessions in which all youths have participated, the administrator should be able to know at that time whether the sessions were completed.

Failure to be realistic will undermine the entire management by objectives approach, for objectives are not concerned with either the how or the why of something, only the what and when.[14] The why is determined far in advance of the final establishment of goals and the how provides the job substance of personnel once the objectives have been specified.

Finally, a very important aspect of objectives is their relation to goals and missions. In other words, once personnel understand the general purposes of the organization, they must be able to see a direct tie-in between these and the specific objectives they are expected to achieve. Consistency throughout the entire management process is extremely important.

The Planning Statement   A planning statement deals with the achievement of objectives. It defines success and states how it may be achieved. The elements of a planning statement are the major courses of action, the specific tasks of various personnel, the precise schedules to be followed, and the resources that will be needed.

Once the basic decisions for a planning statement have been made, additional decision making must follow. The strength of this approach is that the most important decisions are made first. They are arrived at in advance, so that the structure of decision making is orderly and comprehensive.

Planning statements are important because they permit the proper scheduling of all activities. Staff and other workers then know when particular resources will be needed and how they will be used. The consequence is that all levels of management, ranging from the superintendent to the line staff, will save time, money, and energy in solving both short- and long-term problems.

Progress Reviews

Continuous communication among all organizational participants is necessary, especially among those responsible for carrying out the several tasks. One-to-one discussions between supervisor and subordinate provide an understanding of the progress toward goals and determine whether or not the project is on schedule. Feedback must be available to all involved, so that actual progress can be compared with scheduled progress. Decisions can then be made as to whether or not personnel are adequate and resources are sufficient and properly allocated.

Evaluation of Results

When evaluations are made by classically oriented managers, someone usually ends up being "chewed out." These evaluations are threatening, anxiety producing, and understandably, feared. But under MBO, employees consider evaluations in a much more constructive way. The MBO technique is based, it may be remembered, on mutual discussion of goals and objectives and of how they are to be achieved. If a result is not achieved, there must be a reason for it. Possibly the goals, objectives, or methods, or all of them, are unrealistic. If this is the case, all those involved in the project come together again and a reevaluation takes place. Goals, objectives, and methods may have to be modified—but no one gets "chewed out" for failing.

When a personnel problem arises, discussion should be neither punitive nor value laden. Rather, the job is analyzed, roles are discussed, problems are brought into the open, and the person is coached in job performance. Coaching sessions are helping sessions and consist of advising, suggesting, counseling, and encouraging. Their purpose is to educate, inform, and motivate subordinates.[15] In these sessions every attempt is made to avoid any sense of threat that would restrain employees from discussing their difficulties.

Advantages of Management by Objectives

Juvenile corrections personnel can realize many benefits from the management by objectives approach. While this method is not a solution for all problems, it can help many organizations to run much more smoothly. One of the first and major benefits of the approach lies in the advanced planning. Many organizations are managed by crisis; officials who do not plan must of necessity put out fires. This is not to say that problems are absent under MBO; they are definitely present because the organization is always going through change. But the management by objectives approach anticipates many of these problems.

MBO also enables personnel to realize their potential and to experience job growth. People need to grow and expand. When individuals are given the opportunity, they usually thrive on added responsibility, and both they and the organization benefit. As line staff become more committed and effective, the correctional facility's value to society is increased. Too, when personnel share in decision making and have access to greater amounts of information, they tend to talk things over with one another rather than permitting pressures to build to an explosion. As tensions are reduced and communications increase, people come to accept and care for one another, with the result that the workers, their work groups, and the organization all benefit.[16] Managers also benefit, since they become more oriented to staff management than to paper shuffling. Most dictatorial and control-oriented managers, in fact, can make the shift to the new system. The result is that the manager can enjoy greater participation in major decision making, more say in helping and guiding components, less need to maintain a watch-dog mentality, greater all-around satisfaction from being able to manage crisis creatively, and more time to work with staff on a one-to-one basis.

Workers receive the same benefits. They feel more a part of the organization because they help in the decision making. Their jobs are defined in consultation with their managers and peers, so they know what is expected of them. They know, for example, that it is their decision not to let a kid have a home furlough. Since goals, methods for achieving them, and areas of responsiblity have been previously agreed upon, workers need not be ambivalent in making decisions. Increased communication means that they will interact with other members of the facility as a team, and the decisions made will be team decisions. Individuals are freer to share ideas and to make decisions. They have access to any necessary information and can receive feedback from managers, peers, and residents. Personal growth is dramatically increased, and individuals continue to grow as they become more and more involved in organizational affairs and gain status as members of a group.

Probably the greatest benefit of MBO is the correctional facility's change in management from a hierarchically organized, punishment-centered bureaucracy. Power can be shared with staff, who, in turn, participate in the management of the institution. The end result will be higher morale and greater job satisfaction among institutional employees.

MBO is best implemented through a total organizational effort. If this is not practicable, several departments can begin the program on their own, and their successes can provide the impetus for the rest of the organization to follow. Because of the extensive programming involved in MBO planning, everyone should realize that years may pass before the whole organization can shift fully from the old to the new. Six months may pass before the first real changes are perceived, and six years may pass before a large organization adopts the plan totally. Regardless of the time, effort, and costs involved, supporters of MBO believe that the production increases are well worth the effort. (In juvenile corrections, production means returning to the community juveniles able to function as normal citizens.)

The Contingency Theory Approach

An implicit point of the management by objectives approach is that there is no one best way to run an organization. If the total institution milieu is examined, numerous goals are found to be present. Interest and pressure groups, legislators, administrators, middle-management people, treatment and line staff, and residents all vary in their desires. As a result, institutional climates differ from one organization to another. Staff must recognize these differences and plan accordingly. Institutions are managed, in other words, on the basis of their individual purposes.

The major proponent of the contingency approach to leadership is Fred Fiedler. His approach demands that all personnel, jobs, organizational characteristics, and unique situations in an institutional milieu be very carefully analyzed. Fiedler divides these features into three components: leader-member relations, task structure, and position power. Leader-member relations are concerned with rapport between managers and those who work with them. The task structure is concerned with how well jobs are defined, so that staff can know exactly what they are supposed to do. Position power relates to the manager's formal, legitimate power, apart from any personal, charismatic leadership abilities.[17]

Fiedler finds that any number of leadership styles can be effective.

Leaders can be oriented toward person-to-person relations or toward a task-oriented style; they do not have to fit into a tight, preconceived mold, but neither can they simply barge into an organization and begin managing. A thorough analysis of the organization and its people must precede any managing. Once the analysis has been made, leaders can take on or delegate power; help change the structures designed to reach objectives; introduce new goals, members, or groups, or change the climate of the organization and its groups.[18]

SOME CAUTIONARY NOTES

Management by objectives and contemporary management principles are not a panacea for all of the problems faced by correctional administrators. The possibility remains that no management technique can ever be successful in some training schools, detention homes, and other facilities. Their physical design, the nature of the inmate world, and the lack of resources may prohibit their ever becoming any more than custodial warehouses characterized by debilitating conditions. One of the biggest drawbacks, of course, is a clientele that is alienated before entrance and that may never forgive a society perceived to be unjust.

Also, data is lacking on the conditions under which various management techniques will work, for little research, to date, has been done on people-changing institutions. Change should be undertaken very carefully, since change often appears to generate violence; to move too quickly could be disastrous for some facilities. Finally, a first-rate staff-development program and a careful analysis of the institution are necessary before any system-wide organizational change can be implemented.

SUMMARY

Traditional management practices are among the factors contributing to problems in correctional facilities. The more coercive and repressive the management, the more alienated the clientele. Running organizations from the top down in a democratic society simply serves to convince subordinates that they do not really count and that their education, experience, and skills are not respected. For people whose education has trained them to think and whose desires are to achieve respect, responsiblity, and self-growth, authoritarian treatment encourages them only to resist any control that is exercised over them.

However, several techniques are developing that top managers are using to overcome their problems and to increase the viability of their institutions. This general technique is called organization development; its purpose is to make use of the tremendous talent to be found at all levels of the organization, including, in correctional facilities, the residents. Management by objectives is one philosophy of management that enables all participants to become involved in organizational affairs. Whenever this method is used by skilled managers, personnel are integrated with organizational goals. Lower-level participants get to know their superiors and superiors get to know their subordinates. As their missions and goals become uniform, they understand one another and are less likely to work at cross-purposes. The result is a healthier and more productive organization, whose personnel can achieve greater individual satisfaction while fully developing the potential of each.

The trend is clearly in this direction. The National Advisory Commission on Criminal Justice Standards and Goals, for example, recommended that more highly qualified personnel be employed to improve the image of corrections.[19] Such personnel would be invaluable in setting up programs that would enable all levels of employees to understand the new management techniques and thereby reduce any inherent conflict. Whether they function in management or other aspects of the institution, they should have training in all of the disciplines that could aid them in their relationships with others. In addition, they should be promoted on the basis of their interpersonal competence and their ability to work with the diverse staff and resident groups found in correctional facilities.

All personnel, and this now includes residents, should have some say in establishing and in maintaining the goals of the organization, should be involved in both short- and long-term planning, and should be trained to fully and effectively participate with others in decision making. Their understanding of the new management concepts should be enhanced so that those concepts are no longer viewed as threats. Training should include sessions in setting organizational goals, in understanding the objectives of the units in which they work, and in developing the means by which those objectives are to be achieved. The quality of life in juvenile correctional institutions should improve as personnel learn these methods and are rewarded for implementing them.

QUESTIONS

1. Describe from your own experience how a classically oriented manager works.
2. What are the major drawbacks of classical management techniques?
3. What are the differences between a manager who is classically oriented and one who serves as an integrator?
4. What is management by objectives? How does it work and what are its goals?
5. List techniques other than those discussed in this chapter that could be used to reduce intra-institutional conflict.
6. What are the drawbacks to implementing a management by objectives approach?

ENDNOTES

1. Max Weber, *The Theory of Social and Economic Organization,* trans. A. M. Henderson and Talcott Parsons (New York: Oxford University Press, 1947).
2. Douglas McGregor, *The Human Side of Enterprise* (New York: McGraw-Hill Book Company, 1960).
3. Amitai Etzioni, *A Comparative Analysis of Complex Organizations: On Power, Involvement, and Their Correlates* (New York: Free Press, 1975), pp. 27–31.
4. David Street, Robert D. Vinter, and Charles Perrow, *Organization for Treatment: A Comparative Study of Institutions for Delinquents* (New York: Free Press, 1966), p. 177.
5. F. J. Roethlisberger and W. J. Dickson, *Management and the Worker* (Cambridge, Mass.: Harvard University Press, 1935).
6. Abraham Maslow, *Motivation and Personality* (New York: Harper and Brothers, 1954).
7. F. P. Herzberg, J. L. Mausner, and B. Snyderman, *The Motivation to Work,* 2d ed. (New York: John Wiley & Sons, 1959).
8. Street, Vinter, and Perrow, *Organization for Treatment,* pp. 40–55.
9. W. W. Haynes, J. L. Massie, and M. Wallace, Jr., *Management: Analysis, Concepts, and Cases,* 3d ed. (Englewood Cliffs, N.J.: Prentice-Hall, 1975), pp. 11–12.
10. L. Sayles, *Managerial Behavior* (New York: McGraw-Hill Book Company, 1964).
11. W. French, "Organization Development: Objectives, Assumptions and Strategies," *California Management Review* 12 (Winter 1969): 23–24.
12. Paul R. Lawrence and Jay W. Lorsch, *Organization and Environment: Managing Differentiation and Integration* (Cambridge, Mass.: Harvard Graduate School of Business Administration, 1967), p. 146.
13. "Management by Objectives Handbook" (Illinois Department of Corrections, n.d.), p. 11.
14. George L. Morrisey, *Management by Objectives and Results* (Reading, Mass.: Addison-Wesley Publishing Company, 1970).

15. Mark L. McConkie, *Management by Objectives: A Corrections Perspective* (Washington, D.C.: U.S. Government Printing Office, July 1975), pp. 35–36.
16. Edgar F. Huse and James L. Bowditch, *Behavior in Organizations: A Systems Approach to Managing* (Reading, Mass.: Addison-Wesley Publishing Company, 1973), p. 156.
17. Fred Fiedler, "Engineer the Job to Fit the Manager," *Harvard Business Review* 44 (January/February 1965): 118.
18. Ibid., p. 118.
19. National Advisory Commission on Criminal Justice Standards and Goals, *Corrections* (Washington, D.C.: U.S. Government Printing Office, 1973), pp. 459–495.

REFERENCES

Bartollas, Clemens, and Miller, Stuart J. *Correctional Administration: Theory and Practice.* New York: McGraw-Hill Book Company, 1978.
This pioneering text analyzes alternative managerial approaches and issues in corrections.

Beckhard, Richard. *Organization Development: Strategies and Models.* Reading, Mass.: Addison-Wesley Publishing Company, 1969.
This concise and well-written book is an excellent introduction to organization development.

Etzioni, Amitai. A *Comparative Analysis of Complex Organizations and Their Correlates.* New York: Free Press, 1975.
Etzioni's book is quite helpful in understanding the influence of power in various types of organizations.

Huse, Edgar F., and Bowditch, James L. *Behavior in Organizations: A Systems Approach to Managing.* Reading, Mass.: Addison-Wesley Publishing Company, 1973.
This book is a must for students who are interested in organizational analysis and organization development.

McConkie, Mark L. *Management by Objectives: A Corrections Perspective.* Washington, D.C.: U.S. Government Printing Office, July 1975.
McConkie applies the basic concepts of management by objectives to correctional organizations.

13

Issues of Institutionalization

The authors of this book do not approach the subject of institutionalization dispassionately. In our own experience we have attempted to console a number of youths who have been sexually assaulted. We have observed the subtle and sometimes blatant pressures sexual exploiters place on new institutional residents. We have pleaded with youths not to take their lives, and we have been called to the scene of successful suicides. We have also had residents describe how staff sexually exploit them with the promise of an early release. We have been delegated to investigate staff brutality toward residents and have been met by stoney silence from other staff. We have seen juveniles emotionally break apart because of the strain of training school life. We have seen youths rip their faces and arms wide open trying to scale fences because they were so determined to escape from confinement. In short, we have experienced the terrifying impact that the training school has on some youngsters.

But, on the other hand, we have worked with many youths whom we would not want for our next door neighbors. We remember youths who brutally assaulted other youngsters in the community. We recall a boy who knifed another boy simply because he got in his way. We remember the youngster who raped an older woman who had befriended him and then joked about it to his peers. We recall the boy who sexually assaulted and killed a three-year-old child. We have worked with several youths who killed their parents. We remember a youth or

335

two who felt proud of emptying lead into a store owner's stomach. And we recall the youth who made weekend rounds of the college campus seeking women to rape. We have worked with these and many other juveniles who committed violent crimes in the community.

And so we can say with some authority that institutionalization does little good for anyone and sometimes leaves its mark on a youth for the rest of his life. Yet, society is faced with some youngsters who seem to be unable to walk the streets without hurting, intimidating, and stealing from the innocent. They appear to pursue crime as a career, to perceive themselves as criminals, and to have little sensitivity toward the feelings and rights of others.

Thus, the question of institutionalization of juveniles is fraught with conflict. Jerry Miller and others loudly proclaim that all institutions are bad for children and that children must be kept out of them. At the other extreme are those who claim that the violence of youth crime today is directly related to the permissiveness of the juvenile justice system. Those in this position claim that the best medicine for youth crime is to send more youths to training schools, and to use institutionalization widely to protect the community against predatory youngsters.

The purpose of this chapter, then, is to discuss the issues involved in the use of juvenile correctional institutions, most of which are generating interest and controversy among practitioners in the juvenile justice system.

THE NONCRIMINAL YOUTH STAYS LONGER

One of the most widely accepted findings of juvenile corrections is that the noncriminal youth is confined longer than the criminal youth in juvenile institutions.[1] It is, of course, a remarkable irony of justice that the youth who commits no crime can be locked up longer than an armed robber, a rapist, or a murderer. Most noncriminal youths have more difficulty complying with rules and limits than more delinquent youth. All institutional residents are informed of the rules and perhaps even given a list of rules of the cottage and of the institution. Figure 13-1 is one example of cottage rules. But noncriminal youths seem to be more determined to fight the system and to resist the rules. Status offenders, in particular, are quick to challenge authority. The youth who refuses to take a shower, to clean up his room, to do his work detail, or to attend school is almost always a noncriminal youth. The expression, "I won't do it," is one that staff frequently hear from these youths.

More delinquent youths are quickly informed by peers how to get along in the institution and how to please staff. Some, of course, may

FIGURE 13-1   Rules to Follow

1.   Girls wakened at 7:15 A.M. - Must be out of bed by 7:25 A.M. and stay up.

2.   Beds must be neatly made before coming out front in A.M.

3.   All must wash in A.M. - before getting dressed.

4.   All clothes on laundry table must be put away in A.M.

5.   Clothing and shoes in dorm are to be neatly put away in A.M. Cupboard doors and dresser drawers closed.

6.   Iron is only given out at shower time.

7.   All girls must wear P.J. tops and bottoms. Robes must be worn except in dorm area.

8.   Tampax and sanitary pads are to be wrapped in newspaper and put in garbage cans. DO NOT FLUSH DOWN TOILET!!

9.   No glass bottles or deodorant or spray cans are permitted in back area.

10.   Hot combs used in laundry hall only. Used on Tuesday and Thursday, unless special occasion.

11.   GIRLS DO NOT USE WASHER OR DRYER.

12.   Girls are not permitted in any dorm area except their own.

13.   No talking to other cottages or from table to table in dietary. No passing food from table to table or in line.

14.   When sent up from school, girls are to remain in front area of cottage. Control door and front door are to be locked. After being sent up 3 times in a very short period of time, further restrictions may result. This will be done on an individual basis -- to be determined by the reason for being sent up.

15.   No smoking, radio, TV when a girl is sent up from school.

16.   Commissary time - 7:00 P.M. evenings - 2:30 P.M. Saturday, Sunday, and Holidays.

17.   Shower time 8:00 P.M. - all to back at one time.

18.   Control door locked at 6:00 P.M.

19.   No eating or drinking in foyer or living room.

20.   At 11:00 P.M. on Friday and Saturday - all girls must be in the Living Room to watch TV.

21.   Girls must wear shoes to dietary. No bare feet or slippers. Also no P.J. tops are to be worn to Dietary.

22.   All mail is to be given to staff. Girls Do Not Handle It.

choose not to follow this advice for a few weeks or even months, but nearly all eventually play the game of convincing staff that they really have no problems. Institution-wise juveniles accomplish this by staying out of trouble, or "playing it cool," by following the rules of the cottage and the institution, and by complying with the wishes of staff. If they can put on a convincing performance, the consequence should be a prompt release. They remain untouched by any institutional program, do the minimum amount of time, and get out. The ones who need rehabilitation the most are able to escape the institution untouched. The Bartollas, Miller, and Dinitz study of juvenile institutionalization found that the most sophisticated youths in the institution were known as "slicks." Although they had serious offenses on their records and had been institutionalized several times, the slicks usually were released within a year of commitment. Status offenders, in comparison, usually stayed eighteen months and sometimes as long as three years.[2] This is a direct effect of the indeterminate sentence.

Originally, the indeterminate sentence was developed to encourage offenders to cooperate with the staff of the houses of refuge, who, in turn, would be the judges of when a youth was ready for release. Since the length of sentence was indeterminate, it was anticipated that offenders would cooperate when they realized that good behavior would result in an early release. Staff and other instiutional personnel could then release the offenders at the appropriate time, supposedly sooner than if they were given determinate sentences.

That institutional personnel have wide discretion in interpreting rules and in judging when an infraction takes place creates a basic problem. Intransigent staff, staff with personality problems, or staff who have personality conflicts with residents can make it very difficult for a youth they do not like. Residents may have no recourse when a staff member adds time to their stay for no reason or when he argues endlessly that they have not improved.

One youth who came before the cottage review committee for his three-month review was denied release because of a poor attitude in the classroom. He was upset, but still managed in the next three months to get much better evaluations from his teachers. At his next review, he was again turned down because his room was too dirty. Though terribly unhappy that he had to spend another three months in the institution, he finally decided that he would do well in school, would keep his room clean, and would have no problems in any area. Three months later, the youth came to the review confident that justice at last would be done. It appeared for a while that it would be, but then a new staff member objected to his release, "I don't think he is ready to go home. He hasn't been paying me proper respect, and I think another three months here would do him a lot of good." After a lengthy debate, the youth's release was postponed another three months. He ran out of the room screaming, totally beside himself. Later, he said to his social worker, "What in the hell do you have to do to get out of here? They expect more out of me than they can deliver themselves."

As previously noted, the Juvenile Justice Standards Project, jointly sponsored by the Institute of Judicial Administration and the American Bar Association, has recommended that indeterminate sentences should be abolished. The first step in this replacement of the indeterminate sentence has begun with mandatory and determinate sentences for violent juvenile offenders. New York State is the first state to enact a mandatory sentencing law for violent offenders.

Another issue related to the longer stays of noncriminal youth—whether or not noncriminal juveniles should be removed from juvenile court jurisdiction—is one of the most hotly debated controversies in juvenile corrections. Both sides have impressive groups supporting their position. The National Council on Crime and Delinquency, the Juvenile Justice Standards Project, the National Advisory Committee on Juvenile Delinquency Prevention, and a host of other committees and groups have urged that youths guilty of noncriminal behavior should be removed from juvenile court jurisdiction. But, on the other hand, the National Council on Juvenile Court Judges; the Advisory Committee on Standards, established by the Juvenile Justice and Delinquency Prevention Act of 1974; and the vast majority of state legislatures do not agree. The ratio of noncriminal youths in institutional populations is decreasing because some states no longer permit status offenders to be sent to correctional institutions. Nevertheless, the problem remains a real one.

THROWAWAY YOUTH

Society, according to one viewpoint, discards poor and minority children in training schools. Instead of being used only as places to house older and difficult-to-handle youths, this position asserts, these settings too frequently become society's garbage dumps for minority children and the children of the have-nots.[3] The truly throwaway children are the dependent and neglected, the abused, and the mentally ill. Many of these children have not committed any crime, but they are nevertheless committed to correctional institutions simply because no other place is available. Middle-class children, in comparison, are given chance after chance to remain in the community, in either community-based or diversionary programming.

Table 13-1, derived from data of the National Assessment Study of Juvenile Corrections, certainly seems to support the argument that juvenile institutions are racist, since it shows that over half of the confined offenders come from minority groups. The table also shows that juvenile facilities are not places of last resort housing older offenders, for institutional residents are younger than those in either community-residential or day-treatment programs. Consequently, in a country in which minorities constitute less than 15 percent of the

TABLE 13-1 Classification of Offenders by Type of Correctional Program.

	INSTITUTION	COMMUNITY RESIDENTIAL	DAY TREATMENT
Race			
Minority (%)	54	46	66
White (%)	46	54	34
Age			
Mean (years)	15.7	16.7	16.2
Range (years)	8–24	13–24	12–22
Social Class			
Unemployed or			
working-class patient (%)	59	40	60
Sex			
Male (%)	71	62	84
Female (%)	29	38	16
Prior Correctional Experiences			
(mean number of times)			
Arrested	8.0	6.3	6.0
Detention	4.5	4.8	3.4
Jail	3.2	2.0	1.5
Court	5.5	5.7	4.3
Probation	2.0	1.2	1.5
Group or foster home	1.2	1.5	0.3
Institution	1.7	1.0	0.5
(Range of n)	(1269–1341)	(145–152)	(224–238)

national population and in which nearly 75 percent of the arrested juveniles are white, it is appalling that over half of the institutionalized population comes from minority groups and that institutional residents have an average age younger than that of youths left in the community.

Equally as serious as the problem of racism is the placement of the dependent and neglected, the abused child, and the mentally ill with delinquents in training schools. Juvenile correctional facilities simply are not capable of dealing with these special cases. Youths with these special problems are not only going to fail to improve in these settings, but their special handicaps are often made worse by the institutional environment. Indeed, a significant part of the traumatic impact of institutionalization for these youths is the exploitation they receive from more aggressive and delinquent peers.

It is also claimed that sexism is as prevalent as racism and class oppression. Judge Lisa Richette, author of *Throwaway Children,* contends that girls are treated much differently from boys in juvenile institutions. Judge Richette claims that troublesome girls are committed to training schools to save them from the evils and sins of society.[4]

Further sexism is apparent in the offense disparity between boys and girls. Girls are sent to institutions for less serious crimes than are boys. For example, when Giallombardo's list of the juvenile offenses committed by inmates of three training schools for girls is studied, it becomes very clear that few of the girls in these institutions had committed any crimes other than status offenses.[5]

In addition to offense disparity, the charge can also be made that girls, at least in some states, stay longer in institutions. Training schools for girls also lack the number and the quality of programs typically found in training schools for boys. Boys generally have seven or more vocational programs available in a large training school, but girls normally have access only to beauty culture, sewing, and food service classes. Judge Richette, in this regard, adds that the philosophy of treating girls in training schools is to make them good housewives when they are released. Instead, they should be better equipped to find jobs when they return to the community.[6]

Those who challenge these charges of racism and sexism claim that minority children commit more serious offenses. They are sent to institutions in greater numbers and at a younger age simply because their community behavior is so unacceptable. Furthermore, girls who are sent away to training schools are those who have had one chance after another in the community. If these youths are the throwaway youth, it is because they choose to be the throwaway youth, for society has given them every chance to avoid this predicament. The rationale is that it is unfortunate that they have to be placed in an institution, but society cannot condone or tolerate their resistance to authority, their refusal to attend school, their defiance of parents, and their runaway behavior.

This charge that society uses institutions as throwaway housing for its unwanted is very serious. The United States has long maintained that equality before the law is the cornerstone of a democratic society, and that those who are punished are threats to the society and must be punished. Social justice in our society is at stake here. The poor, as well as the rich, deserve equal treatment under the law. So do black as well as white and female as well as male. Clearly, the charges cannot be dismissed out-of-hand; they must be analyzed carefully. But if the criticisms are valid and social justice, indeed, is lacking for some of our children, then we must develop alternative methods to handle them more appropriately and beneficially.

JUVENILE VICTIMIZATION

Bartollas et al. examined victimization in an end-of-the-line male training school in Ohio and came to a number of conclusions.[7]

1. Most victimizations involve the appropriation of personal property. Although personal attacks are far less common, these most demeaning and lurid of all forms of inmate victimization are a good index of the nature and quality of life in some training schools. They tell us a great deal about the overall exploitation patterns, the social organization, the inmate norms or code, and the inmate leadership of a juvenile institution that is normally hidden from even the most perceptive observers.

2. Investigation of sexual assaults on inmates suggests that:

Whites are victimized by blacks out of all proportion to the relative number of each.

After the whites, the weaker blacks are the next most frequently abused group.

Lower-class youths prey on the far less institution-wise and less capable of defense middle-class residents.

Victimization of the normal and the mildly disturbed describes a U-shaped curve on a graph. The more normal (on psychological tests) the resident, the greater the likelihood of exploitation; similarly, the mildly disturbed are also preyed upon more often than chance would dictate.

Normal or sick, black or white, lower or middle class, long-term inmate or newcomer, sexual victims are accorded a pariah status by both inmates and staff—a status not dissimilar to that of a female rape victim, except for its much greater intensity and inescapability in the confines of a closed social setting. It is not easy to grasp the meaning of such a status; to be an outsider among outsiders, stigmatized among the labeled, is an irony that begs a novelist's touch.

3. Staff members are also victimized by inmates. Tough inmates physically intimidate staff. Nearly all inmates learn to manipulate staff by playing physical, psychological, theological, therapeutic, and educational games with them.

4. Staff, like the residents, range from the exploiters to the vic-

timized. Unquestionably, one thing is certain—good intentions are no match against knowledge and use of the pressure points in the system to one's advantage. This fundamental principle is clearly understood by staff bent on exploitation.

5. At the subtlest level, inmates signal or cue each other about their accessibility to victimization. These cues are then tested in daily encounters. The results of this testing lead to the sorting of residents into the various exploitation-victimization categories and defines their social roles and status in the inmate social structure.

6. Inmate victimization is facilitated by diagnostic processing and labeling. The Ohio institution defends itself against community pressures by labeling some youths with an R suffix (dangerous) or E suffix (emotionally disturbed). Some residents, therefore, are confirmed in their toughness, and their preying on weaker residents is merely an extension of their disorder. Similarly, other youths are confirmed in their inability to take care of themselves. They are the easy victims for the exploiter. This is a concrete example of the self-fulfilling prophecy and of the effectiveness of stigma in promoting exploitation and a pecking order within the training school.

7. Enormous suffering and trauma pervade the exploitation system. For extreme victims, running away, attempts at suicide, and resorting to drugs seem to be the only remedies available. These are invariably counterproductive. No such strategy is adaptive and surely none is therapeutic or rehabilitative.

8. The inmate code is detrimental to the weak and beleagured and works to the advantage of the aggressive and strong. Like the criminal code, the inmate code favors the top dogs in the system. In fact, there is no simple justice in the inmate social system, and undoubtedly far less justice and humanity than in the larger social system.

9. The staff code, written as well as unwritten, works against effective rehabilitation. Although it sets limits on staff exploitation of inmates, it does not preclude it. The staff code invariably tends "to place a premium on stability, not change; on holding the fort, not storming the ramparts; on avoiding trouble, not making it." Staff, like the residents, want to do easy time. To accomplish this goal, staff create a gulf between themselves and inmates and use a few inmate toughs to control the cottages and the integrity of the institution. In return, these inmate leaders, or "heavies," are granted personal privileges and considerable leeway in their "management" policies.

10. Two paradoxes in institutional life became increasingly evident throughout this research. The Ohio training school receives the worst of the labeled—the unwanted, the losers, and the outsiders. These young men not only consider themselves to be among the toughest of their counterparts, but also have the societal credentials to prove it. But,

in much the same way that they themselves were processed, they maintain an extremely brutalizing system. If anything, the environment of this institution is less fair, less just, less humane, and less decent than the worst aspects of the juvenile justice system on the outside. Brute force, manipulation, and institutional sophistication carry the day and set the standards that ultimately prevail. In this process, many of the most dangerous and tough delinquents in the outside community become the meek and doubly and triply stigmatized victims within the institution.

The other major paradox is the inversion of black-white relationships. On the outside, "black is beautiful" may be a great slogan, but by heroes, jobs, housing, health, morbidity, relative income, or any other hard or soft measure, the world is white. On the inside, however, the values and norms, privileges and high status, preferred roles and inmate power belong to the black, not the white, community. The black character of the institution—the food, the music, the argot, the body-gesture communication—is derived from the ghetto culture that predominates. Deeper probing forces the conclusion that power and status, indeed, reside in blackness. Whites, in this social order, most often are at the very bottom and blacks at the very top, a most unaccustomed position for both.

Several other studies concur on the pervasiveness of victimization in juvenile institutions.[8] Ken Wooden, who visited juvenile institutions throughout the country, documented the brutal treatment residents received from staff in both private and public training schools. For example, he reports the incident of a boy on work detail who asked to go to the bathroom and defecated in a shed when he was denied permission. Excerpts from legal affidavits contain the reactions of staff.

> The guard grabbed the kid by the hair and dragged him to put his face in the shit. The kid refused. The guard grabbed him by the hair and collar, kicked him to his knees and stuck his face in the shit saying, "That'll teach you to shit in the carrot shed, you cocksucker." The kid got up and tried to wash his face off in the barn sink. Another guard was in the barn and wouldn't let the kid wash his face. Instead he hosed him down from head to foot.[9]

Another boy became ill while eating and requested permission not to eat any more. Staff denied him permission. When he vomited, he "was whacked on the head with a big serving spoon" and was made to do push-ups. According to the legal affidavit:

> After dinner, downstairs, the guard ordered Smith to do push-ups on the line. Smith felt sick again, asked the guard if he could go to the bathroom, was refused, and continued doing push-ups till he finally threw up again,

this time on the floor. The guard ordered Smith to eat his own vomit. Smith kept refusing until the guard started kicking and hitting him. Smith was finally forced by the guard to eat his vomit until the floor was clean. He ate it all. When he was finally excused, Smith went into the bathroom and threw up in the john.[10]

Part of the same legal document:

Another time this kid Hill went to the bathroom and took a shit. He forgot to flush the toilet. The guard didn't hear the toilet flush and so he went into the bathroom to check. He then came back out and grabbed Hill by the hair, brought him back into the bathroom and shoved Hill's head into the toilet bowl which was still unflushed saying, "This will teach you to flush the toilet next time."[11]

The death of Willie Stewart is even more tragic. As a young adolescent, he was taken to Cummins Prison. Upon entering the gates, he was "chased by a car. . . ., shot at, ordered to dunk his entire body in a pool of water, slapped, did thirty-one minutes of push-ups, made to jump up and down holding a hoe pressed to his head and had his hair clipped. . . . and was dumped on a floor by two guards who decided he was faking an illness. . . . He died while being taken to a hospital; his mother was told that he had eaten something that killed him.[12]

To the charges of Bartollas, Miller, and Dinitz, Wooden, and others that "man is a wolf to man" in juvenile institutions, critics claim that the problem of institutional victimization is exaggerated and that these writers only sensationalize the atypical. Defenders of institutions also claim that the rate of exploitation is low and exists only in older, male institutions.

Bartollas and Sieverdes, in an unpublished study of six training schools in a southeastern state, draw these preliminary conclusions:

Coeducational institutions appear to have less sexual victimization.

Older youths become more involved in exploitation, especially sexual, than younger ones.

The degree of victimization rises as institutions become more custodial.

Victimization rises when inmate subcultures develop solidarity.

Victimization rises when the age spread of an institutional population increases.

Institutional residents, even those as young as ten years old, are aware of sexual exploitation and the dynamics involved.

Home visits appear to attenuate sexual victimization.

Staff are unaware of a great deal of the victimization that takes place "backstage."

Staff feel helpless to prevent exploitation among residents.

Treatment-oriented staff seem to be more sensitive to exploitation than custodial staff and, therefore, are able to control it more.[13]

GOAL CONFLICT

Determining the goals that are appropriate for juvenile facilities is one of the stickiest issues in juvenile corrections. Not only do administrators find that different individuals in their institution have different conceptions of where the facility should be going and what should be done with juveniles, but society in general also is equally confused as to what the institutional goals should be.

Street, Vinter, and Perrow classified the basic institutional goals as incarceration/deprivation, obedience/conformity, reeducation/development, and treatment. They only considered the last three because they believed that incarceration and deprivation goals are not found in juvenile correctional facilities. Table 13-2 presents an outline of the basic components of these goals.

Generally, staff in obedience/conformity institutions emphasize rules, keep residents constantly under surveillance, punish them frequently and harshly, and do not otherwise become involved with them. Staff in reeducation/development facilities demand conformity, hard work, and intellectual growth; they are more willing to give additional rewards for conformity to the education/development ideals and they are somewhat closer to the residents. Staff in treatment facilities are much more permissive. Residents are worked with, helped and led, and are permitted to get closer to the staff emotionally.

Among the specific findings related to the institutions in this study is the fact that residents in treatment and reeducation/conformity institutions "tended to report highly developed or positive social relations more often than did those of the obedience/conformity institutions." Also, residents in treatment facilities are more positive toward the institution, develop more primary relationships, and have leaders who are more positively oriented than residents of the obedience/conformity facilities.

Much additional study needs to be done on the goals of juvenile correctional facilities. As well as staff and residents, the entire climate of the institution is affected by these goals. A general climate of conflict is certainly not conducive to high morale or effective functioning among either staff or residents. Also, the nature of goals largely determines the changes that realistically can be made. These goals cannot, incidentally, be ascertained by reading the often-glowing words of the public relations department; a stated official goal is often merely that—an official statement. Administrators or staff coming into a facility are

TABLE 13-2 Institutional Goals

Dimension	Obedience/conformity Institutions	Reeducation/develop-ment Institutions	Treatment Institutions
STAFF PERSPECTIVE			
Assumptions	Inmates would learn to conform out of fear of the consequences.	Inmates possess resources that could be drawn upon and developed.	Deviance could be corrected only by a thoroughgoing reorientation and reconstitution of the inmate.
Strategy to change people	Demanded compliance and submission.	Sought moderate changes through training for a gainful career.	Sought broad changes, altered personalities, and improved interpersonal relations.
Staff attitudes	Staff used coercive methods; staff pessimistic of inmate change.	Used reeducative methods; staff optimistic of inmate change.	Used more differentiated and voluntaristic methods; staff optimistic of inmate change.
Relationship	Staff members perceived staff-inmate understanding as difficult.	Staff members perceived staff-inmate understanding as possible and helpful.	Staff members firmly believed in staff-inmate understanding as a key factor in treatment.
Authority	Cottage staff had most authority.	Balanced distribution of authority.	Clinicians had most authority.
Coordination	Executive's firm direction of all phases of staff performance.	Some coordination.	Coordination of relatively autonomous subordinates.
Routine	Tasks routinized.	Some nonroutinized programs.	Nonroutinized programming.
Discipline	Discipline emphasized.	Balance between discipline and permissiveness.	Permissiveness emphasized.
INMATES PERSPECTIVE			
Perspective	Residents perceived the institution and staff negatively.	Residents perception fairly positive.	Residents perceived the institution and staff positively.
Inmate Organization	Inmates tended to organize themselves cohesively to procure legitimate and illegitimate items of value.	Group formation tended to be more after the pattern of treatment institutions.	Inmates tended to organize more voluntarily around friendship patterms; inmate friendships were not antistaff, and the groups tended to be prostaff.
Leadership	Inmate leadership highly involved in illicit and secret activities. Inmate leaders tended to gather power by controlling illicit rewards, and leaders presented solidary opposition to staff.	The leaders were a good influence for the inmates, and they were not antistaff in any way.	Inmate leadership was positive and constructive in its outlook. There was no need for the leaders to gather power, as there was no quest for illicit rewards. Leaders were prepared to act along with the staff.
Decision Making	Decisions made about inmates without any personal consideration.	Some personal consideration.	Decisions made about inmates with their consent and personal input.

Adapted from Harjit S. Sandhu, *Juvenile Delinquency: Causes, Control, and Prevention* (New York: McGraw-Hill Book Company, 1976), p. 234.

well-advised to determine the institution's climate and the various goals of residents, staff, and former administrators.

ORGANIZATIONAL PROCESSING OF RESIDENTS

A highly controversial issue within juvenile corrections concerns the proper way to initiate and process residents through institutional life. Mortification, deprivation, brutality, boredom, and labeling are descriptive of what happens during the organizational processing of residents.

The Critical Response to Processing

Staff believe, according to critics of traditional institutions, that all facets of the residents' lives that could provide them with a modicum of freedom must be regimented to maintain control.[14] Consequently, residents are stripped of everything that provides security, identity, and independence. Administrators regulate all institutional activities by rules formulated to permit the training school to reach its custodial goals. These rules are considered to be so necessary that staff are expected to enforce them with a vigor seldom found elsewhere in society. Institutional personnel interpret adherence to these rules as a sign that residents are showing progress and will eventually be ready to return to the outside world. Any signs of ingenuity, intelligence, or freedom of the will are regarded as intransigence or sickness.

Furthermore, although censorship of mail is a thing of the past in most training schools, physical movements are still restricted, as staff escort inmates throughout the institutional complex. Search lines are set up periodically to determine whether or not contraband is in circulation within the training school. Staff sometimes search an inmate's room and destroy treasured pictures or other personal property in hunting contraband. Communicating in some juvenile institutions must be done in whispers. The incarcerated are often required to react to their peers as automatons—faceless, humorless, and inhuman beings. Staff are suspicious of deviation from normal behavior and use the slightest infraction by an inmate as an excuse to prolong his institutional stay. In most institutions, misbehaving youngsters are put in isolation, sometimes with disastrous results, as youths locked in isolation may become mentally distraught after a period of time; in the old days, this mental reaction was referred to as being stir-crazy. In spite of the negative effects of isolation, the practice is still used. If they are not watched, such isolated youths—whether normal, emotionally disturbed, or upset—often try to commit suicide, set the rooms on fire, or drive metal and other objects into their arms and bodies. Their desire, obviously, is to escape in any way possible. Through all staff treatment, the youths must exhibit appropriate demeanor and deference, since the failure to do so will result in further punishment.

Mortification.   Society's definition of juvenile offenders as deviants and of their acts as reprehensible is brought home again and again in the juvenile institution. Evidence of outside identities, such as watches, money, rings, clothes, and other personal items, is stripped away and drab institutional clothing is worn by all. This, or course, has an adverse impact on the self-esteem of juveniles. The degrading manner in which the juveniles are treated by staff is also a blow to the self-concept. The barking of orders, the harsh tone of voice, the deriding comments, and sometimes even physical brutality that have long been found in training schools contribute to the residents' concept of staff as hostile, condescending, self-seeking, and indifferent.

The self-esteem of confined offenders is further challenged and devalued, say the critics, by relationships with their peers in the institution. Residents are forced to associate with those for whom they may have personal antipathy. Not only do they find themselves in daily interaction with them, but they also are dependent upon them for status and well-being. The newcomer must prove himself, for in the initial contacts with peers, each new youth is sized up and assigned a place in the inmate hierarchy. If he is sufficiently tough, the youth can become an inmate leader; if he is weak, the neophyte will probably end up at or near the bottom of the inmate social order. Inmates with status can recover some of the rights they forfeited to the institution but those with no status may lose everything.

In male institutions, the constant threat and occasional use of violence brings home the terrifying nature of this social world. If physical strength is not one of his attributes, the new resident either must outsmart and outtalk those who attempt to exploit him or must feign bravery and toughness so convincingly that his bluff is not called. Should his performance fail, he may be subject to the most devastating blow of all—becoming a sexual victim. This traumatic event often destroys any feelings of self-worth and complicates even further the problem of reentry into the outside world.

Female institutions have few, if any, sexual assaults, but they, too, are pervaded by violence. Inmate leaders gain immense power over their cottage, and every one of their whims and wishes must be honored. Passive girls are pushed around by the more aggressive; material possessions are borrowed and never returned. The institutional milieu, at times, creates enormous pressures to become involved in a "marriage," that is, a lesbian relationship with another girl.

Deprivation.   The mortification process leads very naturally into deprivation. For most offenders, being taken from a materialistic society into an institution comes as a genuine shock. Youths begin their stays with almost nothing so that if they are interested in maintaining even a semblance of the life-styles they have been used to on the outside, they must invent ways to get ahead; their quest is for the possessions and privileges taken from them by staff. A politics of scarcity evolves, with rules adapted to institutional living. The enterprising and the strong can achieve a comfort that is almost shocking considering the institutional situation; drugs, street clothes, extra food, sex, and weapons are all available in many institutions. The trick is to be powerful enough to get them.

Boredom.   In addition to the aforementioned problems, youths must cope with the boredom and drudgery of institutional life. Their hours are programmed from the moment of waking, and days appear to be an endless succession of identical time schedules to be met and places to go to for routinized trivia. Free time usually means reading the same magazines, playing the same card games with the same old group, playing basketball or softball, or watching television. This monotonous programming leads youths to dread the endless days and to look forward to their release with a passion only fellow inmates can understand. Little wonder, then, that getting out becomes almost an obsession and that inmates will go to any length possible to convince their keepers of their readiness to go home.

Labeling.   Another form of processing is labeling; all institutions label their residents in some manner. Youths are considered dangerous, not dangerous, emotionally disturbed, normal, passive-aggressive, passive, in need of treatment, not in need of treatment, and so on. The purpose of labeling is to help administrators keep track of residents and to provide an easy identification of residents for placement in institutional programs. In addition, many therapeutic programs have their own system of labels that are tacked on to youths' names and identification numbers. This practice at first appears to be harmless and often of considerable benefit to all concerned. Indeed, in many cases labeling does no doubt achieve the ends for which it was devised, but in other cases, the effects are extremely negative and result in wasted effort.

The major drawback of labels is that they stereotype youths. Others come to expect a youth to act in the manner implied by the label, and he may be forced to live up to these expectations. Also, labels may be assigned dogmatically; that is, youths may be given labels they do not deserve and, as a result, actions are held against them that are of no real significance in the youths' present lives.

Numerous examples of such negative labeling are found in institutional records. Case histories are notoriously inaccurate, often collected by untrained and overworked personnel, and reflect the personal opinion, observations, and recollections of community members. School records, presentence reports, records of early court appearances, records of intake interviews, and the results of psychological tests are all found in the case histories. These records are collected by school teachers, administrators, counselors, politically appointed court intake personnel, psychiatric and nonpsychiatric social workers, and presentence and court investigators. The possibility for error is obviously tremendous, yet these records often constitute the only source of information that institutional workers have at their disposal when the youths enter. These institutional workers then begin their own work-ups on the youths and add their observations to the thickening folder.

The inaccuracies and misperceptions contained in these folders are read as fact. Youths who committed, or who were rumored to have committed, sodomy or fellatio, who had early sexual experiences, or had random problems with the police or community members suddenly find themselves identified by these real or rumored facts as though they had no other existence. The past is continually brought up, and long-resolved problems must be explained again and again.

The Moderate Response to Processing

According to the moderate response to processing, the foregoing position is vastly overstated, as it would seem to indicate that all institutions process residents in this manner. Camps and ranches certainly deal with residents much differently from a maximum security training school. The atmosphere in many training schools is also more relaxed than it has been in the past. Indeed, many of the smaller, professionally administered public and private facilities do their jobs well and compassionately.

Numerous positive changes have occurred in training schools across the country. Residents now may wear their own clothes in many training schools. Coeducational dances with other training schools are a vital part of the social calendar of a number of institutions. College volunteers visit many institutions on a regular basis and provide a variety of activities for residents. Movies, athletic events, rock concerts, and church activities in the community are often privileges for the well-behaved. Many residents are permitted to go home once a month or so. Visiting parents may sometimes take a son or daughter off campus for several hours to enjoy a meal, a movie, or a ballgame. Some youths are even permitted to work or to attend school in the community.

Rules are, of course, a social necessity. Society could not survive without rules and guidelines for human behavior, nor could institutions. Granted that some staff are self-seeking or do use the rules to gratify their own sadistic nature, rules still are a necessary part of institutional life. Adamek and Dager, in their study of a private girls school, found that rules—even though dysfunctional in some ways—do foster identification with the staff. Too, they reported that some of the girls from unstructured backgrounds were actually enthusiastic about rules.[15] Delinquents, especially, need to learn structure and limits. Many of their problems can be traced to their unbridled nature; rules provide offenders with the opportunity to gain internal control and to build internal resources. Therefore, it is not unreasonable to expect youths to keep a room clean, to maintain good behavior in the academic area, to stay out of fights, to be courteous to staff, and to function willingly and well on work details.

Unquestionably, *One Flew Over the Cuckoo's Nest,* for example, poignantly shows the process of the stripping of self in a total institution.[16] But the average training school is not a grand asylum or a fortress-like prison, and the "status degradation ceremony" of these total institutions simply is not found in juvenile correction institutions—according to the moderate response to processing.[17]

Indeed, if the assault on self is too severe or residents are encountering unmanageable problems, they simply escape. Institutional runaways flood our countrysides every year. Some institutions have as many escapes per year as they have residents. Camps and ranches have only minimum security; residents only need to vanish into a nearby woods. Many training schools do not even have fences, but fences are easily scaled by a youth eager to escape. Although some maximum security juvenile training schools are more difficult to escape from, the average cottage-style training school presents few problems for those anxious to abscond.

The assumed power of staff is greatly exaggerated, says the moderate response. In fact, the rise of inmate grievance procedures is one of the salient characteristics of both juvenile and adult corrections. Although youths do not have prisoners' unions as adults in many states do, ombudsmen are available to residents of many training schools. The California Youth Authority has initiated an inmate grievance procedure in one of its institutions in which an outside arbitrator is called in to resolve inmate grievances. In this particular institution, staff find themselves in the uncomfortable spot of being overruled at times. The courts, too, seem to be turning their attention to justice for youths in the training school. The case of *Morales* v. *Thurman* and others appear to reflect a greater concern of the court for fair and just treatment of children in trouble.[18]

Finally, according to the moderate response, the statements on boredom are grossly unrepresentative. On weekends, youths in minimum security facilities often are taken to movies, rock concerts, or other entertainment in town. They may even attend boat races, may go fishing or canoeing, may be taken to the county or state fair, or may attend church. In more secure institutions, a movie is shown nearly every Saturday night; in addition, community groups frequently present concerts, talent shows, and other programs for the residents. Weekends generally are full of recreational activity. And, of course, many youths in both minimum and maximum security facilities go home one or more weekends a month.

As might be expected, the truth probably rests somewhere between the critical and the moderate response. Most training schools do not resemble the punishment-centered, violent, and inhumane atmosphere of the maximum security prison. But some do. That the charges made by the critical response are true in any juvenile correctional setting is a real tragedy, a national disgrace. If we are going to continue sending juveniles to training schools, then we must be certain that they are not made any worse by their experience. No quick and easy solutions are available to make training schools more humane. But somehow, we must make them safer for all youths; we cannot justify having our children sexually brutalized either in the streets or in our institutions. Neither can we condone or accept staff brutality and sexual exploitation of juveniles.

LOCK UP, GIVE UP, OR TRY HARDER

As Chapter 11 described, the evidence is not very positive concerning the effectiveness of treatment in juvenile institutions. Three responses, at least, are made to the philosophical aim of rehabilitating youths in juvenile institutions. First is the claim that nothing works and therefore treatment is a waste of time. Supporters of this position often challenge the viability of the treatment philosophy in a coercive correctional setting that houses basically lower-class offenders. The best strategy to pursue, according to this position, is to give up the rehabilitation ideal and to devote our energies into making juvenile correctional institutions more humane and less violent. The more important task at hand is to learn how to warehouse youthful offenders in a more civilized manner.

A second position strongly recommends that deter-incapacitate-punish be substituted for the rehabilitation ideal as the basic purpose of institutionalization. This hard-line approach advocates locking up youths to make them aware of the seriousness of their behavior. Thus, punishment can be made to serve as an important moral function in teaching the consequences of antisocial behavior. This position also contends that offenders who have received this type of correction are far less likely to commit further crimes than those who have been treated, for treatment indulges offenders and excuses them for wrongdoing, thereby doing nothing to deter them from committing further crimes.

A third position advocates that society try harder with the treatment model. How much harder should we try? What is involved in trying harder? Where do we start? These are not easy questions. Supporters of this position are fond of stating that rehabilitation has not failed because it has yet to be tried. But what is involved in trying it? Do we hire more psychiatrists, psychologists, or social workers? Little evidence exists that the present ones are having much success in working with offenders. Do we expend extensive resources on one or two chosen treatment modalities and establish them in every juvenile correctional setting? Which ones? Why these? Do we bring additional ex-offenders into our institutions to serve as therapists?

Regardless of who is questioned—administrators and other institutional staff, juvenile court judges, probation officers, or citizens in the community—nearly everyone wants youths to be rehabilitated in correctional settings. This position, therefore, has much greater public and political support than the positions that advocate giving up or locking up. However, the way to translate the desire into a treatment program that works has eluded institutional administrators to date.

CORRECTING THE HARD CORE

A crucial issue at this time is the treatment of chronic offenders. Too many studies have indicated that a few youths are committing the majority of serious crimes in every community. When these serious or chronic offenders are at last institutionalized, every effort must be extended to turn them around during the institutional process.

Traditionally, chronic offenders have been handled in one of two ways. If they are hostile toward institutional staff, handcuffs, thorazine, corporal punishment or "instant therapy," and isolation in a segregation unit usually are used to control them. Or, if they are not hostile toward staff, they generally are permitted to become the inmate leaders. In control of the inmate subculture, they have their needs supplied and are able to direct peers in how to defeat the treatment efforts of staff.

Positive peer culture makes a valiant effort to mitigate the influence of these hard-core offenders by capturing their lieutenants. Considerable debate, however, is taking place concerning how successful this strategy really is. Reports of increased inmate brutality among residents in training schools that use positive peer culture are countered by an equal number of other reports about delinquent subcultures developing prosocial norms and values. Mann, in reviewing the literature, claims that limited success is being experienced in working with the difficult-to-handle youth. Obviously, more research is needed in this area.

INFLEXIBLE AND UNCHANGING BUREAUCRACIES

A final issue of juvenile institutionalization is the rigidity and unreceptivity to change of juvenile institutions. This should come as no surprise, since these traits characterize most bureaucracies. Major questions exist, however, concerning the sources of the rigidity and whether or not something can be done to change them. Without change, many juvenile facilities will either have to be eliminated or will continue to operate with a violent and inhumane atmosphere.

One reason for the inflexibility of bureaucracies is their basic structure. As different positions are created, each is surrounded by a plethora of regulations and expectations. These rules become formalized into the law of the organization, and changing them requires an extreme effort. Individuals who have always operated according to the rules often see no reason for the change in either the regulations or the positions. Those in authority often want the organization to run without changes since they will know what to expect if nothing new is added. This inertia is one of the greatest hindrances in changing juvenile facilities.

The inevitable human relationships that develop result in still further rigidity within the organization. Because of this fact and the established status structure that people come to accept, many individuals do all that is possible to keep the organization free from the possible disruption that would come from any change.

Juvenile institutions, then, have not only a formal bureaucratic structure, but also a culture that emphasizes stablity. These two components combine to make any modifications very difficult. Top management, middle managers, cottage supervisors, and residents all frequently feel threatened whenever someone attempts to implement change.

SUMMARY

Should juvenile facilities be allowed to continue in their present form? As we have seen so far, and will continue to see throughout the remaining chapters of this book, little in modern correctional facilities is conducive to the effective handling of juveniles. Real problems, in fact, accompany their use.

Large numbers of individuals and groups believe that institutions should be eliminated. Others believe that the institutions that do exist should be made more humane. The likelihood is that some youths will have to be confined for periods of time even if diversion from the system and community-based corrections should become the primary method of handling juveniles. These youths certainly should not be made any worse for their experience.

If the decision is made to change the character of our juvenile facilities, many new problems will emerge. Research will have to be conducted to determine the most effective methods and direction of change. Strategies and techniques will have to be developed to help top-, middle-, and lower-level managers to implement the change. The community will have to be educated as to what is happening in the institutions. Extensive training programs will have to be developed to train staff in new ways of handling people. Sufficient funds to overcome both old and new problems will have to be appropriated. The effort and commitment required to solve all the problems will be one of the most extensive undertakings ever attempted in the juvenile justice system.

QUESTIONS

1. What can be done to keep the noncriminal youth from staying longer than criminal youth in juvenile institutions?

2. Do you agree with the critical or the moderate response to institutional processing? Why?

3. What is your response to institutional victimization of juveniles? How do you feel victimization could be stopped?

4. Why is there such a conflict in goals in juvenile institutions?

5. What is your response to the section on throwaway youth? Do you believe that training schools are racist and sexist? Why or why not?

6. What can society do to treat the hard-core or chronic offender in juvenile correctional institutions?

ENDNOTES

1. Paul Lerman, "Child Convicts," *Trans-action* 8 (July/August 1971): 35–42; Clemens Bartollas, Stuart J. Miller, and Simon Dinitz, *Juvenile Victimization: The Institutional Paradox* (New York: Halsted Press, A Sage Publication, 1976), pp. 151–168.
2. Bartollas, Miller, and Dinitz, *Juvenile Victimization*, pp. 151–168.

3. Lois G. Forer, *No One Will Listen: How Our Legal System Brutalizes the Youthful Poor* (New York: John Day, 1970)
4. Lisa Aversa Richette, *The Throwaway Children* (New York: J. B. Lippincott Company, 1969).
5. Rose Giallombardo, *The Social World of Imprisoned Girls* (New York: John Wiley & Sons, 1974).
6. Judge Richette made the comments during a lecture at the Third Annual Juvenile Justice Conference, 14 to 18 March 1976.
7. Bartollas, Miller, and Dinitz, *Juvenile Victimization: The Institutional Paradox*. New York: Halsted Press, A Sage Publication, 1976, pp. 259–273.
8. Sethard Fisher, "Social Organization in a Correctional Residence," *Pacific Sociological Review* 4 (Fall 1961): 78–93; Alan J. Davis, "Sexual Assaults in the Philadelphia Prison System and Sheriff's Vans," *Trans-action* 6 (December 1968): 9–17.
9. Ken Wooden, *Weeping in the Playtime of Others* (New York: McGraw-Hill Book Company, 1976), p. 113.
10. Ibid., pp. 113–114.
11. Ibid.
12. Ibid., p. 114
13. Clemens Bartollas and Christopher Sieverdes, *Games Juveniles Play: How They Get Their Way* (Unpublished manuscript).
14. Bartollas, Miller, and Dinitz, *Juvenile Victimization*.
15. Raymond J. Adamek and Edward Z. Dager, "Social Structure, Identification and Change in a Treatment-Oriented Institution," *American Sociological Review* 3 (December 1968): 931–944.
16. Erving Goffman, *Asylums* (Garden City, N.Y.: Doubleday Anchor Books, 1961).
17. Harold Garfinkel, "Conditions of Successful Degradation Ceremonies," *American Journal of Sociology* 61 (March 1956): 420–424.
18. *Morales* v. *Thurman,* 364 F. Supp. 166 (E.D. Tex. 1973).

REFERENCES

Bartollas, Clemens, Miller, Stuart J., and Dinitz, Simon. *Juvenile Victimization: The Institutional Paradox*. New York: Halsted Press, A Sage Publication, 1976.
> *Describes juvenile victimization in a maximum security juvenile institution for males.*

Goffman, Erving. *Asylums*. New York: Doubleday Anchor Books, 1961.
> *The classic study on the characteristics of a total institution.*

Richette, Lisa Aversa. *The Throwaway Children*. New York: J. B. Lippincott Company, 1969.
> *Judge Richette lucidly describes how poor children become the rejects of the juvenile justice system.*

Street, David; Vinter, Robert D.; and Perrow, Charles. *Organization for Treatment: A Comparative Study of Institutions for Delinquents*. New York: Free Press, 1966.
> *Compares five juvenile correctional institutions with each other; probably the most important book on juvenile institutionalization.*

Wooden, Kenneth. *Weeping in the Playtime of Others*. New York: McGraw-Hill Book Company, 1976.
> *An investigative study of juvenile institutions in this country.*

part III

AFTER CONFINEMENT AND OTHER ISSUES

14

Juvenile Aftercare

Release is the prime goal of a confined youth. The days, weeks, months, and sometimes years spent in confinement are occupied by thoughts and fantasies of release or even escape. For many, these thoughts and desires become all-consuming passions and govern every action. Youth who have been intractable become compliant, the weak feign strength, the ill pretend health, and the worst become the best. Every action becomes a show for the benefit of those who can expedite release—the line staff, social workers, teachers, chaplains, and others.

The entire juvenile justice system is focused on release. Staff are responsible for guiding residents throughout their confinement. Punishment, education and vocational training, and rehabilitative techniques are used in an effort to guarantee that a resident's return to the community will be permanent and positive. Understandably, too, staff may become emotionally involved with a particular youth, and they are concerned about what will happen once he "hits the streets." Administrators, too, are concerned because they know that they and their decision-making processes will come under fire if he turns to any type of crime after he is released. The parole officer or aftercare specialist is also concerned about whether or not this youth will create problems or will embarrass him. Needless to say, members of a youth's home community are also concerned, for they want a guarantee that the juvenile who is returning will be a law-abiding citizen. But, paradoxically, in spite of the tremendous concern exhibited by all those affected by parole and by aftercare personnel, little has been done in the correctional field to guarantee the desired outcome.

This chapter, then, considers juvenile aftercare, the final episode in the correctional endeavor. Beginning with an overview of the release process and considering it from the several perspectives of resident, staff, and society, it reviews the problems and opportunities facing the parolee, the parole officer, and society once a youth is released. Aftercare is defined, its history and implementation are discussed, and general operational problems are considered. Finally, prediction, recidivism, problems of the parolee, the nature of aftercare programs, and the interstate compact are reviewed.

JUVENILE AFTERCARE: WHAT IS IT?

Juvenile aftercare is concerned with "the release of a child from the institution at the time when he can best benefit from release and from life in the community under the supervision of a counselor."[1] This view of juvenile aftercare, or parole, stresses three very important points: (1) aftercare concerns youths who have been institutionalized; (2) release should come at the optimal point in the youth's confinement—an assumption that implies that officials are able to recognize when that optimal point is reached and to act to release the youth at that time; and (3) aftercare is concerned with far more than release from the facility. Ideally, many things can and should happen to guarantee a successful adjustment to the community. They will be examined later, but first, a brief look at the history of juvenile parole.

The History of Parole

Juvenile aftercare is as old as the juvenile institution. Superintendents of the early houses of refuge had the authority to release youths when they saw fit. Some youths were returned directly to their familes; others were placed in the community as indentured servants and apprentices. After serving as indentured servants or apprentices, they were released from their obligations and reentered the community as free citizens. For some, placement amounted to little more than slavery. They were sent to stores, factories, or farms that needed cheap labor. For others, the situation was more favorable, and some youths in trouble benefitted from placement with caring and responsible families. Nevertheless, the system was not at all formalized; only in the 1840s did states begin to set up inspection procedures to keep watch on those with whom youths were placed.

The movement toward an effective parole system for youthful offenders was far from rapid and the system is underdeveloped even today. Citizens and professionals perhaps thought that institutionalization was sufficient for youth, or they may have been more concerned about adults, whom they feared and mistrusted more. Whatever the reason, not until the twentieth century were any serious efforts made to improve juvenile aftercare systems.

Parole Objectives   A major concern of the past twenty years in juvenile corrections has been the development of a workable philosophy and concept of parole. To achieve this end, the Task Force on Corrections of the President's Commission on Law Enforcement and Administration of Justice has proposed these objectives for parole:

1. Release from confinement at the most favorable time, with appropriate consideration of the requirements of justice, the expected subsequent behavior, and the cost.
2. The largest possible number of successful parole completions.
3. Reduction of crimes committed by released juveniles.
4. Reduction of violent acts committed by released offenders.
5. An increase in community confidence in parole.[2]

The achievement of these objectives requires extensive planning and research. For example, to determine the most favorable time for release requires far more knowledge than is presently available. Many new and innovative research designs must be developed before the needed techniques for prediction can be achieved, and research must enable releasing authorities to compare the costs of leaving individuals in institutions with the possible harm to society if they are released.

A major goal in determining optimal release times is to understand the different types of offenders so well that the probability of their committing crimes can be predicted. The offenders must also be well enough known to permit their assignment to programs that will wean them from further law-violating behavior. Once these factors are known, parole officers can be more confident that their charges will complete parole successfully, will not exceed the minimum number of crimes that could be expected from an offender population, and will commit the smallest possible number of violent acts. The most difficult aspect of this decision making is deciding who are the high-risk offenders. But, once this knowledge is developed, public confidence in parole procedures should increase. Nevertheless, education of the public to the problems and procedures of parole is important.

The management by objectives principles discussed earlier provide a method of implementing the achievement of these goals effectively. Advance planning at all levels of juvenile justice is mandatory; citizens, legislatures, police, judges, probation officers, correctional officials, aftercare officers, and community social service agencies must all be involved. To the greatest extent possible, agreement must be achieved and knowledge must be shared on what constitutes aftercare; both agencies and officials should understand their roles in relation to released youths. Only then can they act effectively to help target youths stay out of trouble. The youths, in turn, must be made to understand that genuine help is available to them from a variety of sources in the community.

Specifically, planning must take place in each institution. Such planning is necessary if the functions of the various community agencies are to be articulated with institutional services. Evaluation procedures must be developed to assist institutions and agencies to determine their success. The general mission of parole must be determined, and realistic goals and objectives spelled out. Then the necessary guidelines for achieving a productive parole policy can be implemented, and arbitrary, whimsical, and idiosyncratic parole revocation by individual aftercare officers will be diminished.

THE OPERATION OF JUVENILE AFTERCARE

Each year, approximately 60,000 youths in the United States are placed on aftercare.[3] The bases on which they are released vary, and so do those individuals responsible for making the release decision. In thirty-four states and in Puerto Rico, the authority for making the parole decision for juveniles rests within the institutions. In the remaining states, the decision is made by boards and agencies that are to some extent independent of the training schools, as indicated in Table 14-1.

Some controversy presently exists about who should make the parole decision. Some feel that staff who work with residents know them best and are, therefore, the best judges of when they should be released. The staff see their charges daily, work with them in therapy, interact with them informally, and observe their interaction with peers. This twenty-four-hour living experience should, according to the proponents of institutional decision making, make the institution and its staff outstanding experts on the progress and character of their youths. Such experience, it is believed, will enable institutional officials to know better than anyone the optimum time for release.

This argument has been countered by another: that institutional officials and staff are prone to overreact to residents' inabilities to get along in the institution. If the offender can stay out of institutional problems and can stay on the good side of the staff, or if he reaches a certain age, or if the institution becomes overcrowded, he is deemed ready for release. But if a youth has a personality conflict with a particu-

TABLE 14-1   Juvenile Parole Authorities Other than Training School Staffs, Seventeen States, 1967

Paroling Authority	Number of Jurisdictions
Youth Authorities	4
Training School Board	3
Institution Board	2
Department of Corrections	2
Department of Public Welfare	2
Parole Board	2
Board of Control	1
Ex-Officio Board	1

From: President's Commission on Law Enforcement and Administration of *Justice, Task Force Report: Corrections* (Washington, D.C.: U.S. Government Printing Office, 1967), p. 65.

lar staff member or fights to protect himself, he may not be able to get out. Staff, according to this view, sometimes are prejudiced or opposed ideologically to what the youth stands for. The accusation also is made that staff occasionally release troublemakers just to get them out of the institution.

Many feel that the decision to release residents should be made by independent agencies and boards that are not swayed by what happens in institutions. One major advantage of setting up independent agencies and boards is that idiosyncratic and irrational decision making by staff would be eliminated. No longer would release be based upon factors irrelevant to a resident's ability to get along in the community. Release would be decided impartially, regardless of whether or not a few rules were violated or a resident did talk back to staff from time to time.

On the other hand, institutional staff feel that those in independent agencies and boards are too far removed from institutions to know what is going on within them. Staff further believe that autonomous boards are unrealistic and uninformed about the problems that staff members and other officials face in working with difficult and troublesome youths. They also believe that important aspects of various cases are ignored by independent boards, resulting in inappropriate decisions at times. Moreover, staff feel that the establishment of these boards downgrades their own professional competence and introduces an unnecessary complication.

Most experts believe that this impasse could be resolved by "a decision-making body within a central correctional agency of the state that controls all releases to the community and returns to institutions. Institutional recommendations and opinions should . . . weigh heavily, but final decisions should rest with the central body."[4] By combining this organizational form with appropriate goal setting and with staff training in the management by objectives format, maximum efficiency and effectiveness could be attained in the parole decision. Basically, the issue comes down to that of being able to predict the success of those released on parole or aftercare.

Prediction   Prediction is common in the sciences. Every field, including political science, psychology, sociology, medicine, and space science, tries to forecast the future. That some are eminently successful becomes apparent when their results are examined. Political science is becoming more and more accurate in predicting the outcomes of elections; psychology, through its testing programs, is beginning to successfully predict learning rates and vocational achievements of students; space science is accurately predicting trajectories of space vehicles to Mars; and medicine, although often less spectacular in its ability to forecast the control of certain diseases, is nevertheless making tremendous strides. It is because of specialized knowledge in medicine, demography, biology, and other fields that the highly profitable insurance industry thrives. Equally efficient predictions are now, and have been, requested of the field of corrections.

Areas in criminology and corrections in which prediction is common are forecasting delinquency and predicting the outcome of aftercare. The principles used in these efforts are basically the same as those in other fields. In aftercare, the most informal approach to prediction takes place when either institutional staff or an independent board attempt to determine when a youth is ready to return to the community. Institutional staff members are charged with observing offenders throughout their stay, recognizing when the optimum time for their release comes, and recommending them for release. The decision generally comes from a staff meeting that is called to evaluate all residents. Staff gather impartial information from cottage parents, counselors, teachers, vocational staff, chaplains, and others. After carefully weighing all such information, they comfortably arrive at the judgment that a youth is rehabilitated and is ready for release. That, at least in theory, is how it is done. However, several studies question whether or not staff members are able to predict when offenders are ready for release.[5]

Statistical Studies.   The prediction methods used by the insurance industry and other fields are also used in release procedures. No attempt is made to predict what an individual will do; rather, the attempt is to predict what *groups* of individuals will do. These methods depend upon sophisticated computer techniques and statistics; only the fundamentals of their development and use will be discussed here.

Prediction, basically, attempts to assemble accurate knowledge about offenders that will help to forecast their later behavior. This information is assembled in units known as *predictor items* and is used to determine whether offenders will remain lawabiding or get into trouble after release. The same principles are used in forecasting delinquency as youths are growing up. The theory is that if these behaviors can be predicted, special programs can be formulated to help the various categories of youths to adjust.

The problem lies in finding valid predictive information. It is difficult to determine which psychological test will be effective in predicting residents' behavior. The Minnesota Multiphasic Personality Inventory, the Jesness Personality Inventory, and other written tests are used. The sociological variables used include family background, size of family, number of siblings, nature of family relationships, and the neighborhood from which offenders come. Criminological variables include such items as prior criminal history, prior institutional history, types and seriousness of offenses, and the length of confinement.

The research goal is to be able to show a high correlation between the test results and the after-release behavior of the youths tested. It is very probable that youths with a long history of serious offenses are more likely to get into trouble than are those without a criminal history. A serious prior criminal history is almost inevitably correlated with trouble after release. As the number and seriousness of any juvenile's criminal acts increases, so do the chances that he will get into additional trouble. Another method determines the percent of youths whose specific characteristics tend to predispose them to either getting into or staying out of trouble. Once these characteristics are known, prediction tables, or, as they are sometimes called, experience tables or base-expectancy tables, can then be constructed. Figure 14-1 is a prediction table set up by Mannheim and Wilkins.

Some researchers have found prediction tables to be trustworthy. Gottfredson impressively points out that prediction tables used in California discriminate at around the 80 percent level.[6] Yet, few hear of them. Why? First, they are far from perfect. Even if 80 percent of the outcomes could be predicted for released juveniles, we do not know which 80 percent. Also, the remaining 20 percent just might commit serious crimes, and many parole-granting agencies do not want to take a chance. These people would rather keep the 80 percent confined rather than take a chance that the remaining 20 percent would get into trouble. Second, many tables do not meet the basic requirements of

FIGURE 14-1 The Mannheim-Wilkins borstal prediction table. To find the estimated probability of boys' "success" after borstal, Mannheim and Wilkins scored each boy on the factors shown in the table below. From the total score obtained in this way, the probability of "success" can be determined from the graph. The points marked A, B, X, C and D on the graph show the mean scores, and corresponding probability of "success", for the five "risk groups" into which Mannheim and Wilkins divided their sample.

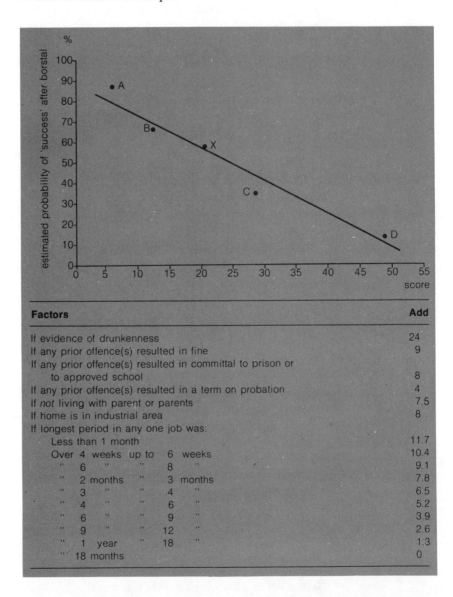

Factors	Add
If evidence of drunkenness	24
If any prior offence(s) resulted in fine	9
If any prior offence(s) resulted in committal to prison or to approved school	8
If any prior offence(s) resulted in a term on probation	4
If *not* living with parent or parents	7.5
If home is in industrial area	8
If longest period in any one job was:	
Less than 1 month	11.7
Over 4 weeks up to 6 weeks	10.4
" 6 " " 8 "	9.1
" 2 months " 3 months	7.8
" 3 " " 4 "	6.5
" 4 " " 6 "	5.2
" 6 " " 9 "	3.9
" 9 " 12 "	2.6
" 1 year " 18 "	1.3
" 18 months	0

"simplicity, efficiency, repeatability, or reliability, and validity."[7] Third, they may be able to forecast fairly accurately for some groups, but the range of delinquent behavior is great. Many subgroups in the delinquent population may require completely different prediction tables than those presently in existence. Too, different treatment modalities may employ other factors for prediction than those in the methods now being used. We simply do not know. Furthermore, the data upon which the tables are presently based are sometimes taken from institutional files that are often of questionable accuracy. Therefore, we do not know whether or not the tables compiled from these data are trustworthy. On the basis of the California base-expectancy studies, they may be, but it is doubtful that data in states with less notable histories in corrections would be sufficiently accurate or complete. Finally, social change may alter important prediction factors, but this is very difficult to determine.

The attitude of parole boards is another factor affecting the use of prediction tables. Board members (as well as institutional staff) do not want to be criticized for making mistakes; they want to make sure that residents have every opportunity to avail themselves of institutional programs; they believe that each case is different and should be treated differently; they often find their hands tied because of minimum or maximum sentencing practices; and often they simply do not believe in the reliability of prediction tables.[8] Rather, they believe that sitting down across the table from offenders, looking them in the eye, and discussing their cases with them gives the boards a far better feel for the person being considered for parole.

RECIDIVISM

The above issues are very important. Until the 1960s, many apparently assumed that once juvenile facilities had worked their magic, juveniles could be released to the community and would not to get into further difficulties. It was almost as if society assumed that institutionalization was all that was needed. Youths were released and almost forgotten. They received attention only from the occasional street workers with whom they came into contact when they rejoined their old gangs. Many county and city parole officers were interested more in the regularity with which juveniles reported than in their welfare.

But, before long, a few researchers began to realize that these youths were getting into trouble at surprising rates; several studies concluded that about 50 percent of all youthful parolees will return to institutions.[9] Obviously, if all the youths who continued to commit crimes were reconfined, this rate of recidivism would no doubt be much higher.

Improving the Effectiveness of Aftercare   The desire to lower recidivism has led to a number of experiments based on the assumption either that the institutions are not doing their job or that conditions in the community prevent parolees from staying out of trouble. On one hand, juvenile corrections has turned its attention to the role of aftercare officers to determine if varying the caseload and using therapeutic intervention might be of help to offenders. And, on the other, considerable attention is being paid to whether or not institutional care affects the success of parole. The following conclusions seem to summarize the often-conflicting studies on juvenile aftercare:

1. No convincing evidence exists that assigning juveniles to parole officers with small case loads contributes significantly to lowering juvenile recidivism.
2. Adequate supervision does appear to increase the chances of success of juveniles on parole.
3. Some parolees do better on aftercare if they have been institutionalized, but the majority do better if they are left in the community.
4. Some evidence exists that the type of institutions in which youths are confined does make a difference in how they respond to parole.
5. Some evidence also exists that early release does not increase recidivism and, indeed, actually reduces it for the majority of youthful offenders.[10]

THE COMMUNITY EXPERIENCE

In spite of various institutional and parole programs, some youths do get into trouble after release. The reasons may range from the extreme fragmentation encountered in the system and the way aftercare is organized to conflict with parole officers, school authorities, parents, and peers. Poor performance in school and the inability to get a job, too, contribute to failure in the community. In this section, these aspects of the release experiences of delinquents will be examined.

Jurisdiction over Aftercare   When youths are released, they are put on supervision. Usually, this means that they must report regularly to an overworked parole officer whose primary function is to see that the rules of parole are followed. But the parole function is changing, and much more concern is expressed now about how the offenders are to be handled. Again, the diversity and fragmentation so apparent throughout juvenile justice become obvious.

One of the major problems is "that in only thirty-four states does the state department which administers the state juvenile institutions also provide aftercare services for juveniles released from these institutions."[11] If aftercare is to be effective, it presumably should be coordinated with the programs presented in the institutions. Little likelihood exists that institutional staff who know the offenders well will have any contact with the supervising aftercare agent; it is obvious, therefore, that an administrative tie-in between the institution and the aftercare agent is vital.

Aftercare agencies are also diverse in form. In fact, no one form exists in a majority of the states. Table 14-2 shows that state departments of public welfare are the agencies most frequently charged with overseeing released youths; next are state youth correction agencies, state departments of correction, institutional boards, and state training school boards. In one state the department of health is responsible for aftercare. This diversity creates a number of problems.

The first is the difficulty in obtaining consistent national standards for aftercare. It is also unlikely that the different states will agree on one philosophy of aftercare and on the passage of laws to implement that philosophy. Additional evaluation studies that include cooperation among the states are needed to determine the relative effectiveness of various programs and the most efficient and effective structure for administering them.

TABLE 14-2   Organizations That Administer Aftercare

Type of Structure	Number of States
State Department of Public Welfare	13
State Youth Correction Agency	12
State Department of Correction	10
Institution Board	6
State Training School Board	4
State Department of Health	1
Other	5
Total	51

From: President's Commission on Law Enforcement and Administration of Justice, *Task Force Report: Corrections* (Washington, D.C.: U.S. Government Printing Office, 1967), p. 151.

Another problem involves the nature of the agencies presently administering aftercare. Fear and parochial attitudes prevent many worthwhile programs from being combined in any field, and corrections is certainly no exception. People feel threatened by change, especially when their jobs may be at stake. Furthermore, as was mentioned in the chapter on management, many people simply do not want to change. They are comfortable in their habit cage and, once inertia sets in, they resist change in every way possible. The effect of these attitudes is that much needed coordination and consolidation of effort never occurs.

Finally, the primary function of many of these agencies is not aftercare. Aftercare is in some cases no more than the responsibility of one small department in a large bureaucracy that is performing many functions, such as adult welfare, home services, and the determination of eligibility of welfare clients. Unless every effort is made to guarantee that the appropriate goals are decided upon and met, aftercare services may be far removed from the level that correctional professionals believe to be desirable.

The solution proposed earlier of "a decision-making body within a central correctional agency of the state that controls all releases to the community and returns to institutions" appears to meet the foregoing requirements.[12] The National Advisory Commission on Criminal Justice Standards and Goals calls this approach the consolidation model. The decision-making authority would be a department of corrections that would retain autonomy in making relevant decisions. This authority also would be responsible for overseeing institutions and their programs as well as aftercare programs in the community. The present trend does seem to be in this direction.

Role of the Aftercare Officer

The youths placed on aftercare require supportive counseling, delivery of certain services, and supervision. But to a very great extent, they have received only supervision, since the caseloads are very high for each officer. This situation has begun to change, fortunately, and the emerging view is that aftercare officers should be experts in providing community services and counseling assistance. Aftercare officers have all the role conflicts of the probation officer described in Chapter 5, and, in addition, they are looked upon even more as law enforcement figures because they can return offenders to institutional confinement.

The Supervisory Role. According to Arnold, "The biggest difference between parolees and those who supervise them is probably in social-class position and in the subculture that goes with class difference."[13] There is concern that the increasing amount of education required of a parole officer will widen the social distance between him and his clients.

Vocabularies, life-styles, and mannerisms set the officers apart from their lower-class, minority-group clients. Many officers aspire to the middle class and consequently may look down upon or disapprove of the actions of their lower-class clients. In this situation, lower-class youths often find that even minor violations of rules lead to parole revocation. Fortunately, the trend toward due process for juveniles is providing them with greater protection from the capriciousness, pettiness, intolerance, and the whims of some aftercare officers.

To understand the resentment toward some aftercare officers, it is necessary to examine some of the rules to which youths are subject. A Pennsylvania county uses the rules set down in Figure 14-2, modified according to each parolee's needs. These rules are read by the juvenile, who then signs the statement, "I, the undersigned, have received a copy, read and understood the aforementioned rules and agree to abide by them." The rules are neither hard to agree to nor hard to break, for most of them are irrelevant to everything in the life-style of offenders. Enforcement of the rules drives youths even farther from genuine communication with officers. On the other hand, lack of enforcement of a formal set of rules gives juveniles the impression that they are free to do as they wish and aftercare officers are left in a bind.

Some youths on release to the community will skip school, talk back to parents, get involved in minor traffic violations, or violate curfew. Most aftercare officers realize that many nondelinquent youths behave in the same manner, but no one would consider confining them. Revocation generally is based upon the attitudes of the youths. Needless to say, an expression of hostility toward the officers sometimes results in recommitment, even if the offenses and behavior are insignificant. The likelihood of revocation is increased as the severity of behavior increases. The commission of misdemeanors and a pattern of delinquency suggests that more serious offenses may follow. Aftercare officers may decide at this point that for the protection of both the youth and the community revocation is necessary. Finally, if felonies are committed, little doubt exists in the minds of most officers that the youths should return to the institution.

Officers who take a supervisory stance in relation to the youths and their behavior sometimes will consider any violation of the rules as sufficient grounds for revocation. In the past, they simply picked such offenders up and took them back to the paroling institutions, ignoring due process. The stepping over of an arbitrary line by the youths was sufficient to warrant taking them into custody. The line often was ill or vaguely defined, and the youths had no idea as to whether or not their behavior was within acceptable limits. In addition, since they seldom saw the officers, the youths could usually count on getting away with anything they tried, but often the parole officer would suddenly appear

FIGURE 14-2

PAROLE RULES FOR _____

DATE _____

PERIOD _____

PAROLE OFFICER _____

1. Obey all Federal, State and Local Laws.

2. Obey your parents or guardians at all times.

3. Maintain a satisfactory adjustment within an employment or educational/ vocational setting.

4. Be in your home by _____ p.m. every night unless you have special permission of your parents to be out later, and only for a specific reason and until a specified time.

5. You must not leave Washington County, Pennsylvania without the permission your Parole Officer unless accompanied by a parent and remain while away with a parent.

6. Notify your Parole Officer of any change in address, school or employment and obtain his/her consent.

7. You must not frequent places of poor reputation or places where liquor is sold or consume alcoholic beverages.

8. You must not be in the company of repetitive delinquent or criminal offenders, or others presently on probation or individuals known to be law violators.

9. You must not own or control a motor vehicle without your Parole Officer's consent.

10. You must report to your Parole Officer as requested.

11. Do not use, sell or possess any narcotic or dangerous drug or marijuana.

12. Cooperate fully with any agency this Office may refer you to for service.

13. Obey all orders given by the Judge at the time of your hearing. The orders which are applicable to you are noted below.

    _____

    _____

14. Pay restitution in the amount of _____ by this date _____

15. You are forbidden to use or carry a firearm in your possession without the express permission of your Probation Officer.

16. Other regulations _____

and the youths would be sent back to the institutions. Revocation depended on chance, the attitude of the youth, and the personal whim of the aftercare officer.

The Social Services Role. The problems faced by juvenile parolees are very possibly completely different from the problems faced by juveniles on probation. Youths who are confined face the shock of complete isolation from their communities. They are exposed to many degrading experiences, are sometimes "messed over" by staff and residents, learn behavior that allows them to survive, are not permitted to practice the decision making they would have to do in the community, and are stigmatized by their stay in the institution. The world they left is changing and perhaps so are they. Consequently, when youths are ready for release, they are not necessarily ready to reenter the community, but there is usually no transition stage from institution to community. In the past, these youths were simply dumped back into that community. But, as the concept of parole changes, more and more parole officers and training schools are giving youths prerelease counseling and are allowing home visits to ease their return to normal life.

Parole officers must develop a caring and understanding relationship with the youths they supervise. In fact, some do choose to overlook antisocial behavior wherever possible, for this approach is more one of treatment than of law enforcement. Even though some juveniles under their care may commit offenses for which others would confine them, these officers try to work with the youths, put them in touch with appropriate social agencies, and help them solve their problems and fulfill their needs. As new needs emerge and new programs are developed to meet them, the characteristics of aftercare officers must change.

Today's aftercare officers should be familiar with the operation of the entire criminal justice system and the basics of psychology, psychiatry, social work, political science, sociology, law, medicine, and any other discipline relevant to their work with juveniles. They must use that knowledge for the benefit of their parolees. They must learn when individual versus group counseling, individual versus family counseling, vocational rehabilitation, and educational counseling are needed. They must know when to be firm with youths and when to leave them alone. They must have a full grasp of the total services offered and needed, and they must know how to integrate the two. That they also must be sensitive and perceptive is obvious.

A bachelor's degree is now required in other segments of the criminal justice system, and many feel that it should also be a prerequisite for a parole officer. Such a degree no doubt does give practitioners in aftercare the benefit of insights gleaned through study of the history and development in the field, but it does not guarantee that an officer will have all of the desired personal characteristics; the ability to empathize is not bestowed by a degree.

Some thought must also be given to the methods aftercare officers should use in managing their charges. Modern management techniques do not require the sensitivity and perceptiveness mentioned above, but the personal characteristics of the modern aftercare officer should include integrity, emotional maturity, tolerance, tact, and the ability to work well with others. Those aftercare officers who believe that their total function is merely to receive report-in phone calls or postcards from parolees have too narrow a conception of their role in modern corrections. Those who are brusque, harsh, and insensitive or who dogmatically adhere to trivial and meaningless rules are doing their communities and future generations a disservice.

Another need for improved aftercare is the ability to determine the character of an offender so that he can be assigned to an appropriate officer. As in most areas of juvenile corrections, the relations between parole officer and parolee have not been fully studied. Geis and Woodson suggest that probation officers, and the same would no doubt hold true for parole officers, should be evaluated on the following factors: "(1) identification traits—sex, age; (2) background, experience, and interests; (3) personality traits as determined by a battery of psychological examinations; and (4) expressed interest in various types of clients."[14] With accurate knowledge of both parolee and officer, the possibility exists that a match-up can be made that will reduce or eliminate the present social distance between the two.

Reducing Arbitrariness. By legally entitling every youth to a hearing before parole revocation, prejudicial, whimsical, arbitrary, and irrational actions on the part of parole officers can be reduced. At present, such laws do not exist in most states, but court decisions on due process proceedings in other areas of criminal justice, such as *In re Gault,* are putting pressure on probation and parole departments to protect the parolee against unfair return. Many courts, training schools, and probation and parole departments are setting up due process hearings to protect themselves from possible court action and lawsuits on behalf of returnees. It is possible that due process proceedings will become mandatory before revocation of parole, requiring the same type of proof of wrongdoing as is necessary for conviction.

The court decisions in *Mempa* v. *Rhay* and *People ex rel.* v. *Warden Greenhaven* probably will help set the stage for such a requirement.[15] These were adult cases, but it is probable that the decisions eventually will be applied to juveniles. The court opinion in the *Mempa* case stated that state probationers have the right to hearing and counsel when accused of probation violations, and some courts have extended this right to parole violations. In *People* v. *Greenhaven,* it was stated that inmates are permitted to have counsel at revocation hearings. But the case that set the rationale for the requirement of due process was *Murray* v. *Page:*

> Therefore, while a prisoner does not have a constitutional right to parole, once paroled he cannot be deprived of his freedom by means inconsistent with due process. The minimal right of the parolee to be informed of the charges and the nature of the evidence against him and to appear to be heard at the revocation hearing is inviolate. Statutory deprivation of this right is manifestly inconsistent with due process and is unconstitutional; nor can such right be lost by the subjective determination of the executive that the case for revocation is "clear."[16]

Community Relationships

Earlier it was stated that recidivism rates probably approach the 50 percent level either because institutions are ineffective or because of adverse community impact on youths. Although there is little question about the dubious quality of institutional life or the sometimes arbitrary decision making by aftercare officers, community factors, such as family, peers, school, job opportunities and relations with aftercare officers, also strongly affect parole performance.

Arnold examined some of these factors in a study of juveniles after their release from an institution. He found that the problem of family control of youths reasserts itself when they return from confinement. Even when both parents are in the home, many find that the youth is still out of control. Many parents resolve to do better and keep their children under constant surveillance for several weeks. But eventually this constant supervision usually proves impossible, and the youths are back on the streets. Other parents admit the situation is hopeless and give up trying altogether. Most fall somewhere between the two extremes and try to at least maintain some form of curfew. But in no cases are parents particularly effective.[17]

Peer groups have the most impact. Arnold's study found that most youths went back to their old group within a day or so of their return and none of the groups failed to accept them. If the old groups no longer existed, the youths then sought new ones. If the family had moved, the problem of influence of antisocial peers was solved by a slowly decreasing rate of interaction with the old group and the gradual establishment of new friends in the new area. The Arnold study supports the contention that youths return to the environments that originally produced their delinquencies and that peer expectations are more important than those of the parents.

Another interesting finding was that the youths did not immediately assume a greater status as a result of the training school stay.

Their own parents, obviously, were upset over them, but so were other parents, who did not want their children associating with the newly released youths. Also, some of the parolees themselves indicated disapproval of the training school experience. Girls, too, tended to shy away from the male parolees. Released youths, in other words, do not necessarily become highly respected members of the peer culture.

Parolees face major, sometimes monumental, problems in returning to school and getting jobs. Parole officers look upon school attendance and jobs as signs that the youths are performing successfully. Yet, many of the youths who did not do well in school before their incarceration do not find it any more acceptable after they return. They usually were behind their classmates when they entered the training schools and they are still behind when they come out. Their classmates have changed, principals are leery of accepting these labeled youths, teachers remember them unfavorably, and the training schools have failed to change their attitudes toward academic courses.

The job situation is not much better. Training school programs are often either of a make-work type or are otherwise irrelevant to actual jobs available in the home community. In other cases the training schools prepare the youths for jobs that are available in the area where the training schools are located but not in the youths' home communities. The youths may be able to do odd jobs, but their immaturity, lack of desire for a job, and inexperience preclude them from looking for anything more substantial.

These factors, then, provide the matrix within which the youths must operate. What leads them to become delinquent again? For some time it has been known that younger parolees are more likely to fail than older parolees, that persons who were involved in crime for longer periods of time are more likely to fail than individuals with short records, that those who begin early are more likely to continue, that individuals more heavily involved in crime are more likely to fail than those not so heavily involved, that persons frequently confined are more likely to fail than those who have not been confined, and that crimes-against-property offenders fail more often than violent offenders. These characteristics, nevertheless, still do not *explain* the conditions that cause a youth to fail.

Arnold has attempted to formulate a theory to answer this question. He points out that delinquency and crime are on-again, off-again affairs. Juveniles usually engage in crime only on occasion and in provocative situations. The risks of getting caught are weighed against gaining status in the eyes of their peers. This need for peer approval leads youths toward delinquency, even if they actually do not wish to participate in illegal activity; they assume that everyone else is going to, so they had better go along also.

So far, the general theory has been applied only to already-delinquent youths, but Arnold believes that they also hold for juveniles on parole. Certainly those on parole return to peer groups that have considerable experience with delinquency. The youths, too, have little or no contact with older persons or with others who would regard delinquent behavior as undesirable. The parolee thus moves into a social situation that affords little restraint from further delinquency. In addition, Arnold feels that youths who become recidivists experience four specific problems:

They have more difficulty adjusting to their peers than do non-recidivists.

They are more likely than nonrecidivists to be in groups to which it is difficult to adjust.

They are more likely than nonrecidivists to maintain interaction with older groups that have a history of delinquency.

They receive less effective antidelinquent teaching than do non-recidivists.[18]

Arnold's theory as stated here has not been researched, but it does seem to have considerable potential.

AFTERCARE PROGRAMS

Aftercare programs are either underdeveloped or nonexistent. In too many jurisdictions, the primary program is one in which parole officers see their clients periodically but have few services to offer them. Many youths are required to do no more than send in monthly written reports to the parole office. As late as 1967, the President's Commission on Law Enforcement and Administration of Justice reported that "no innovative parole programs were found in forty states."[19]

There is a crucial need for the continuation of the services that were provided in the institutions. Educational programs, therapeutic techniques, and other institutional programs should be carried over into community life if institutionalization is to be productive. To suddenly discontinue the support of youths who need help will surely set them adrift. If continuity can be achieved, offenders will be supported by controls and guidelines when they are on the streets, controls and guidelines that have been lacking all their lives.

Recognition that juveniles need help in readjusting to the community is leading some training schools and parole offices to set up prerelease counseling. Offenders are counseled both before and after they leave the institution in an effort to ease the transition. Group homes are also being used as holding places until youths are ready to make it on their own.

One of the most significant trends is the use of social services by local parole offices. Many community agencies that deal with problems ranging from drug and alcohol addiction to poverty, mental health problems, unemployment, medical problems, and family problems are now being used by local parole agencies. Aftercare officers are being educated in the functions and availability of these agencies, and many are making use of the services they offer. Other officers are themselves being trained in therapeutic techniques. Youths in some counties and cities are being offered a full range of services. If this trend continues, more youthful offenders will eventually be offered the type of help they most desperately need.

INTERSTATE COMPACTS

Mobility is a way of life for the American people. The call of better jobs and a better standard of living leads as many as 20 percent of the population to seek new homes each year, and many move to other states. This mobility also encourages many youths to commit a series of crimes in several states or to run to other states to escape prosecution. Thus, an offender may have arrest warrants against him in several states at once, several states may wish to prosecute him at the same time, or one state may be attempting to rehabilitate him when other states are requesting his transfer for prosecution. The dilemmas inherent in these problems have resulted in the drawing up of the Interstate Compact on Juveniles.

Basically, the Compact is an agreement among the states to deal both with the mobility of youths and the need to keep them under supervision. The compact recognizes four basic areas in which the need for cooperation is evident:

> (1) cooperative supervision of delinquent juveniles on probation or parole; (2) the return, from one state to another of delinquent juveniles who have escaped or absconded; (3) the return, from one state to another, of non-delinquent juveniles who have run away from home; and (4) additional measures for the protection of juveniles and of the public, which any or more of the party states may find desirable to undertake cooperatively.[20]

Through the implementation of this compact, parents, police, judges, probation officers, and institutional officials can, by going through the appropriate procedures, facilitate the return or supervision of wanted youths. States are responsible for setting aside one institution for the confinement of delinquent youths, guaranteeing their safety and social welfare, opening the institution for inspection at any time another state party to the compact wishes to conduct an inspection, and permitting the prompt return of youths to the state in which they are wanted.

If a juvenile is to be sent to another state for treatment or rehabilitation, the states within the compact can enter into supplementary agreements that stipulate the rates to be paid for the care, treatment, and custody of out-of-state delinquent youths; provide that the referring state shall at all times retain jurisdiction over these juveniles; and provide that the state receiving them in one of its institutions shall be the sole agent for the referring state.[21]

Admittedly, it is difficult to implement the interstate compact successfully. For example, it states that juveniles should not be "placed in any prison, jail or lockup nor be detained or transported in association with criminal, vicious or dissolute persons."[22] Yet, as we saw in the chapters on institutions, very few states maintain such humane standards and few states actually prohibit by law the placing of youths in jails, prisons, and police lockups. The problem is made worse by the fact that institutional inspections are seldom made even within states, let alone across state lines. Also, as we have seen, treatment and rehabilitation programs are lacking, and supervision of those on parole is very limited. Under these conditions, the interstate compact remains little more than an administrative device, and the possibility of youths being aided by its provisions is very slight.

SUMMARY

Parole, or aftercare, is the least-developed segment of juvenile corrections. Fragmentation and lack of coordination pervade this relatively unknown phase of the treatment of juvenile offenders. States have neither developed comprehensive guidelines for coordinating agencies that work with released youths nor implemented a comprehensive plan for overseeing the administration of parole. Once a youth is released from an institution, community forces are allowed to work upon him indiscriminately, thereby often negating the effect of any positive programs in which the youths participated. It is reasonable to assume that if

> juveniles were provided with comprehensive and integrated complements to institutional programs, their chances of failure while on parole would be far less.

QUESTIONS

1. What are the major shocks a juvenile faces upon release to the community?

2. What is the purpose of parole?

3. What is prediction? How does it work? What are the drawbacks to effective prediction in aftercare today?

4. What programs appear to have the most promise for juvenile aftercare?

5. Discuss how community factors might interfere with a youth's chances of success on parole.

6. Using the information in this chapter, draw up a set of parole rules that juveniles would consider reasonable and that would contribute to their success on aftercare.

ENDNOTES

1. President's Commission on Law Enforcement and Administration of Justice, *Task Force Report: Corrections* (Washington, D.C.: U.S. Government Printing Office, 1967), p. 149.
2. Ibid.
3. Ibid., p. 389.
4. Ibid., p. 66.
5. Stuart J. Miller and Simon Dinitz, "Measuring Staff Officers' Perception of Institutional Impact and Predictions of Success on Parole."(Paper presented to the Interamerican Association of Criminology and the American Society of Criminology, Caracas, Venezuela, 1972).
6. Don Gottfredson, "Assessment of Prediction Methods," in *The Sociology of Punishment and Correction,* 2d edition, edited by Norman B. Johnston, Leonard Savitz, and Marvin E. Wolfgang (New York: John Wiley & Sons, 1970), pp. 807–813.
7. Hermann Mannheim and Leslie T. Wilkins, "The Requirements of Prediction," in Johnston, Savitz, and Wolfgang, *Sociology of Punishment and Correction,* 2d edition (New York: John Wiley & Sons, 1970), p. 774.
8. President's Commission, *Task Force Report: Corrections.*
9. Daniel Glaser, *The Effectiveness of a Prison and Parole System,* abridged ed. (Indianapolis: Bobbs-Merrill Company, 1969), p. 12; Carolyn Jamison, Bertram M. Johnson, and Evelyn S. Guttman, "An Analysis of Post-Discharge Criminal Behavior (Sacramento: State of California, Department of the Youth Authority, 1966); Nancy Van Couvering, "One-to-One Project Final Report" (A Demonstration Program Sponsored by Stiles

Hall, University YMCA in cooperation with the California Youth Authority, Berkeley, California, October 1966).
10. Douglas Lipton, Robert Martinson, and Judith Wilks, *The Effectiveness of Correctional Treatment: A Survey of Treatment Evaluation Studies* (New York: Praeger Publishers, 1975).
11. President's Commission, *Task Force Report: Corrections,* p. 151.
12. Ibid., p. 66.
13. William Arnold, *Juveniles on Parole: A Sociological Perspective* (New York: Random House, 1970), p. 24.
14. Gilbert Geis and Fred Woodson, "Matching Probation Officer and Delinquent," *NPPA Journal* 2 (January 1956): 59–62.
15. *Mempa v. Rhay,* 389 U.S. 128 (1967); *People ex rel. v. Warden Greenhaven,* 318 NYS 2nd, 449 (1971).
16. *Murray* v. *Page,* 429 F.2nd 1359 (10th Cir. 1970).
17. Arnold, *Juveniles on Parole.* The following section summarizes Arnold's theory of parole found on pages 94–131.
18. Ibid.
19. President's Commission, *Task Force Report: Corrections,* p. 190.
20. *Purdons, Pennsylvania Statutes Annotated* 62 PS. Paragraph 731, 1968, p. 82.
21. Ibid., p. 82.
22. Ibid., p. 89.

REFERENCES

Arnold, William R. *Juveniles on Parole: A Sociological Perspective.* New York: Random House, 1970.
> *Arnold's book is an invaluable source for the student interested in aftercare.*

Irwin, John. *The Felon.* Englewood Cliffs, N.J.: Prentice-Hall, 1970.
> *Although this book deals with adult parole, it provides an excellent understanding of the world view and the problems of parolees.*

President's Commission on Law Enforcement and Administration of Justice. *Task Force Report: Corrections.* Washington, D.C.: U.S. Government Printing Office, 1967.
> *The section on parole is a good introduction to the subject.*

Wilkins, Leslie T. *Evaluation of Penal Measures.* New York: Random House, 1969.
> *Students interested in parole prediction will find this study a little heavy but quite helpful.*

15

Research and Theory in Juvenile Corrections

Throughout history, civilizations have developed many techniques for seeking truth. Magic and superstition; the divine right of kings; the guidance of prophets, priests, and philosophers; intuition; and common sense have all been called on to provide the answers to the great questions. The failure of these methods to provide reliable and valid knowledge has led thinkers to search for other, better sources of truth. The contemporary solution is called science, which its proponents feel provides more accurate answers than does any other method yet discovered.

The two basic tools of science are research and theory, which are inextricably bound; each helps to guide and direct the other. Research finds methods to collect data, helps to identify variables to be studied, tests variables for their worth, analyzes related variables, and suggests new directions for theory. Theory points the way to new research, helps derive new variables, builds interconnections among variables, integrates new and old ideas, builds systems of thought, and leads the way to new social and theoretical conclusions. Research collects and theory analyzes; research discovers and theory explains; research disproves and theory reorders. The process is never ending. Without it, we would be doomed to wallow in ignorance, personal prejudice, and inaccurate information. We would also be doomed to repeat harmful and even dangerous practices.

In this chapter, we look at the processes of theory and research:

384

what they are, how they work, and how they apply in juvenile corrections. Certainly we must be very cautious in claiming too much sophistication for research and theory in juvenile corrections, for there are many gaps in empirical studies and theoretical inquiries. The basic concern in this chapter is to help the beginning student who is seeking information on how research and theory relate to juvenile corrections.

ATTITUDES TOWARD RESEARCH

Practitioners within the criminal justice agencies were highly suspicious of "researchers" for many years. They believed, usually with good reason, that investigators often were prying into their affairs to uncover information about sensational murders and rapes that took place in juvenile correctional institutions; then, after the exposure of such events in the media, administrators and other officials were sometimes removed from their positions.

But there is a distinction between investigative reporting and social science research. Investigative reporting often is essentially muckraking, a deliberate seeking out of the spectacular to shock the nation's conscience. This method of reporting is sometimes needed to persuade the nation to live up to its professed ideals. Such accounts as Wooden's *Weeping in the Playtime of Others,* James' *Children in Trouble: A National Scandal,* and Cole's *Our Children's Keepers* are examples of this type of reporting. These writings provide insights into trouble spots and abuses in the juvenile justice system; without such insights, the victimization of youths in trouble is very likely to continue.

Social science research, on the other hand, is generally less sensa-

FIGURE 15-1   Relationship between Theory and Research

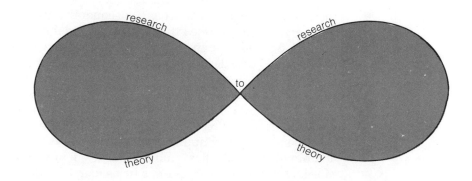

tional. Its investigators generally document their findings in greater detail than do the muckrakers. These researchers spell out their methods of study with greater care and depth, report all data (whether they contradict previously held beliefs or not), and make every effort to guarantee that later researchers can verify their findings. They, too, uncover the spectacular and report it, as honesty dictates they must, but there is a sense of balance and perspective in their methods often lacking in investigative reporting. Another important aspect of social science research is that its methods are universal; they can be used in many areas. Without such universality, the cumulative knowledge upon which science rests could never be collected.

The effects of such research are striking. We find, for example, "what is really out there." Often, our understanding of society and events is personalized—we interpret according to what we observe— but our viewpoint is usually only one of many aspects from which a phenomenon may be studied. Some persons, for instance, long refused to believe that middle-class youths commit crime; research has proved they do. Research, then, gives us another way of seeing; research permits us to test the effectiveness of existing programs; research provides an evaluation of the effectiveness of new programs. If programs are ineffectual, they can be abandoned, as the Massachusetts training schools were in the early 1970s. If two programs are found to have the same effect though one is cheaper than the other, the more expensive one can be dropped. By examining the findings of research, we are able to look in new directions and to arrive at better answers to nagging problems.

Although not all administrators, by any means, are happy with the demands of research, the pendulum appears to have swung in its favor. Several factors seem to be related to this shift in climate. First, more and more education is being demanded of those entering the criminal justice professions. Many agencies require their practitioners to have at least a bachelor of science degree, whether they be police officers or cottage parents. Today's criminal justice practitioners must also be thoroughly trained in research. Consequently, graduates in this field are probably better versed than ever before in the use of the scientific method. Second, Congress, legislatures, foundations, and other funding agencies that desire the maximum benefits from their funds are demanding an accounting of the impact of such funding. Money is available, but only if evaluation research accompanies any proposed project. Needless to say, the ties among projects, money, and research are a major motivating force behind much of today's research. Finally, practitioners are beginning to realize that research can aid them in attaining their goals. Research in ballistics, for example, helps to solve murders and research on prisons helps to reduce riots. In other words, research is useful, and heads of both small agencies and large bureaucracies now realize its benefits.

No one today has all the answers for the vexing problems facing juvenile corrections. But good research, hopefully, will be helpful in arriving at adequate, better reasoned, and more sophisticated solutions.

THE RESEARCH PROCESS

There is no single correct research method, for each has its own advantages and disadvantages. But it is important to examine the various research methods and their effects on the research outcome. Once these effects are known, errors in observation can be reduced.

There are six generally accepted steps to be followed in research: the first is to define the problem; the second is to review the literature; the third is to select the best research method; the fourth is to choose the research design; the fifth is to analyze the data; and the sixth is to report on the results of the study.

Defining the Problem

Researchers must first define the problem clearly and well. They then know their direction and can follow the method that will give them the best chance of success. If the problem is not defined clearly, a conceptual muddiness can pervade the entire research design and reduce or even negate the value of the research.

Reviewing the Literature

Second, researchers must thoroughly review the literature. Their knowledge of the relevant literature, in addition to their personal experiences in dealing with the problem, can do much to sharpen its definition. For example, legal researchers must be familiar with the role of status offense law in relation to the main body of criminal law. To accomplish this, they must turn to specialized legal publications and cases that may assist them to sharpen their focus, define their problem, and propose other, more effective laws.

A review of the literature may also disclose theories that could provide alternative directions. A researcher may initially believe that delinquency can be controlled by psychoanalysis, but he may well decide that guided group interaction is the answer after he has compared the effectiveness of the two methods as they are reported in the literature. Examination of the theories also uncovers important variables that should be included in a study. In addition, studies that are conducted from no apparent theoretical approach may produce variables that are as important as those derived from stated theories.

Researchers may also discover that no research has been done on their particular problem and that the materials at hand are impressionistic and without any empirical base.

Selecting the General Research Design

The third step is to select the best general research design for solving the problem. Generally, research designs are of three types: exploratory, descriptive, and predictive. Exploratory research normally is done in areas in which few findings from previous work are available. The purpose is simply to determine if a problem does exist, to discover its nature and to gather some relevant information about it. Initial attempts at describing the area of study may be undertaken, but, understandably, they may not be very sophisticated.

A strategy that some researchers pursue is to first get as much information as possible through an exploratory study. Then they redesign the plan, using the new information acquired, and proceed to a more comprehensive descriptive study. Giallombardo's initial study of a women's prison, for example, provided many ideas for a later study in three institutions for delinquent girls. In her study of the women's prison, Giallombardo described the informal world of the inmates as a counterpart of the world in men's prisons.[1] She hypothesized "that irrespective of the goals of the formal organization, the structural form of the informal social system evolved by female juvenile offenders will be marriage, kinship, and family groups."[2] Giallombardo then redesigned her study to include three institutions for girls instead of just one. She looked at the structure of the three institutions and tested her hypothesis, providing a basis for comparison.

Descriptive studies are basically just what their name suggests—the subject under study is described in the fullest possible detail. Since some information about the problem already exists, researchers can develop research instruments and techniques to develop more extensive and complete information than possible in an exploratory study. Polsky's *Cottage Six* is a classic example of the descriptive study. Using sociometric analysis, he meticulously and extensively plotted the clique structure of one cottage.[3] Giallombardo successfully described the social structure in the three institutions for girls. The family and role structure clearly and forcefully emerged, thereby adding considerable insight into the social organization of these institutions. Medical, psychological, and other sociological variables could also have been used in these studies, but they would have required considerably more time and effort. Projective tests, case studies, attitude scales, simple observation, interview schedules, and open-ended interviews may be used in many combinations, depending upon the time and resources available to the researchers. These techniques may also be used in exploratory studies, but some of them are of very limited use when little or no prior information is available.

Predictive studies are even more complex, for the task of the researcher essentially is to foretell the future. While this may be little better than crystal-ball gazing in some cases, social scientists are making rapid strides toward better forecasting by using this method. Needless to say, the ability to predict accurately depends on familiarity with many prior exploratory and descriptive studies and on knowledge of many well-defined variables. The Gluecks, for instance, matched 500 delinquents and 500 nondelinquents on age, intelligence, ethnic derivation, and neighborhood conditions before comparing them on approximately 400 traits and factors. On the basis of their analysis, the Gluecks finally decided that accurate information on five factors—discipline of boy by father, supervision of boy by mother, affection of father for boy, affection of mother for boy, and cohesiveness of family—would enable them to prevent delinquency.[4] Craig and Glick contended that the Glueck's scales eventually were validated, but Kahn argued that the scales had not been validated.[5] Such problems of prediction must be solved if prediction is to be a useful tool in solving problems in juvenile justice.

Choosing the Specific Research Design

The fourth stage of research is to choose the specific research design. Whereas exploratory, descriptive, and predictive studies state the researcher's general goals, the specific research design is concerned with how the studies are to be implemented. This phase of the research depends partly upon the amount and kind of research already done. Several of the more popular research designs will be discussed, but first we must understand why different designs are used.

Since the goals of research include accurate perception, researchers must select methods that will most directly assist them in arriving at these goals. The researcher not only is concerned with his own ideas and the ideas of others, but he also seeks to determine the differences among societal occurrences. Therefore, classification of events and of the social variables that constitute them is a must if accurate comparisons are to be made. For example, if riots in training schools are being studied, the researchers will want to know whether or not the nature of administration or the emphasis placed upon treatment contributed to the riot. Researchers will study one riot and the type of administration and then compare these with other riots and other administrations, thereby observing elements they might otherwise have missed.

Comparison, then, is the key to accurate scientific investigation. The more comparisons that are made, the easier it will be to recognize differences, and the sharper the researcher's perceptions will become.

In this way, new variables and insights are gained. For these reasons, skepticism can probably be called the most important factor in scientific investigation. Scientists, therefore, are usually very skeptical about both their own ideas and the research findings of others.

Specific Research designs. Five research designs are discussed in this section: the cross-sectional, the longitudinal, the panel, the ex-post-facto, and the classical experimental. One of the simplest designs used by researchers is the cross-sectional study. This design simply looks at one group of people for one specific period of time. Portune's Cincinnati study of the attitudes of junior high school students toward the police is an example of a cross-sectional study. The attitudes of 1,000 students were studied at one time and were found to vary according to age, sex, race, academic performance, and socioeconomic class.[6] Portune could also have studied groups of delinquents and nondelinquents, as Chapman did, but only a description of one sample at one period of time would have been made in a true cross-sectional study.[7] While this type of study may be useful for many purposes, it provides no information on, for example, how time changes attitudes or how student attitudes toward the police modify as the police change tactics.

Longitudinal study. A second design is the longitudinal, which is an improvement over the cross-sectional design. In a longitudinal study, student attitudes toward the police would be measured at different times—perhaps once a year for as long as the group is in school. This makes it possible to compare later responses with first responses; the effects of the societal change on the attitudes of the students can be measured. However, unless the longitudinal design is structured to include several different groups, we will not learn how one group compares with another, which is a key weakness in this type of study. Longitudinal studies, nevertheless, do provide the researcher with far more information than could be obtained by a cross-sectional study.

Panel study. Another design is the panel study. Here, too, attitudes toward police would be measured at different time periods, but one group—for example, freshmen in school A—is measured in the first time period and another group—freshmen in school B—is measured in the second. Since the two groups obviously differ, the reader may wonder about the validity of the findings. Careful analysis of such student characteristics as age, race, sex, social background, and interpersonal contacts may allow the researcher to match them and thereby reduce the possible differences. But, even if some type of matching is not possible, the researcher is still measuring specifically student attitudes toward police and therefore has some basis for comparison. The researcher can thus gain more information than he would if only one group were measured at only one period of time.

Ex-post-facto study.   The ex-post-facto study design also is well known. The longitudinal and panel studies are known as before-after studies, with which group members are measured first at one time and then again at a later date. The ex-post-facto study is an after-before study. The research must move from the present to the past.

Miller and Dinitz's study measuring perceptions of organizational change is an example.[8] In this study, residents answered questionnaires that measured the degree of the impact of the institution on them. Later the researchers discovered that the institution had undergone organizational changes during the years of testing. Since the institution itself had not been studied by the researchers at that time, a reconstruction of its operation during the periods in question was necessary. Previous descriptions of the institution were found that enabled the researchers to reconstruct its operation sufficiently to complete the study. The data gathered were not as good as they would have been if the institution had been studied at the time the organizational changes were taking place, but valid information was nevertheless gained. The researchers, in other words, went from the present to the past, or from after to before. They were on shaky ground when trying to reconstruct the institution and when making assumptions as to when certain changes had transpired. They might have improved the analysis if they had found additional descriptions rather than just the single one they used or if they had found other studies of institutions comparable to the one being researched. Unfortunately, such studies did not exist, but the researchers still achieved some basis for a comparison and added to their knowledge of organizational change.

Classical experimental design.   The classical experimental design gives researchers some of the best and most accurate comparisons. The key factor in this design is the control group, a group that is compared with the one in which the researchers are interested. Two matched groups are set up and are measured at the same period of time. The group the researchers are primarily interested in is called the experimental group; the other group, the control group, is the one with which the experimental group is compared. The researchers introduce a new variable into the experimental group and then measure the control group against the experimental group at one or more periods.

In the Highfields study, a whole institution was set up as the experimental unit. Youths sent there were exposed to a short-term, treatment-oriented program to determine their "attitudes, values, and opinions toward their families, law and order, and their own outlook on life."[9] Other youths in the study were sent to Annandale (a state reformatory for youths), where they were not exposed to the amenities of Highfields. Those sent to Annandale constituted the control group and had been carefully matched with the Highfields youths. The juveniles in both groups were measured before they entered their respective institutions and again just after they were released. By constructing the study in this manner the researchers were able to achieve both comparison and precision in analyzing the two groups. Many social scientists consider this technique to be the most productive research design.

Certain conditions must be met for research to be authentic. If a research design is changed after it is set up, some of the effectiveness will be destroyed. For example, moving individuals from one group to the other obviously destroys, or at least contaminates, the results of a classical experimental study. Although the classical experimental design and its variations provide some of the best comparisons and the greatest accuracy, using this design is not always desirable, feasible, or necessary. The design chosen depends on the researcher's goals, research background, and the research setting.

Analyzing the Data

The fifth and final stage of the research process is the analysis of the data collected by means of the various research designs. However, many of these designs and the examples described result only in quantitative data; that is, the subject matter is described only in terms of numbers and statistics. Therefore, a frequently used approach is qualitative analysis, which yields the fullest possible information from the assembled data. Ethnomethodology is a productive method used in qualitative analysis. Numbers are not used and no effort is made to interpret data on a quantitative basis. Rather, the researchers immerse themselves in the groups they are studying and try to understand and describe how these individuals feel, think, and act as a group. In other words, the researchers, to the greatest extent possible, become one with the group. These researchers, who are sometimes called participant observers, assume roles in the group; they put themselves in the same position as the people they are observing and try to understand the subjects' behavior from the subjects' point of view.

Although both the Polsky and the Bartollas, Miller, and Dinitz studies also used participant observation, we will here examine only the techniques used in Yablonsky's study of a delinquent gang:

> Approaches used in data gathering included field study methods, participant observation, role playing, group interaction analysis, and sociometry. The data were obtained through close daily interaction with

gang boys over the four-year period during which I was the director of the project.[10]

By using these techniques, Yablonsky was able to examine the social structure of the gang, the reasons youths joined, their emotional needs, their roles, leadership characteristics within the gang, and the functions performed by the gang. This type of approach can be used with any group and is extremely valuable in providing insights and understanding that cannot be gained from statistics alone. A good ethnomethodological study, in fact, may be far more valuable than detailed statistical analysis of the same type of behavior. Again, understanding the viewpoint of the participant is the goal. Many researchers feel that this is really the best type of research.

The authors feel that both qualitative and quantitative research are necessary. Statistical analysis demands quantification and precision of measurement; qualitative analysis gives depth of understanding and insight. Indeed, the two types often complement each other, each suggesting new areas of study for the other and new ways of looking at data. Many researchers use qualitative analysis in the exploratory and descriptive phases of a study and, as variables become defined and relationships are understood, the researchers (or their colleagues) attempt experiments based on the classical experimental model.

Reliability and Validity.   Since all of the research described above is simply a way of observing what is happening, researchers take special pains to insure that two primary research goals are met—reliability and validity. Reliability assumes that a second researcher using the same methods as the original study will observe events in the same manner as the first researcher. If, for example, a researcher uses the same questionnaires and employs the same methods for collecting data on the same kind of sample that a previous researcher used, the second researcher should be able to tell if the method and techniques of the first were reliable. If the findings are the same, the methods and instruments used can generally be considered reliable. Suppose, however, that a research project exactly duplicated Portune's study of youthful attitudes toward the police, but came up with different results. In that case, the findings of the studies would not be considered reliable. Other factors could have thrown off the results, such as a social change about which the follow-up team did not know. Obviously, this is one of the hazards of research.

Validity deals with the authenticity of measurement. A classic example of an invalid measuring instrument is the I.Q. test. Researchers used to think that lower-class youths were less intelligent than their middle-class counterparts because they scored lower on the I.Q. tests. Then it was discovered that these tests actually were measuring the effects of middle- and lower-class upbringing rather than innate intelligence. When researchers began to administer tests controlled for social-class background, the differences between lower- and middle-class groups' scores largely disappeared.

Sampling. Some mention should also be made about statistical analysis and sampling procedures. The reason for sampling is fairly obvious: Populations often are too large to permit the collection of information from every individual. Furthermore, the costs and the time involved would be prohibitive, so researchers select a sample of the population.

Sampling can be either *nonrandom* or *random*. Depending upon which method the researcher chooses, different uses can be made of the data. Nonrandom sampling is used when every element in the population does not have an equal chance of appearing in the sample. Most research in juvenile justice is of the nonrandom variety. Researchers choose these nonrandom populations either because they are close at hand or because the researchers want to use cases of a particular nature. An institution is studied because it is nearby or junior high students are chosen because the senior high school principal would not allow his students to participate. Parolees from one state are chosen over those of another state because the first state has a better reporting system. Nonrandom sampling has produced many excellent studies despite its obvious disadvantages and limitations.

Random sampling offers a better method, since each element of the population has an equal chance of appearing in the sample, and therefore conclusions can be drawn about the population as a whole. Basically, random sampling deals with probability statistics. Mathematicians know that if random samples are used they can state in probability terms whether or not the qualities of the sample are characteristic of the population as a whole. If the researchers, then, want to know about an entire training school population, they can study a random sample of its residents and be confident that within certain known probability limits their sample is, indeed, charactertistic of the entire inmate population. This is the technique that is carefully and meticulously adhered to by those attempting to predict the success of aftercare. If researchers know that an error in drawing conclusions will be made only five times out of a hundred, the odds are considered pretty good that the conclusion is accurate. A parole board that knows that a youth has only five chances in a hundred of getting into trouble again thus considers that youth to be a good parole risk.

The same type of statistical reasoning operates when researchers assign inmates, arrested juveniles, or probation officers to a group that will be analyzed or when they place them in experimental groups. If the members of groups are assigned randomly, certain kinds of statistical tests may be performed when data are analyzed. The researchers can feel confident about the results, since mathematical rules are being followed. Therefore, when researchers request judges, probation officers, training school administrators, parole officers, and others to allow them to randomly place clients in groups, they are simply following good research tactics. One further point should be made. Once research groups are set up, they should not be changed, for reasons which by now should be apparent. Randomness is destroyed, contamination is likely, and the groups may become too small for beneficial analysis.

Writing the Report Writing the report on what has been found in the study is the sixth and final stage of the research process. This report usually includes the methods used, the findings, and the interpretation of the data. Tables and charts are often employed to illustrate findings. Research reports, which are sometimes several hundred pages long, must state clearly the findings of the research project. Acknowledgements of funding and of other help received during the project may also be made.

If the research project was undertaken to examine a problem in a correctional or other type of agency, the findings can be used to improve the services of that agency. If, for example, the research project found that physical and sexual victimization was pervasive in a juvenile institution, administrators would then have the responsibility of using the findings to make the training school safer and more humane for its residents.

PROMOTING RESEARCH IN THE JUVENILE JUSTICE SYSTEM

Administrators need research and evaluation to manage their organizations advantageously. But, if research is to be accepted by staff, administrators must inform them of its purpose and how it is being conducted. Once this is done, the rationale for the following suggestions becomes clearer.

The need for well-kept records is obvious, and poor record keeping is the bane of good research. Incomplete, inaccurate, and poorly written case history files are very difficult, if not impossible, to decipher. Budget limitations, of course, often prohibit acquiring highly sophisticated case history information. Yet, the information needed over a long time span must be complete if research conclusions are to be accurate. Administrators, then, should confer with research experts to determine what information is of greatest importance. Such meetings should be held periodically. As new requirements become apparent, additions can be made to the kinds of data to be collected. If this is done, data collected can be limited to what is important and to what can be gathered in usable form.

To facilitate data gathering, standardized forms should be developed and staff should be carefully trained in how to complete them accurately and fully. Standardized forms mean the same information will be gathered on every case, a very important requirement for good research. Standardized language, too, is important. If different researchers use different words to mean the same thing or the same words to mean different things, misinterpretations can arise. Terms must be defined, and the people filling out the forms need to understand exactly what each term means. Doubt as to what information is being collected is thereby reduced.

Standardized forms also allow for ease in computer analysis. Standardized data can easily be fed into various computer programs, which will facilitate the use of such information—for example, to determine the treatment an individual needs, or which personnel are most compatible with and will have the greatest effect on juveniles, or the kind of administrative program that is most feasible for that particular population. It is difficult to determine the research questions that will be important in the future, but it is necessary to try to anticipate them.

Research Ethics

Researchers do not have a license to do as they choose.[11] When research is conducted on human beings, care must be exercised to avoid violating their rights. The issues are complex; nevertheless, certain basic principles should be followed.

First, once the subjects are told that anything they say is confidential, that trust should not be broken. To punish a juvenile for anything said during a research project is irresponsible. To repeat what is said, whether to staff or to an inmate, not only will destroy the trust and rapport between researcher and subject, but also will verify the subjects' suspicions about authority—that all authorities are devious and not to be trusted. The information gained may be used to sharpen perceptions and to probe in a more sophisticated manner, but any other use will work against all concerned.

Second, individuals should not be deceived about the nature of the research. Deception destroys trust, and the subjects will justifiably feel slighted if they were not considered sophisticated enough to be told about the study plan. If disclosing the nature of the research could contaminate the results, the researcher may decide to deceive the subjects temporarily. However, at the conclusion of the project the subjects must be contacted to be given the reason for the deception and to have the true nature of the research explained.

Third, subjects should not be coerced into participating. As human beings, they have the right to say no. Coercion induces stress and resentment and may have harmful long-term effects on the subjects. To some extent, of course, coercion is a matter of degree. Persuading someone to say yes is not the same as forcing him to. Recent laws also prohibit the collecting of information from participants against their will. Researchers should be careful to weigh the possible effects of the methods they use in gathering information.

Finally, although this by no means exhausts the list of ethical questions, subjects should neither be subjected to the risk of injury, forced into demeaning behavior, nor subjected to physical or mental stress without their full cooperation. Promises of favored treatment or threats of harrassment are simply not acceptable. In institutions, particularly, people will do anything to get out, including subjecting themselves to very risky experiments and to possible personal harm. Researchers or administrators who take advantage of the deprived state of those confined to force compliance in dangerous research should not be permitted to hold responsible positions.

Evaluation Research and Juvenile Corrections

Properly conducted research can make invaluable contributions to all levels of the juvenile justice system. The ability to act depends upon the knowledge of how to act. Gone are the days when simplistic answers could be given to complex questions. Juvenile justice practitioners now operate in a complex, urbanized, industrialized society. They have access to sophisticated knowledge about human behavior, must deal with many different types and classes of people, and must understand the many facets of our legal system. The greater their knowledge in these areas, the more challenging and rewarding their jobs can become.

Research can help the police deal more effectively with their clients. Police often complain that they do not receive the respect they deserve and that they do not receive credit for the work they do. A sophisticated research program is not necessary to discover that this is so, but why clients feel as they do is another story. Studies such as those by Portune, Werthman and Piliavin, and Bouma can provide considerable insight into why juveniles act as they do toward the police. Further, if police officers realize that most juveniles do consider them to be nice guys and feel that they are criticized too much, they may begin to approach juveniles in less hostile and aggressive ways and, in turn, receive more positive responses from juveniles.

The courts are greatly in need of information about the effects of sentencing practices. Research in this area is imperative. Judges need more accurate and in-depth information about the institutions to which their clients are sent. They also need more information about the available judicial alternatives and about the experiences awaiting each type of juvenile offender at these placements. Both the law enforcement officer who wants a particular youth "sent away" and the juvenile judge who takes the hard line would probably be horrified if they knew what happens to youths in some juvenile institutions. By supporting an ongoing program of research through the courts, juvenile judges can aid both their own cause and that of youths in trouble.

Detention is another area in which research is badly needed. How can we make our detention facilities more liveable and of greater benefit to their residents? What programs are most worthwhile for residents? We are not certain which type of youth profits the most from ranches, camps, and coeducational facilities; nor do we know whether indeterminate or determinate sentencing is best. We also need more empirical information on how to work more effectively with the hard-core offender. We certainly need insight on how to protect the weak from exploitation. Finally, should we treat, warehouse, or punish residents while they are institutionalized? Should we prepare them for reintegration into the community? Should we respond to different youths in different ways? If so, how can we identify the program that is best suited to specific types of offenders?

Community-based corrections and diversionary programs, too, are in need of examination. For example, what type of youth receives positive help from such agencies as the youth service bureau? What type of youth profits the most from a program like Homeward Bound? When should foster placement be used and when would it be better to place a youth in a halfway house or in independent placement? How can better relations be generated among the various agencies working with troubled youth? What are the ideal personal and psychological qualifications for a foster parent, a halfway house counselor, a day-treatment-facility worker, a probation officer, a youth service bureau worker, and a volunteer youth advocate?

These and many other questions beg answers from research in juvenile corrections. Given the present conditions, only research and evaluation will make our care of children in trouble more just and less criminogenic.

THEORY AND JUVENILE CORRECTIONS

Theory is equally as important as research. Without theory, research findings remain sterile and researchers remain trapped by a myriad of facts and details. Without theory, an understanding of findings may never be discovered. Even those who say they do not believe in theory would, if they examined their beliefs, find that those beliefs that they consider self-evident are no more than early theories and findings. Without ongoing theoretical development, we remain trapped in the folklore of yesterday. Theory gives us new perspective and contributes to our personal growth.

Schrag states that the main task of a theory is to analyze "relationships among classes [in such a way] that (1) the derived statements are logically valid, (2) accurate in their claims regarding observable data, and (3) useful in describing, explaining, and controlling the course of the events with which they are concerned."[12]

Existing theories in juvenile corrections, as judged by these criteria, are weak for two reasons. First, these theories:

> ... lack the abstract and powerful vocabularies, the precise rules of grammar, and the technical dictionaries that are necessary for translating the philosophy of science into viable procedures for handling their distinctive problems. This means that there are no authenticated methods resolving controversies over the definitions of concepts, the acceptability of assumptions and theories, or even the identification of problems that are unique to [juvenile corrections] as a specialized field of inquiry.[13]

Second, most existing theories or quasi-theories in juvenile corrections are employed largely for heuristic or descriptive purposes rather than for the purposes of treatment and control. Indeed, theory in the much older field of juvenile delinquency has focused almost entirely on the cause of lawbreaking rather than on the *control* and *treatment* of juvenile lawbreakers.

But it is not surprising that theoretical development in juvenile corrections is in its early stages. A general distrust of theory existed for some time among practitioners in the juvenile justice system. They failed to see its immediate relevance to their problems and tended to regard it as totally abstract and divorced from reality.[14] Although interest in theory is lagging behind interest in research in juvenile corrections, there is a growing awareness of its importance in this young discipline.

BASIC THEORETICAL STANCES AND ISSUES

Before a look at the various levels of theory and the deductive and inductive approaches to theory in juvenile corrections, an important issue in the philosophy of science merits discussion: the determinism versus free will argument.

Determinism versus Free Will in Juvenile Corrections

The basic issue in this debate is whether human behavior is determined by an external force or humans exercise free will. These issues cannot be answered by either logic or research. The answer is a matter of faith and personal choice on the part of the holder. If a person has faith that one answer or the other is the truth, then little that anyone can say will change that person's mind. The issue is comparable to a belief in one political party over another. A person who believes in one party will hear only that which is compatible with his beliefs and will tend to discount even the best of arguments, rationale, and logic presented in favor of the opposite party. The same types of positions are found in science.

The deterministic position states that all human behavior is caused by factors beyond human control. Human behavior is but one more facet of a universe that is part of a natural order. Laws govern human activities as they do the operations of the planets and stars; but man can study behavior and discover how natural laws operate. Two positions diverge at this point. One view states that since a natural order exists, with its own laws, changing human behavior is impossible. Proponents of this position argue that science should only be used to discover what these laws are so that no one will attempt to interfere with them. The other view is that, just as in the medical, biological and physical sciences, the laws governing human behavior can be discovered and used. The causes of human behavior, then, once discovered, can be modified and many of society's problems eliminated or ameliorated. This is the position accepted by practically all scientists. The concept as it applies to juvenile corrections is called positivism.

Positivism became the dominant philosophical perspective of juvenile justice with the establishment of the juvenile court. It has three basic assumptions.[15] The first is that the character and background of individuals explain criminal behavior. Positivism, relegating the law and its administration to a secondary role, looks for the cause of deviancy in the actor.

The second assumption of positivism is the existence of scientific determinism. Because of this hard determinism, positivism rejects the view that mankind exercises freedom, possesses reason, and is capable of choice. This clearly is too prescientific, so positivism looks upon human freedom as illusory and likens mankind to physical and chemical particles.

The third assumption holds that the criminal is fundamentally different from the noncriminal. The task then is to identify the factors that have made the juvenile offender a different kind of person. Positivism has concluded, in attempting to explain this difference, that the wayward juvenile was driven into crime "by something in his physical makeup, by aberrant psychological impulses, or by the meanness and harshness of his social environment."[16]

Misbehaving juveniles, according to the deterministic viewpoint, do not need punishment. Since they are "driven" to behave as they do, they are not morally responsible for what they do. The juvenile court thus adopted the medical model of psychiatry and social work in order to help wayward children overcome the causes of their delinquency. Using such medical concepts as pathology, prognosis, diagnosis, treatment, and cure, properly trained professionals were expected to diagnose and treat children in trouble.

Positivism, however, does not dictate all parts of juvenile corrections. The classical approach, with its emphasis on due process, its belief in the free will premise of rationalistic philosophy and the concepts of punishment and deterrence, is integrated into at least two dimensions of juvenile corrections. First, the U.S. Supreme Court decisions of *Kent, Gault, Winship,* and *McKeiver* injected due process and procedural rights into the positivistic justice of the juvenile court. Consequently, the due process emphasis of the classical school now accompanies the individualized justice of scientific determinism. Second, practitioners of the juvenile justice system rely upon concepts of punishment, deterrence, and rationalistic free will when scientific knowledge and experimentation prove unable to alter socially unacceptable behavior.[17] In this regard, Faust has said:

> The last resort in the administration of juvenile justice has been acceptance of the premise that, "He simply does not want or choose to be helped, and therefore we must take some action that will protect the community, deter others from doing what he has done, and hopefully encourage him to change his mind, if not about committing anti-social acts, at least about cooperating with our treatment efforts in his behalf." In other words, when ignorance abounds, but the necessity for coping with the behavioral problem remains, the clear tendency has been to fall back upon free will, punishment, and deterrence.[18]

In short, the classical approach intervenes in the positivism of juvenile justice to give procedural rights to juveniles in the adjudicatory stage of the juvenile court and to punish juveniles when the rehabilitation model does not work.

Levels of Theory   Within the philosophy of science, then, the stage is set for the development of theory, which helps us to better understand and change human behavior. Some theory deals with very small aspects of human behavior, whereas other theory is concerned with the explanation of whole societies and the relationships found in them. Such large-scale theory is sometimes called grand theory or macro-theory, whereas other types of theory are considered middle-range and micro-theory.

FIGURE 15-2   Levels of Theory

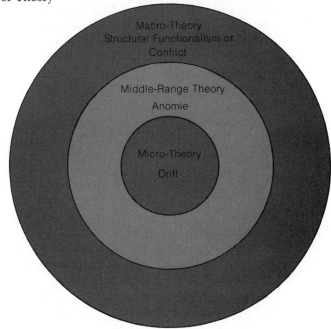

A theory, as previously suggested, is a system of thought that explains something. It should be "tight" and the concepts used in its construction should be related to one another in such a way that they can be tested to prove the theory. A theory that has been proved again and again through repeated testing and research comes to be known as a law. But developing testable theories requires precisely defining their concepts. A major problem in juvenile corrections is that a great many of the ideas are stated too generally or are too loosely interrelated to be considered "tight." The governing concepts also are often either not defined at all or defined so vaguely that operationalizing (testing) them is very difficult.

Grand or Macro-Theory.   Grand or macro-theory, in particular, is stated in such general and loosely interrelated terms that it is almost impossible to prove. Testing it requires experimentation on a societal scale, which obviously is very difficult if not impossible. Another problem with large-scale theory is that its tenets are found in society as ideology rather than as theory. Most people in the United States, for example, have grown up being exposed to a grand theory known as structural-functionalism, consensus theory, or conservative theory.

People in other societies grow up exposed to an opposing ideology known as conflict, or radical theory. A real problem then arises when people base their actions or world view on either of these two theories.

As ideologies, the consensus and conflict models of society are accepted on faith rather than rationality. People hold to them emotionally and refuse to consider alternatives to their tenets. Any attempted testing is looked upon as a threat to cherished ideas; and contrary findings are rejected as being radical or conservative. In spite of the fact that an open-minded consideration of the contrary findings might make life better for all, these findings are rejected out of hand. The point at which scientists differ from the population at large, or at least ideally should differ, is in considering findings that are opposed to prevailing thought systems. Intellectual and scientific honesty requires that new ideas should be used to embellish, modify, or reject existing theories. They are not accepted or rejected simply because they do or do not go along with preconceived notions of the nature of the social order. Only by adopting such an objective stance can science overcome the mistakes inherent in being bound to a restricted set of ideas. In juvenile justice, both the consensus and the radical theories are now providing us with alternative interpretations of the findings of science. Most social scientists finally are slowly accepting them as theories rather than as ideologies. Let us look at these two theories, the consensus and the conflict, more specifically.

Quinney has summarized the main assumptions of both theories. He begins first with the consensus or structural-functional theory:

> (1) society is a relatively persistent, stable structure; (2) it is well-integrated; (3) every element has a function—it helps maintain the system; and (4) a functioning social structure is based on a consensus on values.[19]

This theory implicitly assumes a model of society in which there is a well-integrated, relatively stable consensus on basic values among everyone in the society. People are expected to share the same general objectives, agree on definitions of right and wrong, and engage in mutually supporting activities. Therefore, a young person who violates the law rejects the basic consensus and threatens the stability of the social order.

Quinney then summarizes the main assumptions of the conflict theory:

> By contrast, the conflict model assumes that: (1) at every point society is subject to change; (2) it displays at every point dissension and conflict; (3) every element contributes to change, and (4) it is based on the coercion of some of its members by others.[20]

The conflict theory assumes that society is characterized by diversity and change and that it is held together by force and constraint. Although certain values do dominate, they are supported by dominant interest groups rather than by members of the whole society.[21]

The consensus theory was accepted in juvenile justice until the 1970s. It maintains that the purpose of the juvenile system is to uphold the moral values of society. It claims that all juveniles, regardless of race, social status, or religious creed, are treated kindly and equally. Although juveniles are being arrested by law enforcement officers, are being tried by the juvenile court, or are being confined in institutional or community settings, impartiality and fairness in juvenile justice administration *are,* according to the consensus theory, the order of the day. Supposedly, the upshot of this "benevolent" treatment by the state is that these wayward juveniles are reformed and restored to their rightful place in the larger social order.

The interest group or conflict position is totally in disagreement with this interpretation. Platt and others have suggested that such basic constructs as society, delinquency, and childhood are socially conceived and reinforced by the power group of society, which translates its concepts into law. Law becomes, in fact, an "arm of the ruling class." The haves control the have-nots by creating laws favorable to their own interests and by placing pressure on the justice system to enforce only those laws that will not interfere with their lives. The end result is that the law supports the rich while it exploits the poor. Minority groups and the poor, according to this viewpoint, are thrown away by society and dumped into the juvenile justice system. The defenseless and beaten children of the poor succumb to "the oppressive ideology of the privileged."[22]

Two final comments should be made about these two theories. First, regardless of which one the reader accepts, safeguards must be established to ensure better and fairer treatment of the poor by the juvenile justice system. Suffice it to say that all personnel in the system—members of state legislatures, funding agencies, citizens, and practitioners alike—must give this matter of the exploitation of the poor their closest attention. Second, society must seek the ideal balance between structural functionalism and conflict theory. This balance will be attained only through a comprehensive reform of the present system so that social justice will be available to all children.

Middle-Range Theory.   Robert K. Merton has made an important contribution to our understanding of how deviant behavior is produced by different social structures. According to Merton, "Socially deviant behavior is just as much a product of social structure as conformist behavior. . . . Our primary aim is to discover how some social structure exerts a definite pressure upon certain persons in the society to engage in nonconforming rather than conforming behavior."[23]

In *Social Theory and Social Structure* Merton considers two elements of the social and cultural systems. The first is the set of "culturally defined goals, purposes and interests held out as legitimate objectives for all or for diversely located members of the society." These are the goals that people feel are worth striving for; they may be considered cultural goals. A second important aspect "defines, regulates and controls the acceptable means of reaching out for these goals." Although a specific goal may be attained by a variety of means, not all of these means are positively sanctioned by the culture. The acceptable method is called the institutionalized means. Merton contends that these two elements must be reasonably well integrated if a culture is to be stable and smoothly running. If persons feel that a particular goal is important, they should have a legitimate means of attaining it. When this integration is lacking in a culture, then a state of normlessness, or anomie, result. Merton further affirms that contemporary American culture seems to "approximate the polar type in which great emphasis upon certain success-goals occurs without equivalent emphasis upon institutional means."[24] The lower classes are asked to orient their behavior toward the prospect of accumulating large wealth, while they are largely denied the means of doing so legitimately. It is this opposition of the cultural emphasis and the social structure that creates intense pressure for deviation.

In his essay, Merton develops a typology of the modes of adaptation that may be used when an individual is confronted with anomie. In Table 15-1, five types of individual adaptation are listed: plus (+) signifies acceptance, a minus (−) signifies rejection, and a plus-or-minus (±) signifies a rejection of the prevailing values and a substitu-

TABLE 15-1

Modes of Adaptations	Cultural Goal	Institutional Means
1. Conformist	+	+
2. Innovation	+	−
3. Ritualism	−	+
4. Retreatism	−	−
5. Rebellion	±	±

tion of new ones. These modes of adaptation are used to explain how deviant behavior in general is produced by the social structure, but they can also be applied specifically to juvenile lawbreaking.

To the extent that a society is well integrated (anomie is absent), conformity both to cultural goals and to institutionalized means will be the most common and most widely diffused form of adaptation. The conforming juvenile accepts the cultural goal of society as well as the institutional means of attaining it; he works hard in legitimate ways to become a success.

When adolescents accept the cultural goal but reject the institutional means of attaining it, they may pursue other paths that will frequently not be legitimate in terms of cultural values. Merton expresses the opinion that innovation resulting in deviant behavior is especially likely to occur in a society that offers success as a goal for all, but at the same time withholds from a segment of the population the legitimate means of attaining that goal. Lower-class youths, for example, who have accepted the cultural goal of success are likely to steal if they are denied legitimate opportunities to achieve the goal they have internalized.[25] That is, unable to "make it" in socially acceptable ways, they tend to pursue the success goal in law-violating ways.

Although they have abandoned the cultural goals, some juveniles will continue to abide by the acceptable means for attaining them. Ritualism consists of "individually seeking a private escape from the dangers and frustrations . . . inherent in the competition for major cultural goals by abandoning these goals and clinging all the more closely to the safe routines and institutional norms."[26] Some of these youngsters, for example, while keeping their behavior within the confines of the law, no longer are trying to achieve in school. They go through the motions of attending classes and studying, but actually they have abandoned the goal of being a success in life.

Whereas innovation is a mode of adaptation typical of the lower class, ritualism is encountered more frequently in the lower-middle class because parents of lower-middle-class children exert continuous pressure upon them to abide by the moral mandates of society.

When persons have rejected the goals of the culture and the institutionalized means of attaining them, they have, in effect, retreated from their society. The juvenile drug addict pursues this mode of adaptation. Drug addicts, though divorcing themselves from the cultural goal of success, must break the law to obtain and use their drugs. But, even if they have none of the rewards held out by society, these socially disinherited face few of the frustrations found in continuing to seek those rewards.

Adapting through rebellion consists of rejecting the culture's values and institutions and substituting in their place a new set of values and institutions. A good example of the use of this mode is the juvenile who has committed himself to a political ideology, such as Marxism, that is intent on establishing a new social order that has a "closer correspondence between merit, effort and reward."[27]

Merton used monetary success to exemplify the major cultural goal of our society, but mentioned some of the alternative goals in the repository of acceptable values. Intellectual and artistic achievement, for example, provide alternative career patterns that are not necessarily financially rewarding.

Merton's theory of the middle range—which has been referred to as a conceptual scheme, or an embryo theory—has received much criticism. First, his theory is not logically adequate. The most glaring fault is the absence of intervening steps between retreatism and rebellion. In Merton's definition of conformity, both the cultural goals and the institutional means are accepted. In his definition of innovation, the cultural goals are accepted but the institutional means are not. In ritualism, he rejects cultural goals but he accepts institutional means. In retreatism, Merton rejects both cultural goals and institutional means. In rebellion, however, he establishes new goals and new means. According to logical development, intervening steps belong between retreatism and rebellion. First, a new set of cultural goals should be established and the institutional means rejected; then the cultural goals should be rejected and a new set of institutional means substituted.

The theory also appears to fall short of pragmatic adequacy—which relates to the ability of a theory to offer a solution for the particular problems that initiated the research inquiry—for it only describes the effect of anomie on a success-oriented culture without explaining why and how such behavior occurs. As a result, Merton does not provide solutions to the problem of deviant behavior. Nor does his typology contain practical suggestions for controlling deviant behavior.

Merton appears to be on more solid ground in terms of empirical adequacy—which relates to the degree of agreement between theoretical claims and empirical evidence—because his typology of deviant behavior is exemplified by the lives of youngsters who walk the streets of nearly every city in this country. Conformists, innovators, and retreatists may be more plentiful but rebels and ritualists also can easily be located.

However, this theory lacks operational adequacy—which relates to whether or not it can be tested. Even though this typology describes behavior typical of real behavior in the real world, it has not been developed to the level of a working hypothesis that can be tested.

Furthermore, Merton's theory does not explain why those who have attained success become involved in crime. Neither does it deal with the importance of interaction with peers, a crucial variable in juvenile crime. Nor is adequate consideration given to the psychological characteristics of offenders.

Micro-Theory.   David Matza's drift theory is an example of micro-theory. His thesis is that delinquents drift back and forth between conventional and deviant behavior, choosing first one and then the other. The delinquent "transiently exists in a limbo between convention and crime, responding in turn to the demands of each, flirting now with one, now the other, postponing commitment, evading decision. Thus, he drifts between criminal and conventional action."[28] Matza, in challenging the positivism found in contemporary criminological theory, turns to "soft" rather than "hard" determinism, where both the ability of delinquents to choose and their similarity to nondelinquents are emphasized.

Delinquents, according to numerous theories, have an elaborate set of rationalizations for neutralizing any delinquent acts they commit. But, unless the elements of *preparation* (including the skills, courage, and experience needed to commit the antisocial act) and *desperation* (a fatal feeling of having no choice or control over life) are involved, the youngster probably will not engage in delinquent behavior.[29]

This mood of fatalism is crucial in Matza's conceptual scheme, for he believes that delinquents become fatalistic when they are being "pushed around," or controlled, by external forces. And this fatalistic mood, in turn, puts them in drift.

> Being "pushed around" puts the delinquent in a mood of fatalism. He experiences himself as effect. In that condition, he is rendered irresponsible. The sense of irresponsibility puts him in drift. Drift makes him available for delinquent acts. Whether the drift culminates in delinquency is up to him. Stripped of moral guidance, he momentarily exists in stark and frightening isolation. The precepts of his subculture episodically free him from moral restraint, but in so doing make him even more acutely dependent on the members of that subculture. He turns to peers to rescue him from drift. But that is not their function.[30]

While Matza develops the relationship between will and commitment more fully in a later book, the concept of commitment of the will is an essential part of his argument in *Delinquency and Drift.* The typical delinquent, according to Matza, may flirt from time to time with law-violating behavior, but most of the time this youth is involved in conventional pursuits. Nevertheless, it is possible for such a youth to become committed to delinquency; that is, he will not only be "converted" to a delinquent career, but will be willing to stand up for it.

Micro-theory deals chiefly with the behavior of individuals and small social units. With his particular micro-theory, Matza tries to explain delinquency by the concept of drift. But, in switching from a deterministic frame of reference to one that heavily emphasizes personal choice, Matza incurs philosophical and methodological problems. For example, soft determinism is more concerned with stating the conditions under which delinquency is *possible* than with asserting its *probability*. This, of course, is at odds with the deterministic framework within which science works. Consequently, while theories such as Matza's may provide important insights into the nature of juvenile lawbreaking, they also create serious problems for theory construction and research. It is difficult, if not impossible, to state their propositions in probabilistic terms and even more difficult to test them.[31]

Approaches to Theory   Theory, in addition to fitting into these three levels, can be either deductive or inductive. A deductive general theory or body of ideas serves as the starting point for the development of other more specific ideas (hypotheses). The movement is from the general to the specific. Inductive theory, on the other hand, moves in the opposite direction, from the particular to the general. Beginning with specific findings or data, theoretical development builds up to generalized ideas or theories.

Deductive Theory.   Cloward and Ohlin's Delinquency Opportunity Theory is basically deductive. This theory derives its general substance from value-consensus theory. It is essentially deductive because Cloward and Ohlin primarily restrict themselves to deriving the particular from the general principles of consensus or structural functional framework; they do, however, also work with a few findings from contemporary research. An examination of their theory development shows that they begin their work with Durkheim's idea of the regulations needed in society. These ideas were based on a stable social order that relates means to their goals, so that aspirations do not outstrip the possibility of achievement. However, in a modern industrial society, the norms regulating behavior sometimes break down, and people are left free to achieve whatever they feel able to do. This breakdown of norms is called anomie.[32]

But Merton, as previously noted, took the concept of anomie and modified it to mean more than a breakdown of norms. He claimed that not all individuals have the opportunity to achieve the cultural goal of society, success. The result is that some individuals who want to "make it" in American society must resort to deviant behavior. Cloward and Ohlin take Merton's argument one step further and apply it to a theory of gang delinquency. They state their basic hypothesis in these words:

The disparity between what lower-class youth are led to want and what is actually available to them is the source of a major problem of adjustment. Adolescents who form delinquent subcultures, we suggest, have internalized an emphasis upon conventional goals. Faced with limitations on legitimate avenues of access to these goals, and unable to revise their aspirations downward, they experience intense frustrations; the exploration of nonconformist alternatives may be the result.[33]

Cloward and Ohlin start with ideas that apply to whole societies and work down to a theory that predicts a specific type of behavior. They do use contemporary research findings to buttress their arguments, but the ideas they are working with are related to the value-consensus theory discussed in the last section.

A point of note is that the delinquency opportunity theory was not developed according to the same rigorous methods by which theorems in mathematics are developed. Mathematical theorems are developed logically and in a much more structured manner than most social science theorems. They also predict more accurately than do social science propositions and theories. Although social scientists would like to duplicate the definitive successes of mathematics and some of the physical sciences, that is not presently possible. Many social scientists would no doubt settle for simply achieving isomorphism; that is, making their theories match reality in form. At this point, we are fortunate if we can do as well as Cloward and Ohlin did in moving from the general to the specific and back to the general in developing their theory explaining gang delinquency.

Inductive Theory.   An example of inductive theory is Arnold's theory of parole successes and failures. It is similar to the example of deductive theory, but it, too, is not a pure type. To develop a purely inductive theory Arnold would have had to work entirely from the data at hand and construct a theory from that data. Arnold, however, borrowed from Skolnick the idea that failure on parole is a developmental process. Arnold then used the concept of risk of being caught or of remaining free as developed by Short and Strodtbeck, Matza's analysis of the way delinquents interact in drifting either toward or away from delinquency, and Glaser's conceptualization of the zigzag path felons take toward and away from crime.[34] In other words, Arnold skillfully interwove ideas from a number of respected theories and research findings in the development of his theory. He moved, basically, from research findings, theoretical generalizations, and specific ideas to a more general theory.

Grounded Theory.   Grounded theory differs from inductive theory in one basic respect—inductive theory can start from single ideas that do not have their basis in research; grounded theory starts with research findings and builds the theory from them.[35] Actually, some of Arnold's ideas presented above fall into the grounded theory category because he generated data through research and then constructed a theory of failure on parole. By adding ideas from other researchers and theoreticians, he was able to inductively construct a theory to explain both success and failure. Arnold also was comparative in his approach. His use of findings from diverse studies on the same phenomenon gave his theory a breadth that would not have been possible otherwise. Grounded theory relies heavily on different studies because of the comparative advantages obtained.

Glaser and Strauss suggest that by relying solely on data obtained from research, a systematic discovery of theory is possible. Since such theory is based entirely upon research findings, a close fit will be obtained between the theory and the data. The theory does not become so expansive and removed from what "really exists" that it becomes worthless. Such theory is less likely to be refuted and is more likely to last.

Glaser and Strauss take the position that grounded theory may be generated from either qualitative or quantitative data. Their method consists of systematically building up new research findings that can be compared with previous research findings. Their strategy, then, is one of comparative analysis, in which units of any size can be used for comparison. However, the researcher must make sure to describe the methods used in both the data collection and the theory building processes. As new concepts are generated from the data, they are linked with other concepts reflecting other data until an explanation of the findings is generated.

In the Bartollas, Miller, and Dinitz study, for example, victimization was initially conceived as a clear-cut phenomenon: the strong victimized the weak. As the study progressed, data indicated that victim exploitation was neither simple nor clear-cut. From the viewpoint of grounded theory, the interesting theoretical point was the need to redefine strength as data were collected. The initial assumption was that those who were physically the strongest would be the exploiters. As both quantitative and qualitative data were collected, the definitions of strength emerged. Added to physical strength were race, social class, population characteristics of the institution, the ability to maintain eye contact, tone of voice, seriousness of offense, aggressiveness, treatment of blacks by whites in the community, and the deprived character of inmate life. These features all intermeshed to provide a theory, although untested, of what brings on victimization of the weak.

From the viewpoint of Glaser and Strauss, the theory as developed to this point is substantive theory; that is, the theory applies to one narrow area of study only; in this case, confined males in a maximum security institution. More research on the theory is needed and other findings must be added to them. It should be remembered that further development of the theory can take place only as long as the data are systematically generated and are applicable to the area of study.

The next step, according to Glaser and Strauss, is to develop formal theory. This may be done by rewriting the substantive theory and omitting all references to the substantive elements of the theory, such as the institutional setting in the Bartollas study. The substantive theory then becomes more general and applies to any type of victimization of anyone anywhere. All that one would have to do is to substitute certain societal characteristics, such as the fact that some classes are deprived and some are not, and the possibility of a general theory of victimization emerges.

The best way to generate such a formal theory of victimization would be to locate a number of reserch studies that analyze victimization among all types of groups. The comparative basis gained, provided the data were appropriate or related to the question at hand, would allow for the development of a formal theory. Again, all references to the substantive areas of study would be dropped, and the remaining theory would be generally and abstractly stated.

NEEDED THEORY IN JUVENILE CORRECTIONS

Despite all the criticisms leveled against confinement, little evidence exists to support the view that the mere avoidance of institutionalization of juvenile offenders will result in a more successful adjustment to the community. We do know that some youths do well if they are left in the community, but we also know that some violent and hard-core offenders cannot be trusted to remain in the community. Furthermore, we are fairly confident that confinement of status offenders does reduce their chances for a successful community adjustment. But theoretical statements on incarceration need to be tested with much more extensive empirical investigation before any definitive statements can be made.

Deciding the most viable model for treating juvenile offenders is another important problem. Although the medical, adjustment, crime control, and least-restrictive models are four different models being used in working with offenders, different models may be needed for various types of offenders; this is the basic assumption of the differential-treatment approach. Only by developing theoretical models to the point where they can be tested will correctional administrators be able to provide better guidance to youthful offenders.

An additional important theoretical concern is the clarification of the goals of juvenile corrections. Any attempts to define correctional goals are presently so disorganized by attempts to capture society's concern for both revenge and reform that their effectiveness is seriously hampered. As Wheeler and Cottrell have said, "Delinquency is too serious a problem to be lodged in a labyrinth of bureaucratic settings with little in the name of logic, program, or coordinating mechanism to tie them together."[36]

Probation theory, too, needs attention. Probation officers are expected to play incompatible roles; they are expected to be treatment officers as well as authority figures. Traditional theory has not provided adequate guidelines to allow the probation officer to fulfill these conflicting roles successfully. Gibbons has noted that the probation officer "is not prepared to function within the special structure of corrections in which he is both a representative of the punitive social control system as well as a helper."[37] However, generic casework theory, upon which probation is based, has focused almost entirely upon helping the individual adjust to his environment. This theory has largely ignored the impact on the offender of social pressures and environmental influences. The offender's subcultural and cultural matrix is, of course, highly influential in defining acceptable goals and standards of conduct.[38]

It appears that in terms of theory juvenile corrections would be wise to move away from the causation argument and to concentrate more on the issue of commitment to societal norms. Too, continued effort to differentiate offenders from nonoffenders seems to be counter-productive; self-report studies have clearly demonstrated the folly of continuing to spotlight the juvenile offender as different (in background, experiences, personality characteristics) from those who have not been delinquent.

Another important theoretical concern relates to the necessity of designing a more humane juvenile justice system. Developing a more humane perspective requires focusing upon the juvenile offender as a person. Instilling a sense of justice in applying punishment may be a fruitful theoretical area for developing a more humane justice system. The question of clients' feelings of injustice toward the justice system also appears to be an exciting and productive area of inquiry. Matza originally raised the question of injustice in *Delinquency and Drift,* and Giordano empirically investigated it.[39] However, these feelings should be examined more carefully as a factor in continued delinquent behavior.

Finally, the rights of children deserve theoretical consideration. Some of the many important questions suggested by this line of inquiry are: What rights do children have? When should parents lose their rights over their children? What can society do to insure that the rights of both children and parents will not be abused?

But once theories are developed, they must be tested. An examination of all the theories in this chapter shows most of them to be too broad and vague to be tested directly. A researcher who wishes to test them, therefore, must break them down into simpler statements. A research hypothesis is a general statement that can eventually be tested. For reasons well known in logic and philosophy, the research hypothesis must be stated as a null hypothesis; that is, it must be stated in the negative so that it can be disproved by statistical analysis. Finally, the concepts of the hypothesis may be vague or ambiguous, so they too must be defined and operationalized before they can be tested on a quantitative basis.

SUMMARY

Research and theory presently play important roles in juvenile corrections. If they are to become even more important, careful consideration must be given to those issues that presently diminish their effectiveness. More attention should be paid to the many types of research design. All too often, information is lost, or more information could be gained by small but significant changes in research design. More descriptive studies must be conducted to give comparative researchers a basis for study. Whenever possible, too, the classical experimental design should be used, to maximize information and to control variables that are apt to influence the outcome of studies. Knowledge of these problems and of the method of overcoming them must become common among the practitioners of juvenile justice.

The development of good theory is equally as important as the development of good research. Theory is responsible for the interpretation of research and gives it direction; theory allows for the transcending of the prejudicial, idiosyncratic, and particular. At the same time, all levels and types of theories are important; neither micro-theory, middle-range theory, nor macro-theory has an intrinsic advantage over the others. They all add to knowledge and understanding and help to order the relationships found in the world. One qualification must be added, however, and that is that all theories, whether they are macro or micro, whether they are grounded, deductive, or inductive, must be tested. Without their marriage to research they will remain no more than speculative statements about the nature of human behavior. This does not mean they must be capable of immediate testings; this would rule out the acceptance of much macro-theory. Rather, the problems of testing should be studied, techniques should be developed to allow for partial or future testing, and continued thought must be given to their logic and construction to assure that the final product will be as representative as possible of reality.

Juvenile corrections is handicapped in all of the above areas. Research is sparse, and theory is underdeveloped. Time and time again the authors of this text were faced with only one or two studies available on the topics they were analyzing. In other cases, there were no studies nor even impressionistic writings available from which conclusions could be drawn. Experience in juvenile corrections, discussions with experts, and findings in adult corrections were therefore necessarily the bases for some of the materials presented. One serious drawback was the almost complete lack of repeated studies. For science to move forward, findings have to be tested again and again. Further, although some studies have findings comparable to those in adult corrections, we do not know whether or to what degree the two areas, juvenile and adult corrections, are actually comparable.

Of all the possible research areas, probably none is so lacking as is evaluation research. The many new and model programs mentioned in this book must be studied to determine their effectiveness. Information systems and adequate research personnel must be developed, together with data banks, criteria, and strategies for evaluation.[40]

In Wilkin's words, "Once the process of evaluation is started, it can continue to be improved and made more powerful. The information derived from evaluative studies provides the information which can be the mechanism facilitating the evolution of the system. Unless information about the working of a system is fed back into the system, the system lacks the means for its self-development."[41]

QUESTIONS

1. What are some of the factors that can be said to "determine" human behavior? With which position, determinism or free will, do you agree? Why?

2. How would you go about setting up a research study? What type of study

would you conduct? What factors must you consider in making your decision? What specific design would you develop? Why?

3. How do research and theory complement each other?

4. What is the difference between qualitative and quantitative research? Which do you prefer and why?

5. From what you have read in this book, how adequate is research and theory in juvenile justice? Support your answer with examples.

6. How do ideology and theory differ?

7. What are the different levels of theory? Give examples of each.

8. Explain induction and deduction.

ENDNOTES

1. Rose Giallombardo, *Society of Women* (New York: John Wiley & Sons, 1966).
2. Rose Giallombardo, *The Social World of Imprisoned Girls* (New York: John Wiley & Sons, 1974), p. 12.
3. Howard W. Polsky, *Cottage Six: The Social System of Delinquent Boys in Residential Treatment* (New York: Russell Sage Foundation, 1962).
4. Maude Craig and Selma J. Glick, "Ten Years' Experience with the Glueck Social Prediction Table," *The Sociology of Punishment and Corrections,* 2d ed., edited by Norman B. Johnston, Leonard Savitz, and Marvin E. Wolfgang (New York: John Wiley & Sons, 1970), p. 781.
5. Alfred J. Kahn, "Public Policy and Delinquency Predictions," Johnston, Savitz, and Wolfgang, *Sociology of Punishment and Corrections.*
6. Robert Portune, *Changing Adolescent Attitudes toward Police* (Cincinnati: W. H. Anderson Company, 1971).
7. Donald Bouma, *Kids and Cops* (Grand Rapids, Mich.: William E. Eerdman Publishing Company, 1969).
8. Stuart J. Miller and Simon Dinitz, "Measuring Perceptions of Organizational Change," *Journal of Research on Crime and Delinquency* 11 (July 1974): 180–194.
9. Ashley Weeks, "The Highfields Project," in *Juvenile Delinquency: A Book of Readings,* edited by Rose Giallombardo (New York: John Wiley & Sons, 1976), pp. 535–547.
10. Lewis Yablonsky "The Delinquent Gang as a Near Group," in Giallombardo, *Juvenile Delinquency.*
11. The ethics section is largely adapted from Clare Selltiz, Lawrence S. Wrightsman, and Stuart Cook, *Research Methods in Social Relations,* (New York: Holt, Rinehart and Winston, 1976), pp. 200–249.
12. Clarence Schrag, "Elements of Theoretical Analysis in Sociology," in *Sociological Theory: Inquiries and Paradigms,* edited by Llewellyn Gross (New York: Harper & Row, 1967), p. 229.
13. Ibid., p. 244.
14. LaMar T. Empey, "Contemporary Programs for Adjudicated Juvenile Offenders: Problems of Theory, Practice, and Research," in *Juvenile Justice*

Management, edited by Adams et al. (Springfield, Ill.: Charles C Thomas Company, 1973), p. 441.

15. David Matza, *Delinquency and Drift* (New York: John Wiley & Sons, 1964), p. 5.
16. Donald C. Gibbons, "Differential Treatment of Delinquents and Interpersonal Maturity Level: A Critique," *Social Forces Review* 44 (1970): 68.
17. Frederic L. Faust, "A Perspective on the Dilemma of Free Will and Determinism in Juvenile Justice," *Juvenile Justice* 54 (May 1974): 58.
18. Ibid.
19. Richard Quinney, *The Social Reality of Crime* (Boston: Little, Brown and Company, 1970), p. 9.
20. Ibid., p. 9.
21. Ralf Dahrendorf, "Out of Utopia: Toward a Reorientation in Sociological Analysis," *American Journal of Sociology* 67 (September 1958): 127.
22. Barry Krisberg, *Crime and Punishment* (Englewood Cliffs, N.J.: Prentice-Hall, 1974).
23. The following analysis of social structure and anomie is adapted from Robert K. Merton, *Social Theory and Social Structure, 2d edition* (New York: Free Press, 1957).
24. Morton Deutsch and Robert M. Krauss, *Theories in Social Psychology* (New York: Basic Books, 1965), p. 198.
25. Richard Cloward and Lloyd E. Ohlin, *Delinquency and Opportunity: A Theory of Delinquent Gangs* (New York: Free Press, 1960).
26. Merton, *Social Theory and Social Structure,* p. 151.
27. Ibid., p. 155.
28. Matza, *Delinquency and Drift,* p. 28.
29. LaMar T. Empey and Steven G. Lubeck, *The Silverlake Experiment: Testing Delinquency Theory and Community Intervention* (Chicago: Aldine Publishing Company, 1971), p. 144.
30. Matza, *Delinquency and Drift,* p. 89.
31. Empey and Lubeck, *Silverlake Experiment,* pp. 144–145.
32. Cloward and Ohlin, *Delinquency and Opportunity,* p. 78.
33. Ibid., p. 86.
34. Jerome Skolnick, "Toward a Developmental Theory of Parole," *American Sociological Review* 25 (August 1960): 546; James Short and Fred Strodtbeck, *Group Process and Gang Delinquency* (Chicago: University of Chicago Press, 1965); Matza, *Delinquency and Drift;* Daniel Glaser, *Gross Personal Characteristics and Parole Outcome* (New York: National Council on Crime and Delinquency, 1964), p. 466.
35. Barney Glaser and Anselm L. Strauss, *The Discovery of Grounded Theory* (New York: Aldine-Atherton, 1967), pp. 2–6, 77–79.
36. Stanton Wheeler and Leonard S. Cottrell, *Juvenile Delinquency: Its Prevention and Control* (New York: Russell Sage Foundation, 1966).
37. Don C. Gibbons, *Changing the Law Breaker* (Englewood Cliffs, N.J.: Prentice-Hall, 1965), pp. 224–225.
38. Empey, "Contemporary Programs," pp. 450–451.
39. Peggy C. Giordano, "The Sense of Injustice: An Analysis of Juveniles' Reactions to the Justice Systems," *Criminology* 14 (May 1976): 93–112.
40. President's Commission on Criminal Justice Standards and Goals, *Corrections* (Washington, D.C.: U.S. Government Printing Office, 1973), pp. 496–533.
41. Leslie T. Wilkins, "Evaluation of Penal Treatment," in *Correctional In-*

stitutions, edited by Robert M. Carter, Daniel Glaser, and Leslie T. Wilkins (New York: J. B. Lippincott Company, 1972), p. 515.

REFERENCES

Brodbeck, May. *Readings in the Philosophy of the Social Sciences.* New York: Macmillan Company, 1968.
> *Presents a good introduction to positivism.*

Glaser, Barney G., and Strauss, Anselm L. *The Discovery of Grounded Theory.* New York: Holt, Rinehart and Winston, 1976.
> *Invaluable in showing the relationship between theory and research and in demonstrating how research can generate theory.*

Matza, David. *Delinquency and Drift.* New York: John Wiley & Sons, 1964.
> *This book has become a classic in the field. The drift hypothesis, whether one accepts it or not, is an important concept in juvenile corrections.*

Schur, Edwin M. *Radical Non-Intervention: Rethinking the Delinquency Problem.* Englewood Cliffs, N.J.: Prentice-Hall, 1973.
> *One of the most widely read texts in juvenile corrections, this book reviews various approaches to delinquency and concludes with the advice to leave the kids alone whenever possible.*

Selltiz, Claire; Wrightsman, Lawrence S.; and Cook, Stuart W. *Research Methods in Social Relations.* New York: Holt, Rinehart and Winston, 1976.
> *A good introduction to social research methods.*

16

Social Policy and Juvenile Corrections

Juvenile crime is both a serious matter and a common phenomenon today. The majority of juveniles work through the antisocial phase of their lives and go on to become law-abiding citizens. Some youths commit serious offenses, including violent crimes, and a few pursue crime as a way of life.

The mission of juvenile corrections is to rehabilitate youthful offenders so that they will neither return to the juvenile justice system nor continue on into the life of an adult criminal. As this book has repeatedly documented, there is a long way to go to achieve this goal.

Indeed, the opposite often appears to be true, for once troublemaking youths are processed through the correctional system, the chances of their returning are increased, not reduced. Juvenile corrections often breeds rather than reforms offenders.

Certainly all methods of treatment, rehabilitation, and correction have been tried in order to accomplish this mission. They have included diversion, community-based corrections, radical nonintervention, the closing of training schools, mandatory sentencing, punishment, guided group interaction, positive peer culture, behavior therapy, work release, home furloughs, and coeducational institutionalization. Upon evaluation, however, these strategies are seen to fall far short of accomplishing the goal of preventing youngsters from being returned to the system.

Few would not agree that change is desperately needed on all levels if juvenile corrections is to fulfill its mission. Nevertheless, the present state of juvenile justice does not readily allow significant social policy advances.

BASIC PROBLEMS IN THE ADMINISTRATION OF JUVENILE JUSTICE

The administrative problems facing juvenile justice practitioners are formidable and extensive. Inadequate funding, fragmentation within the system, the lack of a unifying philosophy, a sharp upsurge in the public's fear of the criminal, a gross lack of compassion, a spurious moralism, poorly developed prevention strategies, and the overuse of intervention constitute some of the many problems that demand solutions if the offending juvenile is to be successfully reintegrated into the daily life of the community.

The meagerness of the funding of juvenile justice sorely handicaps social policy advances. Juvenile justice presently is a relatively marginal area of governmental concern. Regardless of how large certain budget-line items for justice may seem, or how pressing litigation or code revision may be to some, the dollars involved are almost insignificant compared to the state resources allocated to public education, or to overcoming energy shortages and unemployment, or even to adult corrections. The low level of funding is also demonstrated by the very small portion of state Law Enforcement Assistance Administration funds allocated to juvenile corrections and is further emphasized in a state legislator's report of his difficulties in getting juvenile justice on any agenda, from that of the general public to the state legislature. Consequently, it is not surprising to find that juvenile justice has no general backing among the states, that few interest groups regularly support it, that coalitions of interest groups and political and governmental leaders seldom push for change, and that reports on important events relating to juvenile justice (other than incidents of crime) are usually relegated to the back pages of the newspapers. It becomes much easier to explain why progress does not occur in this area than to trace the reasons for its varying directions and rate of change among the states.[1]

The fragmentation of the juvenile justice system also presents a barrier to those who would bring change to juvenile corrections. Fragmentation clearly prevents juveniles from receiving just treatment under the law, since state and local units operate autonomously, with little coordination or cooperation at any level. Furthermore, the policy and program concerns of some states are quite different from those of other states; "in fact, the policy, structure, or program solutions chosen by some states represent the problems rejected by other states."[2]

The lack of a unifying philosophy is another barrier to change. Should our child-saving philosophy be based on the treatment, adjustment, punishment, or least-restrictive model? Should our strategy with juveniles in trouble be nonintervention, diversion, deinstitutionalization, institutionalization? If a juvenile must be institutionalized, should our aim be treatment, punishment, or merely warehousing? The field is rent by conflict among those who hold different convictions about how to handle troublesome youths. The net effect of these philosophical differences works to form pressure groups and professional associations. These groups take specific, sometimes narrow, positions as each attempts to convince others that its position is the only one that deserves to be heard. Each stance is defended emotionally, and often more effort goes into argument than into a genuine concern with the needs of children.

Furthermore, a sharp upsurge in the public's fear of crime is beginning to create a national mood of "let's get tough with criminals." This attitude is producing a rise in institutional populations and a loss of support for community-based corrections and diversion. There is increasing interest in mandatory sentencing, which has become the established policy in one state, and more and more juveniles who have committed serious offenses are being transferred to the adult court. Institutional runaways are also becoming a serious concern as pressure is being placed on correctional administrators to tighten the standards for work release and home furloughs. For example, district attorneys in some jurisdictions are requesting that they be given the name of institutionalized youths who will be sent home each weekend on furlough. Obviously, the crime control, or punishment, model is gathering momentum, while the other approaches to youth crime are slowly losing ground. As a result of the pressure of the hard-liners, retrenchment rather than change is becoming the predominant characteristic of juvenile corrections.

Compassion also seems to be lacking in the juvenile justice system. Richette has noted, "The system [juvenile justice] as a whole has a clinical coldness about it."[3] Juveniles, in spite of the problems they might have in following community norms, are sensitive, have the same feelings as everyone else, are easily hurt, and are alienated by uncaring and unsympathetic treatment. This lack of caring is often reflected in the denial of basic human rights to these youths; but due process and procedural rights must be granted juveniles in trouble. Indifferent or hostile staff only increase the alienation of these troubled youths. Luger has observed that we have been primarily interested in "making bucks off kids" and consequently have communicated to children in trouble "that we don't give a damn."[4]

The juvenile justice system has too long been a disposal unit for the children of the poor. The lack of social justice for poor and minority groups is a grave indictment of our society. At the same time that the heavy-handed ministrations of the state have harshly processed the poor, the justice system has worked very hard at saving the "saved"— the middle-class youths who have committed minor offenses. These juveniles are usually the ones diverted from the system, placed on probation, and retained in community-based corrections.

Noncriminal youths typically stay longer and have more painful experiences in the juvenile justice system; nothing testifies so well to the fact that the juvenile justice system does not work as the tossing of all youths into the same bag, the rapist with the runaway. Beyond the rhetoric is the reality that the system cannot sort the youths who come into it.[5] The unfortunate consequence is that youths who either are noncriminal or have committed only minor offenses often end up being confined for months longer than those who have committed violent crimes. Not only are noncriminal youths confined longer, they also tend to become the institutional scapegoats and sometimes choose to take their own lives because they cannot survive in the institutional context.

A spurious moralism—especially outside large urban areas—still pervades juvenile justice. Too many juvenile courts still act as moral busybodies in their attempts to enforce a standard of morality on all adolescents. For them, the *parens patriae* philosophy has deteriorated into what is almost an obsession with the concept of proper moral behavior. Girls, particularly, suffer at the hands of this moralism. Institutionalization often becomes a legal chastity belt for them, and they are sent to training schools for the purpose of protecting their morality. Other examples of this moralism are required attendance at church, the ban against smoking, curfews, and the establishment of dress and hair length standards, including the prohibition against beards. Preoccupation with these concerns clouds the larger issues of juvenile justice and the need for change.

In addition, juvenile institutionalization is for many youngsters a dehumanizing, brutal, and criminogenic experience. Exploitation has reached epidemic proportions in some training schools, where the weak give up everything, including their bodies, to the strong. Youngsters tend to emerge from this time of "correction" much more committed to crime as a way of life and further alienated from conventional values and institutions than before their stay.

Prevention strategies are underdeveloped and inefficient. We have not been able to prevent delinquency, and once youngsters become involved in lawbreaking behavior, we have not been able to exercise control. Problems in prevention strategies emerge on at least three fronts: first, although crime prevention must begin in the local community or on the grass-roots level, little progress has been made in community organization since the Chicago Area Projects; second, basic concepts in the prevention field are not precise, and few attempts have been made to design programs around theoretical constructs; and third, we have failed to appreciate fully the negative effects of removing juvenile offenders from such mainstream institutions as the home and school to rehabilitate them.[6]

Many social institutions use the police and the juvenile court as dumping grounds. Schools, in particular, use the courts to solve their problems. Although compulsory-school-attendance laws make it necessary to refer some youths to the courts, social institutions in this country—the family, the community, and the school—are too quick to use the legal system to deal with their own problems.

The overuse of intervention has too frequently characterized juvenile corrections. We have usually required all youths to participate in treatment programs because of our desire to help them. Faced with the options of locking up, giving up, or trying harder, we have tried harder to treat juveniles. Consequently, a treatment sprawl has resulted, in which offenders are faced with what must seem like an endless variety of ways to "recycle" them. The treatment goes on and on, sometimes involving contradictory methods.

Closely related to overintervention is the failure of many community-based and diversionary programs to deliver. Too many programs set their goals too high and promise too much in order to obtain federal funding. In effect, each program promises to be the panacea for youth crime, which has sometimes led groups to disastrous competition for federal dollars. Not only are these programs unable to achieve their ends, but they also tend to evade accountability for the quality of their work with youths. For example, while they may do the necessary evaluation for funding renewal, they do not carry out any pertinent follow-up on program effectiveness, with the result that poor programs are sometimes perpetuated rather than allowed to die.

Furthermore, juvenile corrections is in a quandary on what to do with the hard-core or difficult-to-handle juvenile. Thorazine, handcuffs, and corporal punishment are usually reserved for these youths who are shipped to the maximum security juvenile facilities. But our strategies and programs are not rehabilitating these youngsters. The public says that these youthful criminals must be locked up because the innocent deserve protection, but in our places of confinement these youths become inmate leaders and set the mood and the rules for a violent, delinquent inmate subculture.

Finally, juvenile justice is dependent on federal support for funding community programs and for developing national standards. The President's Commission on Law Enforcement and Administration of Justice and the National Advisory Commission on Criminal Justice

Standards and Goals had a pervasive influence on juvenile corrections in the late 1960s and early 1970s. The standards developed by the Institute of Judicial Administration and the American Bar Association Joint Commission on Juvenile Justice Standards, the Juvenile Justice Task Force of the National Advisory Commission on Criminal Justice Standards and Goals, and the Standards Committee established by the Juvenile Justice and Delinquency Prevention Act of 1974 promise to have as much if not more influence on juvenile corrections in the late 1970s and the 1980s.

POLITICAL PROCESS AND JUVENILE JUSTICE

A critical examination of juvenile justice easily leads the observer to cynicism and to the feeling that nothing can be done. The agencies that run our political system do not provide enough money for the juvenile justice system to be effective. Some politicians use the superintendencies of training schools and positions on parole boards, in police departments, and in sheriffs' offices as political payoffs. Some correctional administrators permit the hiring of untrained and uneducated individuals for the very delicate one-to-one handling of youths. They sometimes support and even defend staff who brutalize defenseless youths. They also continue to award lucrative contracts for the building of institutions that are unsafe and unneeded. Governors and state legislatures often refuse to pass laws requiring rigorous licensing procedures, with the result that many training schools and other holding facilities are not subject to inspection. Jails and police lockups continue to be used for juveniles. Blacks, the poor, and women all receive discriminatory treatment from the justice system. Innovative methods are fought tooth-and-nail by those who benefit from keeping things the way they are.

Lerman probably has the best answer for modifying the juvenile justice structure. He advocates the formation of interest groups to fight for juveniles:

> What is required is search and experimentation to evolve a variety of social-planning models that can be used adaptively to deal with the existing realities of interest groups, conflicts, and scarce resources. In pursuit of this strategy, planners may have to trade off a value they cherish—rationality—in order to realize other values they prize—humanitarianism, fairness, and effective treatment. . . . other participants in the criminal-justice system have been engaged in trade-offs for a long time. If planners want to have a voice in guiding the system, they may have to become participants and act like an interest group too. This

might compromise their adherence to rationality—but they may have no other choice if they are to exercise influence.[7]

Indeed, if we want a juvenile justice system that works, then we must become members of interest groups working for a more humane and just juvenile correctional system and must thrust ourselves into the political arena. The task of these interest groups will be to influence policymakers at all levels. Such interest groups often will be filled with conflict, for no two people agree exactly on how to prevent and control juvenile crime. Many battles also will be lost, but persistence and intelligence should eventually pay off in positive policy changes affecting juveniles in trouble.

Considerable evidence is available in the literature of the influence of interest groups on the creation and implementation of policy.[8] The Illinois Department of Corrections, for example, planned to transfer youths from the Valleyview Youth Center to another facility and to make Valleyview into an adult prison. The citizens of the community created such an uproar that Governor Thompson met with them in an open meeting. As a result, the adult prison was not opened in Valleyview. Another example is the mandatory sentencing law enacted by the New York State Legislature in 1976.[9] We can be certain that this new law was the result of a conscious and a deliberate effort by interest groups that were reacting to violent youth crime in New York State. A third example is the success of interest groups intent on keeping status offenders out of the juvenile justice system in having their wish enacted into law in several states. These interest groups have had to compete with other groups that are intent on keeping status offenders under the jurisdiction of the juvenile court. Another well-known example is the work of child advocacy groups, which have promoted the special needs and rights of children. The right to treatment law appears to be a direct consequence of their lobbying activity.

Interest groups generally do not find it easy to mobilize support from community organizations because representatives of those organizations tend to protect the vested interests of their institutions. Inertia, fear, and parochialism often stop interest groups before they ever get a chance to establish significant policy changes.

One of the most important tasks of each person interested in reform in juvenile corrections is to determine the standards that should be enacted into policy. The writers of this book hereby recommend standards that are crucial in dealing more effectively and humanely with the problems of youth crime. Most of them are derived from the 1973 report on corrections of the National Advisory Commission on Criminal Justice Standards and Goals. We are less impressed with the juvenile justice standards formulated by the Task Force Report of the National Advisory Committee in 1977.

A CREDO FOR JUVENILE CORRECTIONS

Delinquency prevention and control must be returned to the local community.

A humane and fair system of juvenile corrections must always be the priority of all those concerned with juvenile justice.

The treatment of juvenile offenders must be conducted under the least-restrictive model and, as often as possible, troublesome youths should be handled outside the juvenile justice system.

Total-system planning must be a top priority.

The recruitment, training, and support of all staff throughout the juvenile justice system must be of the highest possible quality.

Persons admitted to practice in the juvenile justice system must be sensitive, caring, and understanding.

1. Delinquency prevention and control techniques will not become more effective in deterring crime until decision making is returned to the local community. Sociologists have argued for decades that the stability of older rural societies kept the residents under control and that as the modern industrial society has developed, a pervasive anonymity has destroyed any possibility of communities once again exercising control. Oscar Newman offers a comparable analysis, saying that architecture and the structure of streets, buildings, and communities are so impersonal and public that everyone feels free to do as he wishes, without ever fearing the consequences of penal sanction.[10] Toffler argues, in *Future Shock,* that the pace of life is so great that people everywhere are overwhelmed by stimuli and that they will soon break down if they do not find some means of getting away from these stimuli.[11]

These themes are reiterated again and again, and their demand is not for punishment, rehabilitation, or therapy; it is, instead, for a flight from alienation, a return to the community, and a return to relatedness, rootedness, and identity, as Eric Fromm put it.[12] Conrad, too, has castigated the modern mass urbanized, industrialized, and impersonalized society. He claims that we need a quest for citizenship and that crime will be reduced only when citizenship has been rebuilt.

When the community allows citizenship to lapse or to lose meaning for its inhabitants, crime is one of its more noticeable consequences. The failure of citizenship is two-sided. We do well to isolate the criminal and make sure that the blame for his crime is correctly assigned. We should also recognize that the criminal's failure as a citizen signals a need to rebuild the community that produced him.[13]

A few must be listening to these warnings. Federal legislation in a number of areas, social security, workmen's compensation, welfare, Medicare, Medicaid, and a host of new proposals are geared to give citizens once again that security that was once provided by our communities. Certainly these efforts are visible as architects, capitalizing on the pioneering efforts of Oscar Newman, build safe housing developments, or, as cities begin to limit their size, develop smaller satellite cities, or build malls that are enjoyable for young and old alike. Their efforts can be seen in old-age homes, where men and women are no longer segregated; in mental hospitals, where patients can sit and have a beer together; in communities, where efforts are underway to reintegrate the elderly, the alcoholic, the mentally ill, and the mentally retarded into society as fully participating and valued members.

In short, community organization seems to be one of the keys to the prevention and control of youth crime. The Chicago Area Projects provide one viable model of community organization on the grass-roots level, but other models are needed. In the Chicago Area Projects, which have now spread throughout Illinois, the institutions of the community—the family, the school, the church, the social and recreational clubs, and others—are not so quick as they once were to turn juveniles in trouble over to the police and to the juvenile court. Citizens of the community expect to discipline and to control those who violate persons and property; they also expect to provide the quality of environment that will reduce social problems and crime.

2. *A top priority of everyone concerned with juvenile justice should be to build a more humane and fair system.* Since the point of initial contact with the juvenile justice system is an especially critical one, every effort must be made to insure that first offenders are dealt with fairly and are guaranteed full rights under the Constitution. All youths, regardless of age, sex, race, creed, or national origin, should be dealt with uniformly and without discrimination. They should not be denied access to any legal recourse, grievance mechanism, or rehabilitative need; nor can they be denied freedom of expression, religion, education, vocation, or recreational and counseling programs. Under no circumstances should suggestions be made, except within a genuine counseling context, that a particular service is not needed by the youth. Ridiculing, harassing, or punishing youths for seeking legal assistance, for filing grievance procedures, or for asking for rehabilitative assistance should be strictly prohibited. Officials are employed to help and guide youths, not to shake their confidence or scare them away

from seeking relationships that will help them attain full and productive citizenship.

Under no circumstances, then, may agencies or their staffs for personal, institutional, or program conveniences strip clients of any of their rights as citizens. Institutional rules that limit individual freedom should be established only after discussion by all parties involved. To guarantee that such rules are, indeed, protective of individual rights, the courts should periodically review the regulations of law enforcement, corrections, probation, and parole agencies. Rules that are punitive should be put in writing for all offenders being processed through the system; sanctions for violation of the rules should also be provided in writing to all offenders coming into contact with agencies. No other sanctions should be used.

If minor rules are violated, offenders must still be guaranteed due process. Offenders should be notified of charges against them and allowed to explain why they acted as they did. If a hearing is requested by an offender, independent personnel or departments should conduct it impartially to determine the offender's guilt or innocence. Serious offenders are a matter for the courts, not for adjudication by police or correctional personnel. Obviously, if offenders are found to be innocent of the charges, any reference to the act in their records should be removed. If offenders are to be reclassified, they should be notified of the pending change and allowed to participate in the decision-making process. If they might be in any way adversely affected by the change, they should be permitted to have an administrative hearing on the validity of the charges. The same holds true when clients have grievances about their treatment at the hands of any juvenile justice system personnel.

These suggested goals are actually no more than a common sense approach to human relations. We all know how we want to be treated by others, and many of these standards do no more than formalize what should be normal and ordinary treatment of human beings. The formulation of such standards and goals provides direction for handling offenders. Offenders who are treated considerately, compassionately, firmly, and fairly will know that someone cares and is available to help them. If we, in this impersonal and anonymous society of ours, can demonstrate through actions toward others that they need not fear reprimands if they ask for help, we may be able to reduce their need to commit criminal acts. All citizens can help each other to become fully participating and respected members of the community. Law enforcement officials have a particularly difficult role in achieving this goal. They must mete out punishments, yet retain the support and respect of those with whom they deal.

3. The treatment of juvenile offenders should be guided by the least-restrictive model and, whenever possible, troublesome youths should be handled outside the juvenile justice system. From the point of first contact, juvenile correctional officials should make every effort to divert youth from the police, the courts, or institutional programs. Whenever possible juvenile offenders should remain with their families or be placed in foster or group homes. Contact with police should remain informal for as long as possible, and providing contact for the youth with a social service or welfare agency should be of high priority. The needs of each youth should be ascertained so the appropriate agencies can be contacted to help him solve his problems. Detention homes or training schools must be used only as a last resort. Juveniles should never be placed in jails, in adult reformatories, or in adult prisons.

Noncriminal youths and status offenders must be kept out of the juvenile justice system at all costs. No evidence exists that their contacts with the system are at all positive, and much evidence testifies to the brutality of this system. The argument that no one will provide for these youths if the juvenile court does not intervene makes it all the more necessary to establish sufficient nonsystem facilities and programs to care for their needs.

Public decision makers must be urged to appropriate the necessary funds to enlarge the community-based corrections of nearly every state. Total deinstitutionalization may not be a viable option today, but the number of community-based facilities and programs must be significantly increased. In order to involve the community positively in these programs, correctional administrators and judges must use the best judgment possible in evaluating and placing the juvenile offender. If too many crimes are committed by program participants, these programs will be placed in jeopardy.

No additional facilities for confining youths should be built, since diversion techniques and community programs can handle all but a very small number of youth in trouble. If replacing a facility or remodeling an old one is deemed necessary, however, certain principles should be followed. Old buildings located some distance from home communities should be abandoned; only those located within a community and within easy access to all services should be remodeled. If a new facility is to be built, it, too, should be located near its client population, as well as hospitals, junior colleges, and social services. All new facilities should be small, with modern living conditions, sanitary facilities, and healthful surroundings. No fortress-like or large rambling structures should be built; those existing should be razed. Dormitories should never be used; youth should, instead, be placed in comfortable single rooms with pleasant decor and in facilities arranged in clusters of no more than ten to twelve youths, so that living units remain small. A single room allows privacy and individuality; the design should consider the development of a sense of territoriality.

Security features should be minimal. Control should be exercised through staffing procedures and intelligent construction, rather than through the use of bars, screens, steel doors, locks, barbed wire, and brick and concrete. Unobtrusive security features should replace those institutional features that give rise to a "total" atmosphere. An open communication system and monitoring without guard stations are positive alternatives to maximum security features. All areas should give a feeling of safety and livability.

4. Total-system planning must be a top priority at both state and local levels. The mission of such planning is to reduce juvenile crime, to divert juveniles from the juvenile justice system, and to facilitate integration into the home communities. This mission should be understood by all agencies and personnel involved with youths. Citizens in the community should be involved in any decision making and planning, as should law enforcement officers, presentencing investigators, judges, correctional institution personnel, and probation and parole officers. Statewide juvenile justice training seminars should be available, as they can provide personnel with an understanding of the broader goals of the system.

Integration of the services of all involved agencies is imperative. A common mission and collaboration among all agencies would guarantee each agency's compatibility with the overall objectives of the system. Such collaboration would also allow each agency to state its own goals precisely, thereby preventing overlap with other agencies. Each subsystem, then, would perform definite, well-delineated functions and would not find itself in unnecessary conflict with other subsystems. Standardized procedures for reconciling the conflicts that do arise should be developed. These procedures would be used for generating and gathering relevant information for solving problems at different levels of the state organization and transmitting it to all who required it. These are the principles of management by objectives.

As each subsystem, law enforcement group, court, corrections agency, and probation and parole department is developed and reorganized, a number of factors must be taken into consideration. Once the goals of these agencies are hammered out by participants from all segments of the system, including offenders, they should be discussed throughout the entire juvenile justice system. The objectives of each subunit of any subsystem should be drawn up in accordance with the goals of the subsystem so that appropriate guidelines can de devised. The specific numbers of clients to be handled, the nature of these clients, their program needs, the costs of all agency functions, the schedules to be followed, and the specific results to be achieved should all be precisely stated so that their measurement is facilitated. Finally, evaluation meetings should be periodically held by all involved so that progress, or lack of it, can be discussed and problems resolved.

The programs and agencies that are a part of the statewide system should be structured to meet community and offender needs, and the best methods for meeting these needs should be a continuing concern of agency and program personnel. Specialized offender programs should be so planned that the extent of the problem is defined, all of the factors that affect the problem are delineated, the alternative paths to the solution of the problems are analyzed, and an effective delivery system developed. Specific goals and objectives should be stated in measurable form and analyzed and revised whenever analysis shows that either offender, community, agency, or state inputs to the problem have changed.

The development of comprehensive statewide research programs is very important in this program. The findings from these programs should be coordinated with those of other states and should provide information that enables top planners and researchers to predict trends and gather data relevant to ongoing programs. These findings also can be computerized in formats that are easily available to and understood by all correctional system personnel. Regional and, where available, institutionally based computer terminals—combined with the development of comprehensive and standardized data collection forms—will allow staff and officials to send and receive information relative to their programs efficiently and speedily. A centralized state, or even national, data center will allow the permanent storage of all information for research purposes. However, data pertaining to specific offenders, such as names, social security numbers, and other information that could be used for later identification of offenders, should under no circumstances be programmed into the system.

Such a research program will permit the evaluation of the total juvenile correctional system as well as of its subsystems, units, and personnel performance. The specified measurable objectives and stated results required by planners can then be analyzed to determine whether or not and to what degree they are being achieved. Administrators and personnel responsible for programs can subject their role performance to analysis and, through planning and discussion with peers and supervisors, modify their approaches to problems whenever necessary. Units and subsystems that do not meet the established standards should be brought into conformity.

5. *The recruitment, training, and support of staff throughout the juvenile justice system is of utmost importance.* Personnel employed by the agencies to oversee programs in juvenile corrections should be well

trained and sensitive. Personal characteristics unrelated to the ability to be caring and understanding should not be used as criteria for hiring. All personnel should be fully informed by their superiors of the duties and expectations of their roles. Training programs should be developed to aid both old and new staff in learning their duties and to supply them with pertinent new information as it is received from the social and life sciences. Personnel should have a good background understanding of the problems faced by adolescents in both urban and rural settings. They should also be trained in how to effectively and extensively use volunteers from all sections of the community.

Practitioners should be deeply involved in helping delinquents learn to live happy and productive lives. Caring staff members, even in the worst institutional environments, always make a difference in the lives of youngsters. However, staff must be respected if youths are to profit from their influence, and staff who know what it is like on the street, who are firm, who are difficult to manipulate, and who "give a damn" are respected. The effective staff member treats his charges as persons of worth and expects them to behave responsibly. Such personnel are skilled in making others feel good about themselves and in knowing how to best reinforce positive behavior. Instead of any particular treatment technique, the key ingredient in success seems to be caring individuals who like kids, who listen to them, and who seem to have an uncanny ability of knowing the right way to help them.

In delivering services to troublesome youngsters, it is not surprising that paraprofessionals—especially minority group members and ex-offenders—appear to be able to relate to and to establish rapport with them in ways that professionals find impossible. Therefore, every effort should be made to employ as many sensitive and caring paraprofessionals and ex-offenders as possible.

In conclusion, the challenge in juvenile corrections is great. If we care for children, we will increase our efforts to diminish the negative effects of the hard-line and the punitive approach to corrections. If we care for children, we will see to it that our ideas are presented forcefully and clearly to policymakers. And if we care for children, we will not wait until the system finally works, but instead, we will reach out and help those youths seeking to find themselves.

QUESTIONS

1. What is social policy? How does it affect juvenile corrections?
2. What is the present status of juvenile corrections in social policy?

3. What is the most serious problem in developing significant social policy for juvenile corrections?

4. What is your reaction to the credo for juvenile corrections?

5. What do you feel is missing from this credo?

ENDNOTES

1. Rosemary C. Sarri and Robert D. Vinter, "Justice for Whom? Varieties of Juvenile Correctional Approaches," in *The Juvenile Justice System,* edited by Malcolm W. Klein (Beverly Hills, Calif.: Sage Publishers, 1976), p. 169.
2. Ibid., p. 169.
3. Lecture by Judge Lisa Richette at the Third Annual Juvenile Justice Conference, 14 to 18 March 1976.
4. Lecture by Milton Luger at the Third Annual Juvenile Justice Conference.
5. William T. Pink and Mervin F. White, "Delinquency Prevention: The State of the Art," in Klein, *Juvenile Justice System,* p. 6.
6. Ibid., p. 7.
7. Paul Lerman, *Delinquency and Social Policy* (New York: Praeger Publishers, 1970), p. 417.
8. Richard Quinney, *The Social Reality of Crime* (Boston: Little, Brown and Company, 1970).
9. The Juvenile Justice and Reform Act of 1976, State of New York.
10. Oscar Newman, *Defensible Space* (New York: Macmillan Company, 1972).
11. Alvin Toffler, *Future Shock* (New York: Random House, 1970).
12. Eric Fromm, *Escape from Freedom* (New York: Holt, Rinehart and Winston, 1941).
13. John P. Conrad, "Looking toward the Year 2000: The Role of Correctional Research," in *Contemporary Corrections: A Concept in Search of Content,"* edited by Benjamin Frank (Reston, Va.: Reston Publishing Company, 1973), p. 337.

REFERENCES

Kahn, Alfred J.; Kamerman, Sheila B.; and McGowan, Brenda G. *Child Advocacy: Report of a National Base Line Study.* New York: Child Advocacy Research Project, Columbia School of Social Work, 1972.
  These researchers have written extensively in the area of child advocacy. This text will provide a good introduction to child advocacy.

Kassebaum, Gene. *Delinquency and Social Policy.* Englewood Cliffs, N.J.: Prentice-Hall, Inc., 1974.
  A good introduction to delinquency and social policy.

Lerman, Paul. *Delinquency and Social Policy.* New York: Praeger Publishers, 1970.
  Contains an excellent selection of readings on social policy and delinquency.

BIBLIOGRAPHY

Adamek, Raymond J., and Dager, Edward Z. "Social Structure, Identification and Change in a Treatment-Oriented Institution." *American Sociological Review* 3 (December 1968): 931–944.

Adams, Gary B.; Carter, Robert M.; Gerletti, John D.; Pursuit, Dan G.; and Rogers, Percy G. *Juvenile Justice Management.* Springfield, Ill.: Charles C Thomas, 1973.

Adams, Stuart. "Assessment of the Psychiatric Treatment Program, Phase I: Second Interim Report." Research Report No. 15. Mimeographed. Sacramento: California Youth Authority, December 1959.

———. "Assessment of the Psychiatric Treatment Program, Phase I: Third Interim Report." Research Report No. 21. Mimeographed. Sacramento: California Youth Authority, January 1961.

———. "Effectiveness of the Youth Authority Special Treatment Program: First Interim Report." Research Report No. 5. Mimeographed. Sacramento: California Youth Authority, March 1959.

———. "Some Findings from Correctional Caseload Research." *Federal Probation* 31 (December 1967): 48–57.

———. "The PICO Project." In *The Sociology of Punishment and Correction,* edited by Norman Johnston, Leonard Savitz, and Marvin E. Wolfgang. New York: John Wiley & Sons, 1970. Pp. 548–561.

Adler, Freda. *Sisters in Crime.* New York: McGraw-Hill, 1975

Advisory Council of Judges of the National Council on Crime and Delinquency. *Guides for Juvenile Court Judges.* New York: National Council on Crime and Delinquency, 1963.

Aichhorn, August. *Wayward Youth.* New York: Viking Press, 1963.

Allen, Harry E., and Simonsen, Clifford E. *Corrections in America: An Introduction.* Beverly Hills, Calif.: Glencoe Press, 1975.

Allen, Thomas E. "Psychiatric Observations as an Adolescent in the Social System and Culture." *Psychiatry* 32 (August 1969): 292–302.

Alper, Benedict S. *Prisons Inside-Out.* Cambridge, Mass.: Ballinger, 1974.

American Correctional Association. *Manual of Correctional Standards.* College

Park, Md.: American Correctional Association, 1974.

Arnold, William R. *Juveniles on Parole: A Sociological Perspective.* New York: Random House, 1970.

Atchley, Robert C., and McCabe, Patrick M. "Socialization in Correctional Communities: A Replication." *American Sociological Review* 33 (October 1968): 774–785.

Augustus, John. *A Report of the Labors of John Augustus, for the Last Ten Years, in Aid of the Unfortunate.* Boston: Wright and Hasty, 1852.

Axelrod, Sidney. "Negro and White Male Institutionalized Delinquents." *American Journal of Sociology* 57 (May 1952): 569–574.

Bakal, Yitzhak. *Closing Correctional Institutions.* Lexington, Mass.: D. C. Heath and Company, 1973.

Baker, Harvey H. "Procedure of the Boston Juvenile Court." In *Juvenile Justice Philosophy: Readings, Cases and Comments,* edited by Frederic L. Faust and Paul J. Brantingham. St. Paul, Minn.: West Publishing Company, 1974.

Barker, Gordon H., and Adams, Thomas W. "The Social Structure of a Correctional Institution." *Journal of Criminal Law, Criminology and Police Science* 49 (January/February 1959): 416–422.

Baron, Roger, and Feeney, Floyd. *Juvenile Diversion through Family Counseling: A Program for the Diversion of Status Offenders in Sacramento County, California.* Washington, D.C.: U.S. Government Printing Office (February 1976).

Bartollas, Clemens. "Runaway at the Training Institution, Central Ohio." Ph.D. dissertation, Ohio State University, 1973

———. "Runaway at the Training Institution, Central Ohio." *Canadian Journal of Criminology and Corrections* 17 (July 1975): 221–235.

———. "Sisyphus in a Juvenile Institution." *Social Work* 20 (September 1975): 364–368.

———. "Unmanageable and Unshareable Problems and How They Contribute to Runaway Behavior." *Sociological Research Symposium.* Vol. 4. Richmond: Virginia Commonwealth University, 1975.

———, and Miller, Stuart J. *Correctional Administration: Theory and Practice.* New York: McGraw-Hill, 1978.

———; Miller, Stuart J.; and Dinitz, Simon. "Boys Who Profit: The Limits of Institutional Success." In *Reform in Corrections: Problems and Issues,* edited by Harry E. Allen and Nancy J. Beran. New York: Praeger Publishers, 1977. Pp. 8–16.

———; Miller, Stuart J.; and Dinitz, Simon. *Juvenile Victimization: The Institutional Paradox.* New York: Halsted Press, 1976.

———; Miller, Stuart J.; and Dinitz, Simon. "Staff Exploitation of Inmates: The Paradox of Institutional Control." In *Exploiters and Exploited: The Dynamics of Victimization,* edited by Emilio Viano and Israel Drapkin. Lexington, Mass.: D. C. Heath and Company, 1975.

———; Miller, Stuart J.; and Dinitz, Simon. "The Booty Bandit: A Social Role in a Juvenile Institution." *Journal of Homosexuality* 1 (1974): 203–212.

————; Miller, Stuart J.; and Dinitz, Simon. "The Exploitation Matrix in a Juvenile Institution." *International Journal of Criminology and Penology* 4 (1976): 257–270.

————; Miller, Stuart J.; and Dinitz, Simon. "The Informal Code: A Gatekeeper to Treatment in a Juvenile Institution." Published by the Program for the Study of Crime and Delinquency of the Ohio State University and used in its annual report to the Administration of Justice Division, Ohio Department of Economic and Community Development, June 1974.

————; Miller, Stuart J.; and Dinitz, Simon. "The Informal Code in a Juvenile Institution: Guidelines for the Strong." *Journal of Southern Criminal Justice* (Summer 1975), pp. 33–52.

————; Miller, Stuart J.; and Dinitz, Simon. "The White Victim in a Black Institution." In *Treating the Offender: Problems and Issues,* edited by Marc Riedel and Pedro A. Vales. New York: Praeger Publishers, 1976.

————, and Sieverdes, Christopher, *Games Juveniles Play: How They Get Their Way.* (Unpublished manuscript).

Baum, Martha, and Wheeler, Stanton. "Becoming an Inmate." In *Controlling Delinquency,* edited by Stanton Wheeler. New York: John Wiley & Sons, 1968. Pp. 153–185.

Bayh, Birch. *Congressional Record,* 121, 17 April 1975.

Bazelon, David L. "Beyond Control of the Juvenile Court." *Juvenile Court Journal* 21 (Summer 1970).

Becker, Howard. *The Outsiders.* New York: Free Press, 1963.

Beckhard, Richard. *Organization Development: Strategies and Models.* Reading, Mass.: Addison Wesley Publishing Co., 1969.

Berger, Peter. *Invitation to Sociology: A Humanistic Perspective.* New York: Doubleday Anchor, 1963.

Berk, Bernard B. "Organizational Goals and Inmate Organization." *American Journal of Sociology* 71 (March 1966): 522–534.

Berman, John J. "Parolees' Perception of the Justice System." *Criminology* 13 (February 1976): 507–520.

Bernard, Jessie. "Teen-age Culture: An Overview." In *Middle-Class Juvenile Delinquency,* edited by Edmund Vaz. New York: Harper & Row, 1967.

Bernard, J. L., and Eisenman, R. "Verbal Conditioning in Sociopaths with Spiral and Monetary Reinforcememt." *Journal of Personality and Social Psychology* 6 (1976): pp. 203–206.

Berne, Eric. *Games People Play.* New York: Grove Press, 1964.

————. *Transactional Analysis in Psychotherapy.* New York: Grove Press.

————. *What Do You Say after You Say Hello?* New York: Grove Press, 1972.

Bixby, Lovell F. "Short-Term Treatment of Youthful Offenders." *Focus* 30 (March 1951): 35–36.

Blackburn, Donald G. "Institutions for Juvenile Delinquents." *NPPA Journal* 4 (January 1958): 12–21.

Blankenship, Ralph L., and Singh, Krishina B. "Differential Labelling of Juveniles: A Multivariate Analysis." *Criminology* 13 (February 1976): 471–490.

Blau, Peter M. *Exchange and Power in Social Life.* New York: John Wiley & Sons, 1967.

————, and Scott, W. Richard. *Formal Organizations.* San Francisco: Chandler, 1962.

Bluestone, Harvey; O'Malley, Edward P.; and Connell, Sydney. "Homosexuality in Prison." *Journal of Social Therapy* 12 (1966): 13–24.

Board of Directors, National Council on Crime and Delinquency. "Jurisdiction over Status Offenses Should Be Removed from the Juvenile Court." *Crime and Delinquency* 21 (April 1975).

Board of State Charities of Massachusetts. *Sixth Annual Report, 1869.*

Bohlke, Robert H. "Social Mobility, Stratification Inconsistency and Middle-Class Delinquency." In *Middle-Class Juvenile Delinquency,* edited by Edmund Vaz. New York: Harper & Row, 1967.

Bordua, David J. "Gang Members and the Police." In *The Police,* edited by David Bordua. New York: John Wiley & Sons, 1967. Pp. 56–98.

————. "Recent Trends: Deviant Behavior and Social Control," *The Annals,* 359 (January 1967): 149–163.

Boston University, Law-Medicine Institute, Training Center in Youth Development. "Educational Counselors: Training for a New Definition of After-Care of Juvenile Parolees, Final Report." Mimeographed. November 1966.

Bouma, Donald H. *Kids and Cops.* Grand Rapids, Mich.: William E. Eerdman Publishing Company, 1969.

Bradley, Harold B., and Williams, Jack D. "Intensive Treatment Program, Second Annual Report." Mimeographed. Sacramento: California Department of Corrections, December 1958.

Breed, Allen F. *National Study of Youth Service Bureaus.* Washington, D.C.: U.S. Department of Health, Education and Welfare, 1972.

Breitel, Charles D. "Controls in Criminal Law Enforcement." *University of Chicago Law Review* 27 (Spring 1960): 427.

Brinkerhoff, Oren R. "The Reformation of Criminals, Ohio Methods—Progressive Steps in Legislation and Administration." In *The Reformatory System in the United States,* edited by S. J. Barrows. Washington, D.C.: U.S. Government Printing Office, 1900. Pp. 171–182.

Brockway, Z. B. "The Reformatory System." In *The Reformatory System in the United States,* edited by S. J. Barrows. Washington, D.C.: U.S. Government Printing Office, 1900, pp. 17–27.

Brodbeck, May. *Readings in the Philosophy of the Social Sciences.* New York: Macmillan, 1968.

Bronfenbrenner, Urie. "Socialization and Social Class through Time and Space." In *Readings in Social Psychology,* edited by Eleanor Maccoby, Theodore Newcomb, and Eugene Hartley. New York: Holt, Rinehart and Winston, 1958.

Brown, Claude. *Manchild in the Promised Land.* New York: Macmillan, 1965.

Brown, Roscoe C., and Dodson, Dan W. "The Effectiveness of a Boys' Club in Reducing Delinquency." *Prevention of Delinquency: Problems and Pro-*

grams, edited by John R. Stratton and Robert M. Terry. New York: Macmillan, 1968.

Bruyn, Severyn T. *The Human Perspective in Sociology.* Englewood Cliffs, N.J.: Prentice-Hall, 1966.

Buckley, Walter. *Modern Systems Research for the Behavioral Scientist.* Chicago: Aldine Publishing Company, 1968.

Burns, Henry, Jr. "A Miniature Totalitarian State: Maximum Security Prison." *Canadian Journal of Corrections* (9 July 1969), pp. 153–164.

Burt, Cyril. *The Young Delinquent.* New York: D. Appleton and Company, 1930.

Byars, George H. "Some Facts about the Sniffing Phenomenon." *Juvenile Justice* 26 (May 1975): 27–34.

Caditz, Sylvan B. "The Effect of a Training School Experience on Delinquent Boys as Measured by Objective Personality Tests." Ph.D. dissertation, University of Washington, 1958.

Carey, James T.; Goldfarb, Joel; Rowe, Michael J.; and Lohmon, Joseph D. *The Handling of Juveniles from Offense to Disposition.* Washington, D.C.: U.S. Government Printing Office, 1967.

Carroll, James L. "Status within Prison: Toward an Operational Definition." *Correctional Psychologist* 4 (September/October, 1970): 49–56.

Carson, Dale. "Police Youth Patrol Program." In *Police Programs for Preventing Crime and Delinquency,* edited by Dan G. Pursuit et al. Springfield, Ill.: Charles C Thomas, 1972. Pp. 390–395.

Carter, Robert M. *Middle-Class Delinquency: An Experiment in Community Control.* Berkeley: University of California, School of Criminology, 1968.

———. "The Police View of the Justice System." In *The Juvenile Justice System,* edited by Malcolm W. Klein. Beverly Hills, Calif.: Sage Publications, 1976. Pp. 124–125.

———, and Klein, Malcolm. *Back on the Streets.* Englewood Cliffs, N.J.: Prentice-Hall, 1976.

———; Glaser, Daniel; and Wilkins, Leslie T. *Correctional Institutions.* New York: J. B. Lippincott Company, 1972.

———; McGee, Richard A.; and Nelson, Kim E. *Corrections in America.* Philadelphia: J. B. Lippincott Company, 1975.

———; McGee, Richard A.; and Nelson, Kim E. *The Challenge of Crime in a Free Society.* Washington, D.C.: U.S. Government Printing Office, 1967.

———, and Wilkins, Leslie T. *Probation and Parole: Selected Readings.* New York: John Wiley & Sons, 1970.

Cartwright, Desmond S.; Tomson, Barbara; and Schwartz, Hershey. *Gang Delinquency.* Belmont, Calif.: Wadsworth Publishing Company, 1975.

Cavan, Ruth Shonle. *Juvenile Delinquency: Development, Treatment, Control.* Philadelphia: J. B. Lippincott Company, 1962.

———. *Readings in Juvenile Delinquency.* Philadelphia: J. B. Lippincott Company, 1962.

———, and Ferdinand, Theodore N. *Juvenile Delinquency.* Philadelphia: J. B. Lippincott Company, 1975.

Chambliss, William J. "The Differential Selection of Juvenile Offenders for Court Appearance." *Crime and the Legal Process*. New York: McGraw-Hill, 1969. Pp. 264–290.

Charlton, T. J. "Juvenile Reformatories of the United States." In *The Reformatory System in the United States,* edited by S. J. Barrows. Washington, D.C.: U.S. Government Printing Office, 1900.

Cheatwood, Derral A. "The Staff in Correctional Settings—An Empirical Investigation of Frying Pans and Fires." *Journal of Research in Crime and Delinquency* 11 (1974): 173–179.

Children's Bureau. *Eighty-five Juvenile Court Statistics*. Children's Bureau Statistical Series. Washington, D.C.: U.S. Government Printing Office, 1965.

Chilton, Roland J. "Middle-Class Delinquency and Specific Offense Analysis." In *Middle-Class Juvenile Delinquency,* edited by Edmund Vaz. New York: Harper & Row, 1967.

Cirourel, Aaron V. *The Social Organization of Juvenile Justice*. New York: John Wiley & Sons, 1968.

Clemmer, Donald. *The Prison Community*. New York: Holt, Rinehart and Winston, 1958.

Cloward, Richard, et al. *Theoretical Studies in Social Organization of the Prison*. New York: Social Science Research Council, 1960.

————, and Ohlin, Lloyd E. *Delinquency and Opportunity: A Theory of Delinquent Gangs*. New York: Free Press, 1960.

Coates, Robert B., et al. "Exploratory Analysis of Recidivism and Cohort Data on the Massachusetts Youth Correctional System." Cambridge, Mass.: Center for Criminal Justice, Harvard Law School, 1975.

Coffey, Alan R. *Correctional Administration: The Management of Probation, Institutions and Parole*. Englewood Cliffs, N.J.: Prentice-Hall, 1975.

————. *Juvenile Corrections: Treatment and Rehabilitation*. Englewood Cliffs, N.J.: Prentice-Hall, 1975.

Cohen, Albert K. *Delinquent Boys: The Culture of the Gang*. New York: Free Press, 1955.

————. "Middle-Class Delinquency and the Social Structure." In *Middle-Class Juvenile Delinquency,* edited by Edmund Vaz. New York: Harper & Row, 1967.

Cole, Larry. *Our Children's Keepers: Inside America's Kid Prisons*. New York: Grossman Publishers, 1972.

Coleman, James S. "Athletics in High School." In *Middle-Class Juvenile Delinquency,* edited by Edmund Vaz. New York: Harper & Row, 1967.

Collins, Craig. "Youth Gangs of the 70s." *Police Chief* 42 (September 1975): 50–54.

Columbia Law Review. "Note: Rights and Rehabilitation in the Juvenile Court." In *The Juvenile Justice Philosophy: Readings, Cases and Comments,* edited by Frederic L. Faust and Paul J. Brantingham. St. Paul, Minn.: West Publishing Company, 1974.

"Community Treatment Project." Research Report No. 5. Sacramento: California Youth Authority, February 1964.

Conrad, John P. "Looking toward the Year 2000: The Role of Correctional Research." In *Contemporary Corrections: A Concept in Search of Content,* edited by Benjamin Frank. Reston, Va.: Reston Publishing Company, 1973.

―――. "We Should Never Have Promised a Hospital." *Federal Probation* 39 (December 1975).

Corrections Magazine 1 (September 1974). *Corrections Magazine* 3 (March 1977).

Craig, Maude M., and Glick, Selma J. "Ten Years' Experience with the Glueck Social Prediction Tables." In *The Sociology of Punishment and Correction,* edited by Norman Johnston, Leonard Savitz, and Martin E. Wolfgang. New York: John Wiley & Sons, 1970. Pp. 781–790.

Cressey, Donald R. "Sources of Resistance to Innovation in Corrections." In *Correctional Institutions,* edited by Robert M. Carter, Daniel Glaser, and Leslie T. Williams. Philadelphia: J. B. Lippincott Company, 1972. Pp. 438–460.

―――. *The Prison: Studies in Institutional Organization and Change.* New York: Holt, Rinehart and Winston, 1966.

―――, and Krassowski, Withold. "Inmate Organization and Anomie in American Prisons and Soviet Labor Camps." *Social Problems* 5 (Winter 1957): 217–230.

―――, and Ward, David A. *Delinquency, Crime and Social Process.* New York: Harper & Row, 1969.

Critfield, B. E. "The Interstate Parole and Probation Compact." In *Sourcebook on Probation, Parole and Pardons,* edited by Charles Newman. Springfield, Ill.: Charles C Thomas, 1954. Pp. 351–358.

Dahrendorf, Ralf. *Class and Class Conflict in Industrial Society.* Stanford: Stanford University Press, 1959.

―――. "Out of Utopia: Toward a Reorientation in Sociological Analysis." *American Journal of Sociology* 67 (September 1958): 115–127.

Davis, Alan J. "Sexual Assaults in the Philadelphia Prison System and Sheriff's Vans." *Trans-action* 6 (December 1968): 9–17.

Deutsch, Albert. "A Journalist's Impressions of State Training Schools." *Focus* 28 (March 1949): 33–40.

―――. *Our Rejected Children.* Boston: Little, Brown and Company, 1950.

Deutsch, Morton, and Krauss, Robert M. *Theories in Social Psychology.* New York: Basic Books, 1965.

Dicerbo, Eugene. "Probation Revocation." In *Sourcebook on Probation, Parole and Pardons,* edited by Charles Newman. Springfield, Ill.: Charles C Thomas, 1968. Pp. 132–145.

Dinitz, Simon; Miller, Stuart J.; and Bartollas, Clemens. "Inmate Exploitation: A Study of the Juvenile Victim." In *Exploiters and Exploited: The Dynamics of Victimization,* edited by Viano and Drapkin. Lexington, Mass.: D. C. Heath and Company, 1974.

Dressler, David. *Practice and Theory of Probation and Parole.* New York: Columbia University Press, 1969.

Dubin, Robert. "Deviant Behavior and Social Structure: Continuities in Social Theory." *American Sociological Review* 24 (April 1959): 147–164.

Duffee, David, and Siegel, Larry. "The Organization Man: Legal Counsel in the Juvenile Court." In *Juvenile Justice Philosophy: Readings, Cases and Comments,* edited by Frederic L. Faust and Paul J. Brantingham. St. Paul, Minn.: West Publishing Company, 1974.

Dunham, Warren H. "The Juvenile Court: Contradictory Orientations in Processing Offenders." *Law and Contemporary Problems* 23 (Summer 1958): 508–527.

Dyson, Frank. "School-Community Guidance Center." In *Police Programs for Preventing Crime and Delinquency,* edited by Dan G. Pursuit et al. Springfield, Ill.: Charles C Thomas, 1972.

Eldefonso, Edward. *Law Enforcement and the Youthful Offender.* 2d ed. New York: John Wiley & Sons, 1973.

———, and Coffey, Alan R. *Process and Impact of the Juvenile Justice System.* Beverly Hills, Calif.: Glencoe Press, 1976.

———, and Hartinger, Edward. *Control, Treatment, and Rehabilitation of Juvenile Offenders.* Beverly Hills, Calif.: Glencoe Press, 1976.

Ellenberger, Henri. "Relations Psychologiques entre le Criminal et la Victime." *Review Internationale de Criminologie and de Police Technique* 2 (April/June, 1954).

Elliott, Delbert S. "Delinquency, School Attendance and Dropout." In *Prevention of Delinquency: Problems and Programs,* edited by John R. Stratton and Robert M. Terry. New York: Macmillan, 1968.

———. "The Prevention of Delinquency through Youth Development: Strategy and Project Evaluation." Cited in Center for Action Research Document 34. Boulder: University of Colorado, Bureau of Sociological Research, February 1971.

Ellison, T. E. "The Indiana Prison System." In *The Reformatory System in the United States,* edited by S. J. Barrows. Washington, D.C.: U.S. Government Printing Office, 1900. Pp. 183–213.

Emerson, Robert M. *Judging Delinquents: Context and Process in the Juvenile Court.* Chicago: Aldine Publishing Company, 1969.

Empey, LaMar T. *Studies in Delinquency: Alternatives to Incarceration.* U.S. Department of Health, Education and Welfare, Office of Juvenile Delinquency and Youth Development, Publication No. 9–1. Washington, D.C.: U.S. Government Printing Office, 1967. Pp. 1–11.

———. "Contemporary Programs for Adjudicated Juvenile Offenders: Problems of Theory, Practice, and Research." In *Juvenile Justice Management,* edited by Adams et al. Springfield, Ill.: Charles C Thomas, 1973. Pp. 425–493.

———, and Erickson, Maynard L. "Hidden Delinquency and Social Status." *Social Forces* 44 (June 1966): 546–554.

———; and Scott, Max. "The Provo Experiment: Evaluation of a Community Program." *Correction in the Community: Alternatives to Incarceration.* Sacramento: California Department of Corrections, 1964.

————, and Lubeck, Steven G. *The Siverlake Experiment: Testing Delinquency Theory Intervention.* Chicago: Aldine Publishing Company, 1971.

————, and Newland, George E. "Staff-Inmate Collaboration." *Journal of Research in Crime and Delinquency* 5 (January 1968): 1–17.

————, and Rabow, Jerome. "The Provo Experiment in Delinquency Rehabilitation." *American Sociological Review* 26 (October 1961): 679–696.

England, Ralph W., Jr. "A Theory of Middle-Class Juvenile Delinquency." In *Middle-Class Juvenile Delinquency,* edited by Edmund Vaz. New York: Harper & Row, 1967.

————. "What is Responsible for Satisfactory Probation and Post-Probation Outcome?" *Journal of Criminal Law, Criminology and Police Science* 47 (1957).

Ennis, Phillip H. "Crime Victims and the Police." *Trans-action* 4 (June 1967): 36–44.

Erickson, Maynard L., and Empey, LaMar T. "Court Records, Undetected Delinquency and Decision-Making." *Journal of Criminal Law, Criminology and Police Science* 54 (December 1963): 456–469.

Escobedo v. *Illinois.* 378 U.S. 478, 1964.

Etzioni, Amitai. *A Comparative Analysis of Complex Organizations.* New York: Free Press, 1961.

————. *A Comparative Analysis of Complex Organizations: On Power, Involvement and Their Correlates.* New York: Free Press, 1975.

————. *Modern Organizations.* Englewood Cliffs, N.J.: Prentice-Hall, 1964.

Fannin, Leon F., and Clinard, Marshall B. "Differences in the Conception of Self as a Male among Lower-and Middle-Class Delinquents." In *Middle-Class Juvenile Delinquency,* edited by Edmund Vaz. New York: Harper & Row, 1967.

Faust, Frederic L. "A Perspective on the Dilemma of Free Will and Determinism in Juvenile Justice." *Juvenile Justice* 24 (May 1974): 54–60.

————, and Brantingham, Paul J. *Juvenile Justice Philosophy: Readings, Cases and Comments.* St. Paul, Minn.: West Publishing Company, 1974.

Felkenes, George T. *The Criminal Justice System: Its Functions and Personnel.* Englewood Cliffs, N.J.: Prentice-Hall, 1973.

Ferdinand, Theodore N., and Luchterhand, Elmer G. "Inner-City Youths, the Police, the Juvenile Court and Justice." *Social Problems* 17 (Spring 1970): 510–527.

Ferguson, Elizabeth A. *Social Work: An Introduction.* Philadelphia: J.B. Lippincott Company, 1963.

Fiedler, Fred. "Engineer the Job to Fit the Manager.": *Harvard Business Review* 44 (January/February 1965): 141–155.

Fisher, Sethard. "Social Organization in a Correctional Residence." *Pacific Sociological Review* 4 (Fall 1961): 87–93.

Flammang, C. J. *Police Juvenile Enforcement.* Springfield, Ill.: Charles C Thomas, 1972.

Folks, Homer. "Juvenile Probations." *NCCCC Proceedings* (1906). Pp. 117–122.

Forer, Lois G. *No One Will Listen: How Our Legal System Brutalizes the Youthful Poor.* New York: John Day, 1970.

Foster, Robert M. "Youth Service Systems: New Criteria." In *Closing Correctional Institutions,* edited by Yitzhak Bakal. Lexington, Mass.: D. C. Heath and Company, 1973. Pp. 33–37.

Fox, Vernon. *Introduction to Corrections.* Englewood Cliffs, N.J.: Prentice-Hall, 1972.

———. "Michigan's Experiment in Minimum Security Penology." *Journal of Criminal Law, Criminology and Police Science* 41 (July/August, 1950): 150–166.

Fox, Sanford F. *Juvenile Courts in a Nutshell.* St. Paul, Minn.: West Publishing Company, 1971.

Frank, Benjamin. *Contemporary Corrections: A Concept in Search of Content.* Reston, Va.: Reston Publishing Company, 1973.

French, W. "Organizational Development: Objectives, Assumptions and Strategies." *California Management Review* 12 (Winter 1969): 23–24.

Fromm, Eric. *Escape from Freedom.* New York: Holt, Rinehart and Winston, 1941.

Fry, Margery. *Arms of the Law.* London: Gallancz Press, 1951.

Gagon, John H., and Simon, William. "The Social Meaning of Prison Homosexuality." *Federal Probation* 32 (1968): 23–29.

Gain, Charles R. "Officer Friendly." In *Police Programs for Preventing Crime and Delinquency,* edited by Dan G. Pursuit et al. Springfield, Ill.: Charles C Thomas, 1972.

Garabedian, Peter G. *Becoming Delinquent: Young Offenders and the Correctional System.* Chicago: Aldine Publishing Company, 1970.

———. "Legitimate and Illegitimate Opportunities in the Prison Community." *Sociological Inquiry* 32 (Spring 1962): 172–184.

———. "Social Roles and Process of Socialization in the Prison Community." *Social Problems* 2 (Fall 1963): 139–152.

Garfinkel, Harold. "Conditions of Successful Degradation Ceremonies." *American Journal of Sociology* 61 (March 1956): 420–424.

Garmire, Bernard L. "Be a Good Guy." In *Police Programs for Preventing Crime and Delinquency,* edited by Dan G. Pursuit et al. Springfield, Ill.: Charles C Thomas, 1972.

Geis, Gilbert, and Woodson, Fred W. "Matching Probation Officer and Delinquent." *NPPA Journal* 2 (January 1956): 59–62.

Gelber, Seymour. "The Prosecutor in Juvenile Court—New Doors for the DA." *The Prosecutor* 2 (1975).

George, William R. *The Junior Republic.* New York: D. Appleton and Company, 1910.

Gemignani, Robert. "National Strategy for Youth Development and Delinquency Prevention." In Center for Action Research Document No. 34. Boulder: University of Colorado, Bureau of Sociological Research, October 1971.

Gerard, Roy. "Institutional Innovations in Juvenile Corrections." In *Penology: The Evolution of Corrections in America,* edited by George G. Killinger and Paul F. Cromwell, Jr. St. Paul, Minn.: West Publishing Company, 1973. Pp. 149–162. See also, *Federal Probation* 34 (December 1970).

Giallombardo, Rose. *Society of Women.* New York: John Wiley & Sons, 1966.

———. *The Social World of Imprisoned Girls.* New York: John Wiley & Sons, 1974.

Gibbons, Don C. *Changing the Law Breaker.* Englewood Cliffs, N.J.: Prentice-Hall, 1965.

———. *Delinquent Behavior.* Englewood Cliffs, N.J.: Prentice-Hall, 1970.

———. *Delinquent Behavior.* 2d ed. Englewood Cliffs, N.J.: Prentice-Hall, 1976.

———. "Differential Treatment of Delinquents and Interpersonal Maturity Level: A Critique." *Social Forces Review* 44 (1970): 22–33.

———. *Society, Crime, and Criminal Careers.* 2d ed. Englewood Cliffs, N.J.: Prentice-Hall, 1976.

———, and Blake, Gerald F. "Evaluating the Impact of Juvenile Diversion Programs." *Crime and Delinquency* 22 (October 1976). Pp. 411–420.

Gibbs, Jack P. "Conceptions of Deviant Behavior: The Old and the New." *Pacific Sociological Review* 9 (Spring 1966): 9–14.

Giordano, Peggy C. "The Sense of Injustice: An Analysis of Juveniles' Reactions to the Justice System." *Criminology* 14 (May 1976).

Glaser, Barney G., and Strauss, Anselm L. *The Discovery of Grounded Theory.* New York: Holt, Rinehart, and Winston, 1976.

Glaser, Daniel. "Five Practical Research Suggestions for Correctional Administrators." In *Correctional Institutions,* edited by Robert Carter, Daniel Glaser, and Leslie T. Wilkins. New York: J. B. Lippincott Company, 1972. Pp. 499–508.

———. *Gross Personal Characteristics and Parole Outcome.* New York: National Council on Crime and Delinquency, 1964.

———. *The Effectiveness of a Prison and Parole System.* Abridged ed. Indianapolis: Bobbs-Merrill Company, 1969.

———. "The Prison of the Future." In *Penology: The Evolution of Corrections in America,* edited by George G. Killinger and Paul F. Cromwell, Jr. St. Paul, Minn.: West Publishing Company, 1973.

Glasser, William. *Reality Therapy: A New Approach to Psychiatry.* New York: Harper & Row, 1965.

Glueck, Sheldon, and Glueck, Eleanor T. *Criminal Careers in Retrospect.* New York: Commonwealth Fund.

———, and Glueck, Eleanor T. *Unraveling Juvenile Delinquency.* Cambridge, Mass.: Harvard University Press, 1950.

Goffman, Erving. *Asylums.* Garden City, N.Y.: Doubleday Anchor, 1961.

———. "Characteristics of Total Institutions." In *Deviance: Studies in the Process of Stigmatization and Societal Reaction,* edited by Simon Dinitz, Russell Dynes, and Alfred Clarke. New York: Oxford University Press, 1967. Pp. 472–485.

Gold, Martin, and Reimer, David J. *Changing Patterns of Delinquent Behavior among Americans 13 to 16 Years Old, 1967–1972.* Ann Arbor: University of Michigan, Institute for Social Research, 1974.

Goldfarb, Ronald. *Jails: The Ultimate Ghetto.* Garden City, N.Y.: Doubleday Anchor, 1975.

———, and Singer, Linda. *After Conviction: A Review of the American Correctional System.* New York: Simon and Schuster, 1973.

Goldman, Nathan. *The Differential Selection of Juvenile Offenders for Court Appearance.* New York: National Council on Crime and Delinquency, 1963.

Gottfredson, Don M. "Assessment of Prediction Methods." In *The Sociology of Punishment and Corrections,* edited by Norman Johnston, Leonard Savitz, and Martin E. Wolfgang. 2d ed. New York: John Wiley & Sons, 1970. Pp. 745–771.

———. "The Base Expectancy Approach." In *The Sociology of Punishment and Corrections,* edited by Norman Johnston, Leonard Savitz, and Martin E. Wolfgang. 2d ed. New York: John Wiley & Sons, 1970. pp. 807–813.

Gough, A. R. "The Expungement of Adjudicatory Records of Juveniles and Adult Offenders: A Problem of Status." *Washington University Law Quarterly* 2 (April 1966): 147.

Gouldner, Alvin. *Patterns of Industrial Bureaucracy.* New York: Free Press, 1954.

Governor's Commission on Juvenile Justice, State of California, 1959.

Greco, Marshall C., and Wright, James C. "The Correctional Institution in the Etiology of Chronic Homosexuality." *American Journal of Orthopsychiatry* 14 (1944): 304–305.

Grosz, Hanus J.; Stern, Herbert; and Feldman, Edward. "A Study of Delinquent Girls Who Participated in and Who Abstained from Participating in a Riot." *American Journal of Psychiatry* 125 (April 1969): 1370–1379.

Grusky, Oscar. "Guided Steps." Columbus: Ohio Youth Commission, 1964.

———. "Organization Goals and the Behavior of Informal Leaders." *American Journal of Sociology* 62 (July 1959): 59–67.

———. "Role Conflict in Organization: A Study of Prison Camp Officials." *Administrative Science Quarterly* 3 (January/March 1958): 452–472.

Gula, Martin. *Agency Operated Group Homes.* Washington, D.C.: U.S. Government Printing Office, 1964.

———. "Community Services and Residential Institutions for Children." In *Closing Correctional Institutions,* edited by Yitzhak Bakal. Lexington, Mass.: D. C. Heath and Company, 1973. Pp. 13–18.

Guttman, Evelyn S. "Effects of Short-Term Psychiatric Treatment on Boys in Two California Youth Authority Institutions." Research Report No. 36. Processed. Sacramento: California Youth Authority, December 1963.

Hackler, James C. "Boys, Blisters, and Behavior—The Impact of a Work Program in an Urban Central Area." In *Prevention of Delinquency: Problems and Programs,* edited by John R. Stratton and Robert M. Terry. New York: Macmillan, 1968.

Hage, Jerald, and Aiken, Michael. *Social Change in Complex Organizations.* New York: Random House, 1970.

Hahn, Paul H. *The Juvenile Offender and the Law*. Cincinnati: W. H. Anderson Company, 1971.

Hall, Edward T. *The Hidden Dimension*. Garden City, N.Y.: Doubleday Anchor, 1969.

Halleck, Seymour L., and Hersko, Marvin. "Homosexual Behavior in a Correctional Institution for Adolescent Girls." *American Journal of Orthopsychiatry* 32 (1962): 911–917.

Hammer, Max. "Homosexuality in the Women's Prison." *Journal of Social Therapy* 11 (May 1965): 168–169.

Handler, Ellen. "Family Surrogates as Correctional Strategy." *Social Science Review* 48 (December 1974): 539–549.

Hardy, Richard C., and Cull, John G. *Fundamentals of Juvenile Criminal Behavior and Drug Abuse*. Springfield, Ill.: Charles C Thomas, 1975.

Harlaw, E.; Weber, R.; and Wilkins, L. T. "Community-based Correctional Programs." In *Issues in Corrections,* edited by Edward Eldefonso. Beverly Hills, Calif.: Glencoe, 1974.

Harris, Thomas A. *I'm OK—You're OK*. New York: Harper & Row, 1967.

Haskell, Martin R. and Yablonsky, Lewis. *Juvenile Delinquency*. Chicago: Rand-McNally College Publishing Company, 1970.

Haynes, F. E. "The Sociological Study of the Prison Community." *Journal of Criminal Law and Criminology* 39 (November/December 1948): 432–440.

Haynes, Norman S. "Parole Boards' Attitudes towards Predictive Devices." In *The Sociology of Punishment and Corrections,* edited by Norman Johnston, Leonard Savitz, and Martin E. Wolfgang. 2d ed. New York: John Wiley & Sons, 1970. Pp. 839–843.

———. "Washington State Correctional Institutions as Communities." *Social Forces* 21 (March 1943): 316–322.

Haynes, W. W.; Massie, J. L.; and Wallace, M., Jr. *Management: Analysis, Concepts and Cases*. 3d ed. Englewood Cliffs, N.J.: Prentice-Hall, 1975.

Hazelrigg, Lawrence E. "An Examination of the Accuracy and Relevance of Staff Perceptions of the Inmate in the Correctional Institution." *Journal of Criminal Law, Criminology and Police Science* 58 (June 1967): 204–220.

Healy, William, and Alper, Benedict S. *Criminal Youth and the Borstal System*. New York: Oxford University Press, 1941.

Heaps, Willard. *Juvenile Justice*. New York: Seabury Press, 1974.

Heffernan, Esther. *Making It in Prison: The Square, the Cool, and the Life*. New York: Wiley-Interscience Press, 1972.

Henderson, Charles Richmond. *Prison Reform*. Philadelphia: Fell Press, 1910.

Herzberg, F. P.; Mausner, J. L.; and Snyderman, B. *The Motivation to Work*. 2d ed. New York: John Wiley & Sons, 1959.

Hindelang, Michael J. "New Direction in Processing of Juvenile Offenders: The Denver Model." Washington, D.C.: U.S. Government Printing Office.

Hirschi, Travis. *Causes of Delinquency*. Berkeley: University of California Press, 1969.

Hirsh, Nathaniel. *Dynamic Causes of Juvenile Crime* (Cambridge, Mass.: Sci-Art Publisher, 1937).

Ho, Man Keung. "Current Trends and Practice in the Rehabilitation of Juvenile Delinquents." In *Fundamentals of Juvenile Criminal Behavior and Drug Abuse,* edited by Richard E. Hardy and John G. Cull. Springfield, Ill.: Charles C Thomas, 1975.

Hoffman-Bustamante, Dale. "The Nature of Female Criminality." *Issues in Criminology* 8 (Fall 1973): 117–136.

Hood, Roger G. "Research on the Effectiveness of Punishments and Treatments." In *Collected Studies in Criminological Research I.* Strasburg: Council of Europe, 1967.

———, and Sparks, Richard. *Key Issues in Criminology.* New York: McGraw-Hill, 1970.

Hopson, Dan, et al. *The Juvenile Offender and the Law.* New York: Da Capo Press, 1971.

Huffman, Arthur V. "Problems Precipitated by Homosexual Approaches on Youthful First Offenders." *Journal of Social Therapy* 7 (1961): 170–181.

Huse, Edgar F., and Bowditch, James L. *Behavior in Organizations: A Systems Approach to Managing.* Reading, Mass.: Addison-Wesley Publishing Company, 1973.

Hussey, Frederick. "Perspectives on Parole Decision-Making with Juveniles." *Criminology* 13 (1976).

Illinois Department of Corrections. "Management by Objectives Handbook." Springfield, Ill.: Illinois Department of Corrections.

In re Barbara Burns. 275, N.C. 517, 169 S.E. 2d, 879, 1969.

In re Gault. 387 U.S. 1 18 L Ed 3d 527, 87 S.Ct. 1428, 1967.

In re Winship. 397 U.S. 358, 90 S.Ct. 1968, 25 L Ed 368, 1970.

"Interstate Compact on Juveniles." In *Purden's Penna. Statutes Annotated: Title 62, Poor Persons and Public Welfare.* Philadelphia: George R. Bisel Company. Pp. 82–91.

Irwin, John. *The Felon.* Englewood Cliffs, N.J.: Prentice-Hall, 1970.

———, and Cressey, Donald R. "Thieves, Convicts and the Inmate Culture." *Social Problems* 10 (Fall 1962): 142–155.

Jacobs, Jane. "Violence in the City Streets." In *The Changing Metropolis,* edited by Federick J. Tietz and James E. McKeown. Boston: Houghton Mifflin Company, 1964.

Jacobson, Frank, and McGee, Eugene. "Englewood Project: Re-education: A Radical Correction of Incarcerated Delinquents." Mimeographed. Englewood, Col.: July 1965.

James, Howard. *Children in Trouble: A National Scandal.* New York: Pocket Books, Simon and Schuster, 1971.

"James Marshall Treatment Program, Progress Report." Processed. Sacramento: California Youth Authority, January 1967.

Jamison, Carolyn B.; Johnson, Bertram M.; and Guttman, Evelyn S. "An Analysis of Post-Discharge Criminal Behavior." Sacramento: California Youth Authority, 1966.

Jeffery, Ray. C. "Theoretical Structure of Crime Control." In *Juvenile Justice*

Philosophy: Readings, Cases and Comments, edited by Frederic L. Faust and Paul J. Brantingham. St. Paul, Minn.: West Publishing Company, 1974.

Jensen, Gary J., and Eve, Raymond. "Sex Differences in Delinquency: An Examination of Popular Sociological Explanations." *Criminology* 13 (February 1976): 427–448.

Jesness, Carl F. "The Fricot Ranch Study: Outcomes with Small versus Large Living Groups in the Rehabilitation of Delinquents." Research Report No. 47. Processed. Sacramento: California Youth Authority, October 1965.

————; DeRisi, William J.; McCormick, Paul M.; and Wedge, Robert F. *The Youth Center Research Project.* Sacramento: American Justice Institute, 1972.

————; Baca Joseph, C'de; McCormick, Paul M.; and Wedge, Robert F. *The Youth Center Research Project: Differential Treatment of Delinquents in Institutions.* Institute for the Study of Crimes and Delinquency, the National Institute of Mental Health, and the California Department of the Youth Authority, 1969.

John Augustus, First Probation Officer. Montclair, N.J.: Patterson-Smith Company, 1972.

Johnson, Bertram. "An Analysis of Predictions of Parole Performance and of Judgments of Supervision in the Parole Research Project." Research Report No. 32. Sacramento: California Youth Authority, 31 December 1962.

————. "Parole Performance of the First Year's Releasees, Parole Research Project: Evaluation of Reduced Caseloads." Research Report No. 27. Mimeographed. Sacramento: California Youth Authority, 31 January 1962.

Johnson, Daniel. "Designation of R-Suffix." Columbus: Ohio Youth Commission, March 1968. Chapter E-3.

Johnson, Elmer H. "Sociology of Confinement: Assimilation and the Prison Rat." *Journal of Criminal Law, Criminology and Police Science* 51 (January/February 1961): 528–533.

Johnson, Lois. "TA with Juvenile Delinquents," *Transactional Analysis Bulletin* 3 (1969).

Johnson, Thomas A. *Introduction to the Juvenile Justice System.* St. Paul, Minn.: West Publishing Company, 1975.

Jones, Maxwell. *Social Psychiatry in Practice.* Baltimore: Penguin Books, 1968.

Junker, Buford J. *Field Work: An Introduction to the Social Sciences.* Chicago: University of Chicago Press, 1960.

Jurjevich, Ratibor M. "Personality Changes Concomitant with Institutional Training of Delinquent Girls." *Journal of General Psychology* 74 (April 1966): 207–215.

Juvenile Justice Reform Act of 1976. State of New York.

Juvenile Probation and Detention. Sacramento: California Youth Authority, 1971.

Kadushin, Alfred. "Institutions for Dependent and Neglected Children." In *Child Caring: Social Policy and the Institution,* edited by Donnell M.

Pappenfort, Dee Morgan Kilpatrick, and Robert W. Roberts. Chicago: Aldine Publishing Company, 1973.

Kahn, Alfred J. "Public Policy and Delinquency Prediction." In *The Sociology of Punishment and Correction,* edited by Norman Johnston, Leonard Savitz, and Martin E. Wolfgang. 2d ed. New York: John Wiley & Sons, 1970. Pp. 791–800.

————. "Social Work and the Control of Delinquency." In *Delinquency and Social Policy,* edited by Paul Lerman. New York: Praeger Publishers, 1970. Pp. 422–427.

————; Kamerman, Sheila B.; and McGowan, Brenda G. *Child Advocacy: Report of a National Base Line Study.* New York: Child Advocacy Research Project, Columbia School of Social Work, 1972.

Kassebaum, Gene. *Delinquency and Social Policy.* Englewood Cliffs, N.J.: Prentice-Hall, Inc., 1974.

Katkin, Daniel; Hyman, Drew; and Kramer, John. *Juvenile Delinquency and the Juvenile Justice System.* North Scituate, Mass.: Duxbury Press, 1976.

Keller, Oliver J., Jr. and Alper, Benedict S. *Halfway Houses: Community-Centered Correction and Treatment.* Lexington, Mass.: D. C. Heath and Company, 1970.

Kenney, John P., and Pursuit, Daniel G. *Police Work with Juveniles.* Springfield, Ill.: Charles C Thomas, 1965.

Kent v. *United States.* 383 U.S. 541, 86 S.Ct. 1045, 16L Ed 2d 84, 1966.

Killinger, George G., and Cromwell, Paul F., Jr. *Corrections in the Community: Alternatives to Imprisonment, Selected Readings.* St. Paul, Minn.: West Publishing Company, 1974.

————, and Cromwell, Paul F., Jr. *Penology: The Evolution of Corrections in America.* St. Paul, Minn.: West Publishing Company, 1973.

Kilpatrick, Morgan Dee, Pappenfort, Donnel M., and Kuby, Alma M. *Institutions for Dependent and Neglected Children.* Vol. 1, 2, 3, 4, of A Census of Children's Residential Institutions in the United States, Puerto Rico, and the Virgin Islands: 1966, comp. Pappenfort and Kilpatrick, Social Service Monographs, 2nd No. 4, 7 volumes, Chicago: School of Social Science Adm., University of Chicago, 1970.

————. "Issues in Police Diversion of Juvenile Offenders: A Guide for Discussion," In *Juvenile Justice Management,* edited by Gary Adams, Robert Carter, John Gerletti, Dan Pursuit, and Percy Rogers, Springfield, Illinois: Charles C Thomas Publisher, 1973.

————. *Juvenile Gangs in Contect.* Englewood Cliffs: Prentice-Hall, 1967.

————. *The Juvenile Justice System.* Beverly Hills, California: Sage Publications, 1976.

————. "Some remarks on gangs," *Delinquency Prevention Report.* Washington, D.C., U.S. Department of Health, Education and Welfare, pp. 3–6, 1970.

Klapnuts, Nora. "Community Alternatives to Prison." In *A Nation without Prisons,* edited by Calvert R. Dodge. Lexington, Mass.: D. C. Heath and Company, 1975.

Klein, Malcolm W. "Issues in Police Diversion of Juvenile Offenders: A Guide for Discussion." In *Juvenile Justice Management,* edited by Adams et al. Springfield, Ill.: Charles C Thomas, 1973.

——. *Juvenile Gangs in Context.* Englewood Cliffs, N.J.: Prentice-Hall, 1967.

——. "Some Remarks on Gangs." *Delinquency Prevention Report.* Washington, D.C.: U.S. Department of Health, Education and Welfare, 1970. Pp. 3–6.

——. *The Juvenile Justice System.* Beverly Hills, Calif.: Sage Publications, 1976.

Klockards, Carl B., Jr. "A Theory of Probation Supervision." *Journal of Criminal Law, Criminology and Police Science* 53, no. 4, 1972.

Knudten, Richard D. *Crime in a Complex Society.* Homewood, Ill.: Dorsey Press, 1970.

Kobetz, Richard W. *The Police Role and Juvenile Delinquency.* Gaithersburg, Md.: International Association of Chiefs of Police, 1971.

——, and Bosarge, Betty B. *Juvenile Justice Administration.* Gaithersburg, Md.: International Association of Chiefs of Police, 1973.

Kobrin, Solomon. "The Chicago Area Project—A Twenty-five-Year Assessment." In *Prevention of Delinquency: Problems and Programs,* edited by John R. Stratton and Robert M. Terry. New York: Macmillan, 1968.

——. "The Conflict of Values in Delinquency Areas." *American Sociological Review* 16 (October 1951): 653–661.

Konopka, Gisela. "Institutional Treatment of Emotionally Disturbed Children." *Crime and Delinquency* 8 (January 1962): 52–57.

——. "The Social Group Work Method: Its Use in the Correctional Field." *Federal Probation* 20 (July 1956): 26–27.

Koontz, H., and O'Donnell, C. *Principles of Management.* New York: McGraw-Hill, 1968.

Kosofsky, Sidney, and Ellis, Albert. "Illegal Communication among Institutionalized Female Delinquents." *Journal of Social Psychology* 48 (August 1958): 155–160.

Krisberg, Barry. *Crime and Privilege: Toward a New Criminology.* Englewood Cliffs, N.J.: Prentice-Hall, 1975.

——. *Crime and Punishment.* Englewood Cliffs, N.J.: Prentice-Hall, 1974.

Kvaraceus, William and Miller, Walter B. "Norm-Violating Behavior in Middle-Class Culture." In *Middle-Class Juvenile Delinquency,* edited by Edmund Vaz. New York: Harper & Row, 1967.

Lackey, Wilford A. "Puppet for Moppets Solves Big Problem for Florida Police." In *Police Programs for Preventing Crime and Delinquency,* edited by Dan G. Pursuit et al. Springfield Ill.: Charles C Thomas, 1972. Pp. 356–361.

Laulicht, Jerome, et al. "A Study of Recidivism in One Training School: Implications for Rehabilitation Programs." *Berkshire Farm Monographs* 1 (1962): 11–22.

——, et al. "Recidivism and Its Correlates: The Problems of Statistical Research." *Berkshire Farm Monographs* 1 (1962): 23–36.

——, et al. "Selection Policies, Recidivism and Types of Rehabilitation Programs in a Training School." *Berkshire Farm Monographs* 1 (1962): 37–48.

Law Enforcement Assistance Administration. *Report of the Advisory Committee to the Administration on Standards for the Administration of Juvenile Justice.* Washington, D.C.: U.S. Government Printing Office (September 1976).

Lawrence, Paul R. and Lorsch, Jay W. *Organization and Environment: Managing Differentiation and Integration.* Cambridge, Mass.: Harvard Graduate School of Business Administration, 1967.

Lefstein, Norman; Stapleton, Vaughan; and Teitelbaum, Lee E. "In Search of Juvenile Justice—*Gault* and Its Implementation." In *Juvenile Justice Philosophy: Readings, Cases and Comments,* edited by Frederic L. Faust and Paul J. Brantingham. St. Paul, Minn.: West Publishing Company, 1974.

Lefton, Mark, and Rosengren, W. R. "Organizations and Clients: Lateral and Longitudinal Dimensions." *American Sociological Review* 31 (December 1966): 802–810.

Lemert, Edwin M. *Instead of Court: Diversion in Juvenile Justice.* Washington, D.C.: U.S. Government Printing Office, 1971.

———. "The Juvenile Court—Quest and Realities." In *Juvenile Delinquency and Youth Crime.*

———. *Social Pathology.* New York: McGraw-Hill, 1951.

Lerman, Paul. "Child Convicts." *Transaction* 8 (July /August 1971): 35–42.

———. *Community Treatment and Social Control: A Critical Analysis of Juvenile Correction Policy.* Chicago: University of Chicago Press, 1975.

———. *Delinquency and Social Policy.* New York: Praeger Publishers, 1970.

———. "Evaluative Studies of Institutions for Delinquents." *Social Work* 13 (July 1968).

Levinson, Robert B., and Kitchener, Howard L. "Demonstration Counseling Project." 2 vols. Mimeographed. Washington, D.C.: National Training School for Boys, 1962–1964.

———, and Kitchener, Howard L. "Treatment of Delinquents: Comparison of Four Methods for Assigning Inmates to Counselors." *Journal of Consulting Psychology* 30 (1966).

Lewis, Diana. "What Is Probation?" *Journal of Criminal Law, Criminology and Police Science* 51 (July/August 1960): 189–208.

Lewis, Orlando F. *The Development of American Prisons and Prison Customs, 1776–1845.* Montclair, N.J.: Patterson Smith, 1967.

Lipton, Douglas; Martinson, Robert; and Wilks, Judith. *The Effectiveness of Correctional Treatment: A Survey of Treatment Evaluation Studies.* New York: Praeger Publishers, 1975.

Lochman, J. D. *The Handling of Juveniles from Offense to Disposition.* Mimeographed. Washington, D.C.: U.S. Government Printing Office, 1963.

Lofland, John. *Deviance and Identity.* Englewood Cliffs, N.J.: Prentice-Hall, 1969.

Lohman, J. D. *The Handling of Juveniles from Offense to Disposition.* Original draft mimeograph. Washington, D.C.: U.S. Government Printing Office, 1963.

Loranger, R. L. "Drug Abuse Rehabilitative Training (DART) Program." In *Police Programs for Preventing Crime and Delinquency,* edited by Dan G. Pursuit et al. Springfield, Ill.: Charles C Thomas, 1972.

Lunden, Walter A. *Statistics on Delinquents and Delinquency.* Springfield, Ill.: Charles C Thomas, 1964.

Mabry, James. "Alternatives to Confinement." In *Penology: The Evolution of Corrections in America,* edited by George G. Killinger and Paul F. Cromwell, Jr. St. Paul, Minn.: West Publishing Company, 1973.

Machover, Karen. *Personality Projection in the Drawing of the Human Figure.* Springfield, Ill.: Charles C Thomas, 1949.

MacDonald, George J., et al. "Treatment of the Sex Offender." (Fort Steilbacoon, Wash.: Western State Hospital, 1968).

MacIver, Robert M. "Planning for the Prevention and Control of Delinquency." In *Delinquency and Social Policy,* edited by Paul Lerman. New York: Praeger Publishers, 1970. Pp. 443–446.

Mack, Julian W. "The Juvenile Court." In *Juvenile Justice Philosophy: Readings, Cases and Comments,* edited by Frederic L. Faust and Paul J. Brantingham. St. Paul, Minn.: West Publishing Company, 1974.

Maddox, George L., and McCall, Beverly C. "Patterns of Drinking and Abstinence." In *Middle-Class Juvenile Delinquency,* edited by Edmund Vaz. New York: Harper & Row, 1967.

Maher, B. and Stein, E. "The Delinquent's Perception of Law and the Community." In *Controlling Delinquents,* edited by Stanton Wheeler. New York: John Wiley and Sons, 1968.

"Management by Objectives Handbook" Illinois Department of Corrections, N.D.

Manella, Frank L. "Aftercare Programs." *NPPA Journal* 4 (January 1958): 74–80.

Mann, D. *Intervening with Convicted Serious Juvenile Offenders.* Santa Monica, Calif.: Rand Corporation, July 1976.

Mannheim, Hermann, and Wilkins, Leslie T. *Prediction Methods in Relation to Borstal Training.* London: Her Majesty's Stationery Office, 1955. Pp. 53, 65.

———, and Wilkins, Leslie T. "The Requirements of Prediction." In *The Sociology of Punishment and Correction,* edited by Norman Johnston, Leonard Savitz, and Martin E. Wolfgang. 2d ed. New York: John Wiley & Sons, 1970. Pp. 772–776.

Marks, Rachael B. "Institutions for Dependent and Delinquent Children: Histories, Nineteenth-Century Statistics and Recurrent Goals." In *Child Caring: Social Policy and the Institution,* edited by Donnel M. Pappenfort, Dee Morgan Kilpatrick, and Robert W. Roberts. Chicago: Aldine Publishing Company, 1973. Pp. 9–68.

Marris, Peter, and Reim, Martin. "Dilemmas of Social Reform." In *Delinquency and Social Policy,* edited by Paul Lerman. New York: Praeger Publishers, 1970. Pp. 465–482.

Martin, John M. "The Creation of a New Network of Services for Troublesome Youth." In *Closing Correctional Institutions,* edited by Yitzhak Bakal. Lexington, Mass.: D. C. Heath and Company, 1973. Pp. 1–12.

Martinson, Robert. "The Age of Treatment: Some Implications of the Custody-Treatment ·Dimension." In *Crisis in American Institutions,* edited by Jerome H. Skolnick and Elliott Currie. Boston: Little, Brown and Company, 1973. Pp. 463–483.

———, and Wilks, Judith. *Knowledge in Criminal Justice Planning.* New York: The Center for Knowledge in Criminal Justice, 1977.

Maslow, A. H. *Motivation and Personality.* New York: Harper and Brothers, 1954.

Mathiesen, Thomas. *Across the Boundaries of Organization.* Berkeley: Glendessory Press, 1971.

Matza, David. *Becoming Deviant.* Englewood Cliffs, N.J.: Prentice-Hall, 1969.

———. *Delinquency and Drift.* New York: John Wiley & Sons, 1964.

———, and Sykes, Gresham M. "Juvenile Delinquency and Subterranean Values." *American Sociological Review* 38 (October 1961): 712–719.

Mazur, Alan. "A Cross-Species Comparison of Status in Small Established Groups." *American Sociological Review* 38 (October 1973): 513–530.

McCleery, Richard. "Communication Patterns as Bases of Systems of Authority and Power." In *Theoretical Studies in Social Organization of the Prison,* edited by Cloward et al. New York: Social Science Research Council, 1960. Pp. 56–61.

———. "Policy Change in Prison Management." In *Complex Organizations: A Sociological Reader,* edited by Amitai Etzioni. New York: Holt, Rinehart and Winston, 1961. Pp. 376–400.

McConkie, Mark L. *Management by Objectives: A Corrections Perspective.* Washington, D.C.: U.S. Government Printing Office, 1975.

McCord, Joan; McCord, William; and Thurber, Emily. "The Effects of Foster-Home Placement in the Prevention of Adult Antisocial Behavior." In *Prevention of Delinquency: Problems and Programs,* edited by John K. Stratton and Robert M. Terry. New York: Macmillan, 1968.

McCord, William and McCord, Joan. "Two Approaches to the Cure of Delinquents." *Journal of Criminal Law, Criminology and Police Science* 44 (May 1953): 442–467.

McCorkle, Lloyd W. "Social Structure in a Prison." *Welfare Reporter* 8 (December 1956): 5–15.

———; Elias, Albert; and Bixby, Lovell F. *The Highfields Story: An Experimental Treatment Program for Youthful Offenders.* New York: Henry Holt, 1958.

———, and Korn, Richard. "Resocialization within Walls." *Annals of the American Academy of Political and Social Science* 293 (May 1954): 88–98.

McEachern, A. W. and Bauzer, Riva. "Factors Related in Disposition in Juvenile Police Contacts," in *Juvenile Gangs in Context,* edited by Malcolm W. Klein. Englewood Cliffs, N.J.: Prentice-Hall.

McGregor, Douglas. *The Human Side of Enterprise.* New York: McGraw-Hill Book Company, 1960.

McKeiver v. *Pennsylvania.* 403 U.S. 528, 535, 1971.

Mempa v. *Rhay,* 389 U.S. 128 (1967).

Mendelsohn, B. "The Origin of Victimology." *Excerpta Criminologica* 3 (May/June 1963): 239–241.

Mennel, Robert M. *Social Theory and Social Structure.* London: Free Press of Glencoe, 1957.

——. *Thorns and Thistles: Juvenile Delinquents in the United States.* Hanover, N.H.: University Press of New England, 1973.

Merton, Robert K. *Social Theory and Social Structure,* 2d ed. New York: Free Press, 1957.

—— ; Broom, Leonard; and Cottrell, Leonard, Jr. "The Study of Social Disorganization and Deviant Behavior." In *Sociology Today,* edited by Robert Merton, Leonard Broom, and Leonard Cottrell, Jr. New York: Basic Books, 1959.

Miller, Jerome G. "The Politics of Change: Correctional Reform." In *Closing Correctional Institutions,* edited by Yitzhak Bakal. Lexington, Mass.: D. C. Heath and Company, 1973. Pp. 3–8.

Miller, Stuart J. "Post-Institutional Adjustment of 443 Consecutive TICO Releases." Ph.D. dissertation, Ohio State University, 1971.

——; Bartollas, Clemens; Jenifer, Donald; Redd, Edward; and Dinitz, Simon. "Games Inmates Play: Notes on Staff Victimization." In *Exploiters and Exploited: The Dynamics of Victimization,* edited by Emilio Viano and Israel Drapkin. Lexington, Mass.: D. C. Heath and Company, 1975.

——; Bartollas, Clemens; Roberts, James; and Dinitz, Simon. "The Heavy and Social Control." *Sociological Research Symposium.* Vol. 4. Richmond: Virginia Commonwealth University, 1974.

——, and Dinitz, Simon. "Measuring Institutional Impact: A Followup." *Criminology* 11 (November 1973): 417–418.

——, and Dinitz, Simon. "Measuring Perceptions of Organization Changes." *Journal of Research in Crime and Delinquency* 11 (July 1974): 180–194.

——, and Dinitz, Simon. "Measuring Staff Officers' Perceptions of Institutions' Impact and Predictions of Success on Parole." Paper presented to the Inter-American Association of Criminology and the American Society of Criminology, Caracas, Venezuela, 1972.

Miller, Walter B. "Adolescent Culture and Drug Use," *Proceedings of International Seminar, Sociocultural Factors in Nonmedical Drug Use,* Institute of Criminal Justice and Criminology, University of Maryland, College Park, Md. (3-5 November, 1975), pp. 59–69.

——. "Inter-Institutional Conflict as a Major Impediment to Delinquency Prevention." In *Juvenile Delinquency: A Book of Readings,* edited by Rose Giallombardo. New York: John Wiley & Sons, 1966. Pp. 559–565.

——. "Lower Class Culture as a Generating Milieu of Gang Delinquency." *Journal of Social Issues* 14 (Summer 1958): 5–19.

——. *Operating Philosophies of Criminal Justice and Youth Service Professionals in Twelve Major Cities.* Cambridge, Mass.: Center for Criminal Justice, Harvard Law School.

——. "Violence by Youth Gangs and Youth Groups as a Crime Problem in

Major American Cities." Washington, D.C.: U.S. Government Printing Office, August 1975.

Miranda v. *Arizona.* 384 U.S. 436, 1966.

Mitchell, B. F. "Recruiting Ideas That Get Results." *Public Personnel Association* (Chicago, N.D.).

Moos, Robert. "The Assessment of the Social Climates of Correctional Institutions." *Journal of Research in Crime and Delinquency* 5 (July 1968): 174–188.

———. "Differential Effects of the Social Climates of Correctional Institutions." *Journal of Research in Crime and Delinquency* 7 (January 1970): 71–82.

Morales v. *Thurman,* 364 F. Supp. 166 (E.D. Tex. 1973).

Morris, Norval. "Impediments to Penal Reform." In *Correctional Institutions,* edited by Robert M. Carter, Daniel Glaser, and Leslie T. Wilkins. Philadelphia: J. B. Lippincott Company, 1972. Pp. 461–487.

Morris, Terrence; Morris, Pauline; and Beily, Barbara. "It's the Prisoners Who Run this Prison." *Prison Service Review* 3 (January 1961): 3–11.

Morrisey, George L. *Management by Objectives and Results.* Reading, Mass.: Addison-Wesley Publishing Company, 1970.

Mosier, Craig Horlan. "Delinquents' Perceptions of Institutional Impact." Ph.D. dissertation. Ohio State University, 1972.

Mouledous, Joseph C. "Organizational Goals and Structure Change: A Study of the Organization of a Prison Social System." *Social Forces* 41 (March 1963): 283–290.

Murphy, Fred J.; Shirley, Mary M.; and Witmer, Helen L. "The Incidence of Hidden Delinquency." *American Journal of Orthopsychiatry* 16 (October 1946): 686–696.

Murphy, Patrick T. *Our Kindly Parent—The State.* New York: Viking Press, 1974.

Murphy, Patrick V. "New York's Diversified Youth Program." In *Police Programs for Preventing Crime and Delinquency,* edited by Dan G. Pursuit et al. Springfield, Ill.: Charles C Thomas, 1972. Pp. 174–181.

Murray v. *Page,* 429 F. 2d 1359 (10th Cir. 1970).

Myerhoff, Howard L., and Myerhoff, Barbara G. "Field Observations of Middle Class Gangs." In *Middle-Class Juvenile Delinquency,* edited by Edmund Vaz. New York: Harper & Row, 1967.

Narlock, R. P.; Adams, Stuart; and Jenkins, Kendall J. "Characteristics and Parole Performance of California Youth Authority Early Releases." Research Report No. 7. Mimeographed. Sacramento: California Youth Authority, June 1959.

National Advisory Commission on Criminal Justice Standards and Goals. *Corrections.* Washington, D.C.: U.S. Government Printing Office, 1973. Pp. 389–436.

National Council on Crime and Delinquency. "Corrections in the United States." *Crime and Delinquency* 13 (January 1967).

———. "Jurisdiction over Status Offenses Should Be Removed from the Juvenile Court." *Crime and Delinquency* 21 (April 1975).

————. "Washington, D.C.: Juvenile Detention Needs." New York: NCCD, 1970.

"National Survey on the Value of Rehabilitation Programs," *Corrections* 1 (May–June 1975).

"National Victimization Survey Finds No Increase in Violent Street Crimes from 1973 to 1974." *Criminal Justice Newsletter* 7, no. 12.

NCCD News 50 (1971).

Neese, Robert. *Prison Exposure*. Philadelphia: Chilton, 1959.

Newman, Charles. *Sourcebook on Probation: Parole and Pardons*. Springfield, Ill.: Charles C Thomas, 1972.

Newman, Oscar. *Defensible Space*. New York: Macmillan, 1972.

New York State Department of Correction, Division of Parole. "Parole Adjustment and Prison Education Achievement of Male Adolescent Offenders, June 1957–June 1961." Mimeographed. September 1964.

Nold, Joseph, and Wilpers, Mary. "Wilderness Training as an Alternative to Incarceration." In Dodge, *A Nation without Prisons*. Lexington, Mass.: D. C. Heath and Company, 1975.

Norman, Sherwood. *The Youth Service Bureau: A Brief Description of Five Programs*. Paramus, N.J.: National Council on Crime and Delinquency, 1970.

————. *The Youth Service Bureau: A Key to Delinquency Prevention*. Paramus, N.J.: National Council on Crime and Delinquency, 1972.

Novick, Abraham G. "Institutional Diversification and Continuity of Service for Corrected Juveniles." *Federal Probation* 28 (March 1964): 40–47.

Nuernberger, Wilfred W., and Van Duizlend, Richard. "Development of Standards for Juvenile Justice: An Overview." *Juvenile Justice* 28 (February 1977): 3–6.

Ney, F. Ivan, and Short, James F., Jr. "Reported Behavior as a Criterion of Deviant Behavior." *Social Problems* 5 (Winter 1958): 207–213.

————; Short, James F.; and Olson, Virgil J. "Socioeconomic Status and Delinquent Behavior." In *Middle-Class Juvenile Delinquency,* edited by Edmund Vaz. New York: Harper & Row, 1967.

"Officials Say Juvenile System Works." *Corrections* 1 (June 1975).

Ohlin, Lloyd E. "Institutions for Predelinquent or Delinquent Children." In *Child Caring: Social Policy and the Institution,* edited by Donnel M. Pappenfort, Dee Morgan Kilpatrick, and Robert W. Roberts. Chicago: Aldine Publishing Company, 1973.

————. "The Reduction of Role Conflict in Institutional Staff." In *Prison within Society,* edited by Lawrence Hazelrigg. Garden City, N.Y.: Andover Books, 1969. Pp. 497–508.

————; Coates, Robert B.; and Miller, Alden D. "The Rights of Children." *Harvard Education Review* 44, Special Issue, Part II, The Rights of Children (February 1974).

————, and Laurence, William C. "Social Interaction among Clients as a Treatment Problem." *Social Work* 4 (April 1959): 3–14.

————; Miller, Alden D.; and Coates, Robert B. *A Preliminary Report of the*

Center for Criminal Justice of the Harvard Law School. Washington, D.C.: U.S. Government Printing Office, N.D.

————, et al. "Major Dilemmas of the Social Worker in Probation and Parole." *National Probation and Parole Association Journal,* 2, 1956. Pp. 211–225.

O'Leary, Vincent, and Duffy, David. "Correctional Policy: A Classification of Goals Designed for Change." *Crime and Delinquency* 16 and 17 (October 1971), pp. 377–385.

Ohmart, H. "The Challenge of Crime in a Free Society." *Youth Authority Quarterly* 21 (Fall 1968).

Palmieri, Henry J. "Private Institutions." *NPPA Journal* 4 (January 1958): 51–56.

Pappenfort, Donnel M.; Kilpatrick, Dee Morgan; and Roberts, Robert W., eds. *Child Caring: Social Policy and the Institutuion.* Chicago: Aldine Publishing Company, 1973.

People ex rel. v. *Warden Greenhaven,* 318 N.Y.S. 2d 449 (1971).

Persons, Roy W. "Psychological and Behavioral Change in Delinquents Following Psychotherapy." *Journal of Clinical Psychology* 22 (1966): 337–340.

————. "Psychotherapy with Sociopathic Offenders: An Empirical Evaluation." *Journal of Clinical Psychology* 21 (1965): 205–207.

————. "Relationship between Psychotherapy with Boys and Subsequent Community Adjustment." *Journal of Consulting Psychology* 31 (1967): 137–141.

————, and Pepinsky, Harold B. "Convergence in Psychotherapy with Delinquent Boys." *Journal of Counseling Psychology* 13 (1966): 319–324.

Perrow, Charles. "Reality Shock: A New Orientation Confronts the Custody Treatment Dilemma." *Social Problems* 10 (Spring 1963): 374–382.

Pettit, M. L. and Holmberg, B. K. "Let's Put It All Together: An Integrated Approach to Criminal Law and Justice." *Journal of Police Science and Administration* 1 (March 1973).

Phase I Assessment of Youth Service Bureaus. Summary Report of Youth Service Bureau Research Group for LEAA. Boston: Boston University, 1975.

Phelps, Thomas R. *Juvenile Delinquency: A Contemporary View.* Pacific Palisades, Calif.: Goodyear Publishing Company, 1976.

Piliavin, Irving, and Briar, Scott. "Police Encounters with Juveniles." *American Journal of Sociology* 70 (September 1964): 206–214.

Pink, William T., and White, Mervin F. "Delinquency Prevention: The State of the Art." In *The Juvenile Justice System,* edited by Malcolm W. Klein. Beverly Hills, Calif.: Sage Publications, 1976.

Pitchers, Peter T. "School-Related Police Program." In *Police Programs for Preventing Crime and Delinquency,* edited by Dan G. Pursuit et al. Springfield, Ill.: Charles C Thomas, 1972. Pp. 316–321.

Platt, Anthony M. *The Child Savers.* Chicago: University of Chicago Press, 1969.

————. "The Rise of the Child-Saving Movement: A Study in Social Policy and

Correctional Reform." *Annals of the American Academy of Political and Social Science* 381 (January 1969): 21–38.

———. "The Rise of the Child-Saving Movement: A Study in Social Policy and Correctional Reform." In *Juvenile Justice Philosophy: Readings, Cases and Comments,* edited by Frederic L. Faust and Paul J. Brantingham. St. Paul, Minn.: West Publishing Company, 1974.

Police Services for Juveniles. Children's Bureau Publication No. 344. Washington, D.C.: U.S. Government Printing Office, 1954.

Polier, Justice. "The Future of the Juvenile Court." *Juvenile Justice* 26 (May 1975): 3–10.

Polsky, Howard. "Changing Delinquent Subculture: A Social Psychological Approach." *Social Work* 4 (October 1959): 3–16.

———. *Cottage Six: The Social System of Delinquent Boys in Residential Treatment.* New York: Russell Sage Foundation, 1962.

———, and Closter, Daniel S. *The Dynamics of Residential Treatment.* Chapel Hill: University of North Carolina Press, 1968.

Porterfield, Austin. *Youth in Trouble.* Fort Worth: Leo Potishman Foundation, 1946.

Portune, Robert. *Changing Adolescent Attitudes toward Police.* Cincinnati: W. H. Anderson Company, 1971.

Pound, Roscoe. "The Juvenile Court and the Law." *National Probation and Parole Association Yearbook* 1 (1944).

President's Commission on Law Enforcement and the Administration of Justice. *Task Force Report: Corrections.* Washington, D.C.: U.S. Government Printing Office, 1967.

———. *Task Force Report: The Challenge of Crime in a Free Society.* Washington, D.C.: U.S. Government Printing Office.

———. *Task Force Report: Juvenile Delinquency and Youth Crime.* Washington, D.C.: U.S. Government Printing Office, 1967.

"Profile of OYC Institutional Population and Youth Leader Staff." Mimeographed. Columbus: Ohio Youth Commission, 1974.

Purdons, *Pennsylvania Statutes Annotated* 62 PS. Paragraph 731, 1968, p. 82.

Pursuit, Dan G.; Gerletti, John D.; Brown, Robert M., Jr.; and Ward, Steven M. *Police Programs for Preventing Crime and Delinquency.* Springfield, Ill.: Charles C Thomas, 1972.

Quinney, Richard. *Criminology: Analysis and Critique of Crime in America.* Boston: Little, Brown and Company, 1975.

———. *The Social Reality of Crime.* Boston: Little, Brown and Company, 1970.

Robey, Ames; Rosenwald, Richard J; Snell, John E., and Lee, Rita E. "The Runaway Girl: A Reaction to Family Stress." *American Journal of Orthopsychiatry* 34 (1974): 762–767.

Reckless, Walter C., and Dinitz, Simon. *The Prevention of Juvenile Delinquency.* Columbus: Ohio University Press, 1972.

———; Dinitz, Simon; and Murray, Ellen. "Self-Concept as an Insular against

Delinquency." *American Sociological Review* 21 (December 1956): 744–756.

————, and Smith, Mapheus. *Juvenile Delinquency*. New York: McGraw-Hill, 1932.

Reed, Amos F., and Hinsey, Cecil W. "A Demonstration Project for Defective Delinquents." *Crime and Delinquency* 11 (1965): 375–383.

Reiss, Ira L. "Sexual Codes in Teen-age Culture." In *Middle-Class Juvenile Delinquency*, edited by Edmund Vaz. New York: Harper & Row, 1967.

Rendleman, Douglas R. "Parens Patriae: From Chancery to the Juvenile Court." In *Juvenile Justice Philosophy: Readings, Cases and Comments*, edited by Frederic L. Faust and Paul J. Brantingham. St. Paul, Minn.: West Publishing Company, 1974.

Renn, Donna E. "The Right to Treatment and the Juvenile." *Crime and Delinquency* 14 (October 1973): 477–484.

"Report Urges Radical Changes in Dealing with Young Criminals." *New York Times*, 30 November 1975, p. 149.

Reuterman, Nicholas A. *A National Survey of Juvenile Detention Facilities*. Edwardsville, Ill.: Southern Illinois University, Delinquency Study and Youth Development Project, February 1970.

Richette, Lisa Aversa. *The Throwaway Children*. New York: J. B. Lippincott Company, 1969.

Robinson, James, and Smith, Gerald. "The Effectiveness of Correctional Programs." *Crime and Delinquency* 15 (January 1969): 67–80.

Robinson, Sophia M. *Juvenile Delinquency: Its Nature and Control*. New York: Henry Holt and Company, 1960.

Roethlisberger, J., and Dickson, W.J. *Management and the Worker: An Account of a Research Program Conducted by the Western Electric Company, Hawthorn Works, Chicago, Illinois*. Cambridge, Mass.: Harvard University Press, 1939.

Roos, Robert, and Ellison, Terri. "The Mentally Ill Juvenile Offender: Crisis for Law and Society." *Juvenile Justice* 27 (February 1976): 25.

Rose, Arnold M., and Wilson, George H. "Change in Attitudes among Delinquent Boys Committed to Open and Closed Institutions." *Journal of Criminal Law, Criminology and Police Science* 52 (August): 166–177.

Rose, Gordon. "Status and Groupings in a Borstal Institution." *British Journal of Delinquency* 9 (April 1959): 258–273.

Rosenheim, Margaret K. "Detention Facilities and Temporary Shelters." In *Child Caring: Social Policy and the Institution*, edited by Donnell M. Pappenfort, Dee Morgan Kilpatrick, and Robert W. Roberts. Chicago: Aldine Publishing Company. Pp. 252–303.

Ross, Sid and Kupferberg, Herbert. "Shut Down Reform School?" *Parade* (September 1972).

Roth, Loren J. "Territoriality and Homosexuality in a Male Prison Population." *American Journal of Orthopsychiatry* 41 (April 1971): 510–513.

Rothman, David J. *The Discovery of the Asylum*. Boston: Little, Brown and Company, 1971.

Rubin, Ted, and Smith, Jack F. *The Future of the Juvenile Court: Implications for Correctional Manpower and Training.* College Park, Md.: American Correctional Association, 1971.

Rubin, H. Ted. "The Eye of the Juvenile Court Judge: A One-Step-Up View of the Juvenile Justice System." In *The Juvenile Justice System.* Edited by Malcolm Klein. Beverly Hills, Calif.: Sage Publications, 1976.

Rushing, William A. "Organizational Rules and Surveillance: Propositions in Comparative Organizational Analysis." *Administrative Science Quarterly* 10 (March 1966): 423–443.

Rutherford, Andrew. "The Dissolution of the Training Schools in Massachusetts." Columbus: Academy for Contemporary Problems, 1974.

———, and Bengur, Osman. "Community-Based Alternatives to Juvenile Incarceration." Law Enforcement Assistance Administration Phase I Report. Washington, D.C.: U.S. Government Printing Office, N.D.

———, and McDermott, Robert. *National Evaluation Program Phase I Summary Report: Juvenile Diversion.* Washington, D.C.: U.S. Government Printing Office (September 1976).

Rutherford, James W. "Police-School Cadet Program." In *Police Programs for Preventing Crime and Delinquency,* edited by Dan G. Pursuit et al. Springfield, Ill.: Charles C Thomas, 1972. Pp. 322–325.

Saleebey, George. "Hidden Closets." Special Edition. Sacramento: California Youth Authority, February 1976.

Salisburg, Harrison E. "The Suburbs." In *Middle-Class Juvenile Delinquency,* edited by Edmund Vaz. New York: Harper & Row, 1967.

Sanders, Wiley B. "Some Early Beginnings of the Children's Court Movement." In *Juvenile Justice Philosophy: Readings, Cases, and Comments,* edited by Frederic L. Faust and Paul J. Brantingham. St. Paul, Minn.: West Publishing Company, 1974.

Sarri, Rosemary C. "The Detention of Youth in Jails and Detention Facilities." *Juvenile Justice* 24 (November 1973): 2–18,

———. *Under Lock and Key: Juveniles in Jails and Detention.* Ann Arbor: University of Michigan, National Assessment of Juvenile Corrections, 1974.

———, and Vinter, Robert O. "Justice for Whom? Varieties of Juvenile Correctional Approaches." In *The Juvenile Justice System,* edited by Malcolm W. Klein. Beverly Hills, Calif.: Sage Publications, 1976. Pp. 161–200.

Sayles, L. *Managerial Behavior.* New York: McGraw-Hill, 1964.

Scarpitti, Frank F. and Stephenson, Richard M. "A Study of Probation Effectiveness," *Journal of Criminal Law, Criminology and Police Science* 59, 3 (1968): 361–369.

Schafer, Stephen. *The Victim and His Criminal.* New York: Random House, 1968.

———. *Theories in Criminology: Past and Present Philosophies of the Crime Problem.* New York: Random House, 1969.

Scheier, Ivan H. and Berry, Judith A. *Serving Youth as Volunteers.* Boulder, Colo.: National Information Center on Volunteers in Courts (February 1972).

Schrag, Clarence. "Elements of Theoretical Analysis in Sociology." In *Sociological Theory: Inquiries and Paradigms,* edited by Llewellyn Gross. New York: Harper & Row, 1967.

———. "Leadership among Prison Inmates." *American Sociological Review* 19 (February 1954): 37–42.

Schramm, Gustav L. "The Juvenile Court Idea." In *Juvenile Justice Philosophy: Readings, Cases and Comments,* edited by Frederic L. Faust and Paul J. Brantingham. St. Paul, Minn.: West Publishing Company, 1974.

Schulberg, Herbert C. "From Institutions to Human Service." In *Closing Correctional Institutions,* edited by Yitzhak Bakal. Lexington, Mass.: D. C. Heath and Company, 1973. Pp. 39–47.

Schultz, Leroy G. "The Victim-Offender Relationship." *Crime and Delinquency* 14 (April 1968): 135–141.

Schulze, Suzanne. *Creative Group Living in a Children's Institution.* New York: Association Press, 1951.

Schur, Edwin M. *Labeling Deviant Behavior: Its Sociological Implications.* New York: Harper & Row, 1971.

———. *Radical Non-Intervention: Rethinking the Delinquency Problem.* Englewood Cliffs, N.J.: Prentice-Hall, 1973.

Schussler, Karl, and Cressy, Donald R. "Personality Characteristics of Animals." *American Journal of Sociology* 55 (March 1950): 476–484.

Scott, Joseph F. "The Massachusetts Reformatory." In *The Reformatory System in the United States,* edited by S. J. Barrows. Washington, D.C.: U.S. Government Printing Office, 1900. Pp. 80–101.

Scott, Joseph W., and Hissong, Jerry B. "Changing the Delinquent Subculture: A Sociological Approach." In *Readings in Juvenile Delinquency,* edited by Ruth Shonle Cavan. Philadelphia: J. B. Lippincott Company, 1975.

———. and Vaz, Edmund. "A Perspective on Middle-Class Delinquency." In *Middle-Class Juvenile Delinquency,* edited by Edmund Vaz. New York: Harper & Row, 1967.

Seckel, Joachim. "The Fremont Experiment: Assessment of Residential Treatment at a Youth Authority Reception Center." Research Report No. 50. Mimeographed. Sacramento: California Youth Authority, January 1967.

———, and Fuller, Douglas W. "Assessment of a Vocational Rehabilitative Program." In *Status of Current Research of the California Youth Authority, Annual Report.* Sacramento: California Youth Authority, April 1966.

Sellin, Thorsten. "The Origin of the 'Pennsylvania System of Prison Discipline'." In *Penology: The Evolution of Corrections in America,* edited by George G. Killinger and Paul F. Cromwell, Jr. St. Paul, Minn.: West Publishing Company, 1973. Pp. 12–22.

———, and Wolfgang, Marvin E. *The Measurement of Delinquency.* New York: John Wiley & Sons, 1971.

Selltiz, Claire; Jahoda, Marie; Deutsch, Morton; and Cook, Stuart. *Research Methods in Social Relations.* New York: Holt, Rinehart and Winston, 1961.

———; Wrightsman, Lawrence S.; and Cook, Stuart W. *Research Methods in Social Relations.* New York: Holt, Rinehart and Winston, 1976.

Sheridon, H. William. *Standards for Juvenile and Family Courts.* Washington, D.C.: U.S. Government Printing Office, 1967.

Sherman, Lawrence W. "Youth Workers, Police and the Gangs, Chicago, 1956–1970." M.A. thesis, University of Chicago, 1970.

Shireman, Charles. "Casework in Probation and Parole: Some Considerations in Diagnosis and Treatment." Federal Probation 51, 1963.

Shore, Melton F. "Psychological Theories of the Causes of Antisocial Behavior." In *Contemporary Corrections: A Concept in Search of Content,* edited by Benjamin Frank. Reston, Va.: Reston Publishing Company,1971. Pp. 285–299.

Short, James F. "Youth, Gang and Society: Micro and Macro Sociological Processes." *Sociological Quarterly* 15 (Winter 1975).

————, and Strodtbeck, Fred L. *Group Process and Gang Delinquency.* Chicago: University of Chicago Press, 1965.

Shyne, Ann W. "Research on Child-Caring Institutions." In *Child Caring: Social Policy and the Institution,* edited by Donnell M. Pappenfort, Dee Morgan Kilpatrick, and Robert W. Roberts. Chicago: Aldine Publishing Company, 1973.

Sieverdes, Christopher, and Bartollas, Clemens. "Modes of Adaptation and Game Behavior at Two Training Schools." In *International Perspectives on Juvenile Justice and Youth Crime,* edited by Paul C. Friday. New York: Praeger Press, 1978.

Silverman, Ira J.; Vega, Manuel; and Agcardi, John. "Police Perceptions of Female Criminality." Paper presented at the annual meeting of the American Society of Criminality, Toronto, Canada, 30 October–2 November, 1975.

Simon, Rita. *Women and Crime.* Lexington, Mass.: D. C. Heath and Company, 1975.

Simmons, J. C. *Deviants.* Berkeley: Glendessary Press, 1964.

Simpson, Jon E.; Eynon, Thomas G.; and Reckless, Walter C. "Institutionalization as Perceived by the Juvenile Offender." *Sociology and Social Research* 48 (1963): 13–23.

Skoler, Daniel L. "Comprehensive Criminal Justice Planning." In *Delinquency and Social Policy,* edited by Paul Lerman. New York: Praeger Publishers, 1970. Pp. 456–464.

Skolnick, Jerome H. *Justice without Trial.* New York: John Wiley & Sons, 1966.

————. "Toward a Developmental Theory of Parole." *American Sociological Review* 25 (August 1960): 542–549.

Smith, Corrine N. "Ohio Youth Commission: State of Ohio." Columbus: Bureau of Communications, Ohio Youth Commission, 1974.

Smith, Kenneth C. "A Profile of Juvenile Court Judges in the United States." *Juvenile Justice* (August 1974).

Smith, Paul M. "Trooper Island." In *Police Programs for Preventing Crime and Delinquency,* edited by Dan G. Pursuit et al. Springfield, Ill.: Charles C Thomas, 1972. Pp. 382–389.

Stapleton, W. Vaughan, and Teitelbaum, Lee E. *In Defense of Youth.* New York: Russell Sage Foundation, 1972.

"State Prisons in America, 1787–1937." In *Penology: The Evolution of Corrections in America,* edited by George G. Killinger and Paul F. Cromwell, Jr. St. Paul, Minn.: West Publishing Company, 1973.

Stouffer, Samuel. "Some Observations on Study Design." In *The Sociological Perspective,* edited by Scott G. McNall. Boston: Little, Brown and Company, 1974.

Stratton, John R., and Terry, Robert M. *Prevention of Delinquency: Problems and Programs.* New York: Macmillan, 1968.

Street, David. "The Inmate Group in Custodial and Treatment Settings." *American Sociological Review* 30 (February 1965): 40–55.

————; Vinter, Robert D.; and Perrow, Charles. *Organization for Treatment: A Comparative Study of Institutions for Delinquents.* New York: Free Press, 1966.

Strodtbeck, Fred L., and Short, James F., Jr. "Aleatory Risks versus Short-Run Hedonism in Explanation of Gang Action." *Social Problems* 11 (Fall 1964): 127–140.

Struggle for Justice: A Report on Crime and Punishment in America. Prepared for the American Friends Service Committee.

Sullivan, Clyde E., and Mandell, Wallace. "Restoration of Youth through Training: A Final Report." Processed. Staten Island, New York: Sakoff Research Center, April 1967.

Supreme Court of Pennsylvania, 1905. "Commonwealth versus Fisher." In *Juvenile Justice Philosophy: Readings, Cases and Comments,* edited by Frederic L. Faust and Paul J. Brantingham. St. Paul, Minn.: West Publishing Company, 1974.

Sutherland, Edwin H., and Cressey, Donald R. *Principles of Criminology.* New York: J. B. Lippincott Company, 1966.

Sykes, Gresham. "Men, Merchants and Toughs: A Study of Reactions to Imprisonment." Social Problems (October 1966): 130–138.

————. *Society of Captives.* Princeton, N.J.: Princeton University Press, 1958.

————, and Messinger, Sheldon L. "The Inmate Social System." In *Theoretical Studies in Social Organization in the Prison,* edited by Richard Cloward et al. New York: Social Science Research Council, 1960.

Szakos, Joseph and Wice, Paul B. "Juvenile Probation Officers: Their Professional Paradox," *The Quarterly,* Vol 34, No. 1 (March 1977), pp. 21–30.

Szurek, S. A. "Some Impressions from Clinical Experiences with Delinquents." In *The Antisocial Child: His Family and His Community,* edited by S. A. Szurek and I. N. Berlin. Palo Alto, Calif.: Science and Behavior Books, 1969.

Tannenbaum, Frank. *Crime and the Community.* New York: Columbia University Press, 1938.

————. *Crime in the Community.* Boston: Ginn and Company, 1938.

Tappan, Paul W. *Crime, Justice and Correction.* New York: McGraw-Hill, 1960.

————. *Juvenile Delinquency.* New York: McGraw-Hill Book Company, 1949.

————. "Treatment without Trial." In *Juvenile Justice Philosophy: Readings,*

Cases and Comments, edited by Frederic L. Faust and Paul J. Branting-ham. St. Paul, Minn.: West Publishing Company, 1974.

Taylor, A. J. W. "An Evaluation of Group Psychotherapy in a Girls' Borstal." *International Journal of Group Psychotherapy* 17 (1967): 168–177.

————. "The Significance of Dads or Special Relationships for Borstal Girls." *British Journal of Criminology* 5 (October 1965): 406–419.

Teeters, Negley K., and Reinemann, John Otto. *The Challenge of Delinquency.* Englewood Cliffs, N.J.: Prentice-Hall, 1950.

Terry, Robert M. "Discrimination in the Handling of Juvenile Offenders by Social Control Agencies." *Journal of Research in Crime and Delinquency* 4 (July 1967): 218–230.

————. "The Screening of Juvenile Offenders." *Journal of Criminal Law, Criminology and Police Science* 58 (June 1967): 173–181.

Thomas, Charles. "Are Status Offenders Really so Different? A Comparative and Longitudinal Assessment." *Crime and Delinquency* 8 (October 1976): 440–442.

————. "Toward a More Inclusive Model of the Inmate Contraculture." *Criminology* 8 (November 1970): 251–262.

————, and Fitch, Anthony W. "An Inquiry into the Association between Respondents' Personal Characteristics and Juvenile Court Dispositions." Williamsburg, Va.: Metropolitan Criminal Justice Center, College of William and Mary, 1975.

————, and Foster, Samuel C. "Prisonization in the Inmate Contraculture." *Social Problems* 20 (Fall 1972): 299–339.

————, and Foster, Samuel C. "The Importation Model Perspective on Inmate Social Roles." *Sociological Quarterly* 14 (Spring 1973): 226–234.

————, and Poole, Eric D. "The Consequences of Incompatible Goal Structures in Correctional Settings." *International Journal of Criminology and Penology* 3 (1975): 27–42.

————, and Sieverdes, Christopher M. "Juvenile Court Intake: An Analysis of Discretionary Decision-Making." *Criminology* 12 (February 1975): 413–432.

Thornberry, Terence P. "Race, Socioeconomic Status and Sentencing in the Juvenile Justice System." *Journal of Criminal Law, Criminology and Police Science* 64 (March 1973): 90–98.

Tittle, Charles R. "Inmate Organization: Sex Differentiation and the Influence of Criminal Subcultures." *American Sociological Review* 34 (August 1969): 492–505.

————. "Social Organization of Prisoners: An Empirical Test." *Social Forces* 43 (December 1964): 216–221.

————. *Society of Subordinates.* Bloomington: Indiana University Press, 1972.

Toffler, Alvin. *Future Shock.* New York: Random House, 1970.

Toigo, Romulo. "Illegitimate and Legitimate Cultures in a Training School for Girls." *Proceedings of the Rip Van Winkler Clinic* 13 (1962).

Tolman, Norman G., and Smith, Merle E. "Significant Alterations of Self-Concept and Defensiveness during Training School Residence." *Mental Hygiene* 47 (1963): 267–274.

Treger, Harvey. *Police-Social Service Project: A New Model for Interprofessional Cooperation*. A University Demonstration Project in Manpower Training and Development. Chicago: University of Illinois at Chicago Circle, Jane Addams School of Social Work, 1973.

Trojanowicz, Robert C. *Juvenile Delinquency: Concepts and Control*. Englewood Cliffs, N.J.: Prentice-Hall, 1973.

Troyer, Joseph G., and Frease, Dean E. "Attitude Change in a Western Canadian Penitentiary." *Canadian Journal of Criminology and Corrections* 17 (July 1975): 250–262.

Truax, Charles B; Wargo, Donald G.; and Silber, Leon D. "Effects of Group Psychotherapy with High Accurate Empathy and Nonpossession Warmth upon Female Delinquents." *Journal of Abnormal Psychology* 71 (1966): 267–274.

Tunley, Roul. *Kids, Crime and Chaos: A World Report on Juvenile Delinquency*. New York: Harper Press, 1962.

Twelfth Annual Training Institute for Probation, Parole and Institutional Staff. "Delinquency as Culturally Patterned and Group-Supported Behavior." Mimeographed. San Francisco, 1960.

U.S. Department of Health, Education and Welfare. *Better Ways to Help Youth: Three Youth Services Systems*. Washington, D.C.: U.S. Government Printing Office, 1973.

————. *Juvenile Court Statistics, 1971*. Washington, D.C.: U.S. Government Printing Office, 1972.

————. *Juvenile Court Statistics, 1972*. Washington, D.C.: U.S. Government Printing Office, 1973.

————. "Delinquency and the Schools." In *Prevention of Delinquency*, edited by Office of Education. New York: Macmillan, 1968.

————. *The Challenge of Youth Service Bureaus*. Washington, D.C.: U.S. Government Printing Office, 1973.

U.S. Department of Justice. *Children in Custody: A Report on the Juvenile Detention and Correctional Facility Census of 1971*. Washington, D.C.: U.S. Government Printing Office.

————. *Children in Custody: Advance Report on the Juvenile Detention and Correctional Facility Census of 1974*, Law Enforcement Assistance Administration. Washington, D.C.: U.S. Government Printing Office (February, 1977).

————. *Uniform Crime Reports in the United States*. Washington, D.C.: U.S. Government Printing Office, 1975.

————. *National Jail Census*. Washington, D.C.; U.S. Government Printing Office, 1970.

U.S. Law Enforcement Assistance Administration. *Children in Custody: Advance Report on the Juvenile Detention and Correctional Facility Census of 1972–1973*. Washington, D.C.: U.S. Government Printing Office, 1975.

————. *Children in Custody: A Report of the Juvenile Detention and Correctional Facility Census of 1971*. Washington, D.C.: U.S. Government Printing Office.

————. *Report of the Advisory Committee to the Administrator on Standards for the Administration of Juvenile Justice.* Washington, D.C.: U.S. Government Printing Office, 1976.

Upshur, Carole. "Delinquency in Girls: Implications for Service Delivery." In *Closing Correctional Institutions,* edited by Yitzhak Bakal. Lexington, Mass.: D. C. Heath and Company, 1973. Pp. 19–30.

Van Couvering, Nancy, et al. "One-to-One Project, Final Report." A demonstration program sponsored by Stiles Hall, University YMCA in cooperation with the California Youth Authority. Berkeley: October 1966.

Van Waters, Miriam. "The Socialization of Juvenile Court Procedure." In *Juvenile Justice Philosophy: Readings, Cases and Comments,* edited by Frederic L. Faust and Paul J. Brantingham. St. Paul, Minn.: West Publishing Company, 1974.

Varnes, Walter. "Cops on Campus." In *Police Programs for Preventing Crime and Delinquency,* edited by Dan G. Pursuit et al. Springfield, Ill.: Charles C Thomas, 1972.

Vaz, Edmund. "Explorations in the Institutionalization of Juvenile Delinquency." *Journal of Criminal Law, Criminology and Police Science* 62 (December 1971): 532–542.

————. "Juvenile Delinquency in the Middle-Class Youth Culture." In *Middle-Class Juvenile Delinquency,* edited by Edmund Vaz. New York: Harper & Row, 1967.

————. *Middle-Class Juvenile Delinquency.* New York: Harper & Row, 1967.

Vedder, Clyde B. *The Juvenile Offender: Perspective and Readings.* New York: Random House, 1954. Pp. 192–228.

Vetter, Harold J., and Simonsen, Clifford E. *Criminal Justice in America.* Philadelphia: W. B. Saunders Company, 1976.

Vinter, Robert D.; Downs, George; and Hall, John. *Juvenile Corrections in the States: Residential Programs and Deinstitutionalization.* Ann Arbor: University of Michigan, National Assessment of Juvenile Corrections, 1975.

————, and Janowitz, Morris. "Effective Institutions for Juvenile Delinquents, A Research Statement." In *Prison within Society,* edited by Lawrence Hazelrigg. Garden City, N.Y.: Doubleday Anchor, 1969.

————, and Lind, Roger. *Staff Relationships and Attitudes in a Juvenile Correctional Institution.* Ann Arbor: University of Michigan, School of Social Work, 1958.

Von Hentig, Hans. *The Criminal and His Victim.* New Haven: Yale University Press, 1948.

Vorrath, Harry H. and Brendtro, Larry K. *Positive Peer Culture.* Chicago: Aldine Publishing Company, 1974.

Waite, Edward E. "How Far Can Court Procedure Be Socialized without Impairing Individual Rights?" In *Juvenile Justice Philosophy: Readings, Cases and Comments,* edited by Frederic L. Faust and Paul J. Brantingham. St. Paul, Minn.: West Publishing Company, 1974.

Wallenstein, James S., and Wylie, Clement J. "Our Law-Abiding Law Breakers." *Probation* (April 1947), pp. 107–112.

Waller, Irvin. *Men Released from Prison.* Toronto: University of Toronto Press, 1974.

Waller, Willard. "The Rating and Dating Complex." In *Middle-Class Juvenile Delinquency,* edited by Edmund Vaz. New York: Harper & Row, 1967.

Ward, David A., and Kassebaum, Gene G. *Women's Prison: Sex and Social Structure.* Chicago: Aldine Publishing Company, 1965.

Ward, P. G. "Validating Prediction Scales." In *The Sociology of Punishment and Correction,* edited by Norman Johnston, Leonard Savitz, and Martin E. Wolfgang. 2d ed. New York: John Wiley & Sons, 1970. Pp. 801–806.

Warner, Florence M. *Juvenile Detention in the United States.* Chicago: University of Chicago Press, 1933.

Warren, Marguerite Q. "The Community Treatment Project: History and Prospects. In *Law Enforcement Science and Technology,* edited by S. A. Yefsky. Washington, D.C.: Thompson Book Company, 1972. Pp. 193–195.

———. "The Community Treatment Project." In *The Sociology of Punishment and Correction,* edited by Norman Johnston, Leonard Savitz, and Martin E. Wolfgang. 2d ed. New York: John Wiley & Sons, 1970. Pp. 671–683.

Wattenberg, William W., and Bufe, Noel. "The Effectiveness of Police Bureau Officers." In *Prevention of Delinquency: Problems and Programs,* edited by John R. Stratton and Robert M. Terry. New York: Macmillan, 1968.

Weber, George H. "Conflict between Professional and Non-professional Personnel in Institutional Delinquency Development." In *Prison within Society,* edited by Lawrence Hazelrigg. Garden City, N.Y.: Doubleday Anchor, 1969. Pp. 426–454. Also see *Journal of Criminal Law Criminology and Police Science* 48 (May–June 1957).

Weber, Max. *The Theory of Social and Economic Organization.* Translated by A. M. Henderson and T. Parsons. New York: Oxford University Press, 1947.

Weeks, Ashley H. "The Highfields Project." In *Juvenile Delinquency: A Book of Readings,* edited by Rose Giallombardo. New York: John Wiley & Sons, 1976. Pp. 535–547.

Weinstein, Noah. *Supreme Court Decisions and Juvenile Justice.* Reno: National Council of Juvenile Court Judges, 1973.

Weis, Joseph. "Middle-Class Female Delinquency." Paper presented at the annual meeting of the American Society of Criminology, Toronto, November 1975.

Wellford, Charles. "Factors Associated with the Adoption of the Inmate Code." *Journal of Criminal Law, Criminology, and Police Science* 58 (June 1967): 197–203.

Werthman, Carl, and Piliavin, Irving. "Gang Members and the Police." In *The Police,* edited by David J. Bordua. New York: John Wiley and Sons, 1967.

Westley, William A. "Violence and the Police." *American Journal of Sociology* 49 (August 1953): 34–41.

———, and Elkin, Frederick. "The Protective Environment and Adolescent

Socialization." In *Middle-Class Juvenile Delinquency,* edited by Edmund Vaz. New York: Harper & Row, 1967.

Wheeler, Stanton. "Socialization in Correctional Communities." *American Sociological Review* 26 (October 1961): 697–712.

———, and Cottrell, Leonard S., Jr. *Juvenile Delinquency: Its Prevention and Control.* New York: Russell Sage Foundation, 1966.

Wicks, Robert J. *Correctional Psychology: Themes and Problems in Correcting the Offender.* New York: Canfield Press, 1974.

Wilkins, Leslie T. *Evaluation of Penal Measures.* New York: Random House, 1969.

———. "Evaluation of Penal Treatments." In *Correctional Institutions,* edited by Robert M. Carter, Daniel Glaser, and Leslie T. Wilkins. New York: J. B. Lippincott Company, 1972. Pp. 508–523.

———. "The Borstal Prediction Study." In *The Sociology of Punishment and Correction,* edited by Norman Johnston, Leonard Savitz, and Martin E. Wolfgang. 2d ed. New York: John Wiley & Sons, 1970. Pp. 777–780.

———, and Smith, MacNaughton P. "Predictive Attribute Analysis." In *The Sociology of Punishment and Correction,* edited by Norman Johnston, Leonard Savitz, and Martin E. Wolfgang. 2d ed. New York: John Wiley & Sons, 1970. Pp. 814–827.

Williams, Jay R., and Gold, Martin. "From Delinquent Behavior to Official Delinquency." *Social Problems* 20 (Fall 1972): 209–229.

Williams, Robin. *American Society: A Sociological Interpretation.* New York: Alfred A. Knopf, 1970.

Williams, Vergil L., and Fish, Mary. *Convicts, Codes and Contraband: The Prison Life of Men and Women.* Cambridge, Mass.: Ballinger, 1974.

Willman, Herb C., Jr. and Chun, Ron Y. F. "Homeward Bound: An Alternative to the Institutionalization of Adjudicated Juvenile Offenders." In George G. Killinger and Paul F. Cromwell, Jr., eds. *Alternatives to Imprisonment: Corrections in the Community.* St. Paul, Minn.: West Publishing Company.

Wilson, James Q. "Dilemmas of Police Administration." *Public Administration Review* 28 (September/October 1968).

Wilson, John M., and Snodgrass, Jon D. "The Prison Cell in a Therapeutic Community." *Journal of Criminal Law, Criminology and Police Science* 60 (1969): 472–478.

Wilson, O. W., and McLaren, Clinton Ray. *Police Administration.* 3d ed. New York: McGraw-Hill, 1972.

Wise, Nancy Barton. "Juvenile Delinquency among Middle-Class Girls." In *Middle-Class Juvenile Delinquency,* edited by Edmund Vaz. New York: Harper & Row, 1967.

Wolfgang, Marvin E.; Figlio, Robert M.; and Sellin, Thorsten. *Delinquency in a Birth Cohort.* Chicago: University of Chicago Press, 1972.

Wooden, Kenneth. *Weeping in the Playtime of Others.* New York: McGraw-Hill, 1976.

Yablonsky, Lewis. "The Delinquent Gang as a Near-Group." In *Juvenile Delin-*

quency: A Book of Readings, edited by Rose Giallombardo. New York: John Wiley & Sons, 1966.

Yefsky, S. A. *Law Enforcement Science and Technology.* Washington, D.C.: Thompson Book Company, 1972.

Young, Frank W. "Reactive Subsystems." *American Sociological Review* 35 (April 1970): 297–307.

Young, Don J. "Recent Appellate Cases." *Juvenile Justice* 26 (May 1975).

Zald, Mayer Ń. "Comparative Analysis and Measurement of Organizational Goals: The Case of Correctional Institutions for Delinquents." *Sociological Quarterly* 4 (Summer 1963): 206–320.

———. "Organizational Control Structure in Five Correctional Institutions." *American Journal of Sociology* (November 1962), pp. 335–345.

———. "Power Balance and Staff Conflict in Correctional Institutions." In *Prison within Society,* edited by Lawrence Hazelrigg. Garden City, N.Y.: Doubleday Anchor, 1969. Pp. 397–425.

———. "The Correctional Institution for Juvenile Offenders: An Analysis of Organization 'Character'." *Social Problems* 8 (Summer 1960): 57–67.

———, and Street, David. "Custody and Treatment in Juvenile Institutions." *Crime and Delinquency* 10 (July 1964): 249–256.

Zetterberg, Hans L. *On Theory and Verification in Sociology.* Totowa, N.J.: Bedminister Press, 1965.

Zingraff, Matthew T. "Conflicting Processes of Socialization among Juveniles in the Prison Community." *Georgia Journal of Corrections* 2 (August 1973): 63–70.

———. "Prisonization as an Inhibitor of Effective Resocialization." *Criminology* 13 (November 1975): 366–388.

Zivan, Morton. "Youth in Trouble: A Vocational Approach." Final Report of a Research and Demonstration Project, 31 May 1961–31 August 1966. Processed. Dobbs Ferry, N.Y.: Children's Village, 1966.

Zweig, Franklin M., and Morris, Robert. "The Social-Planning Design Guide." In *Delinquency and Social Policy,* edited by Paul Lerman. New York: Praeger Publishers, 1970. Pp. 447–455.

Name Index

Subject Index